The Battle of Waterloo was one of the most horrific actions fought during the Napoleonic Wars. There have been several studies of battlefield injuries and the field care that casualties received during the campaign of June 1815. However, what happened to the many thousands of injured men left behind as the armies marched away is rarely discussed.

In June 1815, around 62,000 Allied and French wounded flooded into Brussels, Antwerp, and other towns and cities of the Kingdom of the Netherlands and swamped the medical services. These casualties were eventually cared for by a wide mix of medical personnel including hundreds of 'Belgian' surgeons, most of whom had trained in the French Service de Santé and who assisted in the dispersal, treatment, and rehabilitation of thousands of casualties after the battle.

New data concerning the fate of the thousands of Allied and some French casualties has emerged from the library of the University of Edinburgh. This has revealed a collection of over 170 wound sketches, detailed case reports, and the surgical results from five Brussels Hospitals. The sketches were carried out by Professor John Thomson, who held the first Regius Chair in Military Surgery appointed by the University of Edinburgh. Most accounts are of Allied wounded, but certainly not all. The accounts, drawings and surgical results dramatically alter our understanding of the management of military wounded in the Georgian army.

Michael Crumplin is a retired consultant and general surgeon living in North Wales. Before and after retirement, he took an interest in the human aspects of conflict. He has written four books which focus on medicine and surgery, in both the Army and Royal Navy during the French wars of 1792-1815. He has also written book chapters, many articles, and has, since 2000, delivered around 400 lectures. He was education lead for Waterloo 200 and since 2015, with the generous support of a local businessman, has donated his medical collection and set up a unique museum of surgery in the farm used as the principal field hospital during the Battle of Waterloo at Mont St Jean.

Gareth Glover is a 58-year-old ex-Royal Navy officer, who has studied the Napoleonic Wars for forty years. He has spent the last 15 years discovering and publishing numerous accounts of soldiers who fought in the Napoleonic Wars, to date he has published over 70 books and monographs.

Waterloo: After the Glory

Hospital Sketches and Reports on the Wounded following the Battle

Michael Crumplin and Gareth Glover

Foreword by the Duke of Wellington

Helion & Company

Helion & Company Limited
Unit 8 Amherst Business Centre
Budbrooke Road
Warwick
CV34 5WE
England
Tel. 01926 499619
Email: info@helion.co.uk
Website: www.helion.co.uk
Twitter: @helionbooks
Visit our blog at http://blog.helion.co.uk/

Published by Helion & Company 2019. Reprinted in paperback 2022
Designed and typeset by Mach 3 Solutions Ltd (www.mach3solutions.co.uk)
Cover designed by Paul Hewitt, Battlefield Design (www.battlefield-design.co.uk)

Text © Michael Crumplin and Gareth Glover 2019
Case drawings are open source images courtesy of the University of Edinburgh Library; other illustrations as credited.
Cover: Belgian Wagon Conveying Wounded from the Field After the Battle of Waterloo, 1815, by John Augustus Atkinson.

ISBN 978-1-915070-92-0

British Library Cataloguing-in-Publication Data.
A catalogue record for this book is available from the British Library.

For details of other military history titles published by Helion & Company Limited, contact the above address, or visit our website: http://www.helion.co.uk

We always welcome receiving book proposals from prospective authors.

Contents

List of Plates

Foreword

I am very pleased to write a short foreword to this most interesting book. My ancestor the 1st Duke of Wellington was, unusually for his day, always most concerned about the welfare of his soldiers. Indeed, part of his success as a general has often been ascribed to his great attention to detail about the food, clothing, and medical care of his troops. There is no better example of this than the note which he wrote during the battle in his own hand to instruct the officers during the burning of Hougoumont to '…Take care that no Men are lost by the falling in of the Roof, or floors'.

This book gives the reader a lot of information about the treatment of the wounded both near the battlefield and in the base hospitals in Brussels and Antwerp. It is difficult to imagine how the medical staff, with the primitive instruments then available and with no anaesthesia, tried to look after the great number of men who were wounded in the three day campaign.

I am sure that my ancestor would have much approved of this book. He always suffered great pain and anguish at the numbers of killed and wounded after each battle.

In his despatch to Lord Bathurst he says in describing the Battle of Waterloo 'Your Lordship will observe that such a desperate action could not be fought without great loss. And I am sorry to add that ours has been immense'. And elsewhere he wrote 'My heart is broken by the terrible loss I have sustained in my old friends and companions and my poor soldiers. Believe me, nothing except a battle lost can be half so melancholy as a battle won with the loss of so many friends'.

Duke of Wellington
Apsley House, No. 1 London
26 November 2018

Introduction

This book has been born out of the discovery of some remarkable medical records in the archives of Edinburgh University Library, relating to the care of the wounded following the momentous but extremely costly Battle of Waterloo, fought on 18 June 1815.

Michael Crumplin, 'Mick' to his friends, is an ex-surgeon and has studied military surgery through the ages for much of his life, so when he brought these records to my attention and asked me to co-write this book I did not hesitate to agree. A huge amount has been written on the Waterloo Campaign, which consisted of four major battles fought in lightning succession between the 16 and 18 June 1815. However, whilst much has been written regarding this pivotal European conflict, which finally ended almost 23 years of near continuous warfare, little of this voluminous literature adequately details the sacrifice and suffering of the soldiers who fought these wars. Few publications concerning the Battle of Waterloo and the other related actions, give more than a fleeting account of the fate of the tens of thousands of casualties and who cared for them, nor indeed where they were tended. Understandably, many of the surviving participants only sought to forget the horrors of the conflict and the hardships they had endured, in an effort to progress with their lives and aspirations. However, this unfortunately hides from historians their real challenges, and the historiography of the period can only be enriched by addressing these very human aspects of conflict. This is not an aspect that is ignored in the histories of the two World Wars, particularly the first of these: perhaps we can be psychologically more detached in our views of earlier wars, but that cannot be right.

Those who study the medical and surgical aspects of this period of military history struggle to comprehend the incredible stoicism of many; not only of the victims, but also the dilemmas and failures of medical staff and their simple and often ignorant therapies. Certainly, expectations of pain relief, survival, and life expectancy in general were far less than today. This was a time when men in the 'lower echelons' of society could only expect a lifespan of 40 or a few more years. Their wives and children were prone to early demise and the labours of both men and women were brutal and harsh. Such tedious work over very long hours came with little reward and enabled them to only just survive at subsistence level. Most of the labouring class would likely be physically strong and expect little from life in the way of pain relief, effective therapy, or comfort when they became ill or were injured. Medical men would also frequently have had early hopes of survival for their patients, only to see these dashed by unexpected complications or due to their still-primitive methods.

The material found in the University of Edinburgh Library archives goes some way to help us understand the fate of many of the victims of this notorious battle. A large number of

fascinatingly detailed case reports written by senior surgeons on the scene, and line drawings of over 170 patients indicating their wounds, accompanied in many cases by personal
identification of the individuals, detailed descriptions of their injuries and their surgical
outcomes, bring the fate of the casualties into the stark light. The line drawings attached to
each set of notes are simple and certainly far less sophisticated illustrations than Sir Charles
Bell's paintings of the victims of Corunna and Waterloo, or those by Henry Tonks during
World War One. These still remain an important visual record of the experience of warfare
at this time. This is further enhanced by a host of general casualty returns indicating the
numbers and types of operations performed and their outcomes from a number of diverse
hospitals in both Brussels and Antwerp. These records represent all or part of a series of
official returns submitted to the Army Medical Board following Waterloo, in an attempt to
educate and improve future generations of military surgeons.

Michael Crumplin and Dr Martin Howard have both previously produced books on
military medicine/surgery in the French Revolutionary and Napoleonic Wars, detailing the
organisations set up by both the British and the French, the characters involved, and the
methods then in use, with a few case histories. This book is therefore designed to both
complement and expand upon these works, to take our knowledge further forward, by
describing how the allied surgeons (for with the rapid retreat of the French army, they were
the ones largely left to deal with the wounded of all the protagonists), supported by both the
Belgian[1] military and civilian surgeons and even by a significant influx of British surgeons,
who travelled over in the weeks after the battle to aid the humanitarian effort. The exact
numbers of the wounded during this lightning campaign are not known, but conservative estimates say that there were at least 50,000 French, British, Prussian, Dutch, Belgian,
Brunswick, Hanoverian, and Nassau troops requiring medical assistance. Such numbers,
simply overwhelmed the medical services of the armies involved and the aid of civilians to
collect the wounded, transport them to makeshift hospitals and civilian surgeons to operate
on them, was vital for the saving of many of these casualties' lives.

Their story has yet to be fully told, so finally here it is.

---

1   During the campaign of 1815 Belgium and Holland were amalgamated into the Kingdom of the Netherlands. The
terms 'Belgian' or 'Belgium' are used in the text purely to designate those emanating from the southern provinces of
the Netherlands.

Acknowledgements

Any work of this nature must inevitably rely on the support and advice of a great number of experts and thanks should be given to Renée Van Tiggelen MD, retired radiologist & curator of the Belgian Museum of Radiology; Dr Pierre Lierneux, expert at the Museum of Military History and the Armed Forces; and Thierry Rengoir, who kindly supplied us with a copy (in French) of E. Evrard's *Esculape aux Armées, 500 ans de médecine militaire en Belgique.* (Brussels: Sociéte Scientifique du Service Médical Militaire, 1997).

A great deal of work has been undertaken to identify the many buildings used as hospitals in each city and we must offer our sincere thanks to Ronan Burgess for his help in locating the various hospitals in Antwerp and the selection of proclamations produced in this book: to Roland Reynhaert MD, Colonel Dubois, and Patrick Nefors of the Belgian Army Museum in Brussels for supplying a number of useful documents, and Bernard Wilkin who kindly supplied transcripts of the letters of Surgeon Goffin.

However, more than anyone, we must note our appreciation for the excellent work done by E. Evrard on the Dutch/Belgian military medical services during the Napoleonic wars, which greatly helped us in our research of this very poorly studied area. His articles in the *Revue Belge d'Histoire Militaire* are of an extraordinary depth and those consulted are 'Chirurgiens militaires britanniques à la bataille de Waterloo et dans les hôpitaux de Bruxelles en juin 1815' (Issue XXIV-5 March 1982), and 'Le Service de Santé militaire hollando-belge à la bataille de Waterloo et dans le hôpitaux de Bruxelles en juin 1815' (Issue XXV-1 March 1983).

We must also register our grateful thanks to our editor Andrew Bamford who believed in this project when other publishers could not see its potential.

Michael Crumplin and Gareth Glover

Medical Glossary

Acetabulum: the cup-shaped synovial lined socket, which, with the head of the femur, makes up the large hip joint.

Acromion process: the prominent piece of bone, part of the scapula, which gives prominence at the outer end of the shoulder.

Adnexae: adjoining appendages of organs; for example, the ovaries and Fallopian tubes are the adnexae of the uterus.

Alvine: refers to anything relevant to the abdomen or intestines.

Amaurosis: an old term for weakness or loss of vision caused by any disease or wound, not affecting the eye.

Anasarca: significant and widespread swelling of the tissues and thus swelling of the body, due to escape of fluid into the extracellular space. This usually occurs with liver, kidney or right heart failure – also as a result of extreme starvation or sepsis as a result of malnutrition and severe protein loss.

Antimony tartrate: medication used as an emetic

Anti-phlogistic regimen: when there was incipient or actual infection or signs of severe inflammation, the patient's 'excitable' state was reduced by bleeding, vomiting, and purgation. The regimen was considered essential to render the patient less liable to sepsis. These usual and unpleasant manoeuvres were usually coupled with a simple ('low') diet.

Aorta: the main central large artery of the body, carrying oxygenated blood from the left side of the heart, to all parts, via branches, including the subclavian, carotid, renal, and femoral arteries.

Apoplexy: an old term for a stroke or seizure.

Axilla: the area of the armpit.

Brachial nerve plexus: The collection of major nerve roots and branches, in the neck, supplying the arm

Calcaneum: the main heel-bone, which articulates with the tibia, fibula and bones of the forefoot.

Callus: a hard area of skin or bone as, in the former case, a result of constant wear and pressure. A bony callus is the description of an area of early bone healing and repair.

Carotid artery: the principal artery arising from the aorta which supplies the head, neck, and brain. The common carotid artery splits into the internal and external carotid branches, the former supplies the brain and the latter the structures of the head and neck.

Carpus: the collection of bones lying between the forearm and the metacarpal bones.

Caserne: a military barracks in a garrison town.

Cataplasm: an older name for a poultice or plaster placed on the skin for comfort.

Cathartic: refers to a substance that causes a bowel evacuation often part of the anti-phlogistic regimen.

Cerebellum: the part of the brain, lying beneath and behind the principal cerebral lobes, that is concerned with regulating motor function, equilibrium, coordination, and posture.

Charpie: a light fluffy tangle, made up of linen waste. It was often used to keep open, dress, and drain gaping wounds.

Cicatrix: new tissue that then forms a scar.

Cinchona (bark): derived from several trees or shrubs of the madder family and of the genus Cinchona, which are found in South America, Java and India. The bark of the trees, when treated, yields quinine and other alkaloids. 'Bark', sometimes known as 'Jesuit's Bark' of a red and yellow variety was often prescribed to combat malaria (intermittent and remittent fevers) and any febrile conditions.

Clavicle: the collar-bone.

Clyster: see Glyster

Coagulum: can be a congealed mass of solidified material such as blood (a clot), originating from a liquid form.

Compound Fracture: a fracture where the skin is broken, which heightens the risk of infection and makes a successful outcome far less certain, with inevitable sepsis.

Condyle; tibial, medial, and lateral: the condyles are smooth surfaces at the end of a bone that form part of a joint. Two important condyles sit on the upper surface of the tibial bone, which is the largest of the two leg bones. They form part of the knee-joint.

Conjunctiva: the very delicate and thin linings of the outer surface of the eye – the sclera –and also line the inner surfaces of the eyelids.

Contre-coup injury: this occurs when the skull is forcibly displaced and the brain, with a jelly-like substance, is not only injured at the point of impact, but is forced against the opposite side of the cranium and is there damaged by that secondary impact.

Cordial: a beverage, in this context, a mixture of alcohol and fruit juice, such as lemonade.

Cranial nerves: the twelve specialised pairs of nerves, emanating from the brain, which serve the organs of sight, smell, hearing, cardiac, respiratory and other functions.

Cranium: that part of the bony skull that encloses the brain.

Cricoid bone: forms the lowest of the three fragile bones that make up the larynx. These protect and enclose the glottis and vocal cords.

Débridement: literally means 'unbridling' or releasing tension in a wound. It has, however come to mean thorough cleansing and cutting away all dead and dying tissue, be that skin, fat, muscle, fascia, ligament, cartilage, or bone. This is a vital procedure in the management of war wounds.

Deltoid muscle: a large muscle arising which forms the rounded bulk of the shoulder prominence. It arises from the collar-bone, acromion process and spine of the shoulder-blade. It inserts into the humerus and moves the arm at the shoulder-joint.

Demulcent: a coating substance that helps reduce inflammation

Diaphoretic: a medication that induces perspiration; for example antimonial and mercurial preparations.

Diplöe: the narrow space filled with spongy bone that lies between the two sheets of bone of the skull.

Dissection: an old term for a post-mortem examination.

Diuretic: a drug that induces urine flow from the kidneys (increased micturition) for example, squill and cream of tartar

Dossil: a rolled-up piece of material such as lint or cotton. Often placed in a wound or incision in order to prevent closure of the wound and allow drainage of fluids out – it was alternatively known as a tent.

Dropsy: a swelling of the body and legs as a consequence of the fluid retention, for example from heart or kidney diseases.

Dura mater: the tough outer membrane (there are two other membranes) that envelopes the brain and spinal cord, a breach of which constitutes a real risk of infection.

Emetic: a substance that will induce vomiting – another 'ingredient' of the anti-phlogistic regimen.

Emollient: a word to describe a substance that can sooth or smooth the skin.

Emphysema, surgical: an accumulation of air, escaped from the chest/lungs in the superficial tissues of the chest wall.

Empyema: a collection of purulent fluid in the chest cavity.

Ensiform cartilage: another name for the xiphoid cartilage, which is attached to the lower end of the sternum (breast bone).

Epigastrium: the upper central area of the abdomen, lying just below the front of the rib cage.

Excoriation: an area of damage or removal of part of a surface, a graze.

Exfoliation: shedding material (for example, dead or infected matter) from a surface.

False ribs: the costal cartilages found at the end of the bony ribs.

Febrifuge: a drug that encourages fevers to resolve, for example quinine, peppermint.

Femur: thigh-bone

Fibula: the smaller of the two leg bones on the outside of the limb.

Fistula: a track lined by epithelium or granulation tissue that communicates between two surfaces, for example the bowel and skin.

Foetid: describes something foul-smelling.

Fungus cerebri: an inflamed, infected swollen protrusion of the brain.

Glenoid cavity: a shallow cavity at the end of one bone that forms part of a joint. The term usually applied to the shoulder joint.

Glutei: the large buttock muscles.

Glyster (syn. clyster): an older term for an enema.

Goulard, oil of: a solution of lead acetate and lead oxide, to act as an astringent agent.

Granulation tissue: a form of healing in which a raw area reacts to infection. There is a fairly florid outgrowth of friable tissue in the area.

Haemoptysis: coughing up blood – 'spitting blood' was a term used to denote tuberculosis.

Haemostasis: proper arrest of haemorrhage in an area.

Haemothorax: a collection of blood in the chest cavity.

Hay's Wash: we have been unable to trace this medication

Hernia: a protrusion of abdominal, thoracic, muscular parts through a containing wall, for example an inguinal hernia, or groin rupture.

Humerus: long bone of the upper arm.

Hyoid bone: uppermost of the three delicate bones forming, guarding, and containing the larynx.

Iliac artery: the common iliac arteries are the two principal divisions of the lower aorta. These common iliac vessels divide further into the internal iliac, supplying the pelvic organs, and the external iliac, most of which carries on as the common femoral artery in the thigh.

Iliac bone (ilium): the curved sheet of bone which forms the upper of the three pelvic bones on each side, which form the pelvic girdle.

Integuments: the natural coverings of the body – skin, fat, muscle and ligaments.

Intermittent fever: the old name for what we know as malaria, in all its varieties.

Ischaemia: caused by a lack of blood supply and thus oxygen and nutrients.

Itch: an irritation of the skin. In old parlance, it implied the skin disease scabies.

Jaundice: a yellow colour of the skin, due to a build-up of bile products in the circulation.

Latissimus dorsi: a large flat muscle on the back. The muscle arises from several spinal vertebrae and inserts into the humerus. It has several actions on the arm and is the largest muscle in the upper body.

Lazarette: a hospital largely for housing patients with contagious diseases.

Ligation: the process of tying off a structure, for example a blood vessel.

Ligatures: lengths of linen, silk or animal 'gut' for tying off structures.

Linea alba: a line of sturdy fibrous tissue (that is to say, a white line), formed by the union of abdominal muscles in the midline of the front of the abdominal wall.

Lunar caustic: copper sulphate used, in solid form, for cauterising tissue that needs removal.

Magnesium sulphate: a chemical used as a purgative – for instance as part of the anti-phlogistic regimen.

Malleolus: a bony protuberance on either side of the ankle, at the lower end of the tibial and fibula bones.

Mandible: jaw-bone.

Maxilla: the prominence in the face that we call the cheek-bone.

Medulla oblongata: a cone shaped structure in the brain stem, below the brain, which controls the autonomic, or involuntary functions of the body, for example cardiac and respiratory functions and regulation of the blood pressure. It is the most important part of the brain.

Meninges: the thin covering membranes of the brain and spinal cord. They consist of (from outside inwards), the dura, arachnoid, and pia mater. These, whilst intact, form an important barrier to infection.

Mesentery: the peritoneal-lined fatty sheets that carry blood vessels, nerves, and lymphatics to the bowel.

Metacarpal: the bones between the wrist bony structures and the finger-bones.

Metatarsal bones: the bones between the bones that make up the ankle joint (the tarsus) and the bones of the toes

Mortification: death or gangrene of a part, usually following ischaemia or sepsis or both.

Necrotising fasciitis: a severe, life-threatening infection caused by a mixture of aerobic (for example gram staining positive cocci) and anaerobic bacteria (for example clostridia and Bacteroides) which, by production of their toxins, interrupt blood supply to the tissues. The infection is more common in those victims who are immunocompromised. It requires urgent surgery and other supportive measure. It carries a mortality of around 25 percent today.

Neuropraxia: the loss of muscular and sensory function as a result of temporary nerve damage. The nerve and muscular functions normally will recover over time – usually around six to eight weeks.

Neurotmesis: a usually permanent loss of motor and sensory function as a result of nerve division or ischaemia. Occasionally, partial function may return.

Nosology: classification of diseases.

Occiput: an area of the cranium or brain at the rear of the head.

Oedema: abnormal accumulation of fluid in a part of the body, for example brain or leg.

Olecranon: a part of the ulna bone. It is the prominent area of bone felt at the elbow tip, just beyond (behind) the joint.

Ophthalmia (or Trachoma): is an infection with chlamydia trachomatis, which inflames, infects and can scar the cornea. It may cause blindness. Many cases emanated from the early 19th century Egyptian campaigns and the disease became the reason for the first medical disability pension in the British Army.

Osteomyelitis: infection (acute or chronic) of bone and periosteum.

Palsy: paralysis.

Parietal bone: a large curved plate of bone, part of the skull, lying at each side of the skull.

Parietes: the investing layers of any hollow part, for example the abdominal or chest walls.

Patella: the knee-cap.

Perineum: the area between the genitalia and the anus.

Periosteum: the important nourishing and protective tough membrane that encloses bone. Muscles can arise from it and new bone can be formed from its inner layer.

Peritoneum: the thin lining of the abdominal cavity and covering of the abdominal contents, which allows smooth gliding movements of the organs on themselves and on other parts of the abdomen.

Phagedena: refers to a deep penetrating ulcer resulting in death of a part; for exampler gangrene.

Phrenitis: inflammation of the brain substance; encephalitis.

Plaisters: an old term for plasters.

Pleura: the delicate linings of the lungs and covering of contents of the chest cavity, allowing smooth gliding motions of the viscera within the chest.

Pneumothorax: the accumulation of air within the chest cavity, which will displace the lung.

Poultice: a pad of material – for example cloth, vegetable or breaded – usually heated, which is placed over an area of inflammation or infection, for comfort and to 'draw out' infected material.

Poupart's ligament: the inguinal ligament – an in folding of abdominal muscles in the groin, which helps form the fold there.

Pourriture d'hôpital: translated literally means hospital rot or decomposition. The term is usually applied to septic gangrene.

Pylorus: the sphincter at the outlet of the stomach, which controls the passage of food from the organ.

Quadriceps, muscle and tendon: the quadriceps apparatus consists of the large group of three major thigh muscles, which cause extension of the limb and insert by a strong tendon into the tibial tuberosity, just below the knee-joint.

Rectus Femoris: the central muscle of the quadriceps group.

Remittent Fever: a pattern of fever in which the temperature does not reach normal at any time of the day. It can be ill-defined as contemporary classification of diseases was rather sketchy. Examples might be some cases of malaria, typhoid, viral infection, or brucellosis,

Ricinus: the castor bean or castor oil plant; a species of perennial flowering plant. The drug was used as a laxative.

Roller: is a roll of linen bandage of varying size to be unrolled onto a wounded head, torso, or limb.

Sacrum (sacral bone): the tough bone just above the coccyx, at the base of the spine. It articulates with the pelvis.

Sanies: the term for a thin serous or purulent, often slightly blood-stained, fluid that is discharged from a wound, ulcer, or cavity.

Scabies: a contagious skin disorder caused by the itch mite, *Sarcoptes Scabiei*, which burrows under the skin. A frequent problem 200 years ago.

Scapula: the shoulder blade bone.

Scarlatina: scarlet fever.

Scilla (or Squill): a plant substance used as a diuretic, anti-inflammatory. or expectorant agent.

Sequestrum: a loose or attached portion of dead, infected bone.

Singultus: hiccoughs.

Sinus: refers to a blind-ending tract, often lined by granulation tissue.

Slough: the shedding of effete tissue. In a medical context, it usually refers to dead material produced by loss of blood supply and/or infection.

Sorde: an old word for a sore.

Sphacelate: to become gangrenous; the death of tissue.

Sterno (cleido) mastoid: a muscle – one of a pair – lying diagonally in front of the neck. It arises from into the top part of the breast bone and collar bone and inserts in to the mastoid process of the skull by the ear. It turns the head from side to side.

Subclavian artery: the artery running from the top of the aorta into the arm, whose blood supply it is.

Sudorific: a substance that induces perspiration (synonymous with diaphoretic).

Superciliary ridge: the bony protuberance of the skull, which lies above the eye.

Sutures (lambdoidal, sagittal): lines of fusion of different parts of the cranium; that is to say, they are the immovable junctional areas of the different parts of the skull.

Symphisis: literally means the almost immovable junction of two bones, for example the symphysis pubis, which joins the two pelvic bones in the front pubic region.

Synovial: refers to the lubrication fluid and lining of a movable joint, for example the synovial membrane or fluid of the knee-joint.

Tension pneumothorax: a dangerous accumulation of air trapped in the thoracic cavity, which can fatally compress the heart and other structures in the chest.

Tentorium cerebelli: a fibrous, supportive sheet separating the cerebral cortex from the cerebellum.

Terebinth: another name for turpentine. It is produced by a Mediterranean tree, *Pistacia Terebinthus.*

Thorax: the chest

Thyroid bone: 'the Adam's apple'; the shield-shaped middle of the three delicate bones lying between the hyoid bone and the cricoid bones. It is situated behind the thyroid gland.

Tibia: the largest of the two lower leg bones, lying beside the fibula.

Tic Doloreux: a painful affliction of the face, being an abnormality of the 5th cranial nerve. It is otherwise known as Trigeminal Neuralgia.

Tourniquet: an instrument that obstructs the flow of blood to a part. It acts by pressure. Usually, a tight canvas band operated by a screw or windlass action tightens around a limb or digit. This allows surgeons to operate in a bloodless field.

Trachea: the windpipe

Trapezius muscle: a large flat, paired, triangular muscle that sits on the back of the body. It arises from the occipital skull bone down to the lower thoracic vertebrae and inserts into the scapula, so providing movement of the shoulder-blade and support for the arm.

Trepanning (syn. trephining): a procedure that improves access to a damaged skull by cutting out circular discs of bone, usually from near the fractured area of cranial injury. Thus, unwanted collections of intracranial fluid, such as blood, may be evacuated, or depressed fragments of bone elevated.

Trochanters: are prominent areas projecting from near the upper end of the thigh-bone or femur. The lesser trochanter is on the inside of the femur, the greater trochanter on the outside. These projections form attachments for muscles acting around the hip-joint.

Typhus: incorporates a group of infective diseases, transmitted by the louse, which harbours the Rickettsia organism in its gut. When the skin is scratched the organism enters the body, causing severe symptoms, a rash, and sometime encephalitis. It is a disease of overcrowding and poverty.

Ulcer: a defect in a surface, for example a skin, leg, or gut ulcer.

Ureter: the thin muscular tube lined by epithelium, which runs from the kidney, taking the urine to the bladder.

Urethra: the muscular tube, lying largely in the penis, that takes urine from the bladder to the outside.

Vastus (medialis and lateralis): the two large thigh muscles that sit each side of the rectus femoris muscle; the 'quads'.

Venesection: the therapeutic withdrawal of blood from the patient. Part of the anti-phlogistic regimen, it may entail cutting a vein, using 'wet' cupping, applying leeches, or a single or multi-bladed scarificator.

Vertebra: a structural bone of the spinal column. Each vertebra consists of a solid body in front and a bony arch at the back, which contains the spinal cord structures. The spine is made up of seven cervical, 12 thoracic, and five lumbar vertebrae. These are separated by cartilaginous discs.

Vertebral artery: one of a pair of arteries, arising from the subclavian arteries and taking blood from there to the upper spinal cord, brainstem, cerebellum, and posterior part of the brain.

Vertex: is the top of the skull, formed by four cranial bones.

Vitriol: an archaic name for a sulphate, but usually means sulphuric acid, typically used in dilute form.

Xyphoid cartilage: the small leaf-like cartilage arising from the lower end of the sternum

Zygoma: a bone of the face, which we call the cheek-bone. The temporal skull-bone has a bony arch, which fuses with the zygoma.

1

The Evolution of the Military Medical Services in the Low Countries – 1792-1815

The allied campaigns in the Low Countries against Revolutionary France and the subsequent French Empire were costly and largely ineffectual. In 1793-5, a number of adverse factors and extremely poor logistics ended in a British evacuation, all ending with Holland and Belgium being held firmly by French forces. In 1799, a British force returned to Holland in cooperation with the Russians, but after a short campaign, they again failed completely and it ended ignominiously in a negotiated withdrawal of these forces. A third British venture into this region ended with the military disaster of Walcheren in 1809, which resulted in at least forty times more deaths from malarial and other sicknesses than from combat injuries in the huge British invasion force. The fourth and final British failure in this challenging country came at the botched storming of the fortress of Bergen-op-Zoom in 1814, when the majority of the assailants were eventually forced to surrender.

The combination of contagious disease, poor weather, a very wet locality, and inefficient medical and logistical services led to thousands of British and allied deaths and much suffering. Whilst significant attention has rightly been focussed on sickness in the British army serving in these campaigns in the Low Countries, it should not be assumed that the French army remained well during these sickly seasons. Just as the British soldiers suffered, so did their enemies, although the Dutch troops and the local populace seem to have been better acclimatised. However, it was reported that Dutch troops, sent to Walcheren from Amsterdam, had a similar foreboding to British soldiers when they heard of their posting to the notoriously unhealthy West Indies.

The Dutch physician Laurillard-Fallot, serving with the French army at Walcheren in 1809, attributed his failure to gain promotion from assistant physician to médecin ordinaire to the adverse reports emanating from the hospital where he worked in Middleburg.[1] The low-lying, often sodden ground at Walcheren and on the Beveland islands held as much risk of suffering fatal or debilitating diseases such as benign tertian malaria, dysentery, typhoid, and typhus as they had done, when Sir John Pringle had served there, sixty years previously.[2]

---

1   M. Howard, *Walcheren 1809, the scandalous destruction of a British Army* (Barnsley: Pen & Sword, 2012), p.32.
2   Sir John Pringle (1707-1782), a Scottish physician, has along with two other surgeons been dubbed 'The father of Military medicine'. In 1744 he was appointed by the Duke of Cumberland to be Physician General to the forces in the

Ironically, after so much failure here, the final phase of the war, resulting in the defeat of Bonaparte's army, was to take place in the Low Countries. During the Waterloo campaign the Dutch-Belgian forces, stood alongside the British as allies, but many of their service personnel had not long previously been part of Bonaparte's Grande Armée. However, it was not just military assistance that was to prove essential, but their medical support was soon to become vitally important as well. Fortuitously, the experience gained by many of the Dutch and Belgian medical staff in the French army's *Service de Santé* was to prove of great benefit to both the Allied and French wounded in 1815. The eventual co-operation between Dutch and allied medical staff proved pretty efficient and harmonious in the care of the many casualties after the Battle of Waterloo. Luckily, there was also a good deal less general sickness during the summer months of that year in the Belgian cities than might have been expected. This was undoubtedly at least partly as a result of the organisational abilities of both British and Belgian senior medical staff.

With Napoleon Bonaparte crowned Emperor in late 1804, Belgium and Holland became satellites of the French Empire. Belgium (previously the Austrian Netherlands) had effectively become an integral part of France, whilst in 1806 Napoleon's brother, Louis, was crowned King of Holland. However, as a result of Louis's non-compliant behaviour, this kingdom lasted only four years, before it was also subsumed within greater France. As Bonaparte's empire ended in 1814 a 'United Kingdom of the Netherlands' evolved in 1815 out of the Congress of Vienna, uniting Belgium, Luxembourg and Holland, with the House of Orange becoming a constitutional monarchy.

The population of the southern provinces of the Netherlands had paid a high price in these wars. They had supplied 215,000 men to the French armies, mostly conscripts, which amounted to more than six percent of the total population of the region, of whom 71,000 became casualties. It can therefore be seen that both the nations of Austria and France were to play significant successive roles in shaping the Belgian armed services and the education of military doctors in the closing years of the 18th century into the beginning of the 19th. Those Belgian medical men who provided every support and care for the injured soldiers after the Battle of Waterloo had well established roots in the French and Dutch military services, many of them had been trained in French and Dutch universities or medical centres of instruction.

During these years of Revolution and Empire, there were clear signs of a burgeoning medical education across the whole of Europe. In France during 1793, Metz, Lille, Strasbourg, and Toulon had provided all of the authorised military medical training. This proved insufficient, despite the army having around 4,000 medical officers by 1794, and in that year, three national schools of health were opened in Paris, Strasbourg, and Montpellier. The Austrian medico-surgical academy (the Josephinium) had started at Vienna in 1795, as did a similar unit in Prussian Berlin (La Pépinière).[3] At St Petersburg, a military medical academy was opened in 1798, whilst in Britain, the Royal College of Surgeons of London appeared in 1800 and the first Regius Chair in military surgery was established at Edinburgh in 1806.

Low Countries.

3   G. E. Rothenberg, *The Art of Warfare in the Age of Napoleon* (Bloomington: Indiana University Press 1980), pp. 227-233.

During the period of the French Revolution there was only one Belgian university medical course of studies, which was at Louvain, but with Belgium being incorporated within France, medical students were also able to attend any of the various French institutions. Despite the creation of 'Imperial Universities' at Brussels, Antwerp, Ghent, and Liège in 1806, none of these had any medical faculty until around 1808-1809. Once established, there would have been regular interplay between these faculties and the garrison hospitals in those cities. In Brussels for example, there was interaction between the university and the Jesuit's and St Pierre military hospitals.

After a medical school opened in Antwerp, at the Saint Elisabeth Hospital, Surgeon Sommé of the French army taught there. The renowned Belgian surgeon Jean-François Kluyskens held a chair of surgical pathology in Ghent; however, the school in this city closed in 1814. In Liège there was only very limited surgical teaching for students at the military hospital with places for just six pupils.[4]

The French *Service de Santé* was paramount for the training and employment of Belgian military surgeons. Under this system, the zeal and efficiency of the Republican era demanded much of the people's military medical men. This was exemplified by a demand that there should be a surgeon for every 25 republican soldiers! Although such high aspirations were there, they are unlikely to have been achieved. How different this was, when compared with the provision for the British Army at this time, when the basic allotment of surgeons in the British medical service was provided at the rate of one physician to every 2,000 soldiers and one Staff Surgeon to every 1,000 men. The most junior grade, the hospital mate, was allotted to serve no less than 160 patients in the wards.[5] This was aside from the two regimental surgeons (three after 1803) directly provided for each battalion of around 800 men.

In the French *Service de Santé*, during the Napoleonic period, a great deal of bureaucracy quickly crept in, leading to an overbearing administration and a never-ending parsimony. Although seniority, experience, and commitment certainly could lead to promotion, nepotism and patronage via prominent medical men such as Larrey, Percy, Ivan, Coste, and Corvisart, was fairly rife in the medical profession throughout the entire war.

Napoleon himself showed some interest in public health medicine and disease (particularly in hygiene and vaccination), but he remained a medical cynic and he usually provided less support than was really necessary for the care of his imperial armies.[6] Training and examinations for military medical staff were often rudimentary except for those aspiring to higher positions, such as doctorial status. Many aspiring medical students opted for military medicine, in order to escape conscription into the French army and most of these students would only ever achieve a lowly status in the *Service de Santé*. In 1805 there were 1,986 medical men in the French army, but by 1812, there were 5,112.[7] However, the loss of surgeons in the Grande Armée reached staggering proportions, particularly in the campaigns in the

4   E. Evrard, *Esculape aux Armées – 500 Ans de Médecine Militaire en Belgique* (Brussels: Société scientifque du Service Médical Militaire,1997), p.52.

5   N. Cantlie, *A History of the Army Medical Department* (Edinburgh and London: Churchill Livingstone, 1974), Vol.1, p.179.

6   P. de Callataÿ, 'Napoleon et Medicine, Evolution du Service de Santé Militaire 1815-1997', *Medic,* 1997, pp.37-8.

7   Brice Docteur and Bottet Capitaine, *Le Corps de Santé Militaire en France, 1708-1782* (Paris: Berger-Levrault, 1907), p.171.

Caribbean, Egypt, Iberia, and Russia. For example, among the 4,100 medical staff recruited in the years 1792 and 1793, no less than 1,600 were lost to disease or wounds!

Students could aspire to progress to more senior grades of surgeon or to follow other medical careers (such as physicians or pharmacists). All medical staff members were generically named *officiers de santé*, however, there was some confusion, as the term was also often applied to second-rate civilian practitioners, who had only a limited medical education and had served an apprenticeship. These were not of course as well qualified as the more respected doctors, who had received a much superior basic education and had attended a full course of training at a university or recognised faculty of medical education. To aspire to a doctorate in medicine required influence, money, and required attendance at many hours of courses, working as an *interne* and producing a thesis before obtaining a *certificat de capacité*, which could be exchanged for a doctorate.[8] All young military aspirants from Belgium had to travel to Paris to be examined at the Val-de-Grâce Hospital by a medical board.

Basic medical training for the *Grande Armée* was not a static situation. Jean Dominique Larrey, perhaps the most notable surgeon of these wars, not only implemented and enforced proper courses for military trainees, but encouraged daily practical exercises, employing his ambulances as schools of instruction, not only in surgery, but also in military hygiene –especially for the more junior medical staff.

During the Napoleonic Wars, surgeons (including physicians and pharmacists) were graded into three classes, particularly in the hospital service, according to experience, training and qualification. The senior regimental surgeon was termed a *chirurgien-major*, whilst the lowest level of trainee was known as the *chirurgien-sous-aide* (nicknamed by François Percy, *chirurgiens de pacotille* – 'surgeons with a haversack'). These latter were often very inexperienced young men. The regimental staff usually consisted of a senior *chirurgeon-major* (1st class) and between one and three *aides-majors* (2nd class), with one to four *sous-aides* (3rd class), depending on the number of battalions or squadrons in a particular regiment of infantry or cavalry. In hospitals, surgeons were employed at a number of levels, from senior *chirurgien en chef* down to the surgeons of the three classes. These men would also staff divisional or unit ambulances in the field. A 1st class surgeon would be required to direct an ambulance or services at a divisional level.

The Imperial Guard had a somewhat elite medical service with its own ambulances and staff. However, the efficient provision of ambulances for the Guard was rarely mirrored across line units. There were supposed to be ambulances allocated to corps, divisions, and sometimes even to smaller units. The 'ambulance' was a unit of surgical support, working as close to the site of injury as possible. An ambulance consisted, at full strength, of around 340 personnel and contained medical staff, *brancardiers* or *despotats* (stretcher-bearers), drivers, and others who might carry instruments and dressings. This was a brilliant concept and has been fully described elsewhere.[9] The full ambulance could be broken up to serve units of various sizes –corps, divisions, demi-brigades or regiments. Sadly, Britain failed to emulate this type of service throughout the war.

8   M. Howard *Napoleon's Doctors: The Medical Services of the Grande Armée* (Stroud: Spellmount Ltd., 2006) p.23.
9   J.D. Larrey (Translated from the French by R.W. Hall), *Memoirs of Military Surgery and Campaigns of the French Army* (Baltimore: Joseph Cushing, 1814), Vol.I, pp. 78-83

Of many Belgian surgeons who had gained experience and developed their skills in the *Service de Santé,* some wrote of their personal services. A Belgian military surgeon of particular note was Joseph de Kerkhove. He survived the retreat from Moscow and wrote a number of articles and a book entitled, *Histoire des Maladies observées à la Grande Armée Française pendant la Campagne de Russie en 1812 et Allemagne en 1813* (Antwerp: Janssens, 1836). Other Dutch-Belgian surgeons of note included Lepage, Colson, and Laurillaut-Falot, all of whom worked in the Grande Armée and then in later times in the Belgian Army. It is estimated that around 90 Belgian medical staff worked under the Imperial Eagles.[10] Interestingly, of these, 82 of them later served with the army of the *Pays-Bas* (the army of the Kingdom of the Netherlands in the campaign of 1815). Others would have retired into civilian practice by this time.

A very noteworthy surgeon in Belgian military medical history was Louis Seutin. He was conscripted into the *Service de Santé* after completing his medical courses in April 1813 and then served as a *chirurgien-aide-major* for five months in the Imperial Guard and at military hospitals in Dresden and Leipzig. There he was supervised by none other than Dominique Larrey. Even on campaign, Surgeon Larrey frequently circulated updated instructions concerning the management of establishments to surgeons. One in particular on 14 July 1813 recommended the trimming of wounds, early surgery when indicated (hoping to achieve around a 75 percent success rate), speedy operating, and the rehearsal of surgical procedures on cadaveric material. From Seutin's memoirs we learn that, after the Battle of Dresden, he was sent to Pirna, where in the macabre setting of a charnel house, he directed the rehearsal of amputations on cadavers, brought in by the ambulances. He was carrying out procedures at a young age, more usually attributed to a more senior *chirurgien-major*. Not all young Belgian surgeons were as fortunate in their experience: many young men practiced more limited duties, giving first aid and helping to recover patients from battle, particularly during the campaigns in Russia, Bohemia, and Saxony. The main lesson they learned from the French medical service was to be bold and to react with aggressive intervention.

We must also briefly consider the other branches of medicine; the physicians and the pharmacists. The physicians (*les médecins*) in the *Service de Santé* were, by dint of their status, training, and education, far fewer in number, when compared with the surgical fraternity. They were better paid and far less prominent during combat, being of much less use than surgeons on the immediate battlefield. This became a constant source of friction in all contemporary armies, which unfortunately detracted from the real challenges faced by the profession as a whole.

The senior medical man was the *Médecin en Chef*. He was responsible for hospital and unit appointments and for the quality of care of those with diseases. The fact is that many unit surgeons had also to act as physicians. Napoleon and Larrey seem to have voiced a few derogatory comments about these non-surgical colleagues. Larrey noted at Tilsit in 1807, complaining that with a few hundred sick, there were seven or eight physicians who barely put a foot in the hospital. He threatened to oust them from the hospital if they did not perform their duties! Needless to say, this should not be viewed as a wholesale condemnation

10   Evrard, *Esculape aux Armées*, pp.54-5.

of physicians, since many of them felt side lined when their surgical colleagues were overwhelmed and did their level best to help. Such an example was the Dutch physician, Salomon-Louis Laurillard-Fallot, who whilst working in the *Service de Santé*, assisted his surgical colleagues as best he could. During the Battle of Bautzen in 1813, he did his best to dress wounds and provide basic medical care and Larrey later recalled his spirited efforts.[11]

Also known as apothecaries, military pharmacists practised alongside the branches of surgery and medicine. During the Revolutionary Wars, it was planned that there should be a pharmacist for every 50 patients. Howard reckons that there were several hundred to a thousand serving in the *Grande Armée*, where they were employed in hospitals and with divisions.[12] As with their fellows in the other two specialities, they were designated into three classes. Each significant military hospital had a *Pharmacien-en-Chef*. Trainee pharmacists attended particular military hospitals for instruction. When the three main military teaching centres in France were closed in 1796, apprentice pharmacists were taught in and examined at departmental military hospitals; the young Belgian pharmacists training for ten years before facing examination. After the trainee passed his examination, he would be admitted to the *Service de Santé* as a pharmacist 3rd class. Pharmacists oversaw the stocking and preparation of prescribed medication and were rather like some purveyors in the British Army Medical Department (AMD); a few of them were unfortunately subject to corruption and peculation. Perhaps the best-known pharmacist in the French Empire was Antoine-Augustin Parmentier, prominent for his contributions to studies of nutrition and vaccination. It is stated that they administered sedation and opiates before and during surgery – a practice which was certainly not seen in the British service of this period. There is uncertainty concerning the number of Belgian pharmacists who served with the French *Service de Santé*.[13]

From 1792 until 1814, a number of both temporary and permanent hospitals were created in Belgium under French domination, for the sick and wounded. Following Dumouriez's invasion of the Low Countries in 1792 the French Republican army commandeered a number of religious institutions – principally monasteries and convents and converted them into hospitals. They initially concentrated on utilising to the full, the well-established hospitals at Brussels, Ghent, Antwerp, Louvain, and Liège, but alongside these five principal Belgian military base hospitals, nine others were created under the Convention at Tournai, Mons, Ath, Bruges, Malines, Tirlemont, Tongres, Saint-Trond, and Namur. These were only ever intended to play a lesser and more temporary role, but some of these establishments, such as the one at Malines, were still in use until the early twentieth century.

As regards Brussels itself, the Emperor Joseph II had expelled the members of the Order of Minimes de Saint-François de Paule from the Minimes convent in 1787 and transformed it into a military hospital for the Austrian army. With the entry of Dumouriez's force into Brussels in 1792, the hospital still held 149 sick or wounded Austrian soldiers. These men were evacuated to France and the cases of venereal disease and scabies were transferred to the St Elisabeth hospital. Thus in 1793, the Minimes convent and St Elisabeth barracks were already used as military hospitals in the city. Here, two senior clinicians attached to Dumouriez's

---

11   Howard, *Napoleon's Doctors,* pp.14-15.
12   Howard, *Napoleon's Doctors* pp.5-16.
13   Evrard, *Esculape aux Armées,* p.57.

headquarters, Dr Menuret, senior physician in the French Armée du Nord and senior surgeon Lagresie exploited the St Elisabeth hospital's capacity. At one time there were no less than 1,176 patients in the hospital; 156 were wounded men: 553 had febrile conditions, 304 with scabies, and 163 with venereal diseases. To care for this large number of men, there were three physicians, 48 surgeons and 10 apothecaries. In 1808, when the French took over the large Jesuit convent in the Rue de Ruisbroek, the Minimes hospital became an artillery depot, then a workhouse and later, a tobacco factory and a print-works, it then reverted to being a hospital in 1831.

In Ghent, the convent Riches Claires was opened as a military hospital in 1792. However, it only held 200 patients, so another Augustinian convent was used, known as the Hôpital Militaire de l'Egalité, which became the principal military hospital. During the 1809 epidemic of fever, services were transferred to the

Antoine-Augustin Parmentier, pharmacist, scientist, and nutritionalist. (Gareth Glover's Collection)

Grand Hôpital Biloque, under surgeon Kluyskens and Dr Bouchet. Further units had to be opened and between 1809 and 1810, there was provision for nearly 3,000 patients in all.

Antwerp was a critically important port and stronghold and it had a hospital established in the citadel. In 1793, this was full of Austrian wounded and sick patients when the French seized the town; commendably, they did not eject these cases and the French established a military hospital in the old monastery of the Dames Blanches (also known as the Tersik) at the south west corner of the town. Seven other convents in Antwerp were used as French military hospitals and in 1794 the French army requisitioned a Jesuit convent, which became a substantial medical base, holding 507 patients. Interestingly this hospital was used by the French, Dutch, and latterly by the Belgian army, only closing in 1911. The St Elisabeth Hospital was also requisitioned for military use. In 1809 during the fever epidemics, it served as a transit hospital whilst sick patients were moved to Malines and Brussels.

Louvain also abounded with disused convents. However, the College of Pope Adrien VI became the principal military hospital in the city. In January 1793, it could accommodate up to 200 patients. In 1801, Napoleon created a branch of the Hôtel des Invalides, which was housed in the Faucon College, part of the University of Louvain. No doubt this was the result of how many Belgian soldiers served in the French army and required care in their later lives. This continued to serve as a military hospital until the end of the Second World War. During the 1809 epidemic, typhus swept through the city and the Prefect of the Dyle opened two religious institutions as hospitals – the Abbaye des Prémontrés and the old abbey of Vlierbeek, at Kessel-Loo.

The last of the five major centres containing large military hospitals was the city of Liège. Dumouriez opened a military hospital in the Saint-Leonard convent, which soon housed 300 patients in miserable conditions. This prompted a visit by Danton and three other Directory officials. The visit to the Saint-Leonard hospital and other units revealed some interesting contemporary detail. The hospital was then under the supervision of Surgeon Caput and held 285 patients, who were nursed on the stone floors and were mainly fed on spoiled rice. Severe overcrowding and pressure from some *officiers des santé* had necessitated the opening of two other units – the Val des Ecoliers and the Croisiers in 1793. The Val des Escoliers, run by Surgeon Lagrisie and the senior physician of the Armée du Nord Menuret, held at this time, 380 sick patients and 43 casualties, it was reported to be in a satisfactory state. The des Croisiers Hospital had 244 patients but reportedly lacked a decent supply of linen.

Another convent in Liège had been opened as a hospital in the Saint-Laurent Abbey, which contained 657 patients. These were found to be in a very poor situation. When *Général de Division* Jourdan's forces entered the city in 1794, the St Laurent Hospital was re-established, serving as the only military hospital in the city. The French renamed it the Hôpital de la Liberté. During the campaigns in the Meuse valley, two new hospitals were opened, the Val des Ecoliers (re-named the Hôpital de l'Egalité – now the Fonck Barracks), the other unit was installed in the Chateau Prince Evêque at Seraing. Two further campaign hospitals were opened, one in the Chateau d'Otrange, near Waremme, the other at Stavelot, set up for the treatment of venereal diseases and the management of scabies. A later re-organisation in 1795/6 retained only two military hospitals in Liège (l'Egalité and la Liberté). In 1800 as needs diminished, only the St Laurent Hospital was maintained. It acted as a military convalescent base, a garrison hospital for the cavalry, cripples and military veterans. A glimpse into this unit during 1812 showed that the St Laurent contained 700 patients (300 fever cases, 100 wounded, 200 venereal patients, and 80 cases of scabies). It was staffed by 91 persons – 38 were medical. This hospital later became a barracks for around 1,000 soldiers, then a military prison, a muslin factory, reverting to a Belgian military hospital in 1831.

Many other towns had acted to shelter the sick and wounded in these early campaigns. Tournai on the Scheldt River had a hospital in the south west of the town. This had been opened in 1792 and was sited along an evacuation route. Ath lay not far from the French border and was well-fortified by Sebastien Vauban the celebrated French military engineer. There was a temporary hospital here, sited in a Capuchin monastery. The French re-opened a hospital in Mons in 1792 which had previously been closed in 1773; however in 1801 it returned to civilian use. It was to house many victims of the Waterloo campaign and the hospital here was in use until the end of the Second World War. Bruges harboured a hospital established in a Carmelite monastery, established by the *Commissaires des guerres* (these were agents of military administration). It was however, little used. The French cared for many of their wounded in 1792 in a Dominican convent, situated in the town of Malines. This hospital took in many evacuated patients from Antwerp during the 1809 campaign and there was an outbreak of typhus here. This hospital was used intermittently until 1910. Tirlemont, St Trond, and Tongres were towns situated along the strategic route to the Rhineland, this route passed through Liège, which was, at one time, Dumouriez's headquarters. Namur was an important and strong garrison city. In 1793, there were two military hospitals here – the Caserne and Celestine hospitals, each holding about 200 patients.

During the period of the French Consulate and the subsequent Empire, some calm and order was restored as there was little campaigning in this region and most of the above hospitals settled down to deal with the more mundane civilian disorders, such as febrile illnesses, venereal diseases, and scabies. Napoleon did however maintain a significant military strength and medical presence at the Channel ports such as Antwerp and on the German border at Liège, these vital bases were under constant threat from Allied invasion.[14]

In 1809 victims of fever from the local garrisons in the Walcheren region, as well as thousands of the invasion force who fell ill, filled the Belgian hospitals beyond their capacity. This forced a re-opening of religious institutions and the creation of some other temporary hospitals to cope with the pressure. From hospital reports of the year 1809-10 originating from the Vliebeek (Louvain) and Biloque (Ghent) convent hospitals, we learn of the mortality from diseases such as typhoid, intermittent fever and diarrhoeal afflictions. In the Vliebeek hospital, the mortality was 12 percent and in Ghent, it was nine percent. We do not know the age or fitness of these patients, but these figures are at the upper reaches of the average for the time.

The final campaign of 1814 saw a rather ragged British force of around 12,000 men under Sir Thomas Graham set out to try and capture Antwerp once again. Initial success at Merksem was followed by a disastrous failure at Bergen-op-Zoom. A British hospital had been opened at Willemstadt, under the direction of Dr Robert Grant, who had 30 hospital staff with him. Five hundred men were sick here with bowel and respiratory complaints and the hospital remained open until July 1814.

As with other armies, the medical men from the Low Countries, serving with the French army, possessed varied skills, experience and degrees of devotion to their patients. Most had an inadequate position in military society, a poor remuneration and no substantive military rank. The *Service de Santé* was regarded disdainfully by some, yet many soldiers appreciated the majority of *officiers de santé*. However, there was one serious limitation of the performance by the French service which deteriorated as the war wore on. This was the overbearing influence and control by the *Commissaires de guerres*, administrators who exerted an inexorably powerful domination of the service.[15]

There remained few enough honours for Belgian medical men serving in the French army. Medical staff and their senior colleagues continued to vie in vain for greater recognition and respect during these long wars. For most British, French, Prussian, and Dutch-Belgian surgeons, their greatest reward was gained via some clinical success and the simple gratitude of their patients. For all, this war did provide a catalyst for gradual change to the practice of military medicine. The French services had trained many surgeons, physicians, and pharmacists who had been born in the Low Countries, and these men would certainly prove their worth when called on to care for the casualties of the last great battle of the Napoleonic Wars.

14   Evrard, *Esculape aux Armées* pp.59-67.
15   Howard, *Napoleon's Doctors* pp.45-7.

2

Immediate Battlefield Support for the Wounded during the Waterloo Campaign

As night fell on 18 June 1815, tens of thousands of wounded men lay out amongst the fields of Waterloo with little hope of rapid collection or any pain relief. These wounded men quickly became dehydrated and restless, often pinned down by other casualties or horses and unable to move without pain. As darkness fell the survivors lay exhausted, knowing there was little prospect of them being found by anyone before morning. A profound sense of isolation would have added to both their fear and discomfort. With few dedicated 'stretcher bearers' (regimental musicians, not drummers, in the case of the British), all that they could pray for was the chance of survival, but undoubtedly with a great deal of suffering along the way. People of that time were more inured to suffering and loss than we are today, having already witnessed early death, often from a seemingly minor injury or illness. Not infrequently, men saw their wives bleed to death or perish from puerperal sepsis in childbirth and suffered as a high proportion of their children died with infections or disease.

The modern combat soldier has wildly different expectations, trusting in speedy evacuation by unit paramedics and the Medical Emergency Response Team system. They have a good chance of having their bleeding controlled by tourniquets, haemostatic dressings, and transfusion. They will receive pain relief and later, damage-control resuscitation and surgery. Many will also require corrective surgery, nursing, rehabilitation (both mental and physical), and help back into society. In recent conflicts most patients survived in a major base hospital facility such as Camp Bastion. Here the in-hospital mortality rate over recent wars, with well-trained field ambulance teams, has been around six to seven percent of those patients brought in alive.

At Waterloo the in-hospital fatality rate was actually around a surprising nine percent. However, it must be understood that hundreds of men bled out on the 1815 battlefields, for want of pre-evacuation care and timely removal. Even to reach a hospital in Brussels or a nearby town two hundred years ago was a positive survival indicator. Few of us can possibly imagine the truly apocalyptic scenes on the evening of Waterloo. This battle was the second most sanguinary single day conflict in the long wars against Napoleonic France (the first being Borodino).

Roughly 50,000 casualties lay out on the fields of Waterloo and with around 2,290 wounded men per mile of front, the density of the casualties was about ten times that of the first day of the Battle of the Somme, although the overall number of casualties was much lower. Understandably there is quite a variance between casualty statistics garnered from such diverse sources during the campaign of Waterloo. The late *Colonel* Evrard, a senior Belgian medical officer and renowned historian, quoted a casualty rate across the entire campaign from amongst the 300,000 combatants, at around 89,000, with 23,700 killed and 65,300 wounded (around 30 percent of the total forces employed). He also gives casualty data for Waterloo itself, providing the rather impossibly precise figures of 188,680 combatants, of which 10,813 were killed (5.7 percent) and 35,295 wounded (18.7 percent). However, he does not provide any estimate of the large numbers of 'missing' in these figures nor is any account taken of those who died of their wounds later.[1] These figures are of course, not only inclusive of the wounded from the actions of Quatre Bras, Ligny, and Waterloo, but also include the French and Prussian casualties from Wavre as well. An estimate for Grouchy's losses was around 550 killed and 1,800 wounded, whilst Prussian casualties in these actions were 643 killed and 2,381 wounded. The casualty figures for the Netherlands army are rarely quoted; the total Dutch and Belgian losses being 685 killed and 2,051 wounded, with 1,629 missing.[2]

Therefore, a grand total of around 60-65,000 men required medical support over the four days of fighting. Since many of the French medical staff had left the field with the fleeing army, or had been wounded or captured, most of the medical recovery work after Waterloo fell upon the shoulders of the remaining British, Belgian, Dutch, German, and Prussian surgeons. Estimates of those able to supply this succour are imprecise, but, if we accept that around 300 British surgeons were immediately available during the campaign, we have to assume that at least 200 of these army surgeons would have moved off with their units into France on 19 and 20 June and a similar ratio would apply to all of the allied armies. Thus, perhaps only around 100-120 British army medical staff, a similar number of Dutch-Belgian military doctors, and a scattering of French, Prussian, and other German surgeons would have been available to manage the huge numbers of dispersed casualties of all nations left behind as the armies marched away. Significant assistance was therefore required from the civilian authorities of the new Kingdom of the Netherlands. Their valuable contribution, which has received little recognition, will be featured in this work.

The pitiful state of the casualties and lack of immediate relief resulted from the inertia suffered by the exhausted and hungry combatants. Many units had endured long, tough marches over a number of days, with inadequate food and little sleep, before the battle, culminating with up to nine hours of fighting. The cold night was relatively calm after the cacophony of the day, but it was regularly punctuated by the groans of the wounded and dying, cries for water, and the occasional neighing of limbless or disembowelled horses. Captain Cavalié Mercer's poignant description of that night must have been engraved on his memory:

> Here and there some poor wretch, sitting up among the countless dead, busied himself in endeavours to staunch the flowing stream with which his life was fast ebbing away. Many whom I saw so employed that night were, when morning

---

1   Evrard, *Esculape aux Armées*, p.94
2   Evrard, *Esculape aux Armées*, p.82.

dawned, lying as stiff and tranquil as those who had departed earlier. From time to time a figure would half raise itself from the ground, and then, with a departing groan, fall back again. Others, slowly and painfully rising, stronger, or having less deadly hurt, would stagger away with uncertain steps across the field in search of succour. Many of these I followed with my gaze until lost in the obscurity of distance; but many, alas! After staggering a few paces would sink on the ground, probably to rise no more… Horses, too, there were to claim our pity – mild, patient, enduring. Some lay on the ground with their entrails hanging out, and yet they lived.[3]

The allied forces lost around 2,600 horses killed at Waterloo (British equine losses being 1,577 killed), which probably indicates that there were two or three times as many wounded animals, many of which would have needed to be put out of their misery by their riders or farriers. Whilst most combatants would have fallen into an exhausted sleep, a few did wander out that night, however. Soldiers, eager for plunder, and even some of the bolder female camp followers were the first to roam out onto the battlefield for less than altruistic purposes. There was so little wealth amongst the rank and file, that it was small wonder that pilfering of the dead and wounded, searching for purses, coins, medals, gold braid, rings, and watches was rife. Not a few casualties were injured further or had their throats cut during these nefarious practices. It was not long before the local civil populace was out on the fields joining in this mission. It was routine practice to strip men of their jackets, trousers, overcoats, stockings, and footwear. Such items were seen as fair game and were valuable. These purloined articles were of great use to the farm labourers and their families, whose livelihoods, crops, land, and property had been severely disrupted if not destroyed completely.

The collectors soon began their grizzly task of tapping out teeth from the mouths of healthy young corpses. These could be sold for between a shilling and half-a-crown apiece. Glued or pegged into hippopotamus or walrus ivory they made adequate dentures for those wealthier classes of persons, who were able to afford sugar and who so suffered with carious teeth.

Many regimental fatigue parties were sent out at daylight on 19 June to collect the wounded, but these efforts were soon interrupted by their recall to the units, which were ordered to march on towards France. Some medical officers were appointed to stay behind to assist with their battalion's casualties, but inevitably, many of the French wounded lay out for far longer than the Allied men awaiting collection. The 2/30th Foot was delayed in marching from the area and their very-experienced and humane battalion surgeon, James Elkington, rode out to assist the wounded of various nations. Some wounded men were beyond help and begged for water or an end to their suffering, yet the only certain cases of 'mercy killing' were some recorded as being carried out by members of the Prussian army. These latter events were witnessed by Lieutenant William Hay, serving with the 12th Light Dragoons, who retraced his steps onto the fields around Mont St Jean four days after

---

3   Cavalié Mercer, *Journal of the Waterloo Campaign kept throughout the Campaign of 1815 by the Late General Cavalié Mercer, commanding the 9th Brigade Royal Artillery* (London: Blackwood, 1870) pp.182-3.

Retrieving dead comrades. (Michael Crumplin's collection)

Waterloo. The weather was intolerably hot and the stench unimaginable. He noted groups of Prussians wandering about dispatching some of their own and French wounded, who they considered beyond help. Hay probably at first thought this was a cruel business, but often, if truth be told, at this late stage, it was an act of mercy for most.[4]

When 19 June dawned, Mercer wandered the battlefield, contemplating the miserable scene and he recounted:

> What could I do? All, however, though in more modest terms, craved assistance; and every poor wretch begged most earnestly for water. Some of my men had discovered a good well of uncontaminated water at Hougoumont, and filled their canteens; so I made several of them accompany me and administered to the most craving in our immediate vicinity.[5]

Thirst was a constant problem for injured men accentuated by the heat of the day, the adrenaline surge and the acrid atmosphere of black powder. Those severely injured soldiers who were unable to move, became so extremely thirsty that they were forced to drink from any muddy or bloodstained puddles within reach. For two days following the fighting, the route to the north was clogged with waggons and the detritus of war. Dr John Haddy James, Assistant Surgeon to the 1st Life Guards, commented that:

---

4   W. Hay (ed. Mrs S.C.I. Wood), *Reminiscences under Wellington, 1808-15* (London: Simpkin, 1901), pp.212
5   Mercer, *Journal of the Waterloo Campaign*, p.187.

Most of the wounded were sent back to hospitals in Brussels in carts or any sort of transport that could be found. One's mind shrinks at imagining the suffering they must have endured on that long jolting ride, or that weary tramp, and then only to face in so many cases the pain and disgust of a spreading gangrene.[6]

A large number of wounded were carried to the nearby field dressing station of Mont St Jean, which acted as the Allied 1st Corps dressing station and they then had to endure uncomfortable transportation to Brussels, more than ten miles distant. Often surgery with its inherent complications would be their fate, before eventual repatriation to Britain or their homeland.

Men with upper limb and head wounds wearily struggled on foot the painful ten miles to Brussels, some were fortunate to acquire rider-less horses. Sergeant Anthony Tuittmeyer of the 2nd Line Battalion, King's German Legion, had an arm torn off by a round shot: he managed to procure an abandoned horse and rode north. He reached Brussels and searched for the St Elisabeth hospital towards the north of the city, where he found Dr Christian Bach, a Staff Surgeon of the KGL. After being put to bed, Tuittmeyer fainted and remained insensible for half an hour.[7]

On 6 April, Wellington had requested from the Secretary for War, Lord Bathurst, 'all the spring wagons' he could muster for the sick and wounded.[8] However, most of the less mobile casualties were actually transported by un-sprung requisitioned farm carts, rather than the sprung wagons requested. As the wheels turned on the rough road surface, casualties, particularly those with poorly splinted lower limb fractures, suffered severely. Not only was the pain intolerable, but the risk of haemorrhage and further tissue damage significant.

It was not until the morning of the 19 June that a 48-vehicle convoy of these fourgons lumbered their way down from Brussels and almost missed the battlefield having taken a wrong turning. Deputy Inspector John Gunning, in charge at the 1st Corps dressing station, discovered their error and redirected them off the road to Nivelles and they picked up casualties from Mont St Jean and other localities, and many more in Waterloo village itself including its church. The collection of all the wounded took up to five days, sometimes longer, the few men surviving this long having been given food and water, supplied by thoughtful local peasants or by drinking from the filthy puddles left on the battlefield. Such serious delays predicted poor surgical outcomes. Nevertheless, it is estimated that around 500 (mainly allied) amputations were carried out at Mont St Jean and at the field hospitals of Waterloo prior to being transported to Brussels; and upwards of 2,000 such procedures were carried out over the entire campaign. Some casualties were just too badly injured to be moved, for example, Colonel William Howe de Lancey, Wellington's Assistant Quartermaster General, never left the hovel where he lay dying in the hamlet of Mont St Jean.

6   Jane Vansittart, *Surgeon James's Journal 1815* (London: Cassell, 1964), p.36.

7   M. Crumplin & P. Starling *A Surgical Artist at War, The Paintings and Sketches of Sir Charles Bell, 1809-1815* (Edinburgh: Royal College of Surgeons, 2005) p.82.

8   Lt. Col. Gurwood (ed.), *The Dispatches of Field Marshal the Duke of Wellington* (London: John Murray, 1852), Vol. VIII, p.18.

Sergeant Tuittmeyer. (Courtesy Museum of Military Medicine)

On the western fringes of the battlefield, where the wounded of the 2nd Allied Corps were lying, Belgian farm carts started moving them away from Braine l'Alleud, where a field hospital had been established after the action (probably based at St Etienne church in the village centre, which almost certainly was the Allied 2nd Corps dressing station, during the battle) and where several Dutch-Belgian and even possibly some captive French surgeons laboured away.

Initially, it is estimated that from the three days of fighting, there were around 45 casualties for each surgeon.[9] Casualties continued to pour into Brussels. Sergeant Ned Costello of the 95th Regiment (Rifles) was in Brussels on the 19 June and he observed the initial surge of wounded arriving:

> In the morning [19 June], the scene surpassed all imagination. It baffles description for there were upwards of 40,000 wounded French, Belgians, Prussian and English intermingled with carts, wagons and every other vehicle attainable, which continued to arrive heaped with unfortunate sufferers. The wounded were laid on straw, with avenues between them, in every part of the city, with no discrimination

9   P.J. Haythornthwaite, *Waterloo Men – the Experience of Battle 16-18 June 1815* (Ramsbury: Crowood Press, 1999), p.103

between friends or foes. They were nearly destitute of surgical attendance, but the humane and indefatigable exertions of the fair ladies of Brussels, greatly made up for this deficiency. Numbers were busily employed strapping and bandaging wounds; others were serving out tea, coffee, soups and other nourishments, many occupied themselves dressing them in clean shirts, and other habiliments.[10]

Delays in gathering in all the casualties were hampered by the fact that many French wounded were sheltered by sympathetic Belgians. There was also a strong desire by the French to evade capture (many for a second time), particularly by the vengeful Prussians or dreading incarceration in the prison hulks in the south of England.

For the six-month period during and after the campaign, the Belgian and Allied medical staff created a 'Ville sanitaire' [Sanitary City] and Belgium, could justifiably call itself, 'La sœur de charité de l'Europe guerrière' [The Sister of Charity of European Warriors].[11] As the casualties poured in to Brussels, many patients were temporarily deposited in the Grande Place, in the adjacent park, and in any other large public or private building. Soon, the casualties and medical staff filled Brussels to capacity. However, it was critical for the senior medical men to see that there was a minimum of overcrowding, access to shelter, clean bedding and water, and proper methods of waste disposal, with the real threat of serious contagion hanging over the city in these early summer days.

10   Eileen Hathaway, Costello, The True Story of a Peninsular War Rifleman (Shinglepicker: Swanage, 1997), p285.
11   Edgard Evrard, 'Brève Histoire de l'organisation des soins dispensés aux blessés militaires dans les hôpitaux belges,après la dernière campagne napoléonienne (juin 1815)', Histoire des Sciences Medicales, Tome XXVII, No. 1, 1993, p.32

3

The Dispersal of the British, Netherlands (Dutch-Belgian), Prussian, and French Medical Staff During and After the Battle

The distribution of the hospital facilities of the various armies in this campaign have rarely been examined in any detail. All had previously established organised hospital facilities at key locations, but such a whirlwind campaign of manoeuvre required the additional establishment of field hospitals, near the site of the various battles, often consisting of little more than the local walled farmhouses, with very limited resources. It was essential to establish temporary hospital facilities in convenient large religious or bureaucratic buildings, either at locations without hospitals, or in addition to the permanent medical establishments when these became overloaded with casualties. This was particularly the situation in Brussels.

The British Medical Staff

Before the 1815 campaign commenced, there were already 52 hospital medical staff with the British force in Belgium, the majority having accompanied the troops of the 1814 Flanders campaign, the medical staff having been principally garrisoned at Middelburg, on the Zeeland peninsula. This medical contingent comprised 16 surgeons, three physicians, 22 hospital assistants, seven apothecaries and four purveyors.[1] Deputy Inspector of Hospitals, Dr Robert Grant was chosen as Principal Medical Officer for the forthcoming campaign.[2] From August 1814, these were distributed around the five principal hospitals in Brussels (the Jesuits, St Elisabeth, Annonciate, Gens d'Armerie and the Minimes). Other small medical depots with small hospital facilities were also situated along the casualty evacuation routes, at Antwerp, Ghent, Bruges, and Ostend. A complete garrison company of 4 officers and 107 NCOs and men from a veteran battalion were also sent out to Belgium. The Ordnance Medical Department also had its own battery medical staff serving under Deputy Inspector

---

1   N. Cantlie, *A history of the Army Medical Department* (London: Churchill Livingstone, 1974) Vol.1, p.384.
2   Deputy Inspector of Hospitals Sir James Robert Grant, no. 1307 in Col A. Peterkin & Col. W Johnston, *Commissioned officers in the Medical services of the British Army 1660-1960* (London: Wellcome Library, 1968), Vol.I 1660-1898.

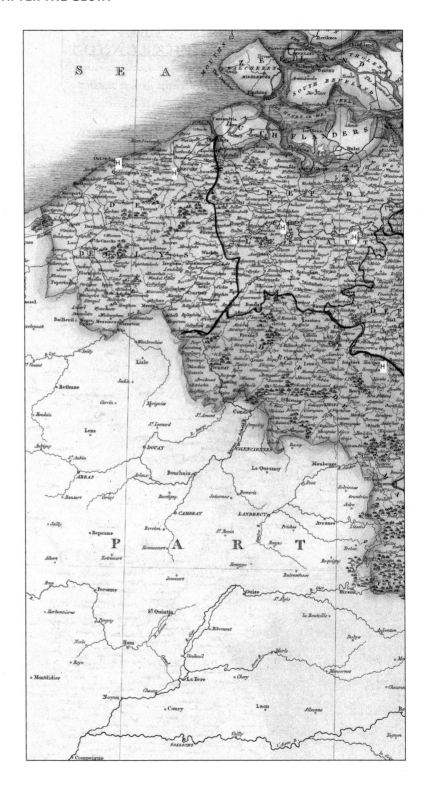

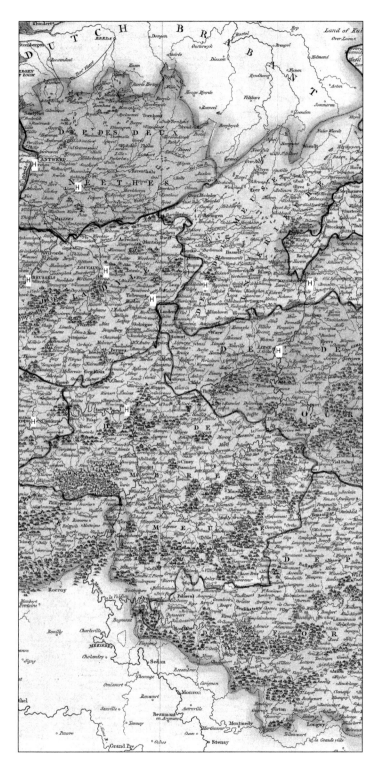

The dispersal of major hospitals or large field hospitals around the Low Countries.

Wittman.[3] Each brigade was allotted a staff surgeon and each division a deputy inspector or staff surgeon.

After 1803, most battalions in the British Army were served by a regimental surgeon and two assistant surgeons. As a rule, the senior of the two assistants would act in the front line, whilst the senior surgeon and the other assistant would stay further back, in a secure and known location for the evacuation of battalion wounded. Some battalions were however short of their surgeon or an assistant surgeon at Waterloo.

At the opening of the campaign and until nearly 48 hours after Battle of Waterloo, there were therefore around 298 medical staff officers available to manage the wounded and the sick. This initial figure included senior surgeons and physicians, junior hospital staff, regimental surgeons, apothecaries, purveyors, and ordnance medical men. After the last battle, the army began its march into France and most of the regimental staff was ordered to accompany the troops in preparation for further fighting, which could potentially lead to high levels of casualties. Of the regimental medical staff, a few assistant surgeons, particularly from the hardest-hit battalions, were allowed to stay back to help in Brussels, at least for a while. The number of medical men available to support the huge numbers of wounded left behind was bolstered by the arrival of a number of late-comers who had arrived at Brussels from Britain, following news of the severe action and the desperate need for medical help. These arrived in a dribble for up to two weeks after the battle, some of them actually civilian surgeons, just keen to help. The Duke of Wellington's personal physician and surgeon, Dr Robert Hume,[4] also remained in the city until July to provide his help. In total it has been estimated in some sources that some 60-odd military surgeons travelled from Britain to help, but the numbers still remained wholly inadequate to the workload.

Those senior staff remaining at Brussels consisted principally of deputy inspectors, hospital staff surgeons to the forces, physicians, hospital assistants to the forces, warranted hospital mates and a few civilian medical staff, apothecaries and purveyors.

Every major hospital controlled by the Allied medical staff in the Low Countries had a senior and experienced staff surgeon in charge of that unit. In the Belgian capital, John Hennen looked after the Jesuits or the principal military hospital in Brussels, [5] hospital assistant Richard Crofton was the resident medical officer there. [6] Dr William Galbraith Wray, an unattached physician to the forces, was in charge of the St Elisabeth Hospital,[7] and David Brownrigg ran the Annonciate Hospital.[8] John Cole looked after the Minimes Hospital,[9] and Theodore Gordon

3   *Deputy Inspector of Hospitals* William Wittman Ordnance Medical Department, no. 1716 in Peterkin & Johnston, *Medical Officers*. He died at Paris on 22 July 1815.

4   Deputy Inspector of Hospitals John Robert Hume, no. 1988 in Peterkin & Johnston *Medical Officers*.

5   Staff Surgeon John Hennen, no. 1971 in Peterkin & Johnston *Medical Officers*. He became a Deputy Inspector of Hospitals on 7 September 1815.

6   Hospital Assistant Richard Crofton, no. 3602 in Peterkin & Johnston *Medical Officers*, retired from the service in February 1816 and died in 1822.

7   Physician William Galbraith Wray, no. 2552 in Peterkin & Johnston *Medical Officers*, he died in Barbados in 1817.

8   Staff Surgeon David Brownrigg, no. 1980 in Peterkin & Johnston *Medical Officers*.

9   Staff Surgeon John Cole, no. 1992 in Peterkin & Johnston *Medical Officers*, he retired in 1821 and died at Boulogne in 1826.

supervised the Gens d'Armerie.[10] Deputy Inspector Summers Higgins had a supervisory role, at first in Brussels, then at Antwerp.[11] On 19 June, Grant applied to Sir James McGrigor, Director General of the AMD in London,[12] for the immediate dispatch of more surgeons from Britain.

In charge of hospital provision in the region was Principal Medical Officer Dr Robert Grant (not to be confused with staff surgeon Robert Grant). He was an experienced physician and surgeon, who had served in Flanders, Cape Colony, and at Walcheren and had given a great deal of assistance to the Russian forces in France in 1814. Initially, he remained busy with making the necessary arrangements for the forthcoming campaign, in Brussels and at Antwerp.

Deputy Inspector of Hospitals John Gunning was Principal Medical Officer to the allied 1st Corps,[13] which was engaged heavily at both the battles of Quatre Bras and Waterloo. Under his command were 138 surgeons of the British and Hanoverian units, which consisted of 11 staff surgeons, 40 regimental surgeons, 86 assistant surgeons, and one junior pharmacist.

It is believed that Lieutenant General Lord Hill's 2nd Corps medical field hospital, run by Staff Surgeon Henry Gresley Emery,[14] which incorporated the Belgian field ambulances, was stationed at Braine l'Alleud during the Battle of Waterloo.

The presence of experienced visiting 'consultant' civilian surgeons provided some interesting medical insight to management and cases. The foremost of these visitors was George James Guthrie of Peninsular War fame. He consulted on many cases but only operated on just two patients, who were a challenge to the extant hospital staff. One patient had a deeply seated intermittently bleeding artery in his leg. Guthrie cut down on the limb and eventually, with some considerable loss of blood, managed to control the vessel. This procedure was unkindly nicknamed by some colleagues, 'Guthrie's Bloody Operation'! This dynamic surgeon also performed and recorded a successful disarticulation of the hip on a French prisoner.

The other notable surgeon to visit the hospitals in Brussels was Sir Charles Bell. He was assisted by his brother in law, John Shaw, and also by Dr Robert Knox (of later notoriety being associated with the Burke and Hare scandal). Bell, we know worked principally at the Gens d'Armerie hospital, mostly on badly delayed and therefore very poorly French casualties. Knox, perhaps overcritical, was unimpressed by Bell's results. In fact, it has been possible to ascertain the identities of only four or five volunteer civilian surgeons who definitely arrived in Brussels after the campaign to help (these were Surgeons Guthrie, Bell, Thomson, Somerville, and possibly a physician, Dr Richard Bright).

The surgeons, physicians, apothecaries and purveyors, were dispersed around the city's hospitals, various public or private buildings which had been requisitioned and even in the parks, where tented or hutted accommodation were quickly set up. But it is clear that there were simply not enough of them.

---

10 Staff Surgeon Theodore Gordon, no. 2340 in Peterkin & Johnston *Medical Officers*, he became Assistant Inspector of Hospitals in September 1815.

11 Deputy Inspector of Hospitals Summers Higgins, no. 1730 in Peterkin & Johnston *Medical Officers*, he died at Cheltenham in 1843.

12 Director General Sir James McGrigor, no. 1182 in Peterkin & Johnston *Medical Officers*, he died in London in 1858.

13 Deputy Inspector of Hospitals John Gunning, no. 1205 in Peterkin & Johnston *Medical Officers*, he died in Paris in 1863.

14 Deputy Inspector of Hospitals Henry Gresley Emery, no. 2054 in Peterkin & Johnston *Medical Officers*, died near Bristol in 1826.

Duties of the Principal Medical Officer in the Management of General Hospitals

There is no indication that any of the Brussels hospitals had a military commandant, as would have been the practice for permanent general hospitals in Britain or abroad at these times. It is feasible that there was a local Dutch-Belgian military or medical officer acting as a liaison for the senior staff surgeons appointed as medical officers to each hospital. The few British physicians present in Brussels would see to the general care and management of the patients, by linking with the staff surgeons and carrying out ward rounds and visiting the apothecaries and purveyors.

The duties of the hospital staff, that is to say surgeons such as Kluyskens and the senior staff surgeons, were also to create reports and returns and keep in touch with the Principal Medical Officer – Robert Grant. His duties included hospital visits to ensure that the professional treatment of patients was 'judicious' and also to see that there was proper diet and drug provision. He was permitted to perform surgery when this was of a serious or difficult nature. In the normal way of things, no capital (that is to say, major) operation, was to have been carried out unless he was present. However, in the chaotic wards of Brussels following the battle, this responsibility was left to the relevant staff surgeons, many of whom were very experienced. In quieter conditions, his other duty was to encourage junior surgeons to attend and watch major surgical procedures or dissections (post-mortems).[15]

It was also a duty of the Principal Medical Officer to see that convalescents were visited daily by medical officers, that patients were not malingering and that they were returned to their regiments or moved on as soon as feasible to base hospitals in Britain, where they might later die, recover to serve in veteran or garrison battalions or be invalided out of the army. This was a particularly important role for Grant to supervise, to minimise the overcrowding in Brussels and Antwerp.

Brussels 26 June 1815

My Lord Duke,
I have the honour to acquaint your Grace, that having now accommodated the wounded and organised the hospitals, I think it right in the present circumstances of the army to lose no time in proceeding to head-quarters and expect to be able to set off tomorrow morning.

On my arrival I shall have the honour of reporting personally the arrangements I have made. In the meantime, as I find the number of wounded prisoners and of the slighter British wounded who are in billets to have been greater than was calculated when I wrote the Adjutant General, I beg to enclose a state which your Grace may rely upon as far as regards the number in the hospitals, but is still conjectural with respect to those in billets, not having been able to obtain, either through the Commandant or Mayor, a statement of them.

---

15   Anon. [probably J. McGrigor], *Instructions for the regulation of Military Hospitals and the Sick with Divisions* (Lisbon: A.R. Galhardo printers, 1813), p.45

I have been prevented, by want of transport, [from] sending the wounded prisoners, or indeed any wounded in the direction of Ghent, Bruges and Ostend, where I had prepared hospitals and proposed embarking many of the wounded, particularly the prisoners.

I shall leave directions to continue to evacuate the hospitals at Bruxelles upon those of Antwerp, with a view to the embarkation of such as are in a proper state. This will give us also room at Bruxelles to take into hospitals the whole of the slight cases that are in billets, and I have already apprised the Mayor that we are ready to receive 500 of the worst of them. What will then remain are [sic] so slight that I expect many of them will be fit to join their regiments in a fortnight.

The conduct of the inhabitants towards the wounded has been excellent, and the exertions of the medical officers great.

I have the honour to be, my Lord Duke, your Grace's most obedient humble servant, J R Grant

State of the wounded as far as can be ascertained:

26 June 1815
Bruxelles   3376
Antwerp   2466
British and Hanoverians   5842
Brunswickers at Merxem and Laeken   900
                                                   6742
French prisoners [wounded] about 2500
NB 1500 of those at Bruxelles are what is calculated to be in quarters of slight cases;
500 of the worst of them are ordered into the hospitals this evening.
J R Grant[16]

Thankfully, local retired medics, civilian practitioners, and even raw medical students were rapidly recruited by the local authorities and gradually filtered into the receiving hospitals to assist with the huge influx of casualties. Data concerning the Dutch-Belgian medical support is of particular interest, since this has been virtually ignored in British accounts of the campaign.

The Dutch-Belgian Medical Staff

A fresh *Service de Santé* had been set up with the creation of the new Netherlands kingdom in 1814, governed by a board of an inspector general and three senior physicians. The senior medical man in the Dutch-Belgian service was Inspector General Professor Sebald Justinas Brugmans (1763-1819), a Dutch physician.[17] Brugmans had four *officiers de santé* serving

16   2nd Duke of Wellington (ed.), *Supplementary Despatches, Correspondence and Memoranda of Field Marshal Arthur Duke of Wellington KG* (London: Murray, 1863), Vol.10, p.598.
17   Evrard, *Esculape aux Armées*, p.73.

under him, with a military pharmacist as secretary to the unit. Until his demise in 1819, Brugmans was the energising force of the *Service de Santé* of the army of the Netherlands. Born at Franken in 1763, he obtained a doctorate in medicine at the University of Groningen in 1785. In the following year, he obtained a chair at Leyden University, lecturing in botany, natural history, chemistry and medicine. Later designated advisor to the *Etats Généraux*, he arranged the care of the sick and wounded left behind when the allies re-embarked after the unfortunate 1793-5 campaigns in Holland.

The French *Service de Santé* took over control when Napoleon forced his brother Louis to stand down as King of Holland in 1810, leaving Brugmans in charge, as director general, but in the new French service of the Low Countries. He was given the same status as Dominique Larrey and Pierre François Percy. Also,

Inspector General Sebald Justinus Brugmans. (Gareth Glover's Collection)

he was awarded the *Legion d'Honneur* and became vice-chancellor of the University of Leyden. This experienced and dedicated clinician devised a strategy of care for the *Service de Santé* and was then charged with its delivery. Most importantly he was a keen military hygienist, with the object of preventing epidemic diseases. Whilst at Leyden in 1798 and at Amsterdam in 1805, Brugmans had surmised that the transmission of hospital gangrene could take place by aerial spread and also by clean wounds being contaminated from the re-use of previously infected materiel. With the enforcement of rigorous discipline and careful inspections, he achieved a great measure of success and gained a high reputation. He had been promoted inspector general by Napoleon and then retained his post under King William, despite Brugmans' prior allegiance to the French empire. At the beginning of June 1815, Brugmans prepared a three-line hospital scheme in preparation for the anticipated casualties – the military hospitals in Brussels and Louvain, with the addition of the civil hospitals in Charleroi, Nivelles, and Termonde were designated as the first reception areas. There were two other primary bases sited further north in Holland.

He selected a Belgian medical officer, Surgeon François Kluyskens (1771-1843),[18] to take control of the surgical services of Belgium. Kluyskens had been born in Alost, and was a reputable and experienced surgeon, who had trained and gained much combat experience with the Austrian army and subsequently served in the French army. He had been surgeon in charge of the military hospital in Ghent, but now his duties were transferred to

18   E. Evrard, *Esculape aux Armées* pp. 42.

the 500-bed military hospital in Brussels (the Jesuits).

The Belgian staff (*officiers de santé*) consisted of five *chirurgiens majors* (1st class – a rank equivalent to a captain and paid 1,600 florins p.a.) and six *chirurgiens aides-majors* (2nd class – equivalent to a 1st lieutenant, paid 900 florins p.a.), who were yet to fully qualify, having previously been situated at the St Pierre hospital in the south of the city, to prepare for their examinations. There were also eighteen *sous-aides* (3rd class – equivalent to a sub lieutenant, paid 500 florins p.a.). These junior surgeons were strictly limited in what they were allowed to practice, and they were certainly not permitted to carry out major amputations. They acted as nursing staff and they had temporarily had to give up their studies.

Surgeon François Kluyskens. (Gareth Glover's Collection)

In general, the Netherlands medical officers of the lower classes were not allowed to marry and were regarded very much as socially inferior. Like the British AMD, this service lacked 'dedicated' stretcher bearers, orderlies, nurses, or dedicated vehicles for casualty evacuation. Thus, the daily care of hospital patients depended purely on the random help offered by designated soldiers or convalescent patients. Leaving first aid care and recovery of casualties to combatants' comrades depleted the fighting force, but strict orders against colleagues helping the wounded would have proven catastrophic for the injured. Whilst in some armies, the evacuation of casualties from the battlefield during the fighting was left to regimental musicians, in 1814-1815 there were no military bands in the army of the Netherlands.

There were 48 Belgian medical officers: one physician (senior medical officer), 41 surgeons (seven of the 1st class, including Kluyskens, 15 of the 2nd class, including Louis Seutinwhose involvement after Waterloo will be dealt with later,[19] and 19 of the 3rd class) and with 6 pharmacists. However, with the inevitability of war and the announcement of the raising of an army of 25,000 men by Prince William to assist the allied cause, there was rather less enthusiasm to serve in the military medical staff than there had been in 1814. From the 1 March 1815 until the 17 June, only 34 medical men, of whom 31 were surgeons and three were pharmacists, had signed up for the army. These were all young men, with far less operational experience than some of their older colleagues. It is very noticeable that there were no Belgian 1st class surgeons, physicians, or pharmacists serving in their medical department. With the enforced union of the northern and southernmost provinces of the

---

19   Evrard, *Esculape aux Armées*, p.54.

new Netherlands, there was bound to be some general Belgian disaffection, but this in no way infers a lack of metal or indeed military performance in the campaign.

The 1st Corps of the allied army included two Netherlands infantry divisions and one of cavalry. The 2nd Corps only had one Netherlands infantry division plus the East India Brigade,[20] stationed in the Hal area, serving under the command of Prince Frederick of the Netherlands. Each infantry division had an ambulance (or mobile field hospital) attached to it, in a similar way to the French medical service. By June 1815, there were five 1st class surgeons and 70 2nd and 3rd class medical men attached to the staff of the three Netherlands infantry divisions and their ambulances. There were also an additional eighteen 2nd and 3rd class medics for the cavalry units. Ambulance *fourgons* were supplied by the commissariat, which also carried the field hospital equipment. For casualty evacuation to the divisional ambulances or to the base hospitals, the requisitioning of army supply wagons was deemed necessary.

On the 5 April, Brugmans conferred command of the medical organisation of the 1st Army Corps (the 2nd and 3rd Divisions) of the Netherlands army to Karl-Georg-Eduard Mergell, a German born at Felsberg in April 1781.[21] He had joined the *Service de Santé* of the army of the Batavian Republic in May 1802 and then, like most of his Dutch and Belgian colleagues, served with the French army from 1805 to 1812 and was promoted *chirurgien-major* in November 1809, during the Peninsular War.

The two divisional ambulances of the 1st Corps had a *chirurgien-major* in charge of each. In the 2nd Infantry Division (Perponcher) it was F.A. Kühn and in the 3rd Infantry Division (Chassé) the *chirurgien-major* was J.C. Croissant. The medical unit attached to the 2nd Corps (the detached Netherlands Corps at Hal) was commanded by *Chirurgien-Major* Schaurich and its 1st Division medical unit was commanded by *Chirurgien-Major* Tesch, with the corps ambulance commander, *Chirurgien-Major* Krabacher. As has been noted previously, no surgeon of Belgian origin held a significant senior role in the two corps or in the three ambulances. Belgian medical officers were however to be found in the Belgian combat units, each regiment having one of the 2nd class, one of the 3rd class and two medical students per regiment and each cavalry brigade. Only a single 3rd class medical officer was supplied to each artillery battery.

In the line regiments, there were 93 regimental surgeons and assistant surgeons attached to the seven brigades of infantry and the three brigades of cavalry belonging to the army of the Kingdom of the Netherlands.[22] In each regiment the appropriate medical equipment was supplied in packs which were carried by horses.

Many military historians from the Netherlands have highlighted the enforced improvisation and the major deficiencies of the Dutch-Belgian medical services during the actions at Quatre Bras and Waterloo. Two illustrious authors, (F. de Bas and J't Serclais de Wommersom) state that Dr Mergell (the Belgian Principal Medical Officer of 1st Corps) and Colonel Reuther (senior administrator to the same corps) were left without adequate instruction and that there had been a woeful lack of preparation. In particular, Reuther actually reported in the aftermath of the battle, that there was a serious lack of transport, an inappropriate distribution of medical supplies, and a lack of precise information on the location of the various medical

---

20   These troops had been recruited specifically to be sent out to re-garrison the Dutch East Indies, which had largely been captured by the British during the wars, but had been handed back to Holland in 1814.

21   Evrard, *Esculape aux Armées*, p.9.

22   Evrard, *Esculape aux Armées*, pp.32-33.

staff during the combat. Mergell also later wrote a confidential report to the administration at The Hague, describing the events of 16-18 June in some detail.

After the fighting of 16 June, *Chirurgien-Major* Kühn and his staff gave support to Perponcher's division as best they could and they evacuated around 1,000 casualties via Genappe. On the 17 June these patients had been collected at Braine l'Alleud. Further casualties had reached Brussels, the first influx having arrived on the night of 17 June.

Mergell, being at the Prince of Orange's headquarters at Braine le Comte, was initially completely ignorant of these events. However, becoming uneasy following the departure of the Prince of Orange to the front on the 16th and the subsequent troop movements, he made his own way to Nivelles. Here he learnt of the events that had occurred, including the engagements involving the 2nd Division, whose bivouac he finally discovered at 11:00 p.m. During the night he collected together about 100 Dutch-Belgian casualties and he had them transported to Nivelles, where he ensured that they were cared for.

The following morning, on 17 June, Colonel Reuther informed Mergell that the headquarters of the Prince of Orange was leaving Braine le Comte, and they were to set themselves up at Waterloo. He therefore promptly ordered the evacuation of all the wounded at Nivelles to Brussels.

Arriving near Waterloo in the afternoon, Mergell collected all of the Dutch-Belgian casualties who were to be found at Braine l'Alleud, Mont St Jean and Waterloo (around 200 in all he estimates), he formed a sick convoy under the care of Surgeons Mahlstede and Scharten, to travel on immediately to Brussels. Mergell was very unhappy with the performance of his medical service at Waterloo, in particular he noted that, the bearers and orderlies had not been seen since the evening of the 17 June, that there was a severe lack of medical equipment and no available wagons. To add to these problems the entire staff of the ambulances of the 2nd and 3rd Divisions of the Dutch-Belgian force had simply disappeared.

Mergell discovered the lost ambulances the following day (18 June) at Brussels and forced them to turn back towards Waterloo, but these two ambulances did not arrive at Braine l'Alleud until after the battle had ended. Mergell had struggled himself to get through the Forest of Soignes and had not arrived on the battlefield until 4:00 p.m. He could not find any of his own forces, only seeing British troops, so he took care of their casualties until the evening, surrounded by British surgeons.

On 19 June, Mergell re-joined his divisional ambulances at Braine l'Alleud. Absent during the battle, they were now able to fully support their own and other allied casualties, housed in St Etienne church and the surrounding buildings.

Towards midday, the two ambulances had to move on and took up their positions with their respective divisions, *en route* to Nivelles as they marched in pursuit of the French. Mergell left some medical staff at Braine l'Alleud, ordering them to remain until the casualties were all evacuated to Brussels. The battalion surgeons had remained with their units during the fighting, but were aware and ashamed of the behaviour of the ambulance staff. The majority of the Dutch-Belgian casualties were therefore treated by British surgeons, probably mostly at Mont St Jean Farm, the 1st Corps dressing station.

Mergell's report of events during the campaign is however circumstantial, attempting to make excuses for the failures, but still quite precise regarding the less-than-glorious behaviour of the medical staff of the 1st Corps ambulances in June 1815. This was a sad blow to him personally, in his first combat.

Netherlands Surgical Results

Despite the shortcomings in the field service, many Netherlands medical staff would be instrumental in bringing great relief to the casualties of the campaign. The activities of the Belgian medical staff from June to August 1815 can be found in a paper, written by Kluysken's son, (Hippolyte, born in 1807), who was also a doctor. This was published in the journal of the Medical Society of Ghent in 1855 and was entitled, *Exposé des Principaux cas de Chirurgie Observés après La Bataille de Waterloo, dans les Hôpitaux à Bruxelles*. This invaluable article was based on his father's contemporary reports and so reflects very much on the work of Joseph-François Kluyskens. Although designed to be an official account, the paper quickly devolves into a first-person account of the city bursting with casualties and of the great charitable efforts made by the citizens. Kluyskens wrote up a summary of the surgical results in the hospitals under his direction and the following data is a résumé of the most salient points:[23]

1 Amputation

Kluyskens estimated from his records, that the number of amputations carried out in the various hospitals and private premises in Brussels amounted to about 300 cases. Commensurate with common injury patterns, these were mostly performed on the lower limbs and interestingly, these were mainly guillotine (circular) amputations. In 160 of these cases the wound incision was closed using adhesive tapes and subsequent bandaging, Kluyskens admits that of these wounds which were closed immediately, only about a quarter healed at the first intention (attempt). The remainder were treated by the wound being left open and packed with charpie (linen waste) or lightly closed, resulting in inevitable suppuration.

The wounds that were immediately closed and had failed to heal by first intention took just as long to heal as those that had not been closed initially. A number of these, (around 19-20 cases) were accompanied by a great deal of pain and distress whilst secondary (later) healing occurred. When any compression of the stump by bandaging was applied, there was in some cases considerable swelling and inflammation. In others, scabbing entirely destroyed areas of skin and subcutaneous tissues.

Another group formed collections of infected and granulation tissue between the skin and the cut bone end. In all of these cases, generally within six to eight days of the operation, it was necessary to remove all bandages and adhesive straps, thus abandoning any attempts at primary healing. Here there was great disruption of the skin and subcutaneous tissues, which had separated from contracted or infected muscles. The infection often resulted in a conical shaped stump, with a purulent discharge exuding from the bone. This complication retarded the recovery of some French patients, so delaying their repatriation. The majority were eventually sent to Dunkirk on the 19 October 1815, but this left around 50 such cases of delayed healing still in the hospitals.

---

23   Evrard, *Esculape aux Armées*, pp.90-93.

This was in stark contrast to those treated by leaving their post-operative wounds open, which healed satisfactorily after a period of suppuration. These patients' wounds were largely healed within six to eight weeks. Kluyskens stated that he only lost 25 of these cases – in the main these were those patients who had primary closure of their operative incisions, this had therefore clearly been an inappropriate initial therapy.

Hippolyte Kluyskens quoted an interesting passage from one of his father's letters to Brugmans, in which he said that the surgical results in the military hospitals in Brussels left little to be desired. The success that they had achieved with their amputees and compound fractures had even surpassed his expectations, but his success appeared to contrast markedly with the less fortunate results of the British surgeons, where he claimed that fewer of their amputees survived. Those soldiers with compound fractures, had almost all succumbed from hospital gangrene which unfortunately flourished in these cramped and over-full hospitals, but this seems to have been a rare occurrence in the patients treated by the Belgian surgeons. They employed the use of a muriatic honey (a mixture of hydrochloric acid and honey) to promote healing. We have however, to regard this as possible surgical hyperbole and unless we know the case mix that the surgeons of the Belgian and British surgeons were presented with, we should be cautious at such an interpretation.

2 Disarticulation at the Shoulder Joint

By the 23 November 1815, there were still 23 patients who had undergone amputations of the arm in the Brussels military hospital. Many of these patients had apparently improperly healed surgical wounds or sepsis and of these, Kluyskens had carried out a disarticulation in two of the cases. He found no favour with Larrey's technique, preferring a high amputation at the very upper extremity of the humerus (upper arm bone), leaving the ball in the socket. Larrey also operated using his own method on two cases, both of whom perished.

3 Complex (Compound, i.e. open) Fractures

Kluyskens, looked after and treated 100 cases of compound fractures, using rather conservative measures, of whom only ten died. Healing of the remainder took around three months. At Namur, on the 17 June, a staggering 886 cases of compound fractures were admitted following the action at Ligny on the previous day.

4 Penetrating Head Injuries

The number of these who actually managed to reach hospital alive was perhaps unsurprisingly, very small.

5 Facial Injuries

There were a large number of wounds of the face, most often inflicted by sabre slashes, healing was effective in almost all of the cases.

6 Thoracic Wounds

Five patients presented with a variety of small arms injuries of the thorax of different levels and were successfully brought in to the military hospital, of whom two survived.

7 Abdominal Wounds

Kluyskens managed some penetrating wounds of the belly, in which no organ had been damaged, and these patients survived. In five cases where the internal organs injured were the gall bladder, the colon, or the bladder, the patients also recovered. In some cases where they had suffered colonic wounds (all of which probably had exteriorised bowel), he removed the dead bits of the gut and created a colostomy (then known as an 'artificial anus'). We have no idea of the number of men who suffered wounds of this type which proved fatal and who never reached hospital, nor of the total number of cases of this type that Kluyskens treated.

8 Genital Wounds

Kluyskens described only two cases of genital wounds. However, at Professor Thomson's visit to the Brussels military hospitals, he sketched seven cases of genital wounds or wounds very close to the genitalia.

9 Ligature of the Brachial Artery

In the main, when the fracture of a limb involved laceration of a major supply artery, amputation was undertaken. Amputation after upper limb wounds involving brachial arteries had fairly consistent survival rates. Establishment of a collateral blood supply (re-established blood flow through the limb via smaller, previously unimportant, blood vessels 'opened up' after the main supply vessel had been obstructed) in the upper limbs was much less of a problem than in the thigh or leg.

10 Wounds of the Joints

In most cases of joint wounds, the Belgian surgeons pursued a conservative regime of treatment. However, this always depended on the movement of the injured joint and the subsequent likely deformity, when healed. This was at variance with British military surgical teaching, where in many more cases of compound joint injury, early amputation was usually mandated to prevent the sequence of pain, immobility, and sepsis.

11 Hospital Gangrene (Necrotising fasciitis, or French, *'pourriture d'hôpital'*)

In September 1815 some hospitals were plagued by a prolific number of cases displaying this dreadful complication. The infection was caused by a 'cocktail' of aerobic and anaerobic organisms. It particularly struck post amputation stumps and infected wounds. In some cases, muriatic honey was successfully used, to the extent that Kluyskens claimed that no cases under his care were lost. This is a questionable claim as it is so out of kilter with the usual outcome statistics, whilst the statement actually goes against Belgian claims that there was no such contagion in their hospitals.

12 Tetanus

This infection was recorded in eight cases, three of which were patients with knee and foot injuries. Of the eight cases that Kluyskens described, only one patient survived, the remaining seven patients finally succumbed having lived for around 15-18 days. Stütz's method of treatment was employed. This consisted of prescribing alternating doses of an opiate and an alkaline preparation. The opiate was administered mixed with wine (two fluid ounces of wine with eight grains of opium, or 80 drops of laudanum in seven fluid ounces of distilled water). The alkali was administered as potassium bicarbonate in distilled water. This therapy seemed to alleviate the violent contractions, particularly of the large back muscles causing spasms. There is no mention by Kluyskens of ablative limb surgery or tube feeding (necessitated by lockjaw-type spasms of the teeth, preventing feeding). The small number of cases of tetanus emphasises the relative rarity of this severe infection, despite the widespread use and presence of horse manure in agriculture and the thousands of equine casualties, which would have contaminated the soil. The excreta of horses and other domestic animals contain the spores of the organism *Clostridium Tetani*, which causes this terrible infection, commonly known as 'Lockjaw'.

The results obtained by Kluyskens and his staff, in the military hospital in Brussels (given the limited contemporary knowledge of these clinicians and their excessive workload), seemed to be very satisfactory. Unfortunately, we do not have the outcome data from the impressive series of 300 amputations performed by Kluyskens, He wrote in a report to Brugmans that his team's success with the wounded and amputees was better than those of his British compatriots. The British surgeons working in Brussels in June and July (largely staff surgeons and their assistants) certainly praised, in their memoirs, the well-ventilated, clean and orderly hospitals. They were also very impressed by the efforts of the Belgian military and civil surgeons working under Kluyskens' direction.

Kluyskens emerges as both a natural, energetic and talented military surgeon and administrator. He was made a Chevalier of the Order of the Belgian Lion by King William of the Netherlands, and King William of Prussia rewarded him with a precious diamond ring, accompanied by a signed letter, thanking him for his care and attention to the wounded Prussian soldiers.

Larrey praised the industry, intelligence, and dexterity of the Belgian surgeons as they carried out their arduous work and he noted a high level of success, particularly with their primary (early)

Surgeon Louis Seutin (Gareth Glover's collection)

amputations. We must however note that there must have been some considerable delay with many of these procedures, in recovering them from the battlefields, perhaps throwing some doubt on the definition of primary or early amputations.

Larrey, although officially a prisoner, personally assisted with a large number of casualties –principally Prussians at Louvain. On 24 June, Larrey, who was then on his parole, was granted leave to visit the Brussels hospitals in order to give advice on the care of the French wounded. He mentions his meeting with surgeon Louis Seutin in his memoirs and he worked with the young Belgian surgeon to carry out a variety of operations. Seutin had been an acolyte of Larrey and had served as a *chirurgien aide-major* in *La Grande Armée* in 1813 at Dresden and Leipzig. Larrey and Seutin operated for four days on the French patients before the former returned to Louvain as he had been instructed by the Prussian authorities. Larrey described Seutin as an active man full of zeal and of unusual intelligence and he recounted in his memoirs,

> Together we performed a considerable number of major operations, such as amputation of the arm at the shoulder joint and others equally difficult, which were generally successful.[24]

Larrey's support of Seutin proved to be a considerable influence on the Belgian surgeon's career, which elevated him to a certain celebrity status.

Prussian Medical Staff

When King Frederick William III of Prussia re-organised his army in 1813, his medical staff was modelled on the French service. Surgeon-General Johann Goercke, a personal friend and colleague of Larrey, was in Berlin, in the equivalent rank of Director General of the Prussian Army's medical services. The distinguished Surgeon-General von Gräfe directed surgical services under Goercke's command.

In Blücher's Prussian Army of the Lower Rhine, the senior surgeon was Surgeon-General Voelzke who was attached to the commander in chief's staff. There were three divisional ambulances/field hospitals for each corps, each under the command of a senior surgeon. These Prussian Principal Medical Officers directed three or four Surgeon-Majors, who worked in each of the field hospitals. The ambulance of the III Corps was still in preparation at Magdeburg and thus did not participate in the Waterloo campaign. During the Prussian manoeuvres of 15-18 June, one can only speculate that the field ambulances of I and IV Corps served in a somewhat haphazard fashion. Front line Prussian medical support was, however, efficiently organised, every regiment having its own experienced surgeon who was responsible for distributing junior assistant surgeons with each individual battalion.

The Prussian medical service, however, suffered from a dearth of medical staff, particularly along its long lines of communication towards the Rhine. This latter issue resulted in a large proportion of Prussian casualties being cared for by British and Dutch-Belgian

24 J.H. Dible, *Napoleon's Surgeon* (London: William Heinemann Medical Books Ltd, 1970), p.241.

medical staff, before these patients could reach the Prussian hospitals situated far in the rear at Liège and Maastricht. After the Battle of Ligny on 16 June, the Prussians sent many of their casualties (around 10-12,000 cases) to Namur. Once the Prussian army had retired to Wavre, however, the great majority of Prussian casualties were treated at Louvain, where Blücher had installed his new Prussian military base around 20 miles north of Wavre.

To prevent the inevitable spread of contagion, consequent on overcrowding, Brugmans had sought to disperse as many cases as possible into other towns as soon as feasible. Kluyskens travelled to Louvain and a number of large buildings were soon requisitioned to create annexes for the military hospital, the

Karl Ferdinand von Gräfe – Military Superintendent of Hospitals. (Gareth Glover's Collection)

largest of these being the Vlierbeek Abbey. At Louvain, alongside the wounded Prussians, there were a significant number of French casualties from the fighting at Wavre, Plançenoit, and Waterloo. First class surgeon A. Van Onsenoort was the local director and was delighted to receive a visit from Baron Larrey there.

Larrey had been captured by the Prussians on the 19 June and narrowly escaped execution, having been initially mistaken for Napoleon! Recognised by a Prussian surgeon, he was taken to Blücher, whose son's life he had previously saved. The Prussian commander gave Larrey some gold *Frederic d'Ors* and sent him to Louvain, where he was to be held a prisoner. Larrey recounts in his memoirs that after resting a while and having advised on the treatment of some of the casualties during the battle, he was subsequently given permission to help with the wounded in Louvain. Too feeble after his head injuries to cope with the performance of major operations himself, he wrote that he simply advised and was regularly consulted by the Belgian military medical staff.

Between 16 June and 15 July, more than 10,000 Prussian and numerous French casualties passed through the Louvain hospitals. Some Prussians were also sent to Antwerp, where a French surgeon Jean Claude Sommé, who had left the Grande Armée in 1806, cared for a large number of Prussian casualties in the civil hospital of St Elisabeth. Other hospitals to receive Prussian and a few French patients were; St Trond, Tirlemont, and Lier; these places being situated along the evacuation route to Germany.

The Belgian Surgeon, Jacques Michel Goffin, from Saint Severin near Huy, served during the 1815 campaign at Louvain. He wrote a short note to his uncle in Liege.

To Mister Richard, Imperial Notary in Liège, Ourte Department
Louvain 30 June 1815

My dear uncle and aunt,
Since the hostilities have started again, I have been busy day and night rescuing the wounded. At this moment I am still surrounded by these unfortunate people who plead for my assistance, that is why I will be brief in this response. I left on the 18th of the month for Antwerp with all the sick who remained, to make way for the wounded and I came back on the 21st. You again give me a new proof of your kindness in your again showing interest in me, which gives me the audacity to inform you that we are ordered to make up our uniforms and as my good aunt already has almost promised one, I dare hope that she will keep her word.

I finish by kissing all of you and receive the assurance of my perfect gratitude.
Your devoted affectionate nephew. Goffin

I'm being asked three hundred francs for the full uniform.
For Jacket 70
Greatcoat 60
Hat 30
Trousers 35
Boots 30
Sword with sword knot 55 and belt

I can after three or four months, repay a third in addition to my pension. I will therefore need two hundred francs to put me out of my embarrassment for the present time. They held my pay for the month of July. Without any help, I won't be able to pay my pension.[25]

French Medical Staff

A dearth of data on the French medical services in this campaign is inevitable due to the chaos and rout after the battle. We do know that the French set up their initial hospital for casualties from the battles of Ligny and Quatre Bras at Charleroi, but the high numbers of casualties flowing in would appear to have caused them to requisition another four large buildings to utilise as ad hoc hospitals.

Caporal Delroeux of the 11e Ligne, whose regiment formed the garrison of Charleroi after its capture by the French on 15 June, recorded:

The mayor having need of manpower to see to the needs of the hospitals that had been established for the wounded (for as the fighting was already heavy, the number continually grew) he pleaded with our commander to send him some good

25   Unpublished letter in the possession of Bernard Wilkin.

non-commissioned officers to help him… Our task was to search for and to take everything that could be used in the hospitals.

On the afternoon of the 17th, the five hospitals that had been established were full; at any moment more wounded could arrive and we were obliged to use several local houses [This should be noted as being prior to the huge number of casualties from Waterloo]. There were insufficient surgeons to carry out the treatment of all the arms and legs that had been mutilated.[26]

At all four battlefields, thousands of lightly wounded French soldiers would struggle away to search for succour, rest, or death. However, many French casualties were immobile and fell to the predations of thirst, bleeding out and excessive pain. They could also expect no mercy; particularly from the Prussians. Some refused surgical aid, preferring a heroic death for their Emperor, whilst many more lay on the battlefield for up to six days, before being transported to hospitals in Brussels, the allied wounded being given priority over them. Some of the surviving regimental staff retired to Laon and Rheims in France with the remnants of their respective units.

Of the 250-300 medical officers serving with the *Service de Santé*, it is difficult to know how many were available to help their countrymen. It is clear from a number of memoirs that many of the surgeons appear to have fled along with the troops once the army routed. It is very possible that some remained with their casualties at the field hospitals and became prisoners, but it is noticeable that no French or allied memoir has yet been found, which mentions anything about doctors being captured with their patients in the hospitals. Baron François Percy, who was rather unwell during the Waterloo campaign and in which he took small part, retired into France, whilst Larrey was held prisoner at Louvain. Some French soldiers with moderate or severe wounds would have eventually made the shelter of one of the 28 military hospitals extant within France whilst many more simply returned home and sought the assistance of their family and local doctor.

---

26   Field Andrew, *Waterloo Rout & Retreat, The French Perspective* (Barnsley: Pen & Sword, 2017) p.54.

4

Definitive Medical Care & the Hospitals for the Allied Wounded in the Kingdom of the Netherlands

Many cities and towns in the Low Countries had adequate facilities to receive casualties, which had been organised previously whilst under the governance of the French Empire. In the new Kingdom of the Netherlands, Brugmans had created regional and garrison medical units, but they were badly understaffed. His first line of base hospitals rested at Brussels and Louvain and he also requisitioned the civilian hospital at Nivelles. Further from the frontier, there would be a need for reception centres forming a second and even a third line of hospitals. The southern provinces of the Low Countries were however to be the all-important zone for supplying medical care. Their territorial medical services relied on the military garrison hospital staff at Brussels, Ghent, Namur, and Louvain. Campaign hospitals were also set up at Charleroi, Nivelles, and Termonde, which acted as support units for the divisional medical staff of both Netherlands army corps, stationed around these towns.

In total, by June 1815, nearly 6,000 beds had been initially created to receive the anticipated battle casualties and measures had soon been taken to augment bed capacity to 8,000. On 30 November 1814, Brugmans commissioned 1st Class Surgeon Kluyskens to take on the role of the senior medical officer of the southern provinces.

In Brussels, the Grand Hospice de St Pierre contained 296 beds. The first training programme had been set up there in January 1809 and consisted of five courses, each under the supervision of a professor. The principal military hospital in the city was however that situated in the Rue de Ruysbroek in the centre of the city: during the French occupation, its capacity had been established at 500 patients. Until the allied forces descended on the city in 1815, there was only a modest sized Brussels garrison of seven companies of the *Maréchausée* and one regiment of *Carabiniers à Cheval* – less than 2,000 men all told. Thus, there had been plenty of bed capacity for a garrison of that size. The Jesuits had also offered instruction in anatomy and had established a working relationship with the St Pierre military hospital.

At Ghent, a school of medicine had been established in 1809 in the Grande Hôpital de la Biloque, where Kluyskens had held a chair in surgical pathology, operative and external medicine. This continued until 1814, when the school was closed. In May 1815, the Ghent military hospital was handed over to the British and Brugmans removed Kluyskens from

St Pierre Hospital, Brussels.
(Gareth Glover's Collection)

The Biloque Hospital, Ghent.
(Gareth Glover's Collection)

The Baviére Hospital in Liège.
(Gareth Glover's Collection)

his command there and posted him to Brussels, as the senior surgeon in the city. We have unfortunately found little data relating to the Ghent hospitals.

In Liège, another medical school had likewise been opened in 1809 which was incorporated in the Hôpital de Baviére. There was limited surgical teaching at the Hôpital Militaire de Saint-Laurent for six pupils only.

Antwerp was a much more secure and logical base for the processing of casualties who were less severely hurt and who might be repatriated within a short duration. Prefet d'Argenson had created a school of medicine at Antwerp in the Hôpital Sainte-Elisabeth in 1809. Surgeon Sommé, a *chirurgeon-major* in the *Grande Armée* had also taught operative medicine there.

To avoid the potential for chaos and disorder in Brussels, packed with casualties, the first measures prepared to deal with huge numbers of casualties entailed moving on or dispersing as many of the walking wounded as was feasible. These were to be scattered further afield throughout the city suburbs and beyond, to help prevent the spread of infection. Huts were hastily constructed around the earthen ramparts and in parks to support this. When news of the fighting arrived, Brugmans travelled from the Hague on the morning of the 19 June to Brussels and he immediately went into conference with Inspector Robert Grant, Principal Medical Officer (PMO) in the British AMD to coordinate their efforts. The talented Kluyskens acted as interpreter (having perfect English) and liaison officer to the allied medical services. In only a few days, order was established and the main priorities had been agreed in a flexible plan, of which the following is a summary of the main principles to be achieved by the respective services:

To avoid a complete shambles, it was necessary to organise the governance and function of both the principal hospitals and all of the temporary hospitals now brought into use in Brussels. Staff Surgeon John Hennen was appointed in charge of the British casualties in the Jesuits, the largest military hospital but overall management of the hospital and its surgical services remained under the direction of Surgeon Kluyskens. The British medical staff officers were however put solely in charge of the Gens d'Armerie and several other hospitals. Kluyskens would remain in charge of the less severely injured and he also took responsibility for those patients (particularly officers) lodged in many of the private premises throughout the city. *Colonel* Evrard's research has found little evidence of disharmony between the British and Dutch-Belgian surgeons.

The immediate need for an increase in surgical staff was the second priority for Grant and Brugmans and they focussed their efforts primarily in Brussels, the key hub for medical care. John Gunning, the PMO for the 1st Corps was granted permission by the Duke of Wellington to retain the medical staff of the headquarters and of the entire 1st Corps, temporarily active at Waterloo and Brussels. John Hume, the personal physician and surgeon to Wellington, was also allowed to remain in Brussels until July. Grant also had the additional responsibility for arranging the eventual repatriation of the surviving severely wounded to Britain, which was to be done via Antwerp rather than the other Channel ports. The small British hospitals previously deployed at Ostend, Bruges and Ghent, were shut down and their attendant staff redeployed to Brussels. The Prussians had little hope of providing medical reinforcements from their own resources, which meant that the expansion of the hospitals in Louvain and staffing them also fell under the direction of Kluyskens.

St Laurent Barracks and Hospital, Liège. (Gareth Glover's Collection)

St Elisabeth Hospital, Antwerp. (Gareth Glover's Collection)

Grant was still under-staffed and he requested further help from the newly-appointed Director General of the AMD, Sir James McGrigor, who had only been promoted on 13 June 1815. Soon, a number of both senior and junior army medical personnel were sent out to assist. Most of the senior men not only carried out some surgery themselves, but also acted in consultative roles.

Belgian medical support was crucial to the cause and vigorous measures had to be imposed to support the excessive hospital work load. On 19 June, Brugmans called up all of the medical staff in and around Brussels and Antwerp who had previously served in the *Service de Santé* of the French *Grande Armée,* the men being allowed to retain their previous rank from the French service. He also called in the medical students from Brussels and Ghent to help bolster the medical support services, these junior staff were employed as *chirurgiens sous-aides majors.* The Commissioner of the Interior for the Department of the Dyle also requisitioned all surgeons, physicians and medical staff – whether retired or actively practising – from the surrounding region to help with the influx. Eventually more than were required were assembled, so he was able to be selective and sent the least able away. Those that were employed were given temporary commissions in the army of the Netherlands and were classed according to both their past military experience and their professional standing. He was eventually able to supply no less than 186 staff in Brussels, consisting of 16 *chirurgiens-majors*, 52 surgeons of the 2nd class, 92 surgeons of the 3rd class, two pharmacists of the 2nd class and 24 *sous-aides* pharmacists. In addition to these, we should add the civilian surgeons of Brussels (who it has proven impossible to quantify with any precision), who also worked under the supervision of Kluyskens.

The requisitioning and supply of clean bedding, dressings, bandages, and drugs was also of prime importance having quickly used up the extant equipment available in the first few days. Kluyskens worked on this problem with great vigour, and Brugmans requisitioned supplies from nearby departments and expedited the transportation of further medical goods stockpiled in the northern Netherlands.

Efforts were made to clear beds from the hospitals in Brussels and Louvain. In all major open spaces in Brussels, tented camps and wooden sheds were hastily erected as temporary accommodation, whilst a number of large public buildings were also requisitioned. The British senior medical staff quickly began to select suitable Allied cases, who were convalescent or who had survived surgery and were well on the road to recovery, for evacuation to Antwerp. Ambulant wounded were moved by road, with rest breaks being taken at both Ghent and Malines. Of the 9,528 wounded and 3,346 sick, many of whom had eventually arrived at Antwerp, a number were evacuated to England very quickly, and only 5,000 or so were still left in hospitals in the Low Countries by the end of June. Most of these would be much more difficult cases which would take longer to recover and were eventually evacuated during the following year. Decanting patients to Antwerp could however mean significant delays in treatment. Waiting three days in Brussels for surgery, Ned Costello was finally sent to Antwerp, where a finger was amputated five days after wounding.[1]

The wounded Netherlands soldiers were moved into Holland as soon as was feasible in sick convoys by road towards, Breda, Bois-le-Duc, and other towns of the northern regions

---

1   E. Hathaway, *Costello. The true story of a Peninsular War Rifleman* (Swanage: Shinglepicker, 1997), p.286.

The Faucon or Valk Military Hospital, Louvain. (Gareth Glover's Collection)

of the Low Countries. At Louvain, Kluyskens requisitioned two large abandoned abbeys, which then formed part of the military hospital group with the Faucon or Valk permanent military hospital. This latter had been a dependant of the *Hôpital des Invalides* at Paris during the French Empire. There was a need to disperse some of the wounded farther to the east. Between the 16 June and mid-July, at least 10,000 Prussian and numerous French casualties had passed through the military hospital at Louvain. Many of the lesser wounds were moved on towards Liège, with organised stops at Tirlemont, Saint-Trond, Lier, Tongre, and other interim towns. Here, many civilian doctors had to be recruited to help cope with the huge numbers.

Despite the measures taken to ease the burden in Brussels, it was also necessary for Kluyskens to consider the thousands of wounded scattered amongst private homes and other buildings in Brussels. For each of the eight regions of Brussels, a team, directed by a military surgeon, was established to make daily rounds of the private houses and make-shift hospitals. In order to take pressure off the medical department, Brugmans requested that all those citizens who had received wounded into their homes, were to place a notice chalked in large letters in their window, giving the nationalities, number of cases and the severity of the wounds. He then delegated 68 *chirurgiens majors* and *aides-majors* and 90 *sous aides* to help in this effort. This was done by dividing the entire medical force available into 23 sections, five serving in the main military hospital and the other 18 taking care of those patients in private houses and temporary hospitals. By the third week of June, 4,156 wounded in private residences of various nationalities had been identified, registered, cared for, and regularly visited. This placement of a large number of the wounded in small separate groups would have helped allay some of the risks from transmittable diseases. There were risks in placing casualties in isolated private dwellings, however. Cavalry officer William Hay found a comrade, Edwin Sandys, in his billet in Brussels. His wounds had been left untreated. Hay rushed off to procure a surgeon, but it was too late and Sandys died. Hay then went off to report to the city's commandant, Major General Adam, who was bed-ridden in another house along with his brigade major, Thomas Hunter-Blair.[2]

Brugmans had remained particularly concerned about the potential spread of infectious disorders during this warm humid period within the overcrowded city. Outbreaks of hospital gangrene, dysentery, typhoid, and typhus were the principal risks that he would have feared. On 22 June he had posted notices throughout the city and also published them in the newspapers. These contained instructions for the management of the casualties advising on the need to incinerate bandages and palliasses once soiled with pus and blood, detailing the appropriate hygienic measures to be taken, recommending the application of dressings, moistened with the *Eau de Goulard* (a solution of lead acetate and lead oxide, to act as an astringent), advice on the diet to be given to the wounded, the importance of bodily cleanliness, proper laundering of bed linen and the regular 'disinfection' of their accommodation. Along with these sensible precautions, he directed that streets and public places should be kept as clean and tidy as feasible. It is a remarkable tribute to Brugmans and his staff that all through the summer of 1815, aside from one small out-break of hospital gangrene, there were no other significant epidemics in the town.

The distinct shortage of wagons for road transport had resulted in very serious delays for many casualties being brought into Brussels from outlying villages. Most of the severely delayed patients were French wounded, who had at least, in many cases, received good care from the local population. Fleury de Chaboulon, Bonaparte's Secretary, wrote,

> French losses would have been considerably more without the generous care that was meted out by the local inhabitants. After the victory at Ligny and Fleurus, they flocked onto the battlefield to console and care for the injured... They recovered the poor French from the field of battle and offered them asylum and all necessary succour.[3]

Similar stories were heard after the conflicts at Quatre Bras, Wavre and Waterloo.

> In order to garner public support, Brugmans even issued posters across the city, containing instructions for residents who were harbouring wounded on basic hygiene of wounds.

> The Inspector-General of the Health Service of the Army and the Navy of S.M. the King of the Netherlands to the inhabitants of Brussels

2   Haythornthwaite, *Waterloo Men*, p.108.
3   P.A.E. Fleury de Chaboulon, *Memoires pour servir a l'histoire de la vie privée du retour et du regne de Napoleon en 1815* (London: John Murray, 1820), Vol.II, p.188.

The poster issued by Inspector Brugmans instructing and encouraging the citizens of Brussels how to care for the wounded and sick after the battle. (Gareth Glover's Collection)

Inhabitants of Brussels,

I am deputised by order of our gracious Serene Majesty, with the mission of assisting the many wounded who have come out of [the] latest battles.

I carried out my first report of the hospitals, where I regulated the service and provisionally put it in as much order as possible.

I have no call to make on your patriotism, nor to your feelings of humanity. You have in this report surpassed everything that could be expected from the most devoted people. You have welcomed into your home, you have gone to pick up on the battlefield as many wounded as your houses can contain. You treat them with the same solicitude that mothers would use for their children; and, without any doubt, you have saved your city from the ravages of a terrible disease.

After organising the most urgent service of the hospital, I had to take care of the needs of your wounded. I have to set into effect, and created divisions of medical officers, who will visit the homes of all where their care will be requested. You will put in one of the front windows of your homes a sign in large letters and bearing these words: one, two, three etc. wounded.

The surgeons, on this notice, will enter your home with dressing linen, and continue to give the wounded the visits that their state demands. In the meantime, you can give them the first aid, for which I have few instructions for you, your common sense and your charity being very good guides on this subject.

Cleaning the wounds, washing the whole body, changing clothes and sleeping comfortably and in well ventilated places, are the most indispensable preliminary conditions, which you have already satisfied. Healthy, light food, largely vegetables, watered wine or refreshing beer, is what suits them. For dressing, you will confine yourself to cover the wounds, after having washed them and their surrounds with a sponge or lint moistened with water of Goulard, and you will hold this lint by a bandage consisting of clean linen. You will lay [lie the casualty carefully] down or let the patient be lifted according to the severity of his injuries. You will not neglect anything, and I cannot recommend you this circumstance too much, that of renewing as much as possible the air of his room, nothing can help more a prompt healing.

It is only the congestion of the wounded in the hospitals that spread diseases: their isolation in the houses does not offer the slightest danger of contagion, and it is under this report that the foresight of your human feelings has preserved you from this scourge.

I will ensure that contagious diseases that result from the meeting of the wounded in the hospitals are also prevented; and, to this end, there will be erected, in the open air, in my view [i.e. his opinion and direction], of the well ventilated and vast tents, where the wounded and sick receive all the relief required in their state, and reward their dedication and courage which deserves so many rights. This curative [sic] service as much as a contraceptive [i.e. for the protection of the patient], will be organized.

Inhabitants of Brussels, redouble your zeal and activity for the relief of our generous defenders. Their cause is yours, and the interest of their well-being is common to you; because an epidemic disease that could be born in hospitals would reach you almost as soon as it reached them.

The whole city is already converted into a vast refuge of sick; and yet several thousand still have to come to us.

Surgeons will, for their part, take care that any germ of contagion is immediately destroyed; They will perfume [i.e. fumigate and clean] places where symptoms of gangrene, a dynamic fever or toxic fever are manifest, either with the muriatic gas oxygen or with nitric vapour [ie a choice of hydrochloric acid or nitric acid compounds], depending on the convenience [i.e. layout] of the place; The first fumigations requiring the rooms or places to be evacuated by patients, and the second that can be made without this condition. The pharmacists of the hospitals will hold ready and, on the orders of the ambulance surgeons, prepare the clean materials for these operations, which are to be established however only in cases of recognised necessity. One of the pharmacists will give the required instructions verbally. If we proceed by muriatic oxygen gas, we put the mixture in a small pot of soil, water it with a little water, place the pot on an ash fire, close all the exits of the place, and pour on the mixture the oil of vitriol [sulphuric acid].

Nitric acid fumigations are more easily practised: just pour in a saucer an ounce of vitriolic oil, warm up the acid on a very-moderate fire of ash, or over the flame of a quinquet [small oil lamp], and throw in small amount of saltpetre powder, until it no longer releases steam. We move the saucer into the corners of the place where the air is the most stagnant. These fumigations can be repeated up to twice a day when the stale air condition and abundance as the nature of the fumes require.

The surgeons, like all those who lodge wounded soldiers, use their full attention to be careful to establish a free flow of air, without regard to complaints that could be formed during the night of the impression of the cold. Preventing serious incidents must be their first goal. Their salvation, the salvation of the wounded and the public are attached to it, and the misunderstood conveniences of the moment must be poorly considered when it comes to the well-being of the future.

Inhabitants of Brussels, you must see in the mission of which I have the honour to be entrusted, the tender solicitude which His Majesty takes about your fate, and a first impression of his gratitude for the marks of attachment which you give to his august person, in the individuals who make up the armed medical services, and those of her high allies I should not recommend you to do, but to continue what by yourself you started.

BRUSSELS, 22 June 1815
The Inspector-General of the Health Service of the Army and the Navy of His Majesty the King of the Netherlands. Brugmans

As to the hospital care in the Netherlands, Kluyskens had impressed his allied colleagues with his achievements whilst he also worked feverishly in the Jesuits military hospital, personally carrying out or supervising around 300 amputations. He also mentored civilian surgeons at the hospices of St Gertrude and d'Ophem. In the main military hospital and its satellites, approximately 2,200 patients were brought in daily, for a few days after the battle.

Up to 250 amputations were carried out each day, activity peaking around the 25 June when the numbers hospitalised had reached around 4,000, many others being put up in private dwellings. Kluyskens was extremely concerned over the dangers of junior surgeons carrying out major surgical cases. These were generally reserved for the more senior staff only. We do know however, that young Louis Seutin, only a second-class surgeon (although clearly a very capable young man), had personally carried out more than twenty amputations in the military hospital. Kluyskens unsurprisingly did not report this to his superiors and he corrected this situation by the time that Brugmans arrived in the city. Seutin had by then been granted the authority to carry out major surgery.

On 28 June, Brugmans was to have proceeded to The Hague, but before he went he helped Kluyskens to resolve another huge problem. This was the scattered nature of the wounded, across the whole area of the campaign, with Charleroi, Nivelles, Braine l'Alleud, and Wavre, all calling out for urgent assistance to help cope with the high numbers of casualties in their vicinities. Possibly inspired by advice from Larrey or Kluyskens, Brugmans set up a mobile 'ambulance' team consisting of ten *chirurgiens aides-majors* and an *économe* (purveyor). This team was to be commanded by Louis Seutin, who Brugmans had now granted the freedom to perform any major surgical procedures necessary. The team was to arrange the evacuation of the lightly wounded whilst those who were unlikely to recover or couldn't survive such a journey, were to receive continuing care in their current locations. This task was continued throughout the entire month of July.

It was not long before all of the hospitals of Brussels were full beyond capacity with the wounded from the various battles. The inhabitants of the city, however, continued to open not only their houses, but their attics, warehouses, outbuildings, and barns to the wounded. Many of the soldiers billeted with particular families before the campaign, returned as casualties to the same places and were welcomed without a moment's thought and were very well cared for. Other citizens supplied their vehicles and horses to help collect the wounded and others supplied material or clothing to be cut up for bandaging, and even refined young ladies, very unused to getting their hands dirty, were seen tending the wounded and nursing them in the best way they knew. They held no favouritism, caring equally for a wounded Belgian, Frenchman or Prussian out of pure compassion and humanity. The calumny propagated in Victorian times, that the Bruxelois wanted nothing to do with the wounded and would not help them, was clearly not the case.

Further afield, there were also thousands of Prussian wounded requiring help. The senior Prussian Surgeon Karl von Gräfe rushed to oversee the medical support at Brussels, but he also had to find surgeons to man hospital units at Antwerp, Louvain, and Namur and along the casualty evacuation routes to Cologne and Mayence, passing through Liège and Maastricht. Hospitals were established in Namur, Louvain, Liège, and Maastricht, designed to house the numerous Prussian casualties. Namur was not employed by Kluyskens for any other than Prussian wounded, but despite the hospital at Louvain being the Principal Prussian base hospital, the surgical staff there actually belonged to the Army of the Netherlands. These were local Belgian surgeons under the direction of the Dutch 1st class surgeon, Van Onsenoort, who encouraged the Prussians to utilise all the local Belgian civilian staff they could find. Von Gräfe supplemented the hospital staff at Louvain with Prussian surgeons and he requisitioned the de Vlierbeek and de Parc abbeys as annexes to Louvain hospital.

The De Vlierbeek Abbey. (Gareth Glover's Collection)

The military hospitals already mentioned at Liège and Maastricht had been given over to the use of the Prussians, but they were full of civilian patients, who had to be dispersed to other locations. In the line of the casualty evacuation route, the Prussian staff commandeered the military hospital in the St Laurent Abbey at Liège and the Abbey of St Agatha was also used as a hospital, making Liège an important medical centre. Further facilities at Maastricht and Aix-la-Chapelle completed the medical evacuation route, base hospitals were then established further away along the axis of the Rhine.

Hassenforder in his account of the history of the French *Service de Santé* wrote: 'The wounded French in this terrible battle were happily recovered and admirably cared for by the Belgians in the hospitals of Brussels and Louvain'.[4] This is an interesting generalisation, informing the reader that if indeed there was any bias towards better care of the allied soldiers, that, there was also reasonable succour given to the French wounded.

A series of Public Announcements or '*Affiches*' were posted up by the governors of Brussels and Antwerp, either requesting supplies or directing how best to help. A series of these consecutive posters has been discovered in the Antwerp Archives and the texts are reproduced here.

---

4   J. Hassenforder, *Le Service de Santé Militaire pendant la Révolution et l'Empire, in Le Service de Santé Militaire de ses Origines à nous jours* (Paris: SPEI, 1961), p.170.

Town Hall Antwerp, 18 June 1815
The Mayor to his citizens.
The current circumstances require sacrifices. The first duty of every citizen is to help those who have come to the defence of the Fatherland with so much courage. The honour and humanity of Belgium require that everyone, according to his means, gives aid to the wounded who have been brought to this city and give them every care they are capable of giving. There is insufficient bedding and time does not allow much to be done. I trust that every private individual will make haste in these times of urgent need to join in bringing in as much bedding as his means allow. These offerings shall be taken into account and shall give them the right to esteem and general recognition. Vermoelen

   Note. The General depot is set up for the long term at Rue Neuve, Section 3, no. 90, and a person will be permanently placed to receive the supplies which the charity of the inhabitants will want to hand over and for which they will be issued a receipt.

Town Hall Antwerp 20 June 1815
The Mayor of the city to the inhabitants of the same.
I have seen with the greatest pleasure the generosity of my fellow-citizens, towards the wounded who have been brought to this city, they have all given them aid and support, to a [such a] degree, that several have voluntarily taken them into their own homes and given them all service and comfort; their well-known humanity, deserves the greatest praise and my special recognition, be reassured, these same will continue with their diligence. The Military Authorities command me to say to those who still have wounded in their houses, that the initial period having passed, they should be moved as quickly as possible to the different hospitals which have been prepared for them, so that the military are brought together, they can make themselves known to Mr Tenbosch, Lieutenant Inspector of the Army Board at the *Groen Plaats* [central market square] who will direct them as to which hospital they should be sent to.

The Town Hall of Antwerp, 24 June 1815
The Mayor requests all inhabitants of this city, who have wounded soldiers or officers staying, to put a notice as soon as possible in large letters in one of their downstairs front windows, stating how many wounded there are in their house, of what nation these are, and to which regiment and company they belong, by which means as best as possible a [sorting out of the] division of lodgings can be achieved. Vermoelen

Antwerp 29 June 1815
The Mayor of Antwerp to its inhabitants
Generous people of Antwerp!
I have seen with satisfaction the efforts you have made to help the brave soldiers who have gloriously defended our Fatherland. My heart has been moved, so I have hurried to inform the government of your beneficence.

The services of the Antwerp hospitals have already been secured, but there are still unfortunates in the general military hospitals of Liège and Namur who are in need of your help. The need in particular is for covering, bed-linen, hoods, bandages, lint and pillows filled with at least wool or horse hair.

I am informed that all the other cities of Belgium have already come to their aid and have delivered more than could have been expected.

No, the people of Antwerp will not be found wanting and your patriotism is my guarantee. Make yet more sacrifices so that the wounded in the two mentioned hospitals may be convinced of your humanity. Their wounds are our wounds and must be healed.

The local College of *Soeurs Noires* has been appointed to receive the donations which I expect from your generosity. Vermoelen

Town Hall of Antwerp 4 July 1815
NOTICE
The Mayor of the city of Antwerp warns the citizens that it is the intention of his excellency the Governor of this city to relieve them of the wounded military who are staying with them, with the exception of the English troops, who will provisionally stay with the civilians, where they will be fed and taken care of by their own administration.

The Belgians and Dutch shall be brought as soon as possible to the Hospital de *Soeurs-Noires, a*nd the Brunswickers and Prussians to the Hospital of *Saint Elisabeth.*

Everyone who has wounded military with them belonging to these various nations, are requested to adhere to the content of this notice. Vermoelen

POLICE
Antwerp 7 July 1815
We the Mayor of Antwerp, having been informed that several wounded prisoners of war have escaped from the city hospitals, forbid anyone from providing civil clothing or any other disguise, to provide shelter or in any way to help them get away, on pain of punishment by the full force of the law. Vermoelen

PRISONERS OF WAR
Antwerp, 8 July 1815
The Lieutenant-General Governor of Antwerp, commander of the first military district, having been informed that many wounded French prisoners of war are abusing the respect and kindness shown to them, by leaving the place provisionally given for their detention, believes that they should be warned to conform to the Law of '9 Prairial year III' [28 May 1795] that all prisoners of war and those held as such, who, without the permission of the government, leaves the place assigned for his detention or his residence, will be punished by 6 years of confinement in irons. Van der Plaat

Important Message [Undated – July?]

The public is notified by the head physician of the English military, that all billeted English wounded must go to the Hotel du Nord, to be cared for there, and that those who are not in a state to get there, will be received in the Minimes Hospital where they can be transported from 3 to 6 in the afternoon.

These interesting instructions and exhortations underline the close co-operation between the city council, inhabitants and medical staff, to provide decent and adequate care for the thousands of wounded men they suddenly found flooding into the city.

5

Mont St Jean Field Hospital

Before many of the wounded from the Battle of Waterloo reached the hospitals of Brussels and Antwerp, they had to pass through the hands of the battalion medical staff performing basic early life-preserving therapy, where feasible, and then on to field hospitals. These latter had been necessary for a marching army and had, in earlier times been named, 'marching,' or 'temporary,' hospitals.[1] They had to be set up separately from smaller regimental medical depots and were either sited in appropriate buildings, or under canvas, near the fighting. These units were occupied by staff surgeons and their assistants and, during combat, the senior regimental staff would join the other surgeons and help with the injured. Working in such cohesive groups meant that opinions and instruments could be shared and a more efficient workforce could operate in a better balance.

Such a unit was sited around 400 metres behind Wellington's position on the ridge at Waterloo. The farm at the hamlet of Mont St Jean had been established since the 14th century (although the existing buildings date from 1719) and was a sizeable Brabant property; it had been owned for a number of generations by the Boucquéau family and in 1815 it was rented to a Mr Berger. It consisted of a long farm building for the family along the north side, where there was a chapel, there were cellars at the west end of this building for the storage of wine and beer – possibly also, grain or flour. The west face of the farm complex had a sizeable gate at its entrance, with large wooden doors. The gateway was flanked by two barns, probably for farm equipment or vehicles. To the south of the square complex there was a large barn, for the storage and drying of farmed products such as rye, oats, wheat, or linseed. It is also possible that cattle were sheltered here. On the eastern face of the farm, there were no buildings, but there certainly was a wall completing the defensive square and a gateway opposite the main entrance. Clearly there may have been less-substantial edifices, such as a lean-to or sheds against the wall. The earlier maps of the farm show a carriage way or cart track passing to the east of the farm, presumably for loading and rear access. It is certain that the principal chaussée, which was centrally paved, passed along the west face of the complex in 1815, as it does today. This would have been the main access for the casualties and medical personnel.

---

1   N.A. Cantlie, *History of the Army Medical Department*, Vol.1, pp.45-46; Crumplin, *Men of Steel*, pp.119-125; Howard, *Wellington's Doctors*, pp. 91-92.

The farm was ideally placed and formed to serve as a large field hospital. It was therefore chosen as the field collection point for the casualties of the centre and left of the allied force consisting of 1st Corps. The right flank and right centre of the allied army, occupied by the 2nd Corps, had access to the 1st Corps field hospital, but along with the Dutch-Belgian units, some of which were stationed there, had reasonable access to the village of Braine l'Alleud. Here there was the large church of St Etienne, which served as a secure and reasonably comfortable hospital station, along with the adjacent houses. In attendance were the local priest and some nuns, who assisted the medical staff there. After the battle was over, many French casualties were gathered here as well.

The principal challenge for a wounded man was to reach Mont St Jean under his own steam, or with the help of other wounded (or unwounded) colleagues. The latter were discouraged from assisting by their officers for obvious reasons. There is little doubt however, that many unwounded men did help casualties to the rear, particularly officers. The patients who were unable to make the journey to Mont St Jean were those suffering with serious blood loss, double leg injuries or bad head, chest, or abdominal wounds. Some regimental bandsmen were designated as bearers, but they proved totally inadequate for this task with the high numbers of casualties. The other problem for mobile yet vulnerable wounded was the fluid nature of the battlefield. Stray round shot, canister, or musket balls were not the only hazard whilst travelling painfully to the rear, but also roaming enemy cavalry squadrons. Nevertheless, thousands of injured men made it to the farm and must have been relieved to do so.

The interior of the church of St Etienne, Braine l'Alleud. (Gareth Glover's collection)

Mont St Jean farm as it might have appeared on 18 June 1815 (Michael Crumplin's collection)

What made Mont St Jean a good field hospital/dressing station was not only its proximity to the combat zone, but also its structure. Although the roof was damaged by stray ordnance, there are no records of any casualties being further injured whilst resting in the farm. The square shape of the farm provided a relatively safe haven in terms of shelter from the fighting and from the elements. Although there were few trees here, there was some shelter from sun or rain in the out-buildings. The dead were collected in out-houses and the human detritus from numerous amputations was simply thrown on the farm's midden. A vitally important issue was an adequate water supply and this was provided by a centrally-placed well. One of the problems that the injured suffered from was extreme thirst. Many of them had filled their wooden canteens (of just over a litre capacity) not with water but alcohol. Plenty of soldiers had already emptied their containers in the heat of the day increasing their dehydration. Water was also needed for sponging down wounds, washing the surgeons' hands, moistening lint for dressings, and cleaning knives and saws.

Interior of Mont St Jean Farm at the turn of the 20th century, with the well in the foreground. (Gareth Glover's collection)

We have few accounts from the farm when it was used as a dressing station. Men treated there would not always be inclined to write of those harsh experiences. Surgeons were overwhelmed by the amount of work. The solution to dealing with thousands of casualties was that these had to be moved on to a more definitive place of care, namely a general base hospital as soon as was possible.

To the east of the farm lay an orchard and undulating fields where the slope ran back from the Allied ridge line to the north. This was the site of the bivouac for the 2nd North British Dragoons (Greys) the night before the battle and provided some shelter for locally wounded men and horses during the combat. One of the sergeants of the Greys, Clarke by name, did venture into the farm before the battle and again after the battle, commenting extensively on his visit later in the day:

> We having arrived at the farmhouse, Mont St Jean, which is situated on the road in short distance in front of the village of the same name, entered the yard, where a most shocking spectacle presented itself. This house and yard, during the time of the battle, had been occupied by some of the British and Belgic surgeons and in it many amputations had been performed. A large dunghill in the middle of the square, was covered with dead bodies and heaps of legs and arms were scattered around! A comrade who stood near me on entering unconsciously muttered 'Of God. What a sight'. To which I made no answer, but felt as he did, for a great number lay by the sides of the houses and basked in the beams of the sun who had only life's last spark remaining and gasped for relief. Some lay with their heads reclining on the lifeless body of some already departed comrade, who, when we offered our assistance to remove them into the shade, declined being disturbed and murmured 'As their hour was near at hand that they preferred meeting it in peace on the spot they already occupied.
>
> I observed with some warmth of national feeling, several highlander's [sic] legs, still wearing the emblem of their country; Auld Scotia's tartan hoe! [The Highlanders wore kilts and long socks at Waterloo]. As also the legs of dragoons in boots and spurs and many others which still wore a part of the garment in which they had proudly paced the causeways of their native land and supported the portly figure of a British grenadier whose exalted spirit had ever forbid him to place in the coward's path that well-turned limb which was now consigned to a Belgic dunghill.
>
> The interior of the house was also crowded with dead and dying, lying indiscriminately together. The buildings had not undergone any great damage, there were, indeed, to be seen, a few ball holes through the walls but no part of the premises burnt.[2]

We cannot be certain whether Mr Berger, the farmer and his family stayed on during the action, but his wife certainly claimed to have stayed (alone) in the roof space of the farmhouse throughout the battle.

---

2   Gareth Glover (ed.), *A Scots Grey at Waterloo* (Barnsley: Frontline, 2018), p208.

All the inhabitants [of Mont St Jean] had fled from this village previous to the action & even Waterloo was deserted. In a farmhouse at the end of the village nearest the field, one solitary woman remained shut up in a garret from which she could see nothing while they were fighting at the very door, while shells were bursting in all the windows & while cannon balls were breaking through the wooden gates into the farm yard and striking against the walls of the house. This farmer's wife was asked by Captain Whale of the Life Guards her motive for this extraordinary conduct replied 'that all she had in the world was there… poultry, cows, calves & pigs and that if she did not stay to take care of them they would all be destroyed or carried off…' The three lower rooms were filled with the wounded British officers.[3]

We can however be sure that the women and children who had followed their husbands to war would have helped with the comfort of the men in the blood-soaked courtyard. These were primarily families who had already been in the Low Countries in early 1815, as there had been discouragement of wives accompanying the additional units deployed during this rapid campaign. The camp followers were likely to have originally taken shelter in the lee of the farm complex, remaining to the north of the buildings. They dressed wounds and prepared dressing material such as lint, cotton, or linen waste or tore up clothing that could be used for bandages or slings. Two of these devoted followers were the wife and daughter of a private soldier, Daniel Gale of the 3/95th Rifles. The wife, whose name is unknown, had her five-year-old daughter, Elizabeth with her. Like so many desperately anxious wives, they were searching for their loved ones during the chaotic mêlée of the closing phase of Waterloo. Having found him, they were able to give succour to those in the farm and in the field. Elizabeth and her mother scraped lint and made up bandages. The little girl dripped water into the parched mouths of soldiers whilst witnessing some horrific wounds. Elizabeth was the last witness of the Battle of Waterloo, dying in 1904.

Not all casualties were housed in the main field hospital. Often senior officers would be looked after in their billets. We know that Henry Paget, Lord Uxbridge, after his knee injury was nursed and operated on in a house belonging to Monsieur Hyacinthe Paris, in Waterloo village. Sir William Howe de Lancey, after his mortal torso wound was cared for in a cottage at Mont St Jean. Many lightly wounded men were moved on to St Joseph's Chapel and nearby houses in Waterloo.

How long it took to clear the field hospital at Mont St Jean, we do not know, but it would have been at least a few days and possibly up to a week. Somewhere around the farm, probably near the north or eastern aspects, there will be mass burial pits and a medical waste pit. These have yet to be discovered. Some memories of the suffering of the thousands of casualties retrieved from Waterloo and the previous actions are to be seen in a small museum dedicated to military medicine, now situated in the farmhouse of Mont St Jean.

---

3   Published as letter 11 in Gareth Glover (ed.) *Waterloo Archive, Volume IV* (Barnsley: Frontline 2012), p32-4. This was clearly used by Charlotte Eaton as part of her *A Near Observer of the Battle of Waterloo* (London: Murray, 1816), Vol.I, p 24.

6

Details of the Principal Receiving Hospitals extant in Brussels and Antwerp after Waterloo

There were in the region of 12,000 allied and around 15,000 French who were more serious casualties, to be cared for after the Waterloo campaign had ended. We know that many of the wounded were initially congregated in large farmhouses and churches near the battlefields, including Mont St Jean farmhouse and the churches of Waterloo and Braine l'Alleud. Yet it must also not be forgotten, that the farmhouses of Quatre Bras, Gemioncourt, Pireaumont and Grand Pierrepont and even the church at Nivelles were utilised for those wounded at the Battle of Quatre Bras two days previously. The French and Prussian wounded from the battles of Ligny and Wavre were again initially housed in every available farmhouse and church in the vicinity, such as Fleurus, Sombreffe, Brye, the upper parts of the village of Ligny which was not destroyed by fire, and also at Wavre itself.

Many of the wounded were then transported as soon as possible to Brussels or the other military hospital locations, which rapidly became overcrowded. The majority were taken to Brussels, where we have already seen that many patients particularly officers were nursed and treated in private houses and where the surgeons were expected to visit them after their hospital rounds. The majority of the other ranks however, were housed in either purpose-built military hospitals but often simply placed in churches, monasteries, markets, convents, and factory buildings, which were initially utilised for all of these patients. The PMO, Doctor Robert Grant – Director General Sir James McGrigor's brother-in-law and also brother of Colquhoun Grant, Wellington's master intelligence agent – promptly requisitioned many such places for the reception of casualties in those first chaotic days after 18 June. He received the full co-operation of the Belgian civil and military authorities.

As noted, five of the largest Brussels hospitals were amalgamated and termed as the 'Grand Hôpital Général de l'Armée Alliée', all others being seen as subservient to these and only temporary. The hospitals soon filled to capacity and overflow facilities were made available in Antwerp, Bruges, Termonde, Louvain, Ghent, Namur, and even Ostend.

Most of the Prussian casualties were located at their own hospitals in Louvain, Namur, Maastricht, and Liege. The French had initially used Charleroi as the main site for their hospitals, but later their wounded were sent to any and all of the nearby hospitals as thought best.

Even at the main medical centre at Brussels, there was little initial triage practised to prioritise urgent cases and men of the same regiment were sent indiscriminately, some to Brussels, others to Antwerp as they literally filled each hospital up. There was some sorting of the wounded beyond those identified as British (or Hanoverians in British pay) being sent to certain hospitals, Dutch-Belgian and Brunswick troops to their own, and Prussian or French prisoners to others again. This was to allow the doctors from each army to look after their own, for ease of language (British and Belgian surgeons also staffing the hospitals for French wounded). It should be noted that very few Prussian wounded are recorded as having been cared for at Brussels and Antwerp. The system was not fool-proof however, and there are often anomalies in the records of each of the hospitals.

The outbreak of fevers was a constant concern, but those wounded who remained at Brussels were found to suffer principally from inflammatory fevers after amputation; whereas those at Antwerp, suffered more from the endemic fevers prevailing at the time, beginning as an intermittent fever and often ending in typhus; showing the influence of malaria in the Antwerp area.

One eyewitness report describing the scene was published in a Brussels newspaper:

> Brussels now becomes one vast infirmary. Fifteen hundred wounded Frenchmen are encamped on the *Place de la Monnaie*,[1] while the illuminations for the *'affaire decisive de la Belle Alliance'* are burning brightly, and the playgoers inside are roaring at the drolleries of 'L'Avocat Patalin'.[2] The Church of the Madeleine and the Salle des Varietes are alike full of the sick and dying; 'Jones, Lieutenant Colonel,'[3] asks for the addresses of wounded officers 'to facilitate the researches of friends; tent hospitals are erected outside the Louvain and Namur gates; for an entire week the peasants are either burying the dead or bringing in the wounded, and a great 'benefit' is organised at the *Monnaie*.[4]

The pressure on the hospitals was so great that the Mayor of Brussels invited fellow citizens to bring any bedding that they could spare to the hospitals.

The Principal Hospitals in Brussels:

The Jesuits Hospital
No. 1 on the Brussels Map
An official military hospital established in 1787 (within the Collège Thérésien, an old Jesuit College) requisitioned by Inspector of Hospitals Sir James Grant. Staff Surgeon John Hennen was placed in charge of the Jesuits Hospital. After the Battle of Waterloo, he had

---

1   The *Place de la Monnaie / Muntplein* still exists and houses the *Theatre Royal de Monnaie*, the Opera House.
2   A French comedy, which translates as *The Town Attorney,* first performed on 4 June 1706.
3   Lieutenant Colonel Sir John Thomas Jones Royal Engineers: he had been sent to Brussels as a member of a commission in March 1815 to suggest improvements to the border fortresses for defence. When Napoleon escaped from Elba and Wellington arrived to command the army, he inspected many of the defence works with him.
4   Published again in the *New York Times* on 6 July 1890.

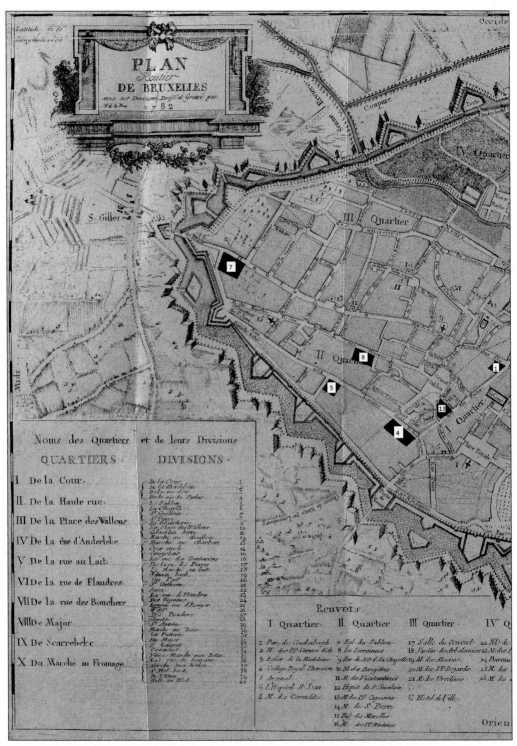

1782 Map of Brussels showing the sites of the main hospitals used after Waterloo. (Gareth Glover's Collection)

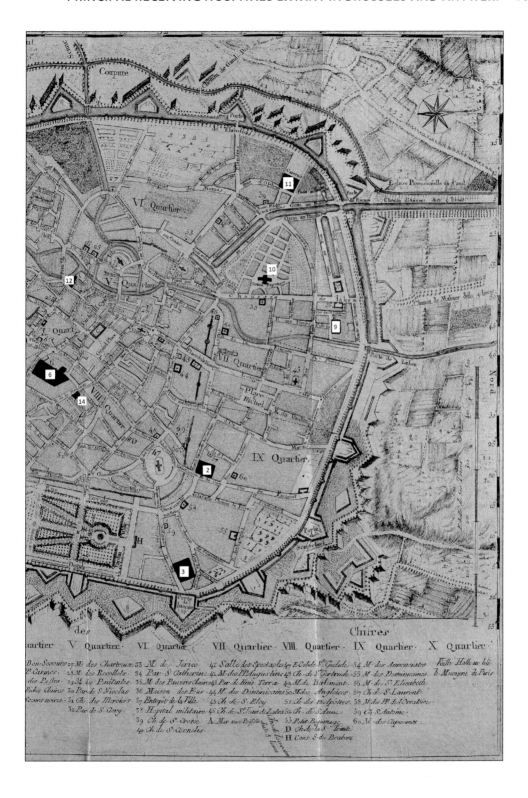

the sole superintendence of the wounded of the General Staff and performed many important operations on this occasion. He continued to direct the duties of the Jesuits Hospital until September 1815, when he was promoted, by Sir James McGrigor. From this hospital we have a list of primary and secondary amputations performed, their types and outcomes (20 June to 20 July 1815), and also a fairly comprehensive list of general wounds and their classifications (up to 16 July). This was written up by Surgeon to the Forces John Hennen and Hospital Assistant to the Forces Richard Crofton who were resident here. The building no longer exists, as it was demolished along with much of this area to allow for the construction of the monumental Palais de Justice in Brussels in 1860. An Eighteenth century map of the city does show a depiction of the Jesuit College (numbered 68)

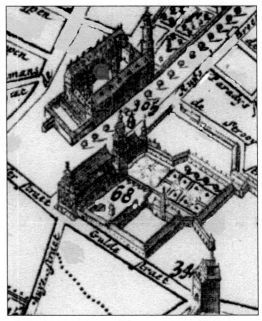

The Jesuit College – from a 1711 map.
(Gareth Glover's Collection)

St Elisabeth (Barrack) Hospital
No. 2 on the Brussels Map

This was another official military hospital established in the first invasion of the Low Countries in 1792. It was also requisitioned by Grant. Data from this hospital includes a list of compound fractures and their outcomes (from 20 June to 6 August), a list of types and outcomes of joint injuries (20 June to 5 August) and a list of operations and outcomes (from reception to 1 August). Dr William Galbraith Wray, Physician to the Forces, wrote up these cases and was the Resident Medical Officer here. His role was to manage incidental and infectious disease and prescribe appropriate medication. The Elisabeth Hospital lay at a low level in Brussels, near the river, but was clean and well ventilated and suffered few cases of gangrene.

The Annonciate Hospital
No. 3 on the Brussels Map

This was a monastery on the Rue de Louvain. It was closed as a religious establishment by the French Army then used as a hospital from 1792 and later used as a barracks. The building was requisitioned by Grant. Data from this hospital includes a list of the variety of wounds (20 June to 20 July) and their causes, also a list of primary and secondary surgical operations and their outcomes (20 June to 31 July). The officer in charge was Surgeon to the Forces David Brownrigg.

The Caserne St Elisabeth Hospital. (Gareth Glover's Collection)

The Gens d'Armerie Hospital
No. 4 on the Brussels Map
The Barracks of the *Maréchausée* or the Gens d'Armerie, was situated on the Rue des Petits Carmes. This requisitioned building housed many French wounded prisoners amongst others. Data from this, extracted from the returns, includes wounds and some operations from 29 June and for the next three days. There is also a list of surgical procedures performed in the Gens d'Armerie, but dates are omitted. The supervising surgeon was Dr Theodore Gordon, Surgeon to the Forces. Intermittent fevers were most prevalent at the Gens d'Armerie which lay in the lower town (filthy in the extreme). Being the last establishment to be opened, it was filled with prisoners of war and probably the worst wounded who could not move off the battlefield themselves. Three hundred men were collected in this hospital, the majority desperately, if not to say incurably, wounded. Among them were one hundred and forty compound fractures, viz, 86 of the thigh, 48 of the leg, and six of the arm. They had been collected from the field later and housed in barns and the like before being transported to Brussels between eight and 13 days after the battle. Dr Knox and Dr Theodore Gordon served at this hospital.

Orpheline Hospital
No. 5 on the Brussels Map

This was an old convent (Couvent de l'Orphelinat) which had been converted into an orphanage; each parish having one). This was requisitioned by Grant. We have no data from this hospital, nor do we know who was in charge of the unit.

The Orpheline Hospital. (Gareth Glover's Collection)

The Saint Jean Hospital
No. 6 on the Brussels Map

This was a civilian hospital run by the city of Brussels and was requisitioned by Grant for care of casualties, possibly of Dutch-Belgian patients, under the care of both military and local civilian surgeons. We have no data or name of the surgeon in charge of this unit.

The St Pierre Hospital
No. 7 on the Brussels Map

This hospital was already a civilian hospital run by the city of Brussels. We have no data or name of the surgeon in charge of this hospital. It was most probably used by Dutch-Belgian patients, under the care of local civilian or military surgeons. We do know, however, that there was a medical educational link with the Jesuits Hospital.

The St Pierre Hospital. (Gareth Glover's Collection)

Minimes Hospital
No. 8 on the Brussels Map

Since 1787, this building had been an Austrian military hospital (the Southern Netherlands had been part of the Hapsburg Empire between 1714 and 1797. Austria relinquished its claim over the province in 1797). There is a return showing the most significant surgical procedures from this hospital from 18 June to 4 August. The surgeon in charge of this place was Dr John Cole, Surgeon to the Forces

Hôpital Militaire
No. 9 on the Brussels Map

This was an old military hospital, which was possibly used by the Dutch-Belgian military for their casualties.

La Grand Béguinage
No. 10 on the Brussels Map

The Grand Hospice of Brussels, also known as Institut Pacheco, was built from 1824 to 1827 by Belgian architect Henri Partoes, on the site previously occupied by the Grand Béguinage. The Hospice is known after the name of the Spanish nobleman Augustin Pacheco whose widow founded the previous institution in 1713, a hospital for the elderly in his memory. At present, the Hospice is a specialised geriatric hospital. The old hospital was used for casualties after the battle. It is sited north west of the Hôpital Militaire.

The Grand Beguinage Hospital (hospice). (Gareth Glover's Collection)

The Barracks of the 'Petit Château' or the Cazerne Rue d'Ophem
No. 11 on the Brussels Map

Sited due west of La Grande Béguinage on the quayside and with its rear on the Rue d'Ophem. This barracks still exists, although rebuilt in the 1840s.

The barracks of the Petit Chateau. (Gareth Glover's Collection)

The Notre Dame Hospital
No. 12 on the Brussels Map
This was the Hôpital Notre Dame de Bon Secours, the nearby Notre Dame de les Soeurs Noires was also requisitioned by Grant.

Ruisbroek
No. 13 on the Brussels Map
An old Belgian hospital in Brussels was situated in the Rue de Ruisbroek, to the south of the Place Royale. This was where the noted Belgian surgeon Dr Joseph-François Kluyskens worked.

The Notre Dame de Bonne Secours Hospital. (Gareth Glover's Collection)

Church of the Madeleine
No. 14 on the Brussels Map
This church, established in the 13th Century by the Brothers of Mercy, was used temporarily to house some one hundred casualties in the early days after the battle.

Chapelle de la Madeleine.
(Gareth Glover's
Collection)

Outside Brussels
A hospital situated at Laeken within two miles of Brussels was run by Dr Pockels, a Brunswick surgeon. It is described as having been sited on a swampy flat through which the Antwerp Canal, the River Dyle and some tributaries ran. This is where the Brunswickers had their hospital. It was situated close to Laeken, since the Brunswickers were stationed at nearby Vilvoorde before the Battle of Waterloo. Nothing is known of the location of this hospital, but it is recorded that almost all amputations performed here terminated fatally.

About 250 French patients were held at Termonde and were looked after by Dr Perkins.[5] The specific location is not known.

---

5   It has proven impossible to absolutely certain of this surgeon's identity, however, it may be John Perkins, who had been an assistant surgeon in the 12th Light Dragoons but had retired in 1813. He may well have been another who responded to the call for medical help. He re-joined the army as a hospital assistant in 1818 and retired again as an assistant surgeon in 1825.

Main Antwerp Hospitals

At least 2,500 casualties were shipped to Antwerp for care.

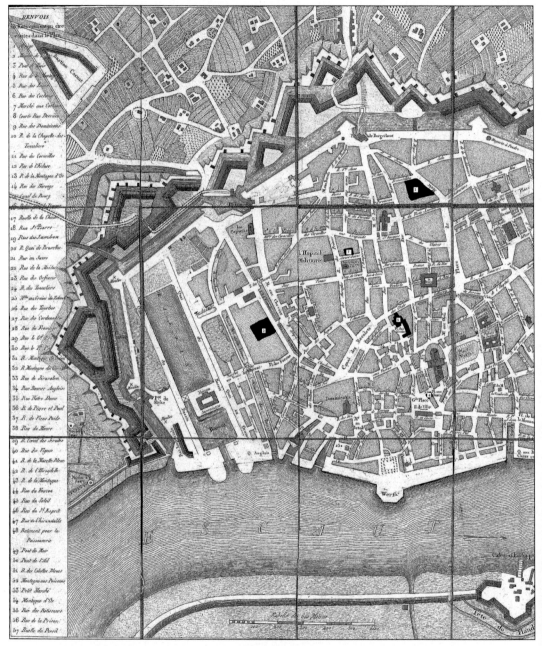

Map of Antwerp in 1810 showing principal hospital sites (Gareth Glover's Collection)

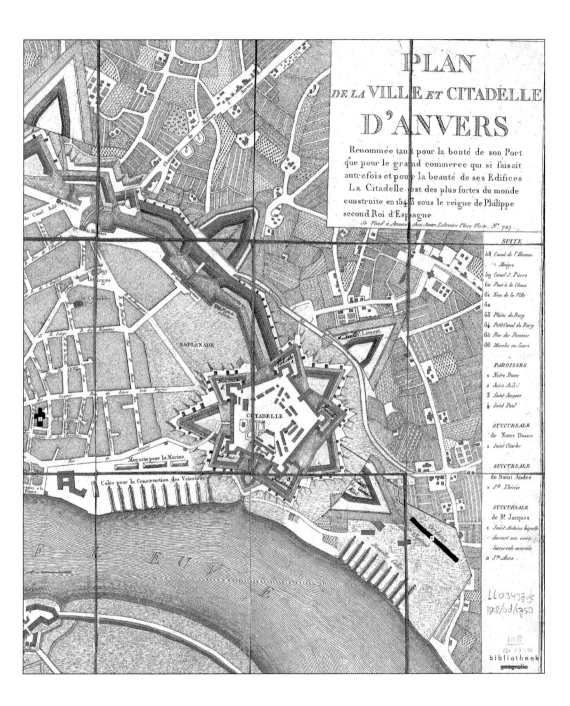

The Minimes
No. 1 on the Antwerp Map
The 18th Century Church of Saint Jean et Etienne aux Minimes, often just called the Church of Minimes was commandeered because of its size and central location.

The Minimes, Antwerp. (Gareth Glover's Collection)

Caserne de Facon
No. 2 on the Antwerp Map
Originally a 14th Century convent known as the Falcon Klooster (named after Falco, Director of the Antwerp Mint) and had an adjoining monastery, but the Austrian Emperor had banned the religious order in 1784 and the convent buildings were converted into a military hospital in 1792. However, the adjoining monastery burnt down in 1795 and the buildings were abandoned. The area was bought by the city in 1810 and Napoleon ordered the ruins to be cleared and a barracks to be built on the site. James Simpson (a British lawyer) accompanied Dr Thomson to Antwerp and he noted that it eventually held 800 British wounded and was apparently very clean and well appointed.

The Facon Barracks. (Gareth Glover's Collection)

Augustine
No. 3 on the Antwerp Map
St Augustine's, a seventeenth century church in central Antwerp was commandeered to take a number of casualties. It has recently been refurbished and is now a concert venue.

St Augustine Church. (Gareth Glover's Collection)

Corderie
No. 4 on the Antwerp Map
This building had been constructed by Napoleon. It was situated beyond the city defences and citadel. The new building formed part of a new naval dockyard and was designed to be a rope work, some 1,300 feet long. It was used to house 1,500 French wounded placed in four long rows of beds from end to end.

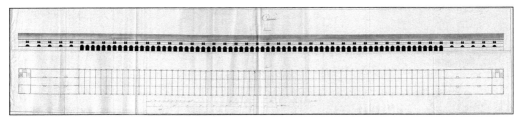

Plan of the Corderie at Antwerp. (Gareth Glover's Collection)

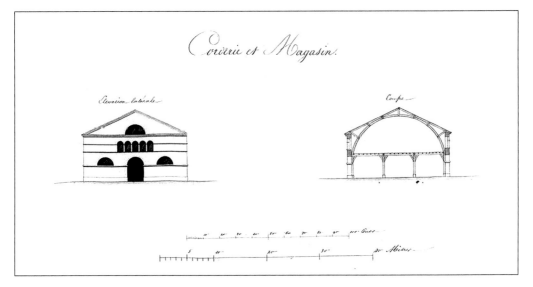

Side Plan of the Corderie at Antwerp. (Gareth Glover's Collection)

The Jesuits Church
No. 5 on the Antwerp Map
Little is known of this hospital except that it held mainly French patients.

The Jesuit's Church. (Gareth Glover's Collection)

Hotel du Nord
No. 6 on the Antwerp Map
This building was a hotel and restaurant in central Antwerp which was used to house British casualties.

The Hotel du Nord – to the right of the church. (Gareth Glover's Collection)

Convent of the Soeurs Noires
No. 7 on the Antwerp Map
This convent of the Black Sisters (or Cellites), followed the Augustine tradition. It was turned into a hospital for the Dutch-Belgian casualties.

Entrance to the Convent of the *Soeurs Noires*. (Gareth Glover's Collection)

Later on, convalescent patients were repatriated to the naval hospitals at Plymouth (Stonehouse), Portsmouth (Haslar), Yarmouth, and Deal. Some were also cared for in Colchester, where there was a military hospital.

We have a description of the patients soon after their arrival at Deal and their memories of the Battle of Waterloo:

> Upwards of ninety soldiers, badly wounded at Waterloo, and afterwards removed from Brussels to Deal Naval Hospital, and whom I separately interrogated on the point in question, not one appeared to have lost complete self-possession for a moment. On the contrary, many of them continued fighting in the ranks of their respective regiments, after having been struck more than once, twice, or three times even, with musket balls: many of those men were wounded with grape-shot; some through the lungs, abdomen, parts of generation, face, neck, vertebral column, joints of the knee, elbow and wrist. Some of this number had also suffered amputation, and there were about eighteen that laboured under gun-shot fractures of the upper and lower extremities. Two or three, from the extensive nature of their wounds and loss of blood, afterwards became faint.[6]

The Royal Naval Hospital at Deal, Kent. (Gareth Glover's Collection)

6   A.C. Hutchinson, *Some Practical Observations in Surgery* (London: Underwood, 1816), pp.6-7.

7

The Report of Observations made in the British Military Hospitals in Belgium after the Battle of Waterloo

John Thomson MD, consulting physician to the Edinburgh new town dispensary & Professor of Surgery to the Royal College of Surgeons, Regius Professor of Military Surgery in the University of Edinburgh and also Surgeon to the Forces, along with his friend Dr Somerville, PMO in Scotland, applied to the Medical Board in London to travel to Belgium as soon as they heard the news of the Battle of Waterloo and of the enormous number of casualties.

Professor John Thomson. (Courtesy Royal College of Surgeons of Edinburgh)

Dr William Somerville. (Public Domain, Courtesy of Art Work UK)

They left London on 4 July and had arrived in Brussels on 8 July 1815, exactly three weeks after the battle had ended and when the work of caring for more than fifty thousand wounded of all nations was well under way. On arrival, they met the senior British medical officers, Mr John Gunning and Dr McNeil.[1] They received permission to visit any of the hospitals and were given carte blanche to enquire into all aspects of the medical care. They were to assist and to report on the care of the wounded in Belgium; and they eventually produced a book entitled, a *Report of Observations made in the British Military Hospitals in Belgium after the Battle of Waterloo, with some remarks upon Amputation.* Published in Edinburgh on 1 January 1816, this was dedicated to the Duke of York, the commander of the British forces. This publication formed almost another official report on the organisation of the medical services in Belgium coupled with the results of surgery in the Low Countries. This report makes interesting qualitative reading, but contains little statistical data, which these authors had collated in other reports and which will be found in the hospital information in the following chapter. The report makes a number of claims and puts forward some hypotheses, which provide excellent examples of medical thinking at the time but clearly indicates the limitations of contemporary knowledge.

The initial comments regarding the time of year are of interest, Thomson stating that the battle had fortuitously occurred some four to five weeks before the usual 'sickly season' in Belgium, possibly based on the malarial season, which was a particular problem in the urban canal areas. This shows that they found little evidence of fevers having spread throughout the overcrowded and unsanitary hospitals even so long after the action. It is also of interest that some more robust patients who had not been removed from the battlefield until two or three days after the battle (some even longer), showed little sign of having suffered inordinately for being left out so long without care. It must however be assumed that without any form of triage on the field, most of the more seriously wounded succumbed well before they were able to be transported to the hospitals and thus the reported hospital survival data will certainly have been significantly skewed.

They discovered that there were still around 2,500 wounded in Belgium (actually there were many more), but by now mainly collected in six hospitals in Brussels, although this would not have included officers billeted in private residences. The hospitals still in use were named as the Jesuits, Elisabeth, Annonciate, Orpheline, Notre Dame and the Gens d'Armerie, the first five being situated in the upper part of the town, renowned as being the healthier area were all largely allocated, to the allied troops. The Gens d'Armerie alone was located in the lower town and was allocated almost exclusively for the French wounded. Here they did find a greater number of patients suffering with secondary fevers.

They surveyed the hospitals in Brussels for a full twelve days and then visited the small hospital at Termonde under the direction of Dr Perkins which contained around two hundred and fifty French wounded, many of whom again suffered with secondary fevers.

They then moved on to Antwerp, where Mr Summers Higgins, the PMO, was in control of five hospitals caring for around 2,500 wounded, mostly French. These hospitals were named Minimes, Facon, Augustine, Hotel du Nord, Jesuits and the Corderie: the last contained no less than one thousand wounded alone. The Corderie and the Jesuits contained exclusively

---

1   Deputy Inspector of Hospitals Donald McNiel, who had also arrived in Belgium after the battle.

French wounded and were overseen by a Dr Vranken who had a number of local Belgian doctors to support him.

Thomson and Somerville returned to Brussels on 29 July, where they visited the hospitals again for a further eight days, before they revisited Antwerp on 7 August. This time at Antwerp, they found that many of the wounded had been discharged and sent home and the remainder had largely been moved from the Augustine, Minimes and Hotel du Nord, concentrating almost all at the Facon. The Corderie was also still in use, but here numbers were down to around 400. Some had died but a far greater number had been sent home to recuperate.

Thomson noted that by this time patients with similar types of injuries had been hospitalised together, so making it easier for the surgeons with any specialist knowledge to handle all similar cases in one place.

The various wounds, their treatment and the ultimate success or failure of therapy, were then detailed in individual chapters, which can be summarised very briefly as follows.

Sabre Wounds

The majority of patients they saw with sabre wounds were French and most injuries were found to be to the head, neck, and shoulders. Adhesive strips were used to close the wounds, but enough room had been left to allow any pus to run out freely. Stitching the wounds had been less frequently practised but Thomson admitted that it could have been of use in some cases.

Puncture Wounds

Most wounds of this kind had been caused by the lance, very few by the bayonet. The lance made a larger wound but interestingly, in general terms, it was found that these wounds healed much faster than those made by bayonets. Lance wounds were frequently found to have extensive areas of inflammation around the punctured area and were often accompanied by a bilious fever (probably a fever accompanying the inevitable sepsis). Tetanus, although a real danger, was found to be very rare (luckily, as there was little effective treatment for this infection, with a mortality rate of over 80 percent).

Lacerated Wounds

These traumatic tearing wounds were caused either by cannonball strikes or from pieces of shell casing. It was found that the shearing stress of this type of wound caused the arteries to shut down (vaso-constrict), which prevented catastrophic losses of blood. They also witnessed wounds that were apparently caused by the 'wind of a ball' in which it was believed that the pressure waves surrounding the ball in flight caused massive internal damage.[2] Thomson discovered some examples of this form of wound but simply concluded that the injury was very difficult to explain.

---

2   This is deemed impossible by modern day physicists. However, the regularity of such extensive bruising without any obvious wound, leads us to believe that there might be something in this. It is however very difficult to replicate in experiments!

Gunshot Wounds

Gunshot wounds were apparently by far the most numerous. They often healed poorly even in the simplest cases. The damage caused by the ball to the various layers of tissue and organs prevented healing as shown by the wound's edges adhering properly. They noted that the routes taken by lead balls through the body cavity were often unpredictable, making it difficult to correctly track the ball from the entry wound to discover where the ball then lodged. On striking bone or solid items of uniform, such as buttons or belt plates, it was quite normal for the lead ball to deform, become deflected, or even split into two. Rather strangely, Thomson observed that lead balls and pieces of fabric dragged into the wound were rarely found to carry infection (this would be at variance with modern bacteriological concepts!) and therefore unless extraction had been carried out at a very early stage (when it was possible to do so without causing too much pain) they could often be left alone to work themselves to the surface over a very long period of time, if ever. This was therefore the preferred method of treating these wounds, except in cases where the ball was lodged in a joint and was causing significant discomfort.

Haemorrhage

Ligation (tying off) of major blood vessels was by now a common place procedure. Ligatures of linen or silk were however, employed with careful selection, but more rarely used as they often resulted in mortification (gangrene) of the affected limb. It was found easier for temporary control to simply apply pressure over the main artery, at the groin for example, or to use compresses of sponge or padded cork to restrict the flow of blood, but not to cut the supply off completely so as to avoid mortification setting in. It was found that secondary haemorrhages (due to sepsis) were frequent in gunshot wounds and they believed them to be caused by injured arteries breaking down later. Surgeons often accounted for relapses in soldier's health by blaming the patients for breaking their 'low diet' regimens by eating an excess of red meat or drinking too much alcohol!

Head Wounds

Most head wounds were found to be caused by sword or small arms missiles, since the more traumatic injuries caused by cannonballs led to immediate fatality.

Glancing blows from sabres often left the brain exposed, which sometimes protruded from the wound, but in time the swollen inflamed brain tissue often returned to within the cranium with little or no permanent damage to brain function. There were many slicing or incised injuries to the back of the neck and they were often found to be accompanied by 'feebleness' in their lower limbs. This was due to bruising or temporary interference with spinal cord function. Direct sword cuts down onto the head were in some cases noted not to cause damage to the brain below (indeed one Frenchman was observed to have suffered thirteen such wounds without noticeable effect). In other cases, where the bone pressed on the brain or fragments of bone were driven into the brain, paralysis did occur, but it was observed that the body was affected on the opposite side to the side of the head injury. Thomson and Somerville were unaware of the cross-representation of the brain at this time. Operations (by trephining or trepanning) were performed to ease pressure on the brain, to elevate or remove bone fragments – also to drain collections of blood or pus.

A stupor was commonly noted in ball strikes on the skull which did not penetrate, there were also noted variations in pupil dilatation (reflecting brain damage or increased intracranial pressure) with such injuries. It was noticed that head injuries did not often display secondary inflammation. This was put down to a strict regime of a low diet and no alcohol. Cranial injury was often accompanied by convulsions and they were viewed as a very dangerous sign for the patient. Elevation or removal of depressed bone fragments of the skull frequently relieved these distressing symptoms.

Facial Wounds

Most sword wounds to the face healed well, (because of the head and neck's rich blood supply) but gunshot wounds healed far slower and often produced extreme pain. This was because the ball often split or flattened and became impacted in the bone. There were also a significant number of wounds incurred where the ball travelled between the temples, behind the eyes, often causing permanent blindness and sometimes loss of smell.

Damage to the jaw or mouth was rarely curable with the salivary glands often found to be permanently injured, in fact most injuries to the lower jaw and accompanying salivary glands proved fatal. Many injuries to the teeth and jaw left permanent facial deformities and made eating difficult.

Neck Wounds

Many were seen with wounds to the neck where the arteries had not been damaged. It was presumed that where the arteries had been cut, they had died immediately. Any wound of the trachea was deemed serious and a number of instances of permanent paralysis in the arms and hands were noted following injuries to the neck as a result of nerve transection. It was observed however, that sabre wounds to the side and back of the neck rarely caused permanent paralysis.

Chest Wounds

It was found that very few wounds to the chest were caused by lance or bayonet, the vast majority being caused by musket balls, and such wounds were found to have a high survival rate (probably many of the most serious, which involved the heart, did not survive long enough to be hospitalised). Damage to the lungs was frequently exhibited by air coming out of the wound, often accompanied by the coughing up of blood (haemoptysis). The track of the ball was often found to have deviated greatly from its original line of flight, having struck the ribs or sternum in its passage through the body. Accompanying haemorrhages were more pronounced in patients wounded by the lance than those with gunshot wounds, but at the same time, lance wounds were found to heal much more quickly than those from musket balls. British surgeons regularly used bleeding (venesection) by the lancet to suppress the coughing up of blood, but it also was thought to have had the advantage of preventing secondary inflammation from any accumulation of pus. It was recommended that a stent (tent in the report – a loose plug of cloth acting as a drain) was fitted to allow pus to run off rather than closing the wound, to avoid the pus accumulating and causing further problems.

Wounds of the Diaphragm

In general, very few wounds of this type were seen and most survived even with two such injuries.

Wounds of the Abdomen

Thomson saw few patients with wounds of the abdomen, having been told that most with such wounds had already succumbed. One particularly impressive example was given. A patient was struck on the right buttock by a shell and a large piece of the shell was subsequently felt under the false ribs on the right side of the abdomen. This was cut out twenty-five days after the wound was incurred and was found to weigh no less than nine ounces! There was however, little sign of inflammation. Some patients survived such wounds, but many suffered from severe inflammation resulting from intra-abdominal sepsis, abscess, and fistula formation, as a result of injury to the bowel. We know that most men with fatal intraabdominal wounds died from blood loss.

Wound of the Liver

A high percentage of such wounds survived, but many suffered frequent heavy haemorrhage before improving and also suffered with jaundice as a result of the spillage of bile intra-abdominally.

Wounds to the Stomach and Intestines

Very few patients with this sort of wound survived and faeces often discharged through the wound (where a fistula had formed). In a number of cases, the lead ball was eventually passed naturally through the rectum the internal healing process having walled off the original gut injury. The treatment was simply to leave the wound alone, enforce a strict low diet on the patients, and hope.

Wounds to the Bladder

Urine consequently issued through the wound for considerable length of time, but use of a catheter relieved many of the symptoms until healing had occurred. However, many men refused to have a catheter passed and consequently suffered badly because of it. Two hundred years ago, it proved difficult to retain a catheter for any length of time.

Wounds to the Pelvis

Such wounds usually healed if a catheter was introduced to allow the passage of the urine. As regards the testes, damage to the sac could be repaired, but greatly engorged, inflamed, and painful testes were routinely removed.

Wounds to the Loins and Pelvis

Many such wounds were found in the hospitals from balls passing through the pelvic area, but a great number appeared not to have damaged any of the vital organs. At the same time, a significant number suffered some paralysis of a lower limb, which Thomson had observed was often accompanied by a severe pain in the affected limb. However, very few were found with paralysis in both lower limbs where damage to the spinal apparatus had occurred.

Hip Wounds

There were a large numbers of such cases, the ball rarely exiting, having been stopped in its track by the thickness of bone in the area. A fracture of the head of the femur always caused severe inflammation and few patients survived.

Wounds to the Thigh

Large areas of muscle carried away by cannon balls did not appear to heal well and were often accompanied by a herniation (protrusion) of the muscle through its investing fascia (tough membrane lining the muscle bulk). The recommended treatment was to bandage reasonably tightly when the patient could bear it. By this means it was found that the swelling would be kept in check.

Many gunshot wounds of the leg were found to cause severe inflammation and abscesses, but the some more superficial wounds were often fairly quick-healing. A fracture of the thigh bone usually ended in the death of the patient. Injuries to the thigh were also noted to cause a permanent shortening of the limb (by the over-riding of fracture fragments).

Wounds to the Knee Joints

A number of these injuries were observed and most were found to have been attacked by severe inflammation, which endangered their lives: because of this amputation was often required. However, where no amputation had taken place it was subsequently noted that most eventually saw a general recovery, with some use of the limb.

Lower Leg Wounds

Wounds of the lower leg often involved the ball smashing into and fragmenting the bone, rather than a simple break. This caused a great number of retained bone sequestra (pieces of infected dead bone), which caused great irritation and so the shattered bone would not heal well, leading to inflammation. Amputation in such cases was frequently found necessary and most patients healed well afterwards.

Wounds to the Ankle and Foot

Such wounds were serious, just like those of the knee. Despite some improvement in a number of cases, it was often found that the pain did not subside and that subsequently amputation had to be undertaken.

Wounds to the Shoulder

Wounds in the shoulder rarely proved fatal although such injuries were often accompanied by paralysis of part of the arm or some movement of the limb being severely restricted permanently.

Wounds to the Elbow

This was a frequent source of injury, with a few caused by a lance or a bayonet but the great majority by musket balls. Some of these injuries required amputation, but many were successfully saved although a proportion of these were left with restricted movement.

When to Operate

From the observations made, Thomson and Somerville determined that early amputation had many advantages and they were clearly advocates of such a regimen. They noted that the surgeons in the Royal Navy routinely did so, but that some army surgeons were yet to fully embrace such a doctrine. They calculated that over five hundred (mainly allied) amputations had been carried out after the Battle of Waterloo, of which a third were estimated to have been carried out before inflammation occurred.

The visiting surgeons recorded a number of advantages to an early (primary) amputation.

The limb ablation would ideally be carried out on the first day of injury, before infection set in. Even in limbs saved from amputation, the patients continued to suffer and inflammation often occurred. At a later stage, the patient was less likely to concur with an operation (termed a secondary procedure) and the outcome if carried out was often far less successful.

They noted the main reasons why surgeons delayed before amputating. These included: the pleas of the wounded, their own doubt as to its necessity, and differing opinions when a number of surgeons were consulted. It was stated that such consultations rarely acted efficiently and decisively or to the ultimate benefit of the patient.

It was also stated that there were undoubtedly a number of situations where immediate amputation was indispensable. These were: when a limb had been shot away; when the bones of a joint were fractured or the bone shattered by a cannon ball; where large portions of the soft tissue had been removed and major blood vessels and nerves had been divided; also, where the bone had been fractured by a spent ball and the soft tissue severely bruised –although it had not broken the skin; when the main artery had been divided and the bone fractured; and where balls had passed through the large joints lacerating the ligaments. All of these wounds if untreated had been found to cause continued or secondary haemorrhage and gangrene. As previously noted, delay often proved fatal to the patient. Other examples of injuries where immediate amputation would prove beneficial were as follows: gunshot wounds to the fingers and toes; injuries to the wrist and ankle and in the forearm, only if bones were fractured and arteries had been divided; lower leg injuries, only in cases where both bones had been broken. In these cases, it was acknowledged that some such amputees might have retained their limbs, but it was argued that significantly improved survival rates were noted when early amputation was carried out. Over all, this philosophy would save many more lives.

Late amputations of upper limb articulating joints, such as the elbow, were found more successful than in the leg. Compound fractures of the arm usually healed well unless the artery was divided, but a fracture through the shoulder joint would usually require immediate amputation. With regard to thigh injuries, these were found to be extremely dangerous to patients and that primary amputations saw a much better survival rate than secondary operations. Overall, however, less than 20 percent of all thigh injuries were found to survive.

Only two amputations at the hip joint were undertaken in Belgium, one by Mr Guthrie and one by Mr Blicke. Both were performed some three weeks after the wound had been received, with just one surviving (Guthrie's patient). It was still extremely rare for disarticulation at the hip to succeed, being at the very cutting edge of current surgical knowledge. As far as the authors know, none of Baron Jean Larrey's seven hip disarticulations survived.

8

Hospital Returns Collected by John Thomson from the Hospitals in Brussels

Report of Dr Gordon regarding cases at the Gens d'Armerie Hospital

Gens d'Armerie Hospital, Brussels 31 July 1815

Sir,

It would be difficult, as it may be unnecessary, to plead any sufficient excuse, for obtruding on your valuable time at the present moment, the following sketch of the Gens d'Armerie Hospital entrusted to my care through the kindness of Mr Gunning PMO,[1] Surgeon in Chief & Dr McNeil, Deputy Inspector of Hospitals,[2] but as it ever has been my practice, to throw together, towards the conclusion of every charge, with which I have been entrusted, a short history of what I have deemed either curious or interesting and as this practice formerly, which in the peninsula met with the approbation of Sir James McGrigor, now Director General; I have presumed to do the same at the present moment, as a small tribute of respect to my superior officer.

The Gens d'Armerie Hospital was appropriated for the reception of as many French prisoners as it could contain computed though erroneously as nearly 300 men – you are aware the more movable cases or those of a more slight description were sent to Antwerp and other stations, in the first instance, the remaining number or such as might be considered immovable, (not to say incurable) were collected after several days in this city and were divided between the St Elisabeth and the Gens d'Armerie – Dr Eyre Physician to the Forces[3] was ordered in charge to this Hospital on the 29 June and before sufficient arrangement as to the cleanliness of the place could be made, he had to receive within its walls 260 [sic. – 259] of perhaps

---

1 Mr John Gunning, Principal Medical Officer to the 1st Corps. (no. 1205 in Peterkin & Johnston *Medical Officers*).
2 Dr Donald McNeil, Deputy Inspector of Hospitals (no. 1442 in Peterkin & Johnston *Medical Officers*).
3 Dr John Eyre Physician to the Forces (no. 2973 in Peterkin & Johnston *Medical Officers*).

the most wretched beings that were ever left on the field of battle. This officer made all those exertions he was so fully competent to do, and great progress had been made in precautionary measures for the timely reparation of such sphacelated cases as presented themselves,[4] thereby an accumulation of disease although the extreme filth of this house and its crowded state for some time prevented the possibility of hindering the formation of fever in the first instance but before I proceed further it will be the most proper place for me to lay before you a return and state of the patients admitted into the Hospital as far as the most minute enquiry, has enabled me to draw it out.

Return of French prisoners admitted on the 30th June & 3 subsequent days[5]

Compound fractures of the thigh	86	In this return only the most severe wounds are mentioned but in many cases there were 2,3 & 4 wounds
Compound fractures of the leg	48	
Compound fractures of the arm	6	
Amputation of the thigh	22	
Amputation of leg	10	
Amputation at shoulder joint	2	
Fracture of the Cranium	6	
Wounds of the head	5	Two of these through the temple
Wounds of the oesophagus	1	
Wounds of the thorax	14	
Wounds of the abdomen	9	
Wounds of the groin	7	
Wounds of the hip joint	4	
Wounds of the knee joint	8	
Wounds of the hand	3	
Wounds of the soft parts	24	
Contusion	4	
Total	259	

By this return you will see that perhaps no one Hospital had within its walls such a number of compound fractures of the thigh, & perhaps it would be difficult to parallel the like number of bad cases collected together at one time, and in one place, in so small a number

4   Cases suffering from gangrene in their wounds.
5   The other returns from this hospital state that the casualties arrived from 29 June. This report is a list of operations and wound types. These figures almost certainly relate solely to some French prisoner of war casualties with significant wounds. It seems that the hospital was opened later and the wounded were in a pitiable state, also the hospital was dirty and unprepared for their reception. The Gens d'Armerie hospital lay in the lower and damper part of the city, near waterways, and was regarded, rightly or wrongly as being less healthy. What remains remarkable is the preponderance of thigh fractures and the greater number of lower limb wounds, when compared with those of the upper limb. Mostly, the list is of the various injuries, but the three operation types, all amputations listed tally with those in the next table in the section 'Performed elsewhere': that is, out-with the hospital.

of men. It now becomes me to draw your attention to the collateral circumstances attendant upon these men & I cannot do better than give you extracts from the reports of the different medical officers, who were attached to this Hospital, at its formation, which at my request they were good enough to draw up; they are the reports of Acting Staff Surgeon Donatt,[6] Surgeon Nieter[7] of the German Legion & Assistant Surgeon Gerson of the same Corps.[8] The character and eminent abilities of the first of these gentlemen you are, I presume, well acquainted with, the latter gentlemen are every way qualified to judge.

The report of Acting Staff Surgeon Donatt, after stating his appointment to this Hospital on the 29th [June] proceeds as follows:

> I found the greater part of the men in the most miserable state; both in respect to their general state of health as well as regards to their wounds, most of them having remained for several days in the field of battle; after the actions of the 16th, 17th & 18th. The greater number of wounds were compound fractures of the lower extremities; the limbs very much shattered & in many cases gangrene had taken place with all the constitutional ills, thereunto belonging several of the above cases, were too far reduced for operation and died in the course of 24 or 48 hours, the cases who there appeared any rational hope from amputation were operated upon by Mr C. Bell[9] and myself, on the two first days of my attendance at the Gens d'Armerie, independent of all the care & attention on my part, many of the operated were sunk after some days, their constitutions not having been sufficiently active to resist the violence committed.

Same report:

> in cases that outlived the first 12 days, by the close attention given to them by the medical officers, nature seemed to be greatly assisted, and the deaths in consequence became much less frequent, their constitutions became much invigorated, the appearances of the wounds & the suppuration therefore much improved, great attention to the digestion organs seems to have been the basis of this improvement which proves the fact of the great want of care, on the part of the men, previous to their coming into the Hospital.

Extracts from the report of Surgeon Nieter appointed 1st July to the 2nd Division, who looked after 65 patients:

---

6   Possibly Dr George Denecke Physician to the Forces, originally of the King's German Legion, who was slightly wounded at Quatre Bras (no. 2457 in Peterkin & Johnston *Medical Officers*).

7   Surgeon Ernst Nieter 2nd Light Infantry Battalion KGL (no. 2369 in Peterkin & Johnston *Medical Officers*).

8   Assistant Surgeon George Hartog Gerson of the 5th Line Battalion KGL (no. 3342 in Peterkin & Johnston *Medical Officers*).

9   Mr Charles Bell, Consulting Surgeon to the Middlesex Hospital. He was a competent surgeon, anatomist, physiologist and artist. He visited Brussels two weeks after the battle.

I found the greatest part of them in a very miserable situation, some of them had not been dressed for 3, 4 and 5 days or even more, & some not since the time they were wounded: a great proportion of them had compd. Fracture, in a gangrenous state and filled with worms [maggots]… Through all this fatigue the patient had undergone, by transportation from the field & from one hospital to another, it could not fail, that the mortality should be great during the first fortnight, particularly the wounds of the thorax and abdomen, as also the compound fractures of the thighs where the bones were much shattered soon becoming gangrenous & ending in death.

Extracts from Assistant Surgeon Gerson, who took charge of a division [within the hospital] on the 4th July; he proceeds to state

That he had in it 21 comp[oun]d fractures of the thigh with great shattering of the bones. The number of slight cases was exceedingly few and eleven had penetrated the great cavities, a great proportion of these cases, had been 4 or 5 days in the field of battle, some as long as eight, without any assistance, many of the wounds were considerably inflamed & in others profuse suppuration had ensued, after intense inflammation. Some of the patients ought to have undergone immediate amputation after the infliction of the wound, but in consequence of the great number, the operation had been deferred till now, in most of these cases, the operation was the only thing that could save the patient, otherwise in a hopeless state.

Having thus I trust, enabled you to form a pretty correct judgement of the state of the Hospital, it will now form part of my plan to enter a little more detail.

The compound fracture of the thigh were in a great proportion of cases, of the upper part of the thigh, many severely splintered, & from the extracts laid before you of the different reports, you will see that little could be done at that time, but laying them in the easiest position, keeping down the inflammation by cold applications. Leeches and *want* of *bandaging*, & occasionally promoting a free discharge, either by the use of warm cataplasms[10] or free dilatations,[11] for the extraction of broken bones & pieces of cloth. In many the symptoms ran so swift, as to carry the patient off within the first fortnight, previously disposed to fever as he was from a variety of circumstances, necessarily attendant on a military life and the privations he had submitted to – the inflammatory stage having subsided, which was not till about the 18th day, profuse suppuration, & hectic fever with dyarhhea [sic],[12] prevented often the surgeon from interposing with the knife, the strength having rapidly failed so much, that the operation could not with safety be undertaken. The previous history will have shewn you that sloughing had even from the first manifested itself, and many I can confidently assert, were obliged to submit to the operation, at a period by no means favourable to final recovery, from the certainty there was, that if time was allowed to elapse in waiting for the most proper time, the patient would have paid the debt of nature in the

10   Poultices of cloth or vegetable.
11   Enlarging the wounds by incision.
12   Patients with severe sepsis would often suffer with diarrhoea.

interim. The mortality has therefore been great in this class of patients, yet I cannot help thinking that all things considered the number of fractures of the thigh that will ultimately do well, or be saved by operation will not be inconsiderable, although under more favourable circumstances by no means what might be expected.

The operations next come to be considered, & here I can be but on[c]e more add to a long list, [of those] who have given the preference to operations [carried out] on the field as being far the most successful mode of treating severe compound fracture. In military hospitals, a crowded Hospital in many instances indifferent ventilation, a comparatively impure state [of] the atmosphere, are but indifferent assistants to aid the cure of such formidable injuries, & ought, I think, always to be taken into account in forming the decision, upon cases of this description, the operations were performed on the field are therefore greater in proportion as to success than those performed at a later period how nicely soever [sic] of the time [that] might have been chosen & I presume depending much on the above circumstances, the operations then are as follows:[13]

Nature of Operation	Perf. In Hospital	Doing well	Doubtful	Dead	Perf. elsewhere	Doing well	Doubtful	Dead	Total operations	Total Deaths
Amputation of Thigh	20	4	4	12	22	9	3	10	42	22
do. of leg	4	3	–	1	10	7	–	3	14	4
do. at the shoulder	1	–	–	1	2	2	–	–	3	1
do. Of the arm	3	2	–	1	–	–	–	–	3	1
Operation for Aneurism	1	–	–	1	–	–	–	–	1	1
Trepan	2	1	–	1	–	–	–	–	2	1
Total	31	10	4	17 [55%]	34	18	3	13 [38%]	65	30 [46%]

13 Of 65 cases undergoing surgery listed here, 30 died (22 of these were delayed thigh amputations). This gives a mortality rate of 46 percent. Some of these cases were almost certainly operated on by Sir Charles Bell, his results evoked criticism from a colleague, but of course he had been given a particularly challenging case-load!

There may be some surprise to see that those who received their operations in hospital could expect a poorer outcome (55 percent died) than those operated elsewhere (38 percent died), but this is certainly to a large extent, an indication of the timing of the operation after injury. Many of those operated on elsewhere were likely to have been operated on sooner at forward field hospitals or occasionally actually on the field. This supports the belief then beginning to be held that early intervention markedly increased the likelihood of a successful outcome. The proportion of the patients 'doing well' was also improved for those operated on 'elsewhere', with only 32 percent of those operated on in hospital doing well compared with 53 percent of those operated on elsewhere. It is also clear that amputations of the thigh carried the greatest risk of poor outcomes (60 percent mortality in the hospital setting and 45 percent operated on elsewhere).

The main issue extracted from this data is that the more severe cases usually got sent to the bigger hospitals, the delay often related more to their transfer and there was a greater chance of becoming infected with a septic wound, or a contagious or water borne infection in a larger hospital. Thus, the more cases that could be treated sooner and closer to their unit and away from a large lazarette, the better the outcome would prove.

Such is the comparative statement of operations performed on the field, or most probably within the first 48 hours: and those performed at the Hospital Gens d'Armerie on the 9th, 10th & 5 subsequent days after the action: not by any means considered as the most proper period, but performed from necessity for the reasons given above.

Fractures of the leg have in general done pretty well aside from the splintering of the bones, it has been necessary to have several of them removed, when they shared the fate of the other operations. The wounds of the head have done wonderfully well. One man has had a ball pass through both the temples fracturing the bones of the orbit of each eye, dividing in one the optic nerve, in the other producing paralysis and amaurosis.[14] This man has had symptoms of inflammation. I cannot say extending to the membranes of the brain but so severe as to require both general and local blood-letting, with the strictest antiphlogistic regimen[15]. He now suffers under a nervous affection much resembling *Tic Doleureux*[16] and he is by no means out of danger, but all things considered is [doing] wonderfully well. Another had a ball enter the squamous suture of the temporal bone & fracturing the parietal bone, lodged in the substance of the brain immediately over the *Tentor[iu]m Cerebelli*,[17] it was extracted by Mr C. Bell, several pieces of bone & a considerable portion of cerebral substance were removed at the same time the depletive and [antiphlogistic] regimen were used. The man does well but he owes much to the indefatigable care & attention of Hospital Assistant Blackadder,[18] the resident Medical Officer of the Gens d'Armerie, to whom I am particularly indebted not only for his attention to the particular duties allotted to him but to his unwearing [sic] assiduity in everything connected to the Hospital. I shall only mention two other cases of fracture of the cranium both attended with *Fungus Cerebri*.[19] The first had several pieces of bone extracted from the parietal bones, at the middle of the sagittal suture[20] – he recovered so far as to be able to speak rationally a little – he continues to labour under a paralysis of the right side – about three days after the extraction of the bones, a fungus shot up, continuing to increase in size daily, but without any bad symptoms, when at the end of 5 days sloughing took place & symptoms of inflammation & suppuration of the membranes of the brain quickly followed bidding defiance to all the means used for his recovery.

On dissection [post-mortem], the lobes of the brain were found filled with matter, and the cerebellum was found to contain an abscess, that extended to the Medulla Oblongata,[21] as far as could be traced. The other had many pieces of bone extracted from the left parietal bone, and had 5 or 6 other wounds, by no means despicable in themselves, in different other parts of the body, this man for many days after the bones were removed, did not recover his

---

14 Blindness.
15 Venesection, purgation and emesis with a 'low' diet.
16 A serious disorder of the Trigeminal (fifth cranial) nerve, characterized by severe pain in the face and forehead on the affected side, extending to the midline of the face and head, triggered by stimuli such as cold drafts, chewing, drinking cold liquids, brushing the hair, or washing the face. Called also trigeminal neuralgia.
17 The tentorium cerebelli is the sheet of the membrane, dura mater, which roofs over the cerebellum and supports the occipital lobes of the brain.
18 Henry Home Blackadder, Hospital Assistant to the Forces (no. 3658 in Peterkin & Johnston *Medical Officers*).
19 A protrusion of infected and swollen brain substance.
20 The sutures knit by interlocking the various skull plates together.
21 A vital part of the upper brain stem beneath the cerebellum.

memory. He did not recollect his own name and seemed to know nothing of Bonaparte. These in some measure regained. He has paralysis of the opposite side, to this hour, but in other respects is doing well.

The wounds of the thorax had almost all died in the earlier days of the Hospital, when accounts could not be kept regularly, but I have understood the lancet was freely and liberally employed, in one the symptoms of Empyema[22] were clearly marked, and at the suggestion of Dr Thomson, Professor of Military Surgery who was kind enough to visit this hospital: the operation [drainage of pus from the chest, by insertion of a metal cannula] was proposed to the poor man; but he would not submit to it. In another the ball had passed through the upper edge of the left lobe, fracturing the 2nd rib, and passing out close to the vertebra behind, this man got over the first symptoms, but on a fresh accession of inflammation and abscess he died; on dissection a spicula[23] of bone was found nearly in the centre of the lobe of the wounded lung with extreme adhesive inflammation & abscess &c. Another has a bayonet wound, or wound from the point of a horseman's sword passing by the edge of the trachea[24] but has no other bad symptom. A low regimen[25] with food of easy digestion is alone taken. The other seemed to have wounded either the kidney or ureter of one side together with the intestines both urine and faecal matter are discharged by the wound, yet present appearances are so promising that I cannot but entertain favourable hopes of his ultimate recovery.

Of the knee joint cases which were 8 in number, two died immediately after their admission into Hospital. 1 or 2 have been obliged to be amputated, and in general under unfavourable circumstances, one or two continue to do well, and promise to do without the operation. The remaining two refuse to submit – here nothing was left to the judgement of the surgeon, in the first instance, as at the time of their admission into Hospital; all the constitutional inflammatory symptoms were in full progress.

The wounds of the hip joint have mostly been fatal, and there still remain six or eight men whose wounds, although they cannot be said to be purely in the hip joint, are yet so connected with the parts in the immediate vicinity of that place, and the bones of the pelvis, as induces me to consider them as cases that will be extremely tedious if not fatal. There has been but one incised wound worthy of notice in the Hospital; and it is the case of wounded oesophagus before mentioned. The wounds of the forearm have been few and have in general done well.

I now come to a subject, which, while it has been the source of the greatest troubles has been so [much] of uneasiness to all concerned and this is the sphacelated[26] state of the sore[s] consequent of on amputation, the second dressing on the 7th, 8th, or 9th days [post operatively], have been the period at which the stumps have begun to put on this appearance. I confine it more particularly to this class of sore, because it has been by far more general in them. The patient becomes restless and uneasy he has a sence [sic] of pricking, shooting, or lancinating [sic] pain in the stump. It cannot be called spasm, he becomes

22   A collection of blood and pus in the chest, with fever, breathlessness and pain.
23   A splinter or fragment.
24   The windpipe.
25   A simple diet of bread milk soups, rice water, gruel, etc.
26   Gangrenous.

hot and thirsty, his pulse is jarring, and the whole arterial system, in a very tumultuary [overworked] state, a rigor and regular paroxism [sic] of intermittent [fever], has in one or two cases about this time intervened, a small dark coloured spot is observable, not always confined to the edge of the sore, its circumference is very tender. The centre itself by no means so, the very reverse, it spreads, the whole face of the stump becomes gangrenous, the constitutional symptoms keep pace with the local ones, the tongue becomes firm, red, delirious with the greatest prostration of strength, and a yellow suffusion of the skin[27] generally closes the scene.

Purging and antimonial medicines have been of use, and the carrot poultice particularly so. The lunar caustic[28] has arrested the progress when conjoined their constitutional remedies, but in general the symptoms have been so rapid, as to defy with any certainty, all the means that have been hitherto, and many local applications have been tried, bark and camphoric[29] rhubarb, the different acids both vegetable and mineral &c. The *solutio arsenicalis* much recommended in hospital gangrene in Spain has not had a fair trial, it being supported, and with some appearance of truth that it was not of the best quality and latterly there was none in store. Upon the whole notwithstanding every attention to the state of the atmosphere in the hospital (and I could refer to the reports of the Principal Medical Officers of this staff on that subject, who have given me their specialised approbation) I am willing to attribute no inconsiderable share of blame to this cause, but still more to the general state of the weather which has been uncommonly rainy and damp, with thunder almost every second day since the action, and if any great difference should appear to exist in respect to this disease as at the other hospitals. I have only to add that I am firmly persuaded it arises from the local situation of the hospital, the site of which is in a very low part of the town of Brussels, surrounded by houses and high walls, and little exposed to the passing breeze. On the subject of the weather it has been remarked, that the thermometer has continued very steady, never above 72, nor under 60 even during the night ever since the thunder storms which occurred on the 17th June.

On the 20th July there was a very thick fog which terminated in a very heavy fall of rain, a number of Medical Officers were suddenly seized with general sickness followed by inflammation of the throat. *Scarlatina*[30] made its appearance at the same time in private families.

On the 27th there was a severe thunder storm followed by a very heavy fall of rain, several of the convalescents were suddenly attacked with fever, and most of the Medical Officers complained of indisposition. In general, much attention to the state of the prima via [the meaning of this is unknown] seemed requisite to prevent an accession of fever. The inhabitants state that in some years, there is a much greater fall of rain than happens usually, that this is one of the rainy years and that during such seasons, there is a very great increase in sickness. Fevers of the typhoid, remittent, and intermittent types being usually the most common, they remarked that when it rains the wind is usually from the west – it may be perhaps unnecessary to add that every attention was paid to the

---

27 That is to say, jaundice.
28 Silver nitrate.
29 Camphor, camphire, afaltum or 'Jew's pitch' was obtained from parts of a Japanese tree, sublimated by the Dutch and was used in inflammatory and febrile and gangrenous conditions also as an 'antiseptic agent' and as a refrigerant.
30 Scarlet Fever.

timely separation of the men,[31] the moment it was possible to detect the smallest appearance of sphacelus, cleanliness was rigidly observed, and the walls of the place have been whitewashed. On this painful subject I will only add, that I should be inclined to give a fair trial to venesection in that state of fever consequent on amputation marked by the hot skin and [re]corded thrilling pulse, where perhaps the little marks of sphacelation had yet time to show themselves. But sphacelation alone would never deter me from the use of the lancet [i.e. bleeding the patient] if symptoms of greater importance should seem to vindicate its necessity, and I have had two cases when notwithstanding their unfavourable result I am convinced I was warranted in the practice, not only by the direct symptoms of pleuritic they showed themselves during life, as fixed pain in the thorax, difficulty of breathing with cough and general restlessness, but by the appearances after death, each had an abscess recently formed in the lungs and each of these men had gangrenous stumps.[32] Should more opportunities unfortunately occur I have it in contemplation to resort to the lancet, and shall certainly inform you of the result. I would be inclined to make a considerable difference between the hospital sore properly so called not infrequently, perhaps generally showing its first appearance without fever from that sore, the consequences of fever which I think may be more properly denominated the endemic fever of the country, always preceding the alteration of the sore and which I have endeavoured to describe, not with all the [completeness?] I could wish, in as much as I have not been able to observe with sufficient exactness its type, I suspect it may be occasionally continued, sometimes remittent, but more generally intermittent fever, and this of the quotidian type,[33] degenerating into the remittent, its causes I fancy are owing to the reduced state of the patient now predisposed on this account to the exciting and many amongst these, the principal is the state of the weather which I have already made a few remarks on, the yellow infusion of the body [i.e. jaundice], and the enormous quantity of faecal matter that may be discharged with advantage, clearly show the gastric organs[34] to be principally affected.

I cannot think it superfluous while on this subject, to state that generally the situation of the men previous to amputation on what may be called the secondary period. It was always the object in these cases of fracture, which probably ought to be operated upon in the field, but now left to take their fate, sometimes complicated with secondary haemorrage [sic] and knee joint cases, to endeavour to conduct them through the stages of inflammation to suppuration with as little loss of health as possible, by local bleeding, cold applications, and diaphoretic medicines[35] with attention to the bowels, and when this stage was clearly established with such an effect on the constitution as to show that the strength of the patient would be unable to bear up against it for a much longer time, and having procured the absence of fever with moist skin and open bowels to proceed to the operation and here again I would beg to have it remarked, that a proportion of the cases

31   An interesting reference to isolation policies.
32   This was probably a consequence of septicaemia and spread of sepsis to the lungs via the blood stream from the gangrenous stump.
33   Attacks of malarial fever that tends to appear daily.
34   The intestines.
35   Medications to induce sweating.

that were admitted into the Gens d'Armerie Hospital were such, as had opportunities occurred on the field, no prudent surgeon would have hesitated in operating on the spot. There have occurred three cases of tetanus amongst the French prisoners admitted into Gens d'Armerie Hospital, two of them before I was attached to it, and the other after amputation of the thigh on the 14th day, when everything favoured a favourable termination. They all died in this last cure. Purgation with moderate doses of opium was all that was used with blisters to the spine.[36]

From the review of my notes that are now before you, I am led to the following conclusions. That in all compound fractures when amputation is not done on the field, or where it may be the intention of the surgeon to attempt the salvation of the limb, he should do as little in the way of surgery as possible in the first instance, splints in the early stages seem prejudicial in the hands of young men peculiarly so, the easy relaxed position, cold applications, leeches, and even along with the feelings of Mr Parkins,[37] warm fomentations are the best local remedies that can be used. The state of the bowels can never be lost sight of. No precise period can be fixed for the abandonment of this practice perhaps from particular circumstances, this period extends further in this hospital than usual, but the tension and tumufaction [swelling] having subsided, and in men of a non-irritable constitution, even a little further the limb may be as to position with daily extension (if from shortening that should be necessary) with splints firmly put on, having in view the prevention of sinuses, and preserving a free discharge much also may be done by the careful application of compresses in the tract of the sinus. This too is the stage where few incisions will be attended with the greatest benefit and the extraction of all loose pieces of bone or foreign matters. The bowels are to be kept open, and the strength supported by nourishing diet, and wine as the last preventative of hospital fever, next to free ventilation, and as proper space for each patient, is the free use of purgation soon after the injury and removal to hospital, purging maybe carried to an extent that can scarcely be believed, by those who have not witnessed its good effects. During the first fortnight after the admission of wounded men I can safely say that I have in no instance had cause to regret the liberal use of purgative medicines during this time, but sometimes to regret that it had not been more freely following up. On this subject I am happy to have the testimony of so respectable a surgeon as Mr Donatt, as may be seen from his report.

In fractures of the cranium or injuries of the head I would almost say, too much abstinence can scarcely be practiced for a very long period, much longer than I have had it yet in my power to carry into effect, but this I am certain of that two days of but a moderate regimen, and a very small proportion of wine, has been seen to do harm in this hospital and would have produced a[n] irremediable disease, but for timely prevention I have been disappointed in not having a greater opportunity of remarking [with this advice] on the thoracic cases.

In the abdominal cases that remain the symptoms have been mild, as only to require abstinence, a very strict regimen, and attention to the stools.

---

36   Viz. cold cupping or the use of cantharides, a vesicant and irritant to produce blistering – i.e. counter-irritation.
37   This possibly refers to Assistant Surgeon John Perkins who had resigned from the army in 1813 but was reinstated in 1818 (no. 3189 in Peterkin & Johnston *Medical Officers*).

But the cases of secondary hemorrhage [sic] have occurred from ulceration of the artery and in one of these, along with rupture of the Posterior Tibial artery, there was an extensive comminuted fracture[38] of the tibia. For several days he would submit to no operation, but after three successive returns of haemorrhage, he submitted to amputation. The other [patient] was likewise complicated with fracture. The femoral artery was tied by Mr Charles Bell. Hemorrage [sic] succeeded from ulceration of the artery and gangrene and they all terminated fatally. It is the one marked in the list for aneurism [sic].

Several secondary bleedings took place but they might with great propriety termed oozings of blood from the whole surface of the sore, but were often repressed by local applications, and from constitutional attending circumstances, generally terminated fatally. They generally happened from the 14th to the 20th day.

On a review of the labours of the officers connected with this hospital, some expression of my own feelings of gratitude to you will I trust be pardoned.

I have at all times, and on every occasion derived the most effective assistance from the able abilities of Acting Staff Surgeon Laisne,[39] and I would express myself, as highly satisfied with every officer doing duty here, and I would trespass on your goodness by soliciting your attention to the merits of the Resident Medical Officer, Hospital Assistant Mr Blackadder, to whom unremitting attention all will have been witness. For myself I am content to rest my defence for this witness on your valuable time on your own urbainity [sic] and love of science and remain with every sensibility, your most obedient humble servant, T. Gordon MD Surgeon to the Forces, In charge of the Gens d'Armerie Hospital.

Classification of the wounds in the *Jesuits* General Hospital Brussels, in charge of Mr Hennen, 16 July 1815

Head						Thorax					Abdomen					
Face	Neck	Calvarium	Total	Convalescent	Died	One Side	Both Sides	Total	Convalescent	Died	Cavity of	Pelvis	Total	Convalescent	Died	Remarks
9	4	7	20	5	3	18	6	42	6	6	4	7	11	4	1	Gun Shot Wounds

38 A fracture of the bone with splintering and resultant multiple fragmentation.

39 Staff Surgeon John Constantine Laisne, who had been put on half pay in 1814, but returned to full pay on 25 June 1815, presumably to attend the wounded in Brussels.

Upper Extremities								Lower Extremities									
Shoulder	Arm	Elbow	Forearm	Hand	Total	Convalescent	Died	Hip Joint	Knee Joint	Thigh	Leg	Ankle Joint	Foot	Total	Convalescent	Died	Remarks
13	35	4	20	8	80	10	2	–	13	91	43	16	11	174	18	16	Gun Shot Wounds
4	5		1	1	11	2				2				2			Incised Wounds
	19		2		21					15	4			19		4	Compound Fractures
			2								2						Simple Fractures
4	8		2		14	3	3			22	11			33	4	16	Amputations

NB – There are no incised wounds in the upper table, which is contiguous with that below

Richard Crofton, Hospital Assistant, Resident.

Signed John Hennen Surgeon to the Forces

Comments

The 327 wounds described here are, in the main serious injuries. This is a fair sample size to make some general observations. 'Convalescent' infers initial recovery but not yet discharged from hospital. A proportion of convalescent patients would have died, possibly around 5-10 percent. This is confirmed by Hodge, who reckoned that, around one in ten men (one in twelve for officers and one in eight for NCOs and private soldiers) died after wounding, that is without major surgical intervention.[40]

We have to assume that the heading 'Gunshot Wounds' refers to musket, carbine and pistol shot injuries. However, we cannot be sure that wounds inflicted by a case round or shrapnel balls were not included. There does not seem to be a reference to any wound caused by ordnance (aside from the above observation). We also have to make the assumption that 'Incised Wounds' have been inflicted by not only sharp cutting edges, but also by straight sabre and lance points.

The bodily distribution of wounds was as follows: head and neck (20) forming six percent; thorax (42) – 13 percent; abdomen (and probably pelvis) (11) – three percent; upper limb (80) – 25 percent and by far the most common site of injury, the lower limbs (174) – 53 percent. Taken in total, the limb injuries formed 78 percent of injuries.

Compound limb fractures are a good deal more serious than simple fractures, where the skin is intact. In the former, the bone ends protrude through the skin, in other words the bone exposed is prone to bacterial ingress and thus sepsis. The problem with chronic osteomyelitis is

40   W.B. Hodge, 'On the Mortality arising from Military Operations', *Journal of the Institute of Actuaries*, Volume 7, Issue 2, 1857, pp.80-90.

that when dead or living bone fragments become infected, they would remain and by their presence, delay healing and in the depths of the limb the sepsis smoulders away in the fragments or parts of bone, particularly if they suffer from a limited or no blood supply. There would be occasional 'flare ups' of infection, with fever, purulent discharge, and general un-wellness. Unless all the septic bone parts (sequestra – removed by sequestrectomy) are removed the wound will take an age to heal, if ever. If there is healing then there is resultant deformity. In these results, there were only two simple fractures, possibly caused by blunt injury or falling from a horse. There were 47 amputations, or disarticulations, four at the shoulder joint and eight of the arm. Three patients died – probably from the 'shoulder' group. The overall mortality rate for the 'Upper Extremity' amputation group was thus quite high at 20 percent. As always, lower limb wounds are twice or three times as likely to be mortal as those to the upper limb. The reasons for this are diverse. The lower limb is a bulkier member, with some large vessels and a larger mass of muscle. Also the thigh and leg are more likely to be contaminated by soil, mud, and a rich cocktail of bacteria that flourish around the groin and upper thigh. It is much more difficult to control deep-seated bleeding in the depths of the lower limb tissue. The arm and forearm are less bulky and the blood vessels are of a smaller calibre and thus easier to control haemorrhage from them. Here there were 33 lower limb amputations – two thirds at the thigh – and 16 died, giving a mortality rate of 48 percent. Surgeon George James Guthrie noted the graded mortality for thigh injury and surgery. The higher the thigh wound or those injuries very near the knee joint, the worse the outcome. Compound knee injuries were also of a more serious nature and threat to life, when compared to penetrating elbow injuries.

Many head, neck and torso injuries would have been instantly or rapidly fatal. The mortality in the Jesuits Hospital for all 327 patients was 9 percent. This figure is roughly double what in-hospital mortality was, in times of non-combat, for example during the Iberian campaigns of 1808-1814. The figure of nine percent seems almost commendable given the limitations of knowledge and understanding of contemporary surgeons. However, we should remember that so many potential patients had already died on the battlefield, purely from haemorrhage, lack of basic first aid, and timely evacuation. The density of injured in this battle would have overwhelmed any medical service.

Number and site of amputations performed in and admitted into the Jesuits General Hospital, Brussels, from the 20 of June to the 20 July 1815

Site of Operation	General Total	Primary Operations	Died	Remaining	Secondary Operations	Died	Remaining	Total Remaining	Proportion Primary Operations	Of deaths Secondary Operations
Shoulder Joint	4	1	–	1	3	2	1	2	No death	2 in 3
Thigh	39	14	5	9	25	13	12	21	1 in 3 nearly	1 in 2 nearly
Leg	36	13	2	11	23	4	19	30	1 in 7 nearly	1 in 6 nearly
Arm	20	4	–	4	16	2	14	18	No death	1 in 8
Forearm	4	2	–	2	2	-	2	4	No death	No death
Total	103	34	7	27	69	21	48	75		

Comments

This series of 103 operations is confined to surgery of the limbs. Seventy-five operations were carried out on the lower limb as compared with 28 on the upper. Early (primary) surgery resulted in a mortality rate of 21 percent, when contrasted with secondary (delayed) operation, which had a mortality rate of 30 percent, not as large a difference as is generally observed. Overall, both in early and delayed operations, amputation of the thigh offered the greatest challenge to the surgeons. With primary amputation at the thigh, the death rate was 36 percent, whilst with secondary limb ablation it was 52 percent. Overall these results reflect a predictable and 'average' performance from one of the larger Brussels hospitals.

Return of Joint cases, treated in the St Elisabeth General Hospital at Brussels from 20 June to 5 August 1815

Joint Wounds	Admitted	Required Amputation	Died	Remaining under Treatment	Remarks
Ankle joints	18	3		15	Doing well
Knee joints	33	6	7	20	Five doubtful, fifteen doing well
Hip joints	4		1	3	Doing well
Shoulder joints	5	2	1	2	Doing well
Elbow joints	14	2	1	11	Doing well
Wrist joints	4	1		3	Doing well
Total	78	14	10	54	

W G Wray MD, Surgeon to the Forces, PMO[41]

Comments

Wounds of the joints were notoriously painful and full of complications during healing. Often the victims were left with chronic sepsis, with discharging wounds or a stiff unusable joint. Here, there is the usual preponderance of lower limb damage (55 cases) as against upper limb joint injury (23 cases). The outcomes from hip joint and knee joint wounds (25 percent and 21 percent died respectfully) are on the better side of average, although it is noted that five of the knee joint injuries remained of concern. It is also commendable that none of the wounds of the ankle joint perished.

41 Surgeon William Galbraith Wray, No. 2552 in Peterkin & Johnston *Medical Officers*. He died in Barbados on 21 January 1817.

Return of Compound Fractures; admitted and treated, in the St Elisabeth Hospital, Brussels, from 20 June to 6 August inclusive

Compound Fractures	Admitted	Required Amputation	Died	Transferred to Gendarmerie Hospital	Under Treatment	Remarks
Upper extremities	86	13	10		63	
Lower extremities						
Thigh	116	14	11	4	87	
Leg	11		1		10	
Ribs	3				3	
Total	216	27	22	4	163	

W G Wray MD, Surgeon to the Forces, PMO

Comments

This is quite a large series of compound wounds. These are all injuries with a high risk of sepsis since they are bony injuries open to bacterial contamination. As usual, there was a preponderance of lower limb wounds (127) as against upper limb injuries (86). A rather small proportion of thigh injuries required amputation and a low mortality rate for this severe injury is surprising (nine percent). Remarkably, the death rate for wounds of the upper limb surgery was higher than for lower limb injuries at 12 percent. The four patients transferred to the Gens d'Armerie Hospital with thigh wounds were probably convalescent French prisoner patients. We do not know the post-amputation mortality rates from this data.

Return of operations in the St Elisabeth General Hospital, Brussels 1 August 1815

Operations	Operations	Recovered	Died	Transferred	Under Treatment	Total	Remarks
Shoulder joints	8		2		6	8	Doing well
Upper extremities	54	6	11	17	20	54	Doing well
Lower extremities	66	6	22	5	33	66	Four doubtful, the rest doing well
Injuries of the head (trephine)	4		3		1	4	Doing well
Hip joints	1				1	1	Doing well
Carotid artery tied	1	1				1	Doing well
Total	134	13	38	22	61	134	

NB In column 'Lower extremities' there are 25 legs and 41 thighs.
W G Wray MD, Surgeon to the Forces, PMO

Comments

Here we have a series of 134 patients undergoing (unspecified) surgery. We should not assume that all limb operations were amputations, since there were 41 procedures carried out on thigh wounds, but we know from the data above, in the previous table, that only 14 patients underwent amputation. The other procedures carried out on the patients with thigh wounds were wound dilatations to extract sequestra, trimming of bone protrusions, and drainage of sepsis. There is a mismatch in the number of shoulder wounds in these tables. Perhaps a few had died between the two dates (1 to 5 August), or several procedures were carried out on the five cases mentioned in the 'joint cases' return. Only a single case of the four patients undergoing trepanning survived. Most of these cases would have been operated on for depressed compound fractures. The high death rate reflects the onset of sepsis or severe underlying brain damage. The single case of carotid artery ligation (for sepsis and then catastrophic haemorrhage) survived.

Classification of the wounds in the Annonciate Hospital at Brussels from 20 June to 20 July 1815

Head			Thorax			Abdomen	Upper Extremities					Lower Extremities								
Face	Neck	Calvarium	On side	Both sides	Cavity of	Pelvis	Shoulder	Arm	Elbow	Forearm	Hand	Hip joint	Knee joint	Thigh	Leg	Ankle joint	Foot	General Total	Wounds	Remarks
2		4	11	5	6	2	9	6	7	11	4		12	50	40	8	3	180	Gunshot Wounds	
2	3	2	1				3		4		1			2	1		1	20	Incised Wounds	
								9		3				28	7	1		48	Compound Fractures	
														1				1	Simple Fractures	
								2		5	1			14	9			31	Amputations	

D Brownrigg, Surgeon to the Forces

Comments

This table is useful as it not only classifies wounds by anatomical region, but also by causation. One of the dilemmas of battlefield injury is that we do not know for certain whether deaths from ordnance fire were more common than those from small arms discharges. A much higher proportion of soldiers hit by round shot, case, grape, or shell fire will die as when compared with those struck by small bore musket, carbine, or pistol shot. Thus, unless we count all the dead on the battlefield and their modes of injury and add these to the wounded who are collected in (some of whom will die before or after therapy), we cannot know the answer to this question. Certainly, many more casualties present to medical staff with small arms wounds than with damage from ordnance.

In this table we must presume that the compound and simple fractures and those cases undergoing amputation are included in the sections labelled 'gunshot' and 'incised wounds'. We also do not know for certain, whether the gunshot wounded cases had their injuries inflicted by small arms alone or some by cannon fire. In this series the ratio of gunshot injuries to incised wounds was 9:1. In the series from the Jesuits Hospital the same ratio comparison was 25:1, the latter place clearly having received less victims of cavalry assault.

Number & site of operations performed in and admitted into the Annonciate Hospital from 20 June to 31 July 1815

Operations	General Total	Primary Operations	Died	Remaining	Secondary Operations	Died	Remaining	Total Remaining	Remarks
Shoulder Joint	3	2	1	1	1	1		1	Doing Well
Thigh	19	14	2	12	5	4	1	13	11 doing well, 2 primary doubtful
Leg	17	13	2	11	4	3	1	12	11 doing well 1 primary doubtful
Arm	10	4	2	2	6	3	3	5	Doing well
Forearm	2	1		1	1	1		1	Doing well
Total	51	34	7	27	17	12	5	32	

D Brownrigg, Surgeon to the Forces[42]

Comments

Here, we see a smaller collection of 51 cases of upper and lower limb compound wounds. The data emphasises the different mortality rates of early and late surgery. We are not sure whether the primary or early surgery refers solely to those cases operated on in the hospital premises or elsewhere as well. Of interest is the fact that, commendably, twice as many patients here had undergone primary surgery. Thirty-four patients underwent early surgery and seven died (21 percent), whilst those having delayed procedures had a 71 percent death rate. The series from this hospital has however a particularly high mortality rate with its secondary operations.

---

42 Surgeon David Brownrigg, No. 1980 in Peterkin & Johnston *Medical Officers*.

Return of Principal Operations performed at the Minimes General Hospital from the 18 of June to the 4 August

Operation	Number of Cases	Recovering	Recovered	Died	Remarks
Securing the Carotid	1			1	Died from the effect of a wound in the oesophagus
Securing the Enlarged Iliac	1			1	Died a week after from low fever
Trephining	4		2	2	Lesion of the Cerebral substance
Shoulder Joint	3	1		2	One from secondary haemorrhage on the 10th day. The other exhausted, the scapula being knocked to pieces *also* on the tenth day
Arm	7		4	3	In all other cases, the constitutional irritation preceded any deterioration of the stump. One was attacked by tetanus & was completely relieved by removing the dressings, fomenting & poulticing the stump – died of low fever week after. No other case of tetanus or any deserving the name of hospital gangrene occurred, although we were at one time very much crowded. Foul and offensive ulcers (of which we received several from billets) were drained & put in a healthy appearance by the frequent application of the raw carrot grated & mixed with vinegar.
Fore Arm	8		7	1	
Thigh	5	1		4	
Leg	5		5		
Penis	1	1			
Total	35	3	18	14	

J Cole Surgeon to the Forces[43]

Comments

This is the last of the five hospital returns, a smaller series than the previous one, solely dealing with patients undergoing surgery. Death rates are recorded and some accompanying remarks. The patients lost were 14 of 35 cases (40 percent) – a high mortality rate. While the patient with a genital injury survived, both the cases requiring major arterial ligation, half the trephined patients and four of five thigh wounds succumbed. It is tantalising to surmise on these below average results. Was there surgical underperformance, a group of particularly sick patients, or a combination of both these adverse factors that affected poor outcomes? We shall unfortunately never know. The comments on the crowded state of the hospital and plethora of infected pressure sores might well have contributed to the problems here. John Cole had been the regimental surgeon to the 68th Regiment for nine years and a staff surgeon for three years before Waterloo. He had an MD and had served in the disastrous Walcheren campaign. The likely issue was that it was the unhealthy case load that presented him with considerable challenges. He certainly 'appears' to be clinically

---

43   Staff Surgeon half pay John Cole, no. 1992 in Peterkin & Johnston *Medical Officers*.

and technically competent from the four, possibly five cases he wrote up and that appear in Chapter 9.

The additional comments, which do not appear in the other four hospital reports, are interesting. The patient who died following carotid artery ligation had been wounded, probably by a sword thrust, in the oesophagus. The patient's food and saliva egressing from the neck wound had infected the area, causing the artery to become weakened and give way. The two deaths after shoulder surgery were due to a secondary haemorrhage and a widely shattered scapula. There was a single case of fatal tetanus, and some patients with bad ulcers (either wounds or pressure sores) sent in from private dwellings.

Return of Capital Operations, Primary and Secondary, performed in General Hospitals Brussels and in the Field, between 16 June & 31 July 1815

Operations	General Total	Primary Operations	Died	Remaining	Proportion of deaths to operations	Secondary Operations	Died	Remaining	Proportion of deaths to diseases	Total Remaining	Of these doubtful	Transferred to Antwerp	Remarks
Shoulder Joint	18	6	1	5	1 to 6	12	6	6	1 to 2	11			
Hip Joint	1					1		1		1			A French soldier who recovered
Thigh	148	54	19	35	1 to 3	94	43	51	1 to 2	86	9	4	
Leg	93	43	7	26	1 to 6	50	16	34	1 to 3	60		4	
Arm	72	21	4	17	1 to 5	51	13	38	1 to 4	55		6	
Fore Arm	39	22	1	21	1 to 22	17	5	12	1 to 3	33		3	
Carotid Artery	1					1		1		1			
Eye	2					2	1	1	1 to 2	1		1	
Total	374	146	32	104		228	84	144		248	9	18	

D McNiel, Hospital Inspector[44]

Comments

Here is a large collected series of cases of capital (larger) operations carried out in the five major hospitals in Brussels and in other places, over a six-week period. It gives us a good idea of surgical outcomes, the chances of death or recovery in a high volume of injuries with a lack of timely evacuation, no anaesthesia or antisepsis, and many of the other facilities that the armed forces are blessed with today. The data is bound to be incomplete, as, for example, we know of at least two 'carotid artery ligations' and the ophthalmic (eye) trauma patients

---

44   Deputy Inspector of Hospitals Donald McNiel, no. 1442 in Peterkin & Johnston *Medical Officers*.

who are not mentioned in this collated data. Many operations would also have been carried out in other buildings or private dwellings and were not therefore included.

If the total number of operations carried out in the five Brussels general hospitals and elsewhere is calculated from each report, the total is 388, which is a slight mismatch compared with the 374 patients in this table. However, considering the general chaos and hopelessly overstretched resources, this is a unique record of surgery, (sadly not yet available to us for any period from the French *Service de Santé*). The overall surgical mortality rate in this group of patients was 116 out of 374 patients, or 31 percent.

One of the most important messages from this data is that lower limb injuries, (242 in this series), which carried such a significantly greater mortality rate for wounds above the knee, were so much more common – twice as frequent – on the battlefield than upper limb wounds (129 included). The reasons for this discrepancy have been discussed previously.

Another significant issue is that there were more secondary procedures (228) carried out than early operations (146). When we take a final look at surgery performed at an early stage (primary operations) – within such a large number of cases – 146 in total, the death rate was 22 percent, whilst the patients whose operations were delayed (secondary) suffered a mortality rate of 37 percent, the difference is noticeable (15 percent). The difference in the results due to the timing of the surgery was found to be most marked in the cases undergoing shoulder and forearm surgery, at 33 percent and 24 percent respectively.

The most remarkable case recorded was that of François de Gay, the French patient who successfully underwent a disarticulation of the hip, performed as a secondary operation by George James Guthrie.

The returns from these five hospitals are unfortunately incomplete as they do not show any data for the Antwerp hospitals, where a large cadre of patients were treated.

	No. Discharged	No. Died	Proportion
General Result of the Battle of Waterloo			
No. of Wounded treated			
6636	4791 (of these, about 1500 may have been invalided)	745	1 in about 9
Number of operations after the battle			
No. of Wounded treated			
508	296(I should think comprehended in the number invalided)	212	1 in about 2½

Note by Thomson – The return of fractures I think is stated erroneously in Brussels, having only 49. It certainly is exclusive of the French hospital, in which alone I had [cared for] 86 of the thigh. I cannot find out the number of fractures at the other stations, nor of course, the causes or mortality in this class.

Comments

Finally, we have a round-up of the wounded 'totals' recorded in these reports and elsewhere, after the campaign. The 6,636 patients had all received some form of treatment. Aside from capital surgery, other procedures would consist of bandaging, probing for foreign bodies, draining sepsis (pus), splinting and resetting fractures, trimming of bone ends and soft tissue injuries, and catheterisation. These treatments were supplemented by sundry drugs and other therapies also low, intermediate and high diets etc. The therapies accompanying the surgery were of very limited value; for example blood-letting, purging or making a wounded soldier vomit in an effort to ward off sepsis. They had no therapeutic benefits and usually engendered harmful results. Analgesics (pain killers) were in very short supply and were rarely given until after major surgery.

Of the 6,636 men treated, 745 died, which resulted in an overall mortality rate amongst the wounded of 11 percent, not far off Hodge's predictions, that one in 12 officers and one in eight NCOs and men would die of their wounds.[45]

Once major surgical procedures had been carried out in numerous locations on the 508 patients listed the mortality rate then rose to 42 percent. This contrasts markedly with the figures of the smaller series of patients in the previous return (at 31 percent), which dealt solely with the five main hospitals in Brussels. Although we have assumed that often a timely primary operation was desirable, and that delayed surgery when the patients were hospitalised frequently gave poorer results, many of all these operations were delayed, or secondary, wherever the location of surgery. Clearly not all of the deaths can be directly attributed to poor surgical techniques, inappropriate timing or type of operation. However, the over-riding salutary observation is that the risk of dying was three to four times as great after being wounded, if surgery was deemed to be necessary.

45 Hodge, *Statistical Society Papers* p.228

9

Thomson's Line Drawings

The following 176 images of 172 individuals wounded during the Waterloo campaign of 1815 (three are duplicated and the last patient has two images numbered 176 & 176a) are reproduced with the kind permission of the University of Edinburgh archives.[1] These line drawings were made by Professor John Thomson MD at Brussels and Antwerp in late June and early July 1815 and are to our knowledge the first known example of individual patient notes with diagrams of the wounds in existence. The accompanying highlighted text is handwritten underneath the diagrams, indicating the name of the individual and regiment they belonged to (where known), which hospital they were in and then a number which must indicate their bed or room. Thomson was appointed as a Staff Surgeon on 21 September 1815.

As to the units/nationality of the patients (where known) sketched in this series, there are:

Breakdown of the cases by nationality

British (not including KGL)	100
French	36
German (Including KGL)	17
Unspecified	21
Total	**174**

Branches of the Service of British Casualties

Infantry	80
Cavalry	14
KGL Cavalry	3
Royal Artillery	4
KGL Artillery	1
Royal Engineers	1
KGL Infantry	8
Unspecified	6
Total	**117**

---

1   Reference Gen 594 Coll – 535

Breakdown of Nationalities by hospital

Brussels	British	French	German	Unspecified	Total
Gens d'Armerie	–	6	–	2	8
Jesuits	13	4	2	1	20
St Elisabeth	27	1	3	–	31
Annonciate	11	–	7	2	20
Minimes	1	–	–	–	1
Antwerp					
Corderie	–	22		13	35
Facon	29		2		31
Augustine	1		1		2
Total	**82**	**33**	**15**	**18**	**148**

The texts also explain the injuries and give some detail of the treatment administered. These form an extraordinary record of a largely forgotten aspect of the Waterloo campaign, but one that is vital to understanding the cost of Napoleonic warfare and the suffering endured by the wounded.

Beneath the original descriptive bold text will be seen further blocks of commentary in italics. These form the additional notes that we have been able to provide regarding the identification of the patients (many names are misspelt), their treatment, and the outcome where it is known. We have also added in further detail, where a particular casualty also appears in one of the various medical publications produced after the war as a special case study.

Unfortunately, despite considerable effort, it has not proven possible to identify all of the casualties, particularly some of the French ones, where little detail is given and rarely even a regiment.

The wounds are categorised by the part of the body damaged and they can be broken down into the following sections:

	Sketch numbers: Total:
Head & neck wounds	– 1–47 (47)
Chest wounds	– 48–86 (38)
Wounds of the Abdomen and Groin	– 87–117 (30)
The Arm	– 118–124 (19 – upper limb)
Shoulder including Scapula	– 125–137
Thigh, leg and Foot	– 134–176a (42 – lower limb)

It can be seen that there is a good sample size and reasonable representation of wounds over the anatomy of patients in this series of sketches.

1. John Beattie – 42nd Regiment

Annonciate Hospital

A splinter of shell struck him over the right eye. He has, also a compound fracture of the left leg, the bones of which were splintered by a musket ball.

> *Private John Beattie was in Captain Mungo McPherson's No. 3 Company 42nd Foot. With such a combination of injuries he was certainly in a risky situation – a fragment of common shell, which probably did not fracture his skull, but the compound wound of the tibia and fibula would put the patient at risk of the inevitable sepsis. John Beattie however survived and he received his Waterloo Prize Money on 17 September 1817.*

2. Moses Wise – 33rd Regiment

Elizabeth Hospital

Musket ball entering at A & it lodged, having fractured the skull by the concussion – part of the Squamous Suture of the temporal bone sloughed away in fragments. Ball supposed to be behind the [Left] parotid.

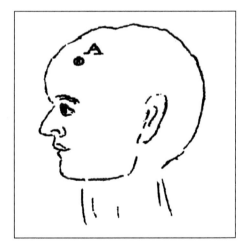

> *This missile fractured Private Moses Wise's skull and burrowed deeply within, tracking and becoming lodged behind the parotid salivary gland. This would be a very painful wound. There is no description of a facial palsy (the seventh craniul nerve of facial expression lying nearby). Sepsis probably intervened and this might have resulted in an abscess, which, when ruptured, would deliver the lead ball. The other recorded complication with this sort of wound was a salivary fistula, when saliva escapes and leaks onto the face. Moses did survive but for some reason he does not appear to have been paid his prize money. He received a pension of 6d per day on 27 August 1816 and died on 24 October 1851 aged 57.*

3. Thomas Reece – 1st Guards 1st Battalion. Pd143

Elizabeth Hospital

Wound from the hairy scalp down to the right eyebrow. The cross incision was made to reach for the ball which was not found, fragments of the bone came away.

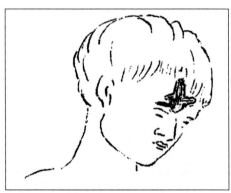

Reece was actually in the 2nd Battalion 1st Foot Guards, in Lieutenant Colonel Fitzroy Somerset's company. The letters and words 'pd 143' presumably related to the patient's ward, row or bed number. Here, the projectile was not found. A cross incision in the scalp has been made to search for it. The appearance of this wound and the surgical incision are similar to the exploratory incision placed over a planned trepanning procedure. Was the ball disrupted before penetrating the brain or did it track elsewhere? Reece survived and was paid his Waterloo Prize Money. He was invalided on 16 March 1816 on a pension of 1 shilling per day. He was living at Carmarthen and died on 1 November 1854. His name is misspelt Reese in the Waterloo Medal Roll.

4. Samuel Pritchard – 4th Foot

Annonciate

Ball entering A fracturing the bone & is lodged. Left eye blind and much swollen.

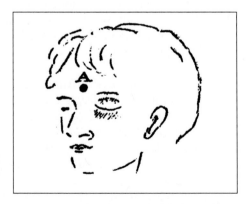

Private Samuel Pritchard was in Captain Robert Erskine's No. 4 Company of the 1st Battalion 4th Foot. This is a difficult case. The ball is known to be lodged behind the left eyeball, which protrudes (proptosis) and Sir Charles Bell, a Scots professor of surgery and artist whose paintings of Waterloo injuries are well known, described the wound. He passed a probe three and a half inches obliquely downwards and proposed to make an incision in the skin probably lateral to the eye socket and reach around with forceps to retrieve the missile, which would prove difficult and painful, but left Brussels before it could be performed. The opposite eye was at risk of sympathetic ophthalmia (an auto-immune reaction to retinal pigment which could auto-destruct the normal eye). He was cared for by Regimental Assistant Surgeon Reid 25th Foot and a letter to Bell from Staff Surgeon Jordan

Roche, dated Brussels 17 August, states that Pritchard was doing well and would be soon sent home, so presumably the operation had been carried out.[2] Treatment today might include enucleation (complete removal) of the injured eye or corticosteroids. Samuel Pritchard was granted a pension of 1 shilling per day on 27 August 1816 and he died on 13 May 1848 aged 65.

5. Andrew Burnett – 1st Foot

Annonciate

Skull fractured by a Musket ball.

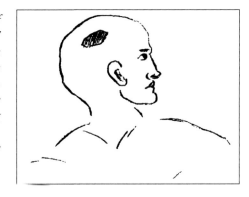

Actually this was Private Andrew Burrell of Captain (brevet Major) George Dodd's No. 7 Company of the 3rd Battalion 1st Foot. There are few details here. Many such patients would survive this type of wound, particularly if the dura mater (the outermost – fairly tough –membrane covering and protecting the fragile brain tissue) remained intact. Andrew Burrell was however unfortunately soon after discharged dead.

6. Sergeant McCormick – 73rd Regiment

Elizabeth Hospital

A musket ball was lodged & flattened between the tables of the skull. The lower table was much compressed. No bad symptoms. The depressed portion raised.

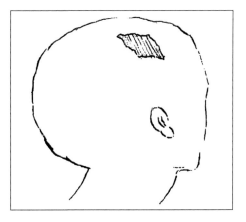

Sergeant Peter McCormick belonged to Captain Duncan Dewar's No. 9 Company of the 2nd Battalion 73rd Foot. Clearly the lead ball was flattened by impact on the cranium and slid on to split the two 'tables' of the skull (the skull is lined by two thin layers or tables of bone, separated by the diploe – a thin layer of cancellous bone). The outer table is thicker

---

2   Crumplin, *A Surgical Artist at War* pp.50–2.

than the inner. It is surprising how often we read of the ball being not just deformed, but split up by bony impact. The ball was removed and the fractured layers of separated skull bone elevated to relieve pressure on the brain. He survived his injury and received his Waterloo Prize Money in 1817. He was sent to England on 17 August 1815 and transferred to the 6th Royal Veteran Battalion on 25 November 1815. He was discharged on 24 May 1816 aged 31 because of 'a severe gunshot wound to the forehead with great loss of bone'. McCormick was born at Kilteghard in Leitrim and his trade was listed as a labourer. He enlisted at Canterbury on 26 December 1811 from the Leitrim Militia. He was promoted to sergeant within a month! He was described on discharge as 5 foot 7 inches tall, with fair hair, blue eyes and of a fair complexion and was given a pension of 1 shilling per day.

7. William Heathy – 79th Regiment

Elizabeth Hospital

Musket ball was lodged between the tables of the skull which it separated.

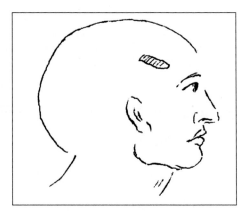

This was actually Private William Hately of Captain Robert MacKay's No. 4 company 1st Battalion 79th Foot. Here is another example of this rare injury, described above in drawing No.6. Hately survived and received his Waterloo Prize Money in 1817. He is shown as Hatley on the Waterloo Medal Roll. He must have pronounced his name as Heatley as his pension document shows his name spelt this way. He received a pension of 9d per day from 9 August 1816 and lived at Halesworth in Suffolk. He was still receiving his pension in 1854.

8. Thibault

Corderie

Exfoliation from the cranium. Palsy of the left arm. Face distorted on both sides but this symptom abating.

A French Prisoner of War. The right side of the cranium has been injured by a fragment of shell, musket ball or a sword cut – the cause is not specified. The injury is sited over the motor area and there is a resultant paralysis of the left arm – i.e. the opposite side to the wound. At this time, the cross- representation in the central nervous system had not been discovered and described. We wonder if the grimacing and distortion of the facial muscles is due to a minor infection with the tetanus bacillus.

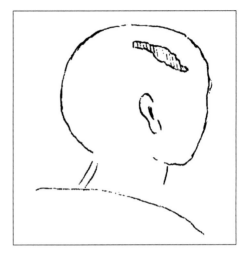

9. Nicholas Toussaint Benard

Corderie

Cut with a sabre. Extensive exfoliation going on. Palsy of the left side.

A French Prisoner of War. The sword stroke has penetrated the right skull and damaged the motor area. This time, the entire right side of the patient has been paralysed. The exfoliation probably refers to protruding damaged brain tissue or possibly excessive amounts of granulation tissue (unhealthy friable and infected healing tissue).

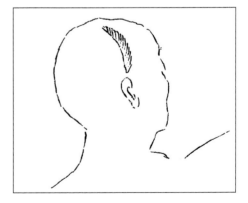

10. Anonymous

Corderie

Musket ball fracture of the skull.

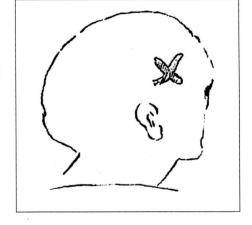

> *The cruciate format of the wound in the drawing suggests that the trephine has been applied by the surgeon. This was a method for elevating depressed bone fragments or letting out trapped blood collection under the skull, which was compressing the brain.*

11. Sergeant Monaghan 69th Regiment

Elizabeth Hospital

A shot laid bare the skull from the temple.

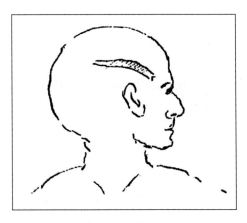

> *Sergeant Thomas Monaghan of the 2nd Battalion 69th Foot received a wound that looks as though it has been caused by a bullet skiting (skidding over a hard smooth surface) along the hard skull, scouring a gutter in the soft tissues. The sergeant survived and received his Waterloo Prize Money in 1817. Thomas Monaghan had been born at Aghalurcher in County Fermanagh and he enlisted in the 69th Foot at Dublin on 13 August 1811 aged 25 for unlimited service. He served with the 69th Foot for a few days short of 17 years (including his two years granted for Waterloo). He had been a private for only 263 days before becoming a corporal and became a sergeant after just over two years further service and remained in this rank during the remainder of his time. At his discharge on 19 June 1827, he was described as being 41 years of age, 5 foot 7½ inches tall, with brown hair, grey eyes and fair complexion. His previous trade is recorded as a weaver. He was discharged because of 'the effects of two old gunshot wounds in the head affecting his memory and health'. It is recorded that he suffered his wound at the Battle of Quatre Bras on 16 June 1815.*

12. Sergeant Davis – 28th Regiment

Facon Hospital – pd.11 A

Musket ball had indented a round piece of the skull at A and forced into the substance of the Brain. Epilepsy & other bad symptoms ensued. He was copiously bled by Mr Wilmore[3] and on removing the piece of bone epileptic symptoms ceased.

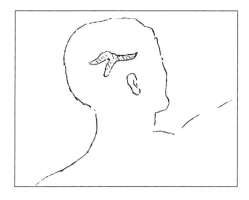

This is Sergeant Thomas Davis of Captain Charles Cadell's No. 3 Company 1st Battalion 28th Foot. Here there is no mention of the musket ball being retrieved from the brain. Maybe the ball went on, after pushing a portion of cranium into the brain. This would cause the epileptic seizures, which seem to have been rapidly alleviated by the elevation and removal of the bone fragment. Whether the epilepsy would return with brain scarring, we will never know for certain, although it is unlikely as he did serve in the army for another nine years and he collected his Waterloo Prize Money in September 1817. Thomas Davis was born in 1783 at Lamorran near Truro in Cornwall and joined the 28th Foot at Fermoy in County Cork on 20 July 1804 at the age of 21 for unlimited service. He had previously served for nearly a year (from August 1803 to July 1804) in the Army of Reserve and served just over 22 years in total, 3½ years as a private, another 3½ years as a corporal and 14½ years as a sergeant (including 2 years for Waterloo). He was discharged from the army on 11 May 1824, when he was 40 years old, being described as 6 feet tall, with brown hair, grey eyes and a fresh complexion. His previous occupation is described as a labourer. He was discharged because of a 'partial dislocation of his left wrist and being worn out'. His wounds are recorded as, severely in the left foot at Talavera on 28 July 1809, at Toulouse on 10 April 1814 (wound not specified) and at Quatre Bras on 16 June 1815. He would appear to have died around January 1874 as a Chelsea in–patient, as his documents at this time note a request for any will and property left by the pensioner.

---

3   Hospital Assistant Frederick Wilmore. It would appear that he had only recently re–joined the Army on 19 May 1815. He had previously joined as a Hospital Mate on 12 October 1809 and served in the Peninsular War and was presumably placed on half pay in 1814.

13. James Young – 79th Regiment

2nd August
Elizabeth Hospital pd. 137

A musket ball fractured the skull and was nearly cut in two having been divided by the table of the bone. The ball was removed [&] many fragments of bone were taken away & the posterior lobe of the right Hemisphere of the Brain was brought into view.

Patient was doing well till continued fever supervened & he is now in danger.

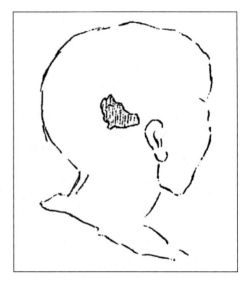

Private James Young of Captain William Marshall's Light Company 1st Battalion 79th Foot received a missile injury at the base of Young's skull. The lead ball was almost cut in two after striking the outer table of the skull. If the cerebral cortex (brain substance) was visible, this meant the dura mater was breached and clearly fatal sepsis was almost inevitable. Young was unfortunately soon after discharged dead.

14. Anonymous

Hospital of Gens d'Armerie

Three sabre cuts on the posterior part of the cranium. The brain protruding at the middle wound. Attended with loss of memory.

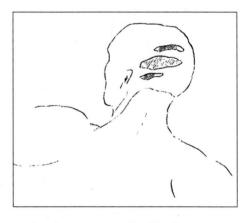

The anonymous patient has received three successive sabre cuts in a short time, the centre one has exposed the man's brain and he was in danger of fatal intracerebral infection. Research has shown that the parts of the brain dealing with memory are; the frontal, anterior cingulate, and parietal cortices and parts of the basal ganglia. Accepting that any part of the brain might have been shaken up, disrupted or received a 'contrecoup' (damage caused to the opposite side of the brain to the side of the injury, as the jelly like substance of the brain collides with the skull and decelerates) type of injury, we have to wonder if the basal ganglia was injured here.

There is good reason to believe that this is the same case as was painted by Charles Bell as an unknown trooper of the 1st or Royal Dragoons (the only thing the patient could remember), which he sketched at the Gendarmerie Hospital on 5 July 1815. The top and middle cuts had effectively separated a section of skull, which Bell recommended to be removed. The operation was performed and there was noticeable relief to the patient soon after. He also noted, that 'the picture is distressing to look upon; yet Mr Shaw[4] mentions that he was told by Dr Macleod,[5] who attended this patient after Sir Charles' departure from Brussels, that the man ultimately survived'.[6]

15. Alexander Kirkland – 3rd Guards

Annonciate Hospital

Skull fractured.

Private Alexander Kirkland of Lieutenant Colonel Charles West's No. 10 company of the 2nd Battalion 3rd (Scots) Foot Guards was possibly attacked by a French horseman. The injury was likely caused by a sabre. Kirkland did survive and received his Waterloo Prize Money in 1817.

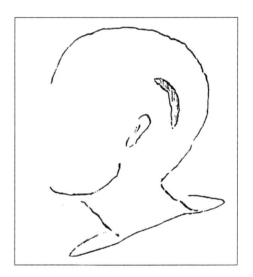

4   Mr Shaw is John Shaw, a brother-in-law and pupil of Sir Charles Bell who travelled out to Belgium with him.
5   Almost certainly Surgeon Swinton Macleod, 42nd Foot.
6   Crumplin, *A Surgical Artist at War* pp.42-44.

16. Anonymous

Annonciate Hospital

Skull fracture – doing well.

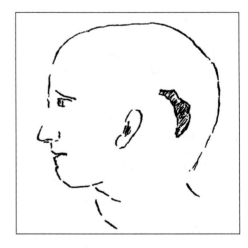

> *The same commentary can be made on this unknown individual as with the previous case.*

17. Janet

Corderie pd.41 1st [August]

An exterior flap laid open by the stroke of a sabre cut. The vertebral arteries seen pulsating.

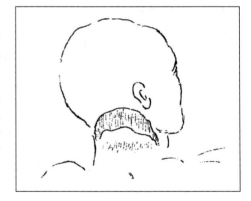

> *This was a French Prisoner of War. The sabre slash has been cut from behind and above but avoided damage to the deeper situated two vertebral arteries. The sabre has largely cut through the neck muscles and a flap of skin, fat, and muscle has been formed. Unless the flap was seen soon by the medical staff, it would become swollen and thickened and then would not close properly. It would have to be stitched, as adhesive straps would not be strong enough to hold it in place.*

18. Etienne Gerarghier

Corderie pd. 68 1st [August]

The lower part of the hairy scalp was turned down by a sabre cut. The flap was adhering.

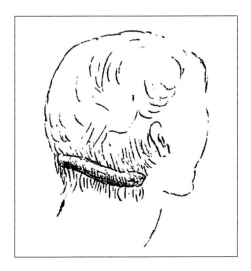

> *Another French Prisoner of War. Here in a similar wound to the back of the scalp, the flap has started to stick back, but there still remains a gap, which would have probably healed as an open granulating wound (called 'healing by second intention'). Many of these types of wound were inflicted by cavalry sabres on opponents who were fleeing, or as a back cut as cavalrymen passed each other in close combat.*

19. François Vergeot

Corderie pd. 41 2nd [August]

Was cut by a sabre which turned down a large flap across the occiput,[7] laid bare the vertebral arteries which were seen pulsating. The pulsations of the cerebellum were evident. The flap was applied & retained in its place, on the 9th August it was adhering, healthy granulations were filling up the gap between A and B.

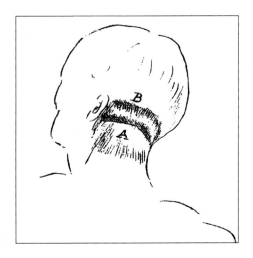

> *This is another French Prisoner of War. Here again the sabre cut has inflicted a flap injury in the occipital region and although the flap has been replaced and has begun to heal (after nearly seven weeks), there is still a gap filled by 'healthy granulations'. The victim was fortunate in not having damage inflicted on his cerebellum (an organ of balance, situated below the body of the brain).*

---

7   The lower back part of the skull.

20. François Chapuis

Corderie pd. 69 2nd [August]

Cut with a sabre across the neck.

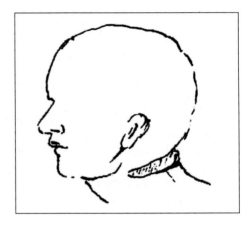

> *Here is yet another of this type of injury. Fortunately, the head and neck has a very rich blood supply and healing is often assured.*

21. Jean Louis le Jeun

Corderie

Cut with a Sabre. The flap adhering & the irregular portion filling up with healthy granulations.

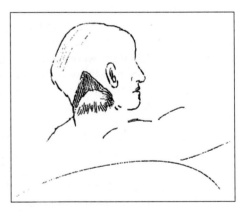

> *What is interesting is that, in none of these cases, has any attempt been made to suture the flap properly into anatomical position. Perhaps, especially in the French patients, as in this case, there had been a great deal of delay in receiving these patients and the healing process has started and the thickened and swollen flap had then become fixed in a lower position than would be ideal.*

22. Mageré

Gens d'Armerie

Sabre cuts.

> The sword injuries are explained by the
> Y-shaped incision, but what, we have to
> enquire, is the cruciate incision, in front of
> the sabre injuries? Was the soldier subjected
> to the trephine? This might have been due to
> signs of raised intracranial pressure.

23. Anonymous

Hospital of Gens d'Armerie

Parts laid open from A to B, brought into
contact and now adhering.

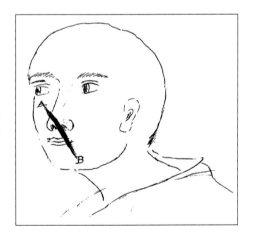

> The patient has a disfiguring slash with a
> sabre – the edges of the wound if seen early
> enough, could be sutured with linen or silk
> sutures or just approximated with adhesive
> plasters. Noses were not infrequently injured
> by gunshot or swords.

24. Terlagande

Corderie

Sabre cuts. Parts adhering.

> *Presumably this was a sabre strike from the hand of an Allied cavalryman. It would have bled profusely. There is no mention here of damage to the left eye.*

25. Anonymous

Corderie

Sabre cut.

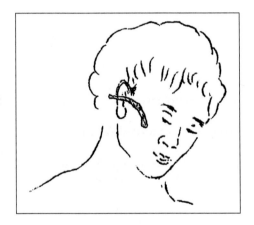

> *As in the previous case, with the ear cut across transversely.*

26. Fractront

Corderie

Sabre wound. Parts re applied & adhering.

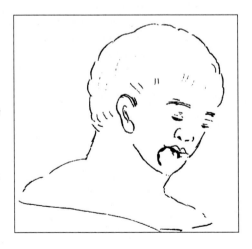

> *Here a flap of the lower lip has been cut by the sword swipe and would have been stitched back into position using sutures of silk or twisted gut (made from part of the lining of a sheep's intestine). Proper reconstruction of soldier's faces would not become feasible until Sir Harold Gillies's pioneering work during the First World War.*

27. Schlem

Jesuits Hospital pd. 107

Musket ball entered on the right side of the neck & came through the thyroid cartilage. Hoarseness very remarkable.

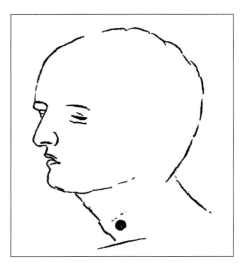

This man is possibly Private Frederick Schlem of Captain Hatorf's Troop of the 1st Light Dragoons KGL. He was fortunate to escape a catastrophic haemorrhage from one of the large blood vessels in the neck. To have the thyroid cartilage damaged (the most prominent piece of which forms the 'Adam's Apple') puts one at severe risk of fatal choking from disruption of the upper airway. He obviously had some damage to his vocal cords or their nerve supply – hence the hoarseness.

28. Robert Stubley – 95th Regiment

St Elizabeth Hospital p. 72

Musket ball entered at A and passed obliquely downwards & out at B.

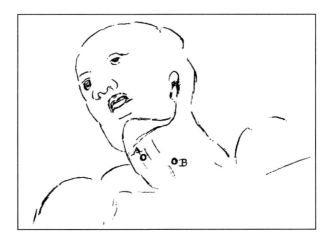

Actually, this man is Private Robert Stubbley of Captain James Fullerton's No. 2 Company, 3rd Battalion 95th Foot. He had similar risks to the last patient, but there is no comment on his breathing or larynx (voice box). This sort of wound could result in fatal pulmonary sepsis, since infected material might track down the windpipe and the patient's coughing would be very difficult and painful. The Waterloo Medal Roll comments that Stubbley died on the 4 August 1815.

29. Anonymous

Corderie pd. 72

Musket ball passed through the gullet. Excessive discharge of saliva. Marasmus.[8] Is fed by a funnel passing the opening.

This may be a French patient. If this was an open, guttered wound made by the passage of a ball across the neck, then how did the trachea (windpipe) escape damage? It lies in front of the gullet (pharynx and upper oesophagus). There is little doubt that the ball damaged the upper part of the food passage, since the saliva trickled out of the wound. Possibly it was an oblique injury, or the surgeon may have made an extension on the incision. An optional method of maintaining the nutrition of the patient was to 'funnel feed' the man, via the external wound in the neck, which would probably have closed spontaneously in five to six weeks. Alternative managements were to pass a gum–elastic via the mouth, into the stomach.

30. Claus Wernier

Jesuit Hospital pd. 8

Musket ball entered the left cheek at A and came out at B right cheek. Left eye blind.

The letters 'A' and 'B' are omitted on the line drawing. There has been some considerable disruption of the left orbit, possibly with fracturing of the surrounding bony structures. The right eye has escaped damage, probably as the missile passed obliquely from left to right.

8   Marasmus – A weakened bodily state as a result of undernourishment

31. François Guillaume

Corderie pd. 58

A musket ball entered immediately behind the left ear at A & came out through the left nostril. The wound is nearly filled up, but he is quite deaf in the left side.

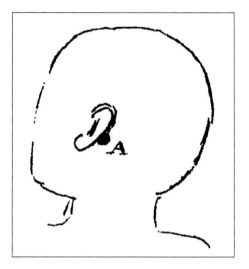

> *This was a very painful, risky, and dreadful wound. Although we do not know the final outcome, we know he was completely deaf in the ear that was struck, as the middle ear hearing mechanism was probably totally disrupted as the ball passed obliquely forwards from the mastoid process, through which it passed.*

32. Wm Ryan – 30th Regiment

Elizabeth

Musket ball entered A came out at B. Left eye injured and blind.

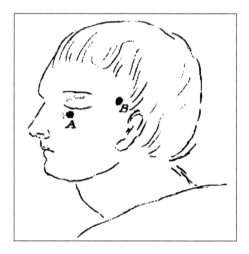

> *This patient is Private William Ryan of Captain James Skerrow's No.6 company of the 2nd Battalion 30th Foot. Here, as in the case of Samuel Pritchard (number 4 in this series), it may be that the right eye is undergoing deterioration from sympathetic ophthalmia. Today, it is a rare complication of penetrating eye injury. He survived but received no prize money.*

33. James McNulty – 1st Battalion 27th Regiment

Elizabeth

Musket ball entered at A fracturing the teeth & jaw. Fragments of the teeth of the left side came out at B.

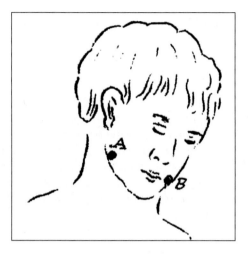

This was Private James McNulty of the 27th's No. 4 company. Bleeding, swelling and pain would ensue after this facial wound. Chewing and swallowing would also be impaired. The patient's diet would be largely liquid and healing would be delayed by ulceration and excessive salivation. He was invalided out of the army on a pension of 9d per day on 26 June 1816 and is recorded as having died aged 60 on 30 May 1854 (although his name is there spelt McNalty).

34. George Carab King's German Legion

Annonciate

Musket ball passed through the face. Entering at A & came out at B.

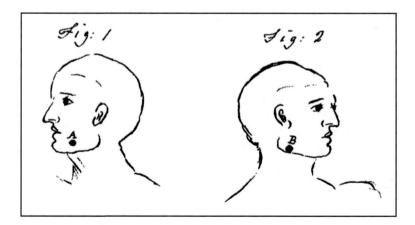

This almost certainly refers to George Kreb of the 3rd KGL Line Battalion. Kreb's jaw was shattered on both sides, possibly with some loss of teeth. He suffered great pain, swelling and would have had difficulty with mastication and swallowing. George Kreb was discharged in 1816 but he still received his Waterloo Prize Money in 1817.

35. Nasier

Corderie see pd. 43

Musket ball entered at A & came out at B.

> *This wound should have destroyed the patient's left orbit and, probably through injuring the left facial nerve in front of the ear, given the patient a facial paralysis. It may have injured the left parotid salivary gland as well.*

36. Major Brown of the 79th Regiment

Was wounded by a musket ball which entered the right cheek at A fig 1: it passed through the mouth, fractured the jaw, practically dislocating it & came out at B fig. 2. Twelve splinters of bone taken out at B. He cannot close the teeth, nor masticate.

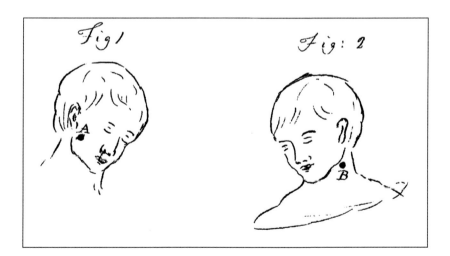

> *Lieutenant Colonel [in the Army, major in the regiment] Andrew Brown was fortunate that the missile did not strike a major neurovascular structure on exit. He had all the other difficulties manifest in the above cases. He however continued to serve in the army until 1831 and he died in 1835.*

37. Anonymous

Corderie

Musket ball entered right cheek at A & came out at B on the right of the cervical vertebrae.

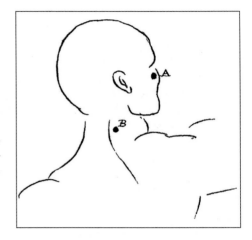

> *One has to wonder whether this anonymous soldier had lowered his head to have these slightly unusual entrance and exit wounds. More likely is that the ball hit his zygoma (cheekbone) and, being part spent, was deflected down to exit through the back of the neck muscles. The passage of the ball might have just tracked under the subcutaneous tissues or passed through his face muscles, jaw, or floor of the mouth and passed out.*

38. Edwards – 1st Guards

Jesuits Hospital

Musket ball entered below [the] right ear, shattering the front teeth & passed out through the hollow under the lower lip.

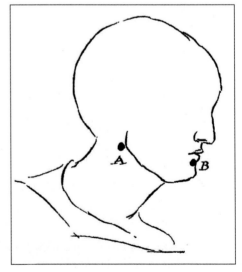

> *This was most likely Private John Edwards of 3rd Battalion 1st Foot Guards. Here, the missile probably passed behind the angle and junction of the vertical and horizontal mandibular rami [the two axes of the jaw bone], forcing its way into the mouth cavity and damaging some of his incisor and canine teeth.*
>
> *There were however five other 'Edwards' in the two battalions of the 1st Foot Guards – David, Rowland, and Robert were in the 2nd Battalion and there were also another John and a James in the 3rd Battalion. They all survived, Rowland is also listed in the Waterloo Roll as, 'wounded 18th June 1815', but John is recorded as having been invalided out of the regiment and he is the most*
>
> *likely candidate, given the wound, which would have made it virtually impossible for him to tear the musket cartridges with his teeth when firing.*

39. Angus MacKinnon – 79th Regiment

Jesuit Hospital

Musket ball entered at A splintered the left side of the Jaw & came out posterior to the left ear.

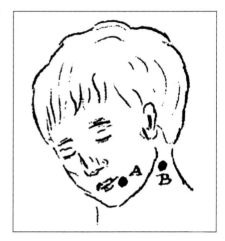

This was almost certainly Private Angus Macmillan of Captain John Christie's No. 2 company. The ball had shattered the inferior ramus of the mandible before exiting. Most of the patients with this type of wound would have to be fed on a liquid diet and would have lost much weight. Today the wound would be tidied up and the debris removed, followed by a wiring or bone grafting of the mandibular bone. His Waterloo Medal was issued incorrectly as McMillen. He did survive to receive his Waterloo Prize Money in 1817. Born at Kilmailey near Fort William in Inverness, he enlisted at Fort William on 25 February 1805 at the age of 22 on unlimited service. He had previously served nearly 4 years in the Lochaber Fencibles from 1799–1802. He served 16 years in the 79th Foot (including his two years for Waterloo) and retired from the army on 24 February 1819 on a reduction in its numbers. His wound must have occurred at Waterloo as he is recorded as having fought at both Quatre Bras and Waterloo. On his discharge he is described as 35 years old, 5 feet 5 inches tall, with brown hair and eyes and a fresh complexion. His previous occupation was recorded as a weaver.

40. Joseph Hallernan – 33rd Regiment

Elizabeth

His head was bent forward to fire his piece [musket] when a musket ball entered at A on the left maxilla[9] & came out on the right of the cervical vertebrae.

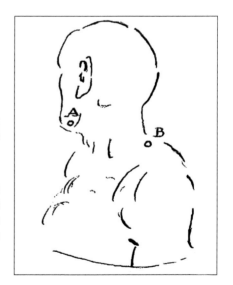

There has been some difficulty in identifying this person. The most likely candidates are Joseph Halliot, Joseph Hartley, Joseph Heaton, or Joseph Hallas. Of these only Joseph Hartley appears to

9   His cheekbone.

have been wounded and ultimately discharged dead, it is therefore most likely that he is our patient. Surgeons often placed their patients in the position they had adopted when receiving a small arms missile, to ascertain the possible track of a ball. Often however, the ball was deflected by bone or clothing, which sometimes made the final destination of the ball hard to locate. Thomson has drawn the entry wound too low for the maxilla. Hopefully this was a fairly superficial tracking wound, just tunnelling under the skin, fat and superficial muscles. He is incorrectly shown as Jonathan Hartley in the Waterloo Medal Roll.

41. Furrier

Corderie

Musket ball entering at A & came out at B having splintered the teeth.

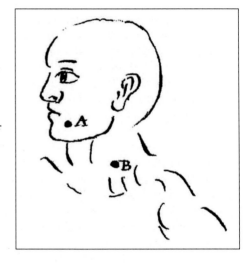

We do not know whether the integrity of the body of the mandible [jawbone] of this Frenchman was spared.

42. Anonymous

Corderie

Ball entered at A & came out at right side of the neck [at] B.

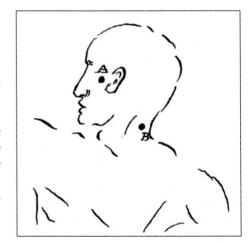

There would have been a facial paralysis after this wounding. The ball appears to have damaged the parotid gland and possibly the facial (VII cranial) nerve.

43. John Luin – 1st Royals

Elizabeth Hospital

Musket ball entered immediately blow the angle of the mouth on the left side & came out below the angle of the jaw on the left side B. A piece of the jaw with two teeth was removed and 4 more teeth are loose.

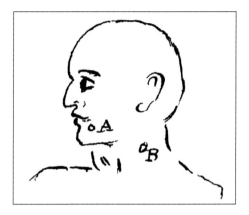

Here, we have almost certainly Private John Levins of Captain John McRae's No. 4 Company 3rd Battalion, 1st (Royal Scots) Regiment. Here is another similar facio-maxillary injury. Levins survived and received his Waterloo Prize Money in 1817.

44. Evan

Corderie, 100 pd. 51

Musket ball entered the right maxilla at A. Came out at B figure 2nd on the right side of cervical vertebrae.

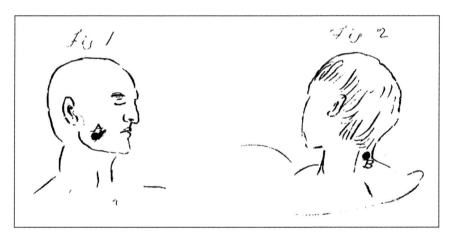

Evan is evidently another French prisoner. The potential for the injury of structures on entering upwards into the right side of the base of this man's skull were consider-able. We can only presume that the great vessels and nerves there (the jugular vein, carotid arteries and (IX – glossopharyngeal, Xth – vagus, XIth – accessory and XIIth – hypoglossal cranial nerves) might not have been injured. The missile may well have tracked superficially.

45. Langes

Corderie

Musket ball entered at A & passed out at B to the right of the vertebra.

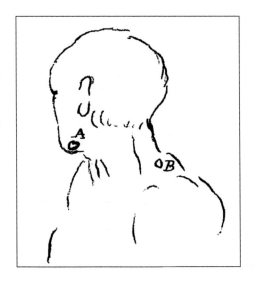

> *It looks as though this might also have been merely a superficial tracking of the ball.*

46. Lieutenant Pagan of the 33rd Regiment

When very close to the enemy, was struck by a nine–pound cannon ball which shaved his ear close off. He has been deaf before the wound and more so. Great purulent discharge from the ear. The same ball afterwards struck Lieutenant Hart[10] & killed him & some men of the regt. He suffers much from headache.

NB I am not quite certain which ear was lost.

> *Lieutenant Samuel Alexander Pagan had an unusual wounding, the external left ear was shaved clean off by the round shot and from the shading on the sketch we can assume that this was indicative of extensive bruising which has tracked down the neck. The officer had a degree of deafness already. The disruption of the external auditory meatus has led to sepsis in the middle ear. The forgetfulness of the author concerning the side of the lost ear in his brief description of the wound may have been due to his writing up the case later, from notes taken in haste! Pagan survived his injury and went on half pay in the 55th Foot on 14 February 1822. He apparently had a later career as a doctor in Edinburgh.*

---

10   Lieutenant James Hart was killed at Waterloo.

47. Olivier

Corderie
9 August

A musket ball entered the neck on the left side & passed out to the right of the spinous processes of the cervical vertebrae producing palsy of the right shoulder joint.

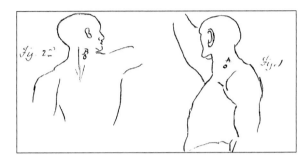

It is probable that the ball has divided the spinal accessory nerve (part of cranial nerve XI), which has thus resulted in some loss of muscle power in the shoulder region. Also, the pain and swelling, nearly two months later would still have made shoulder movements difficult.

48. Lieutenant Forlong – 33rd Regiment

Within about a hundred yards of the enemy a musket ball struck the uppermost button of his jacket on the right breast which gave the ball a deflection upwards & probably lessened its impetus, it then passed into the thorax & lungs & is lodged, it carried in a portion of the clavicle but without fracturing that bone entirely. Great discharge of blood ensued by the wound & by the mouth with difficult respiration, which continued some weeks. He now has much tremor & some pain and stiffness round the right shoulder.

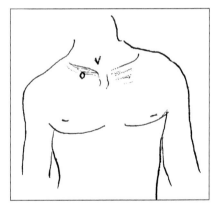

Lieutenant James Forlong (The Waterloo Roll Call mistakenly shows him as an ensign, but he became a lieutenant on 22 December 1814), whose silver-plated button probably saved his life. He was clearly hit by a shot at close range, since the ball still went into his thorax after it had struck the button. The ball broke off a chunk of his clavicle (collar bone), then clearly damaged the intercostal vessels that lie between the ribs, causing significant bleeding. As the ball damaged the top of the right lung, blood was expectorated by mouth. There would be no chance of removing the missile. Occasionally wounds at the top of the chest like this one, could partially damage the right subclavian artery, weakening its wall, and this could lead to an aneurysm (bulging of the artery), which in turn could rupture later in life. Forlong continued to serve for many years only retiring on 17 October 1851. He died at Toronto.

49. Anton Wellonlon, German

Annonciate
14th August

When in the act of firing his musket, a ball struck his left arm at A, passed upwards below the integuments, over the Shoulder Joint & came out at B over the clavicle. Exfoliation of the rib of which a pretty large distinctly marked portion was taken out today.

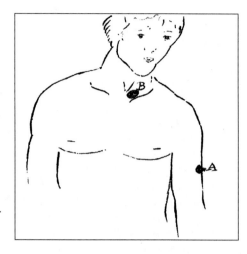

> *This almost certainly refers to Private Anton Wallenton of No.1 company of the 5th KGL Line Battalion. This is a typical example of subcutaneous tracking of a part–spent ball, taking the course of least resistance in the superficial tissues of the arm. Lying close to the clavicle is the 1st rib, part of which has come away either with the strike or with subsequent sepsis. Wallenton appears to have been discharged and certainly did not receive his Waterloo Prize Money.*

50. Morier

Corderie

Musket ball entered at A went through the muscular part of the arm behind, out at B, entered at C passed obliquely downwards and out at D.

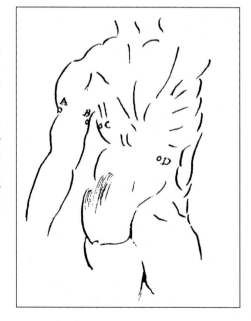

> *With four wounds sustained in the track of this missile wound, Morier has escaped more dangerous injury. There would always remain the risk of sepsis emanating from the bullet track, particularly as there would have been dirty clothing fragments driven through the wound track.*

51. Griffiths – 1st Battalion 95th Regiment

Facon
7th August

Musket ball entered at A and it lodged.

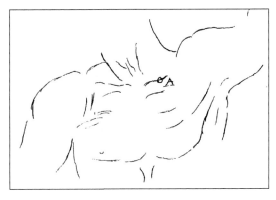

Private John Griffiths served in Captain Jonathan Leach's No.1 company, 1st Battalion 95th Rifles. As the soldier had survived almost two months since his injury, presumably no immediate serious harm occurred. Removal of this bullet might be risky as it would be surrounded by blood vessels and nerves. Presumably digital exploration had revealed a deep lodgement. There could be a risk of later subclavian aneurism (vide supra). John was not paid his Waterloo Prize Money.

52. John Wood

Facon
7th August

Musket ball entered at A and passed out.

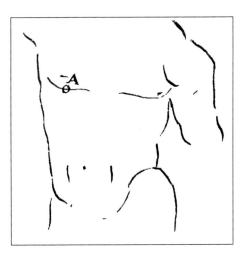

No exit wound has been described in this brief description, (also case number 53). There were a large number of such injuries at Waterloo, but see the next figure, which shows further detail in the same man.

53. John Wood

Musket ball entered at A, an inch and a half below the right nipple & passed out below the last rib on the right side at B. Bilious discharge ensued & afterwards, empyema.[11]

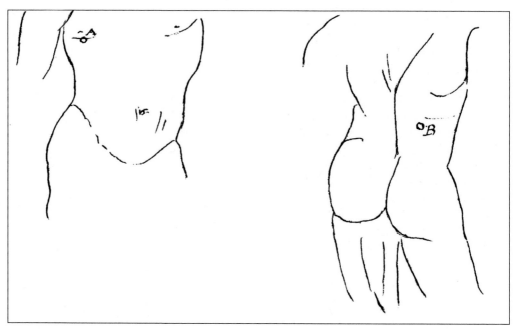

This refers to the same soldier in case 52, but explains his injury. Wood had a through and through injury which had passed across the lower chest and upper abdomen. During the ball's passage through the latter, the ball had scuffed the superior surface of the right lobe of Wood's liver. The bile that had leaked from the damaged liver had gone into both the abdominal cavity and the chest. It had also discharged through the skin. Probably more had contaminated the thoracic (chest) cavity and infection had supervened, causing a collection of bile and pus in the chest (called an empyema). If this had been drained by inserting a metal chest drain or had burst spontaneously, the patient, although suffering a good deal, could survive. This mimics an injury inflicted on George Simmons of the 95th Regiment.[12] Wood has clearly survived a septicaemia and was still alive almost two months later. The chances of a recovery were small and I believe this may refer to Private John Wood of the 2nd Battalion 69th Foot who was discharged dead and did not receive his Waterloo Prize Money.

11　Empyema – An accumulation of pus in the chest cavity or other organs, for example the gall bladder.
12　Crumplin, *Men of Steel*, p.283.

54. Martin Hogg – 27th Regiment

Facon,
7th August

Received a gunshot wound on the right mamma [breast region] which produced a sloughing ulcer of the enclosed space at A.

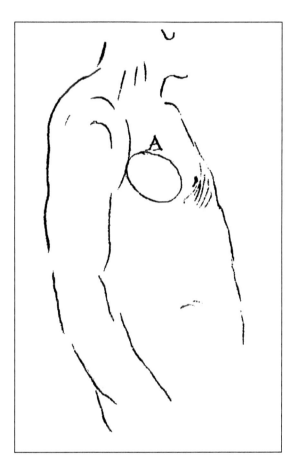

Private Martin Hogg (or Hog) of No. 6 Company 1st Battalion 27th Foot was the injured man. The ball probably damaged the skin, fat and some muscle over Hogg's pectoral region. Infection and lack of local blood supply to the overlying skin caused the skin and superficial tissues to necrose (die). This left an ulcer, which would be cleaned up and dressed with emollients, lint and a linen dressing. Sometimes a vegetable poultice would be laid on the ulcer and any dead tissue cut away or treated with lunar caustic (silver nitrate) – an escharotic (a chemical agent, such as a mineral acid, to destroy old dead tissue). Hogg was invalided out of the army but received his Waterloo Prize Money.

55. Corporal McDonald – 1st Battalion 79th Regiment

Facon
7th August

Musket ball entered through the 8th rib, wounding the liver in its passage & is supposed by Mr Blicke to be lodged in the spleen. Pure bile was discharged for many days but has ceased to appear.

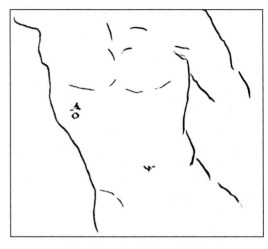

Corporal John McDonald of Captain James Campbell's No. 7 Company 1st Battalion 79th Foot provides us with an interesting case and in its commentary by William Flamank Blicke, Staff Surgeon to the Forces, who had supposed the ball to be in the spleen. This is unlikely as the patient would most likely have been in a critical condition through blood loss, if this were the case. Maybe the patient had pain on the left side in his upper abdomen (possibly caused by blood or bile irritating the diaphragm, which in turn causes pain felt in the left shoulder) which prompted this suggestion. This was likely a part–spent shot and probably the ball lodged in the liver. This would cause blood and bile to leak into the upper abdomen and externally: however, it seems that by 7 August the discharge had ceased. On 19 September 1816 McDonald was discharged from the army and was granted a pension of 9d per day and then lived in Glasgow. He had served for 11½ years, 7 years as a private and 4½ as corporal. His complaint is recorded as 'a gunshot wound through the liver and body, ball lodged'. He was admitted as an in–patient at Chelsea on 24 September 1824 aged 41.

Some additional information is supplied by George Guthrie:

Corporal Macdonald first battalion, 79th Regiment, was wounded on the 16th of June at Quatre Bras, by a musket ball, which entered the abdomen, splintered the eight [sic] rib on the right side, passed through the liver, and was supposed to have lodged on the opposite side, as he says he felt the ball strike the left side, on which he was not able to lie for a long time. Lost but little blood at the time; was dressed superficially and arrived in Brussels on the 19th, labouring under considerable fever. Bleeding to thirty–six ounces. For seven successive days the bleeding was repeated, to from twelve to sixteen ounces each day [roughly 3.5 litres of blood was let over a week!], when a large, bilious, and purulent discharge took place from the wound, on which the inflammatory symptoms appeared to subside, until the 30th of June, when bleeding took place from the wound during the night to the extent of twenty ounces, and then ceased spontaneously. On the 15th of July the haemorrhage recurred with so much fever as to warrant twenty ounces of blood being taken from the arm, and this was repeated next day. The bilious discharge ceased in the middle of August and on the 2nd of September he was discharged [from Hospital] convalescent; the only material inconvenience he suffered from, being a shortness of breath on any exertion.[13]

56. Wm. Williams – 4th Regiment

Elizabeth
2nd August

Musket ball entered cartilage of the rib at A and is lodged.

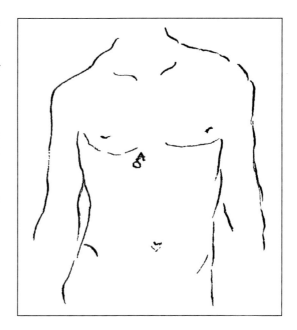

This is Private William Williams of Captain Richard Henry Shaw's No.1 Company 1st Battalion 4th Foot. How deep this gunshot wound was, we do not know. Since there is little other comment, it might have been buried fairly superficially: however, it was clearly not retrievable. Williams survived and received his Waterloo Prize Money in 1817.

13 G.J. Guthrie, *A treatise on gunshot wounds, on injuries of nerves, and of wounds of the extremities requiring the different operations of amputation* (London: Burgess & Hill, 1820), p.530.

57. Louis Bremont

Musket ball entered fig. 1 A behind through scapula & came out in front B through sternum.

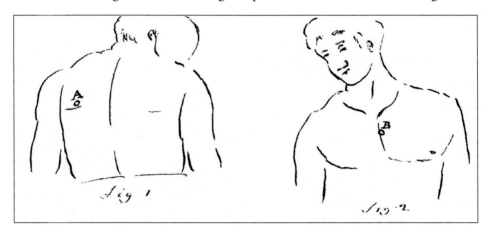

The fact here, that there is little surgical comment shows how little we may deduce from some of these case illustrations. This ball was fired from close range – into the back of the soldier, smashing the scapula and entering the chest by breaking the ribs, passing through lung tissue (missing the heart) and fracturing the sternum, (the breastbone) on exit. So there were three severe bony injuries and a lung or mediastinal (central area of the chest, containing heart, great vessel, trachea, gullet and other structures) wound, bruising and bleeding. He probably did not survive.

58. Frederick Thielman

**Elizabeth
2nd August**

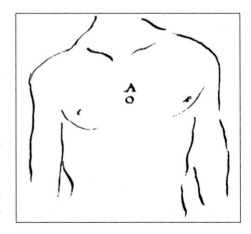

Musket ball entered the Sternum at A & passed out through the ribs on the right side.

This sketch refers to Private Frederick Thielman of no. 3 company of the 2nd KGL Light Battalion. A central chest wound caused by a ball that passed obliquely from front to the right side and out, breaking his ribs. It clearly missed the heart, but may have damaged the right lung, causing air and blood to leak out into the chest cavity.

Thielman survived and received his Waterloo Prize Money in 1817.

59. Robert Gerard 28th Regiment

Elizabeth
2nd August

Musket ball entered at A & is lodged.

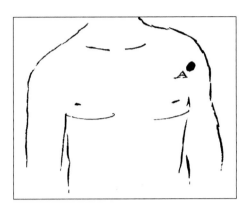

This would almost certainly be Private Robert Gerrett, of Captain Charles Tenlon's Light Company 28th Foot. This missile might well be lodged in the pectoral muscles or chest and/or have damaged the biceps muscle. Gerrett was discharged dead and the Waterloo Roll (which shows him as Garrett) also reports him as dead.

60. Ladovich Ludlen – 2nd Hanoverian Regiment

Elizabeth
9 August

Musket ball entered a little under & inwards from the left nipple[.] It remains lodged. He spat blood copiously for some day[s] after receiving the wound that symptom has now disappeared.

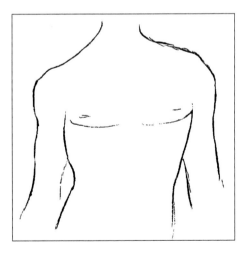

The only possible candidate in the records for this case is Private Henry Ludjens 2nd Light Battalion King's German Legion. The ball had fractured at least two ribs anteriorly and had damaged lung tissue – hence the haemoptysis (coughing up or spitting blood) – vide case 62 – the same patient's case report. Many of these men survived non–exiting chest shots; for example the Earl of March, after the Battle of Orthez in 1814.

61. Demlevy – 69th Regiment

Facon
2nd August

Musket Ball entered at A and is lodged, Bleeding profuse – threatening suffocation.

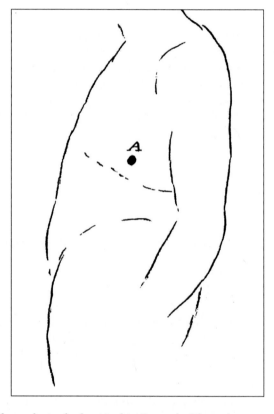

This man was probably Corporal Francis Donhavy (Dunbarry in the Waterloo Prize Roll) of Captain Henry Cox's no.1 company, 2nd Battalion 69th Foot. As this ball entered the left chest, bleeding was mainly from the intercostal (the blood vessels between the ribs) and damaged lung tissue could well have been accumulating in the thoracic cavity (called a haemothorax), threatening to compress his heart and lungs. He did survive his injuries and received his Waterloo Prize Money.

It is certainly the same case as described by George Guthrie:

Corporal Dunrealy [Sic], of the 69th Regiment, was wounded on the 16th of June 1815, at Quatre Bras, by a musket ball, which entered the thorax, fracturing the seventh rib on the fore part of the right side and lodged. He said he had lost a large quantity of blood from the mouth, and some from the wound, between that and the 19th, when he was brought to the hospital in Brussels. The pulse was then quick and hard [bounding], respiration difficult and anxious, and a bloody discharge issued from the wound on every respiration; bowels confined since the accident; was bled to forty-four ounces, saline purgatives, with calomel, antimony and opium were given until the 29th of June, when the wound discharged good pus. From this time, at different periods for six weeks, he lost ninety-two ounces more blood, being strictly placed on a milk diet. Several pieces of rib exfoliated [dead fragments of rib] were ejected from the body. He was sent home on the 31st of August, declaring himself as well as ever he had been in his life; the ball remaining undiscovered.[14]

---

14   Guthrie, *A treatise on gunshot wounds*, p.437.

62. Ludovich Ludlen – 2nd Hanoverian Regiment

Elizabeth
3rd August

Musket ball entered below left mamma at A & remained. Spat blood some days after he was wounded.

A straightforward non–exiting chest injury. This is a duplicate report of case 60 – see above.

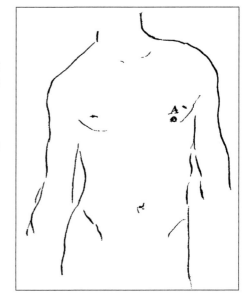

63. Buisson

Corderie

Musket ball entered through Sternum at A & passed through the lungs & out at the right side through the ribs.

Buisson was a French prisoner. The ball had shattered his sternum and passed through lungs and some ribs. No comment on condition or symptoms. Hopefully, he may have survived.

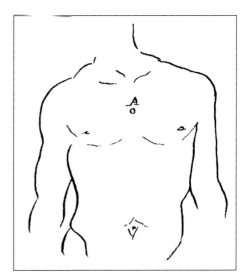

64. Joseph Stenach – 4th Foot

Facon
9 August

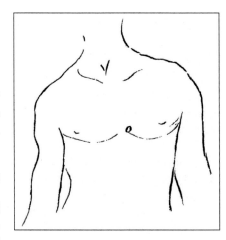

Ball entered on the left of the Cartilage Ensiformis[15] & was cut out two & a half inches to the right of the Spine, at the lowest rib. Had spitting blood and pain of [sic] left shoulder.

> *I believe this refers to Joseph Smart of Captain Kirwan's No. 6 Company 1st Battalion 4th Foot. If the bullet went through to the left of the xiphoid cartilage, it probably was deflected down somewhat and crossed the diaphragm. It was lucky that the missile had missed his heart. The base of his right lung likely suffered some damage. The pain in the left shoulder must have meant that some sub–diaphragmatic irritation by blood or bile, if the liver had been slightly injured. The shoulder pain reflects the nerve supply of the diaphragm which is by the phrenic nerve, which is part of the Accessory Nerve which also supplies the skin of the shoulder region. Smart was discharged from the regiment in 1816 although he still received his Waterloo Prize Money.*

65. William Pearce – 28th Regiment

Elizabeth

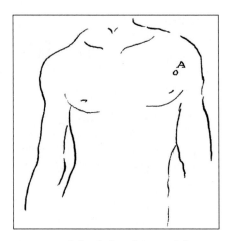

Musket ball entered thorax at A, fractured three ribs & passed out at left [of] scapula. Air discharged at both openings.

> *This was Private William Pearce of Captain Henry Moriarty's No. 2 company 28th Foot. Here, the apex of the left lung has been injured and there is a collection of air in the left chest (i.e. a pneumothorax). Air is blowing in and out of the entry and exit wounds. With luck, the air leak from the lungs would be limited and could escape from the missile wounds. If either of the exterior wounds had closed up and the air leak had continued, there might be a danger of a tension pneumothorax (build-up of air in the chest cavity dangerously compressing the heart). Pearce survived and was discharged from the army and received his Waterloo Prize Money in 1817.*

---

15   The xiphoid cartilage lies at the lower end of the sternum.

66. John Leach

Annonciate

Musket ball entered the thorax at A two & a half inches to the right of the Sternum & passed out behind exactly half way between the Axilla[16] & Spine of Ilium[17] on the right side.

> *The only John Leach at Waterloo was a private in the 15th Hussars. Leach's right lung would have been punctured, but we do not know whether the soldier's liver, diaphragm or any other organs were damaged.*

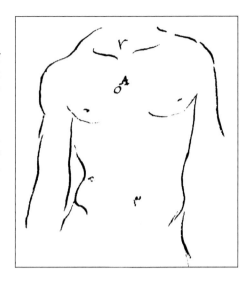

67. Michael Armstrong – 73rd Regiment

Annonciate

Musket ball entered right breast exactly through the nipple A and passed through the thorax & out at the right scapula.

> *This man was Private Michael Armstrong of Captain John Kennedy's Grenadier Company of 2nd Battalion 73rd Foot. His case is another example of a through and through thoracic wound, but no comment on progress were given. Armstrong did not survive, dying on 13 August 1815. He was discharged dead and the Medal Roll also confirms Armstrong as dead. Michael Armstrong had enlisted on 8 January 1813, volunteering from the Kings County Militia. A Waterloo medal was produced for him, but it was returned to the Royal Mint on 5 May 1816.*

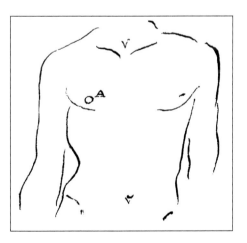

16   Armpit.
17   Upper and larger part of the pelvic bone.

68. Thomas Cooper – 1st Battalion, 95th Regiment

Facon Hospital
7th August

Musket ball entered at A, traversed through the lungs & out through the right scapula. Blood discharged by the mouth copiously at first. He is now quite well.

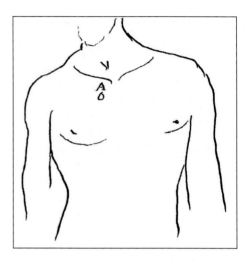

> *Here we have Private Thomas Cooper of Captain Jonathan Leach's No. 1 Company of 1st Battalion 95th Rifles. It is refreshing to note that this soldier recovered from this dangerous through and through chest injury, which broke the right scapula. He received his Waterloo Prize Money in 1817. Cooper was granted a pension of 1 shilling per day from 24 February 1819 and it ceased on his death on 7 September 1855 aged 64.*

69. Charles Mason – 3rd Guards

Jesuits

Musket ball entered an inch below [the] right clavicle[18] passed through the chest & came out by the edge of the Latissimus Dorsi[19] close to the Scapula.

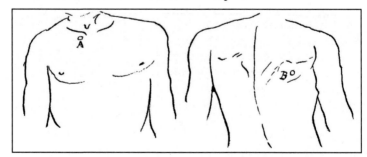

Private Charles Mason of 2nd Battalion 3rd Foot Guards survived although through-and-through chest wounds were far less frequently survived than non–exiting pene-trating chest wounds, caused by spent missiles. Mason was discharged from the army but did receive his Waterloo Prize Money in 1817.

---

18   Collar–bone.
19   A large muscle lying on the side of the chest wall.

70. Georg Recosowitz

Annonciate

Musket ball entered left side of thorax at A & passed thro' the lungs & out below the left scapula – Empyema supervened, but is now recovering.

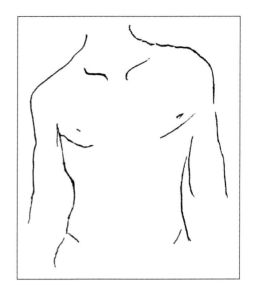

> *No marking letters are seen on this sketch. Another exiting chest wound, hopefully with recovery. How his empyema (a collection of infected material in the chest cavity) was managed would be of interest. Did it surface and burst spontaneously from between the ribs, or did a surgeon incise over a pointing abscess, or, alternatively insert a trocar and cannula to let out the purulent material?*

71. Mayer

Corderie

Musket ball entered at A Fig 1 passed through the lungs & out at B Fig. 2 through the scapula.

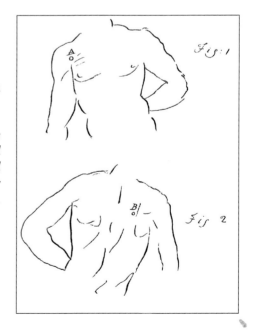

> *This shot wound, which is similar to the preceding ones, must have in part damaged Mayer's right deltoid muscle. If he had survived, this would have made his shoulder movements stiff and sore for a long period. He is likely to have been a French prisoner.*

72. Henry Barnet – 1st Guards

Elizabeth

Wounded in the lungs by a musket ball. The operation for empyema was performed successfully at A.

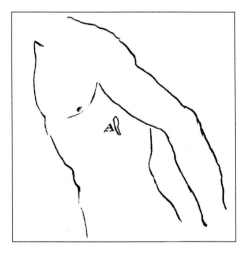

This is most likely Henry Baynon of 3rd Battalion 1st Foot Guards. At length we have a case where treatment for a penetrating chest injury is logged. There were two ways to drain and manage a chest wound, with blood, air, and purulent fluids collecting in the thorax. One was to pass a trocar and cannula in between the ribs, the other was to make an incision, as here, and open the chest cavity in a limited way to let out the fluids. A short wick drain would be placed in the incision to encourage drainage. The procedure was successful and Baynon was invalided out of the army in 1816 and he did not receive his Waterloo Prize Money.

73. Lieutenant Pringle – Royal Engineers

[He] had his spy glass hung in a leather belt across his breast in the direction of the dotted line, a musket ball struck the belt at A fracturing the junction of the first and second ribs with the sternum altho' it did not penetrate the leather but was thrown out by it. There was a deep dent in the leather, & the chest wound was severe.

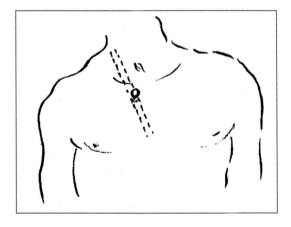

Lieutenant John William Pringle, an engineer officer who was lucky, but obviously suffered a great deal of pain and bruising with the local fractures of the rib–sternal junction. He probably sustained some contusion of the lung and the upper mediastinal structures. He survived and died as a major on 12 October 1861 at Bath.

74. Joseph Clark – 32nd Regiment

Elizabeth, pd 131

Musket ball entered above right Clavicle at A fig 1st passed out through right Scapula at B fig. 2nd.

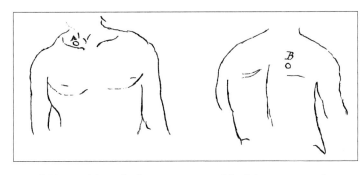

This was almost certainly Corporal Joseph Clarke of Captain Henry Ross Lewin's No. 6 Company 32nd Foot, although there are two with this name on the Prize Money Roll. The shot came from slightly above and passed downwards (or was received whilst he was bending forwards) through the muscles of the neck and out through the scapula. The point about this injury was that, presumably, the missile missed the subclavian artery and vein and also the brachial plexus (the main sheath of nerves supplying the arm, wrist, and hand), since there is no mention of haemorrhage or palsy. Joseph Clarke was invalided on 6 August 1816 and granted a pension of 1 shilling per day. He was drawing it at Salisbury in 1846 and died on 24 May 1853 aged 70.

75. David Williams

Jesuits

A piece of shell wounded him on the right of the Spine between [the] 8th and 9th ribs, it fell from the wound A. Secondary Haemorrhage took place from the intercostal artery on 14th day.

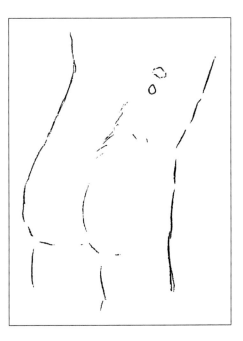

This refers to David Williams of 'G' Troop Royal Horse Artillery. Williams had been hurt by a fragment of common shell, which penetrated as far as the ribs and damaged an artery running along the lower aspect of the 8th rib. Bleeding from the intercostal arteries could pose a significant loss of blood, particularly when concealed within the thoracic cavity. Williams was unlucky to die from this injury.

76. Marshall – 73rd Regiment

Elizabeth
20th August

Musket ball entered left shoulder rather behind but from above, near the letter A and passed through the lungs and out below the left nipple B. The flow of arterial blood by the mouth threatening imminent suffocation and was repeatedly restrained by profuse bleeding[20] repeated as resorted to as required & pulsed till relief was obtained – leeches were abundantly used; & the Anti–phlogistic system pursued in its most rigid form. Two hundred and fifty ounces[21] of blood were drawn by the lancet in eighteen days by staff surgeon Colyear [sic].[22] No symptoms but debility remains & strength returns apace.

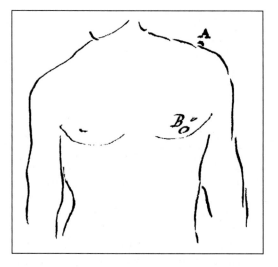

Corporal William Marshall of Captain William Wharton's No. 4 company 2nd Battalion 73rd Foot suffered a musket ball wound to his trunk. After traversing the shoulder muscles, the ball passed through the chest, clearly dividing a large pulmonary (of the lungs) blood vessel, when the ball passed through the lung tissue, it divided a significant division of the right bronchus (main subdivision of the trachea – the windpipe). Blood would then pour into the airways tube and be coughed up and could 'drown' the patient – hence the risk and fear of 'suffocation'. The blood–letting was part of the antiphlogistic regimen (blood–letting, catharsis and administering a drug to promote loose stools). Leeching was another of the blood–letting techniques, each leech would extract around 20–25ccs of blood. Marshall survived and was granted his Waterloo Prize Money in 1817. It was quite an achievement to have overcome both the wound and the therapy! William Marshall had been born at Kings Lynn in Norfolk and he enlisted on 2 June 1813 and was promoted to corporal on 20 November 1814. He was discharged aged 22 on 24 December 1816 in consequence of a 'gunshot wound of the lungs'. He was described as being 5 foot 4 inches tall, brown hair, blue eyes and with a swarthy complexion. He received a pension of 6d per day.

20　That is, by venesection – the letting of blood usually by the arm veins.
21　12 pints!
22　Charles Collier – appointed staff surgeon to the forces in 1812, worked in the Peninsula. He was a correspondent of Sir Charles Bell's.

77. Samuel Brown – 12th Light Dragoons

Elizabeth
2nd August

Musket entered at A, came out at B. Air was expelled at both orifices for some time. The wound at B is now closed, but air is discharged from A when the dressings are removed.

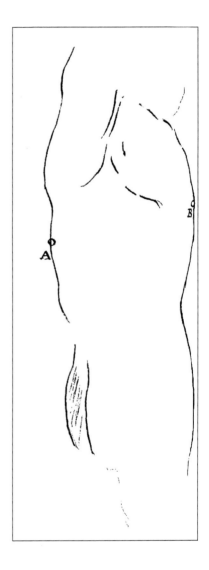

Here we have Trooper Samuel Brown of Captain Houston Wallace's F Troop 12th Light Dragoons. This is now six weeks after wounding and air is still whistling in and out of the rear wound when it is redressed. This would be safe provided the wound stayed open, but it might be risky for the patient if the wound closed as it ultimately would. The risk again here is that an air collection (pneumothorax) could build up pressure in in the patient's right chest which might fatally compress the heart (a tension pneumothorax). However, sepsis and the inflammatory response of the body, in addition to the healing process, often caused the lung tissue locally to adhere to the surrounding chest wall, obviating this complication. There could then not be the space for the air or blood to accumulate. Brown did survive his wounds but was invalided in 1816. He did however receive his Waterloo Prize Money in 1817.

78. Lieutenant Robert Lind – 71st Regiment

An iron canister shot upwards of nine ounces weight entered right clavicle at A, passed through & was cut out at the spine[23] of the left scapula. He vomited blood copiously. He spat blood for three weeks. The wound is healing rapidly. No spitting of blood, strength returning. Shoulder joint rigid, goes to England soon. This is the third type of the sort. Col. Hill – [?].

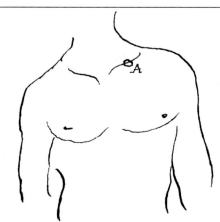

> *The wound is similar to others listed. The officer vomited blood as he had swallowed so much that clearly had spilled over from the trachea.*
>
> *Dalton's Waterloo Roll Call makes the following comment about this officer's wounding: 'Belonged to a respectable family in the county of Antrim. He received a grape shot at Waterloo weighing 10 oz. which he kept as a relic, hooped in silver. The shot entered at the breast and was cut out at the shoulder three days after. Died at Waterloo Cottage, Cookstown, County Antrim, 3rd July, 1851, aged 70'.[24]*
>
> *The significance of the comment about Colonel Hill suffering a similar wound remains unclear as no less than three Lieutenant Colonel Hills were wounded at Waterloo.*

79. David Williams

This is the same case report as no. 75.

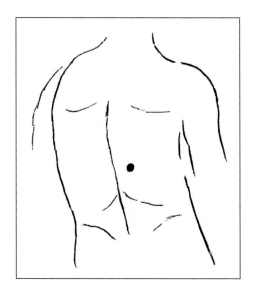

---

23   A ridge of bone lying along the upper part of the back of the shoulder blade.
24   C. Dalton, *The Waterloo Roll Call* (London: Eyre & Spottiswoode, 1904), p.182.

80. Anonymous

Corderie

Musket ball entered at A left side passed upwards & out at B.

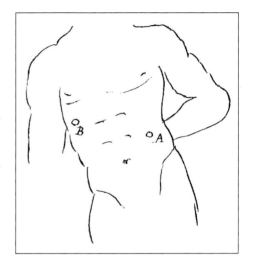

> *There is no comment about damage to the contents of the abdominal cavity, or whether this purely was only a superficial tracking wound. Missiles, usually spent rounds, would pass through the different layers of the muscles, or under the skin in the fat, taking the line of least resistance.*

81. Francis Addis – 1st Foot Guards

Facon
3 August

Ball entered at A & passed out thro' the scapula of same side.

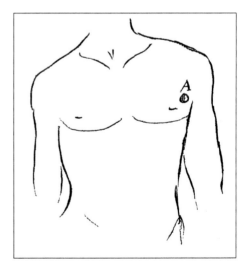

> *Private Francis Addis of Lieutenant Colonel Edward Staple's No. 2 Company of the 3rd Battalion 1st Foot Guards would certainly have had bleeding into the chest cavity, giving the patient a haemo–pneumothorax and a very stiff and painful shoulder movement. He did survive and was awarded his Waterloo Prize Money in 1817, but was invalided out of the army on 26 April 1816 when he resided in London. Francis was granted a pension of 1 shilling per day and he died on 9 December 1846 when aged 72.*

82. Thomas McLualty 13th Light Dragoons

Elizabeth

Musket ball entered at A right arm and came out at B.

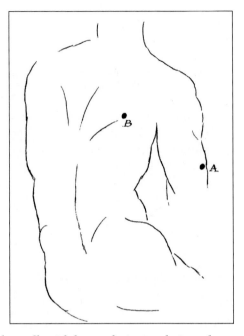

This was almost certainly Corporal Thomas McGaulter of the 13th Light Dragoons. He received a close range shot and we do not know whether there was a fracture of the humerus (upper arm bone) or penetration of the chest cavity by the ball. We get the feeling these might have been soft tissue wounds only. McGaulter continued to serve and received his Waterloo Prize Money in 1817. McGaulter was born at St Quivox in Ayr and joined the 13th Light Dragoons on 5 November 1800, serving for 18½ years (including 2 years for Waterloo) of which he was corporal for the last two. He was discharged on 24 June 1817, 'following gunshot wounds in the right arm and leg suffered at Waterloo'. At his discharge he was recorded as being 42 years old, 5 feet 6 inches tall, with brown hair, grey hair and a fresh complexion. He was a plasterer before joining the army.

83. Anonymous

Corderie

Ball entered at A right side & came out at B left side.

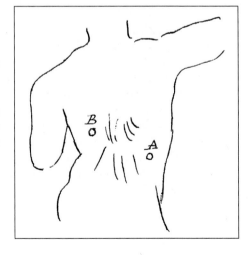

The anonymous soldier was probably a French prisoner. This was almost certainly a superficial tracking wound, injuring soft tissues only.

84. Thomas Jones – 23rd Regiment

Annonciate

A front–rank man was kneeling to fire when a ball entered at A & was cut out of the right side of the scrotum at B.

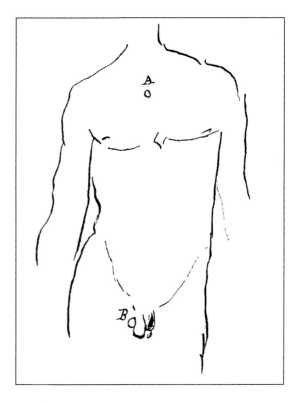

Another interesting case of superficial tracking, this time the missile ran all the way from the sternal region and, having struck the bone was deflected down to the right scrotum. Wounds in the latter area always risked sepsis from anaerobic and intestinal bacteria flourishing in the perineal area. When surgeons were ascertaining the route of a bullet, they would sometimes place the patient in the position he was when he received the injury.

There were four 'Thomas Jones' in the 23rd Regiment, one being recorded as killed on 18 June who served in Captain Charles Jolliffe's No. 8 Company. Of the other three, one served in Captain Harrison's No. 3 Company, one in No. 6 Company and another in Captain Wynne's light company. Only the one in No. 3 Company was invalided shortly after the battle and is likely to be our man, although all received their Waterloo Prize Money. This Thomas Jones was born at Mold in Flintshire, having previously been a weaver. He enlisted on 3 April 1809 aged 20. He was discharged on 24 May 1816.

85. Colonel Hay

Musket ball entered A below scapula on the right side, penetrated and was cut out on the right side [B] passing through the Liver. Bile discharged by the opening in the Thorax.

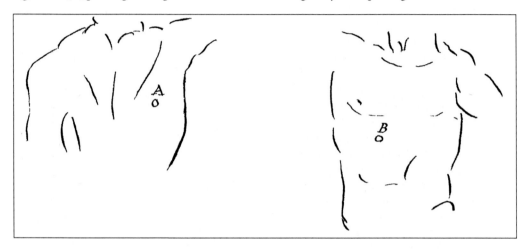

Actually Lieutenant Colonel James Hay commanding the 16th Light Dragoons.
  Guthrie had recorded further details of this wounding:
  Hay was hit at Quatre Bras by a ball that entered through the chest at the level of the 8th and 9th ribs and exiting between the 7th and 8th ribs in front. He bled on and off for three days, but was not moved to Brussels until the 11 July. He had difficulty in breathing and was pale, sweating and jaundiced. His upper abdomen was very uncomfortable and he could not sleep for this. Out of the posterior wound, came bubbles of air and a yellowish (biliary) discharge. He was restless and incoherent and clearly very ill, and up to the 37th day after wounding. There was little hope of recovery. He was bled copiously. ...... by the 1 September, he had quite recovered.[25]
  This had been a potentially lethal wound, should bile and blood have collected in the chest and abdomen. The larger right lobe of the liver had been damaged and there is a bile fistula [a tract lined with granulation tissue or epithelium joining two surfaces – here the skin and the abdominal cavity, from which the bile leaked to the exterior].
  He had also suffered a broken right arm at Salamanca and after the chest injury, was probably kept at Mont St Jean for eight days, until he was fit enough to be moved to Brussels. He was found at Waterloo by Lieutenant William Hay. The colonel was propped up in bed, arranging his will, since he had been told that he would not survive. He did and later became a lieutenant general and colonel of the 79th Foot and died at Kilburn in County Longford on 25 February 1854.

---

25 Guthrie, *On Wounds and Injuries of the Abdomen*, p.51.

86. Lieutenant Simon

Jesuits

Ball entered behind & between 9th & 10th rib passed through & out at A an inch to the right of the xiphoid cartilage. Bile discharged pure from A – jaundice generally.

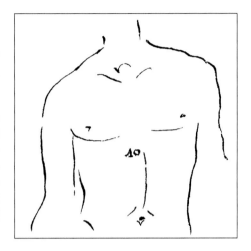

> *Another French Prisoner of War. Whether the jaundice was as a result of widespread absorption of bile or from damage or obstruction to some part of the biliary tree (the bile ducts in the liver, which ultimately drain the bile into the small intestine is hard to surmise. It would not seem to be a good prognostic factor.*

87. James Turner – 1st Guards

Annonciate

Was struck by the splinter of a shell at A. A hardness was felt separately in the space between the dotted lines C–D. The tumefaction at length underlying the hard body was found to be moveable. It was incised at B and was extracted there. It proved to be a piece of shell weighing nine and a half ounces. It was removed the 25th day after the battle. The patience & cheerful disposition of this man contributes to his recovery. The discharge [of pus] has greatly diminished & his strength has increased.

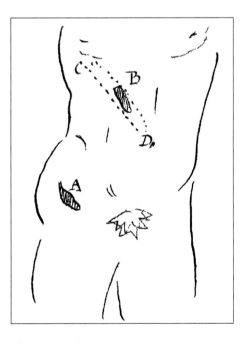

> *Private James Turner of Lieutenant Colonel the Honourable James Stanhope's company of the 3rd Battalion 1st Foot Guards suffered an interesting injury from either an air or ground burst of a common shell. It was fortunate that the chunks of metal did not penetrate deeper. He was invalided out of the army on a pension of 6d per day on 22 August 1816 and resided in London. He was paid his Waterloo Prize Money in 1817.*

88. Sergeant Peter Matthews – 28th Regiment

Elizabeth

A musket ball entered at A & was voided by the rectum.

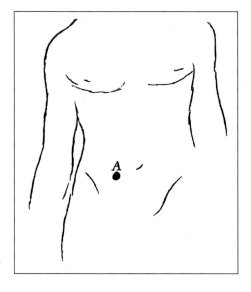

Sergeant Peter Matthews of Captain John Bowie's No.7 Company 28th Foot. This was a fortunate outcome for this man, since many of the wounds of the abdomen were fatal, through haemorrhage and sepsis. The missile had passed from right to left in the abdominal cavity, penetrated either right, transverse (less likely) or the left colon and been voided naturally. The injury to the bowel might have resulted in fatal sepsis, by leakage of faecal material from the colon, but the leakage may have been slight as the mucosa (inner lining of the bowel) would pout and swell, so to an extent sealing the entry wound and thus minimising the leak of gut contents. Also, the body's natural reaction to such an injury would be to wall off the leak area, particularly as the large fatty apron, hanging down from the transverse colon in the abdomen, acts as a sealant to the infected wound site in the gut wall. He did survive and was awarded his Waterloo Prize Money in 1817.

We learn further of this patient from George Guthrie and John Hennen:

Sergeant Peter Matthews of the 28th Regiment, was wounded at Waterloo by a musket ball in the abdomen, about an inch below the umbilicus, a little (three inches) to the right side, which lodged. Scarcely a tinge of blood followed the wound. He did not fall, but walked about fifty yards to the rear; from whence in half an hour, he was carried to a large barn in the village, where he remained for three days, before he was conveyed to an hospital in Brussels, having been bled each day to fainting. He was removed to Brussels, where my attention was particularly attracted to him, in consequence of his having passed the ball (a small rifle one) per annum enveloped in mucus, and unchanged in shape, except for a small groove indent probably from the bayonet or ramrod of the piece, three days after his arrival, or the sixth since receipt of the wound. The wound was healed by the 26th of August; and he felt so well that he marched to Paris with other convalescents, to join his regiment. But had not been there more than ten weeks, when he got drunk, and suffered from an attack of pain in the bowels in the situation of the wound, requiring active treatment. On attempting one day to have a motion, he found, after many efforts, that something blocked up the anus, and on taking hold and drawing it out, he found it was a portion of the waistband of his breeches, including a part of the button hole, a fact verified by Staff Surgeon Dease,[26] who wrote to me an account of this peculiar case. After this the man recovered without further difficulty, although as in all such cases, there was a hernia projection [through the wound site]. He afterwards was subject to costiveness, to pain in the part after a copious meal, probably from the stretch of the adhesions formed between the intestine and the abdominal peritoneum, which inclined him to bend his body forward to obtain relief. In September 1816, Doctor Hennen met him again in the South west of England and immediately recognised him. On examination, his abdominal wound was found perfectly healed, but if he indulged in a full meal or if slow to clear his bowels, the pain in the abdomen was very severe.[27]

89. Pierre Antoine

Gens d'Armerie

Musket ball entered at A & went out at B. Faeces discharged from the colon at A from the 18th till the 26th of June. Now by the natural passage only. Doing well.

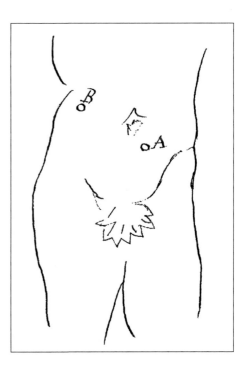

Here again, the colon has been damaged, but because the wound site in the abdomen has been walled off by adjacent tissues and the omentum (an internal fatty apron which acts as a 'policeman' and helps to seal off any septic focus in the abdomen) the faecal leak has been largely external. This faecal fistula has closed in eight days. Most such fistula leaks will close under normal conditions, particularly if there is not obstruction to the bowel below or downstream of the fistula.

26   Assistant Staff Surgeon James Dease.
27   Guthrie, *A treatise on gunshot wounds*, p.523, with further embellishments from John Hennen, *Principles of Military Service comprising Observations on the arrangement, police, and practise of hospitals* (London: Burgess & Hill,1829), p.408.

90. Libelle

Jesuits

Musket ball entered at A came out at B. Faeces pass at B when he coughs, but by his own report at that time only. General health improving.

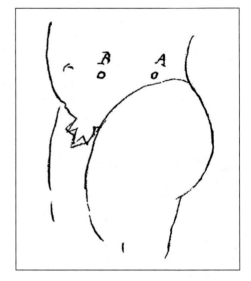

> *Another survivor, whose body had walled off the sepsis and only leaked faecal material when the intra–abdominal pressure was raised by the patient coughing.*

91. Captain – French Prisoner

Jesuits

Musket ball entered at A & remains lodged. Faeces passed by the wound from the 18th June on the evening till the morning of the 25th. Faeces have continued to pass by the proper passage ever since. Doing well.

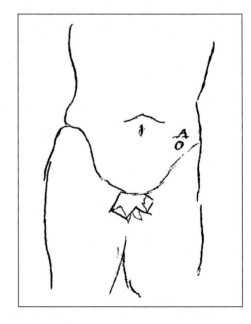

> *Here, the ball has damaged the left (descending) colon and the faecal fistula has been short-lived. This is because the ball had only partly opened the bowel wall. The fistula had closed rapidly in a week.*

92. Christian Wernberg

Facon
8 August

Musket ball entered an inch & a half above spine of Ilium, left side at A & came out between notch of Ilium & sacrum & a little above on the left side. Faeces were discharged at first at A. Is now doing well no faeces by the wound.

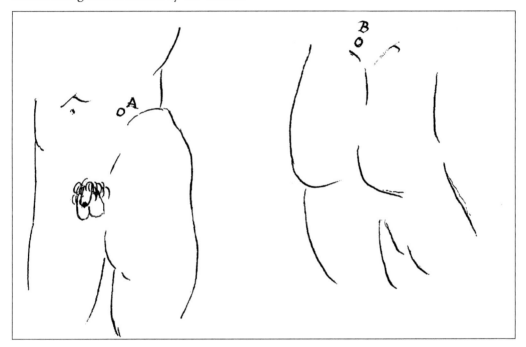

This refers to Private Christian Werneberg of the 1st KGL Line Battalion. The ball has penetrated with great force, but again has only partially wounded the wall of the gut, the fistula has closed. Werneberg survived and received his Waterloo Prize Money in 1817.

93. Anonymous

Corderie
9 August

Musket ball entered through the root of the penis & is lodged. Faeces are daily voided by the wound A.

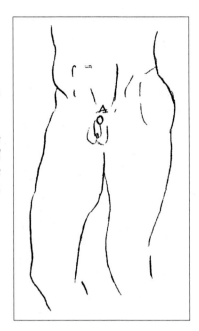

A French prisoner. The ball has passed above the pubic bone and injured some part of the colon, whose faecal contents are still being voided via the wound, but there is no comment on whether the bowels are still opening.

94. Jonathan Carter – 1st Guards

Annonciate

Musket ball entered left groin at A & passed out at right buttock. Faeces discharged by A (during a month) but this had ceased & he was doing well.

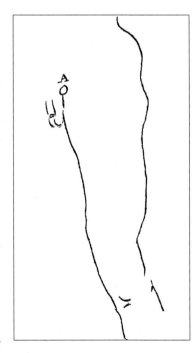

Here we have Private Jonathan Carter of Lieutenant Colonel Fead's No. 4 company of the 3rd Battalion 1st Foot Guards. It is surprising how many soldiers with penetrating lower belly wounds could survive even with bowel damage, without modern interventional surgery and other means of support. The duration of the fistula could be as long as several weeks. The unusual course of the missile and the patient's progress are further explained below. Carter was invalided from the army on 26 April 1816 when he was residing at Bath and he did receive his Waterloo Prize Money in 1817.

Report written by Mr Reid, Assistant Surgeon 25th Foot.

Private John Carter, 2nd Battalion [this is an error], 1st Foot Guards, was wounded at Waterloo, on the

18th of June 1815, by a musket ball, which passed obliquely through the long head of the triceps [an upper arm muscle] adductor of the left thigh [an inner thigh muscle], entered and passed through the lower part of the pelvis below the bladder, wounded the intestinum rectum, and passed out through the inferior portion of the right os ilium, leaving a slight degree of laceration in the gluteus maximus muscle. In order to explain the very extraordinary course of the wound, that the patient, when wounded, was in the act of kneeling on the right knee, in the front rank of his corps, prepara-tory to their receiving a column of French cavalry, which was advancing in front of them. He was brought into hospital, and had his wounds dressed on the third day after the action. During the first six days after his admission into hospital, his stools were passed by the posterior orifice of the wound in the thigh, but no part of them was ever passed by the posterior orifice in the ilium. From this day (27th of June) they were passed partly by the anterior orifice of the wound and partly naturally, at the intervals when he was usually called to stool, until the 20th of July, when the whole of the fecal [sic] discharge took the ordinary course. The only medicine administered during the cure was an occasional laxative to keep his stools liquid. His general health remained good and on discharge from hospital was nearly ready to return to duty.[28]

95. French prisoner

Gens d'Armerie

Musket ball entered [at] A & came out at B having wounded the kidney. Urine & air discharged at B.

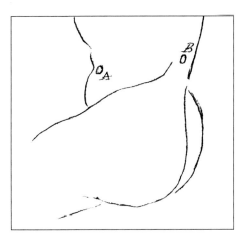

It is difficult to be sure whether the left kidney or the ureter (the thin muscular tube that takes the urine from the kidney to the bladder) had been wounded by the missile. It is most likely that the large bowel had also been wounded as there was an air but not a faecal leak from the wound on the Frenchman's back.

---

28 Hennen, *Principles of Military Service*, p.414.

96. George Walker – 92nd Regiment

Facon
7 August

Gangrene suddenly came on without apparent cause on the scrotum. All the parts greatly enlarged. Had the face of habitual intemperance. About 50 years of age.

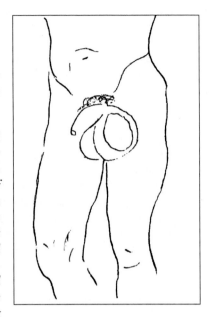

Private George Walker of Captain Donald MacDonald's No.7 Company 92nd Foot may or might not have been wounded preceding this infection and great swelling in the man's scrotum. If this patient was an alcoholic (or a diabetic), his local and general immune system might have been supressed. Had there had been scabies or an insect bite, scratching this area with a dirty fingernail would predispose the area to infection with a cocktail of aerobic and anaerobic bacteria. Walker had a patch of gangrenous skin over the outside of the scrotum. There would be a risk of this spreading with further sepsis and break down of tissue spreading up over the abdominal wall (called Fournier's gangrene). He actually survived his injuries as he received both his Waterloo Medal and Waterloo Prize Money.

97. Sergeant Winstanley – 1st Battalion 23rd Regiment

Annonciate

Ball entered to the left of the roof of the penis, passed through the bladder and out at right hip.

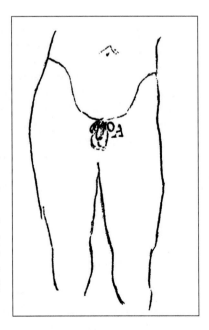

Sergeant Thomas Winstanley of Captain Farmer's No. 7 company 23rd Foot must have been shot at from fairly close range as the ball has gone through the pubic bone, through the bladder, and passing out through a variety of bones at the hip joint. There is no mention of a urinary leakage externally (a fistula) but if urine leaked into the surrounding tissues around the bladder sepsis was inevitable. He survived his wound and received his Waterloo Prize Money in 1817. Winstanley was born at Wigan and enlisted on 10 August 1799 aged 27. He served 21

years in the 23rd Foot (including his 2 years for Waterloo) and 2 ½ years previously in the 63rd Foot. He received a pension of 1 shilling per day when invalided on 9 August 1816 and was recorded as having been wounded in the groin and thigh at Waterloo. He became an in–pensioner on 1 April 1843. He records that he was in action in Holland 1799, Egypt 1801, Copenhagen, Martinique, Albuera, Salamanca, Vitoria, Toulouse, and Waterloo. He was wounded in the wrist in Egypt, in his left leg at Martinique, in his right thigh at Albuera, and also the right thigh and left groin at Waterloo. Whilst an in–patient his family lived in London.

98. Sordois

Corderie
9 August

A musket ball entered close to the root of the penis on the right side & passed out through the left hip posterior to the trochanter major [this is the prominence of the greater trochanter of the thigh bone – femur – felt as the most lateral feeling bone at the hip joint area] but in the line with it. The wound healed readily but a tumour from urinary fistula took place at B.

> *Here is another French prisoner. This is a very similar injury to the previous case. The position of the exit wound is incorrectly drawn*

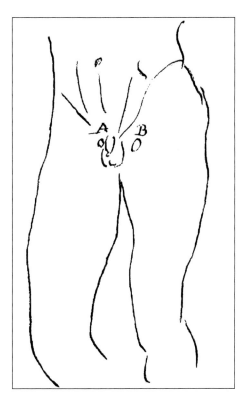

99. Philip Sandford – King's German Legion

Elizabeth
3rd August

Musket ball entered at A and is lodged. Every time he makes water a portion of urine is extended through the wound A.

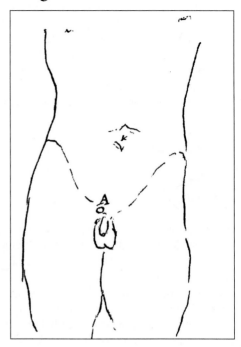

> *This is almost certainly Private Philip Sandvofs, from No. 3 Company 2nd KGL Light Battalion. There will have been only a small bladder defect here, since it took the raised intra–vesical pressure in the bladder, during voiding, before any urine was forced through the defect onto the patient's pubic area. It would soon close. The only risk was infection in the soft tissues surrounding the bladder. This soldier was one of the defenders of La Haye Sainte. Sandvof did survive and received his Waterloo Prize Money in 1817.*

100. Cornibert

Corderie
9 August

Musket ball entered left groin at A. The urine passed copiously by the wound for 3 or 4 weeks, but it has flowed entirely by the urethra lately.

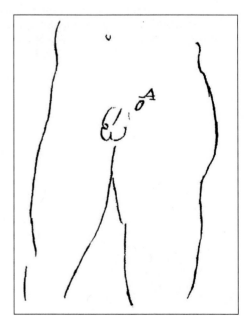

> *Cornibert was most likely a French prisoner. It is impressive in such cases, to witness the ability of the human body to afford survival from internal soiling and/or sepsis to such a degree.*

101. French man

Corderie
9 August

Musket ball lodged, when he makes water, part of it passes by the urethra, part of it by the wound & when the bladder is emptied, a purulent matter is discharged from the urethra.

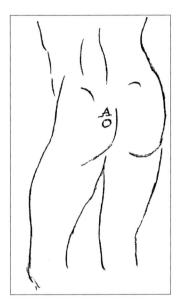

> *This is similar to the last case, except that we have a note that purulent material is discharged via the man's urethra after passing urine. The urethra is the normal passage for the patient's urine externally and here also was a conduit for drainage of the infected material ebbing to and fro, through the bladder wound and lying at the base of the bladder.*

102. Colombier

Corderie
9 August

Musket ball entered left groin at A & passed out through the left hip at B. Urine was discharged at the wound A, for some weeks but it is now almost entirely voided by the urethra & a small portion of it by the rectum.

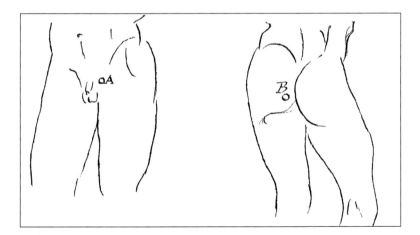

> *Another French prisoner, whose rectum and bladder was damaged by the ball, so urine is voided per rectum. The big risk here was the threatened infection from the large bowel bacteria.*

103. French prisoner

Jesuits

Musket ball entered at A & passed out at B. The kidney was wounded & urine was discharged for 25 days by A. It now flows by the natural passage only.

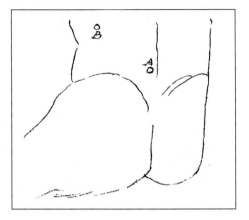

> *In this patient's case, either the left ureter or kidney was damaged and the resulting urinary fistula closed after three weeks or so. Very occasionally the ureter might be strictured (narrowed by scarring) with such an injury – leading to obstruction to the flow of urine from the kidney.*

104. Gondale

Corderie

Musket ball entered left testes, passed through both, entered right thigh, passed through it & came out posterior to the femur. The left testes hung out of the scrotum, was replaced. The wound closing & the patient doing well.

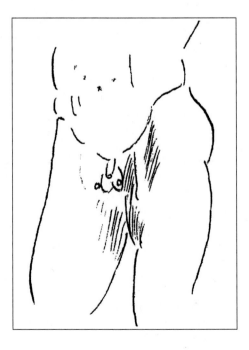

> *This sketch is of a French prisoner with clearly a highly painful, risky and unpleasant wounding. Probably the femur (thigh bone) was spared, but from the drawing there is extensive bruising of the thighs – especially the left. The testis, after replacement, would probably retain some function. If the wound was closed, then the wound edges would be approximated with twisted gut (catgut) sutures, which would be more effective than adhesive straps.*

105. Garnier

A musket ball entered at A, passed through the right thigh, both testes & the left thigh. Doing well.

> *A similar and relatively unusual case in a French prisoner, but the ball entered from behind, injuring both thighs and testes. There was extensive bruising and an unknown quantity of bony damage.*

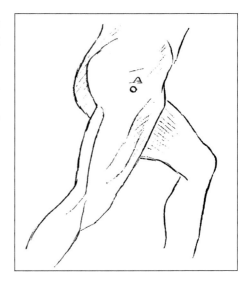

106. Julien

Corderie

Musket ball entered right side of penis at A & passed out through right hip.

> *Was the French prisoner's hip joint damaged? It appears that the penis had escaped trauma.*

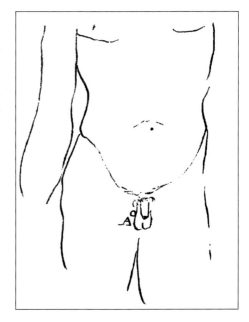

107. Thomas Daws – 71st Regiment

Jesuits

Musket ball entered at A & passed out of right hip.

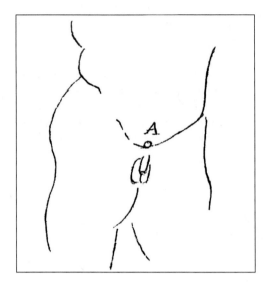

> *Similar wound to the last case. This person has been difficult to identify but would appear to be Private Thomas Dickie of Captain Joseph Pidgeon's company 71st Foot.*

Further information on this soldier is undoubtedly contained in this report by John Hennen:

> *T. D. aged 39, a soldier of the light infantry corps was wounded by a musket ball on the evening of the 18th of June 1815. It entered the pelvis at about one inch and a quarter from the symphysis of the pubes, grazing close to the bone, and came out unaltered in shape, through the buttock of the same side, about three inches from the sacrum. In this course the bladder, which was much distended with urine, was injured; great stupor and pain of the part were experienced on the receipt of the wound, and particularly affected the loins and testicle of the wounded side. He had a strong inclination to void his urine immediately after the receipt of the wound, and in doing so it passed entirely through the anterior opening over the pubes, and not a drop by the natural channel; the efforts to pass it were attended with severe pain (called strangury). At four weeks the urine still passed, but in small quantities, from the upper orifice. The urine had been almost constantly carried off by means of an elastic gum–catheter [i.e. a catheter which had been inserted by a surgeon]. Osseous grit [small bony fragments] passed through with the urine, the largest the size of a split pea. He was sent to England but eight months after, he continued to suffer. He produced a few pieces of bone which he had passed previously, rough and angular and about a third of an inch long.*[29]

---

29 Hennen, *Principles of Military Service* p.429.

108. James Chalmers – 1st Battalion, 95th Regiment

Facon

Musket ball entered at A, passed through & out of the buttock on the right side.

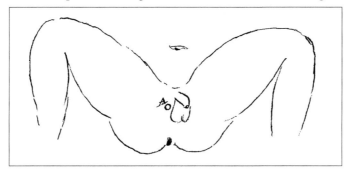

This was Corporal James Chambers of Captain Francis Glass's Company of 1st Battalion 95th Rifles. One has to wonder what position this patient was in when he received this wound. Was he lying down taking cover or kneeling? The ball has traversed the perineum, beside the urethra, and out through the mass of the buttock fat and muscle. Chambers was invalided out of the army in 1816 and did not receive his Waterloo Prize Money.

109. Manque François

Musket ball entered spine of Ilium at A left side, passed obliquely through and out at B right hip.

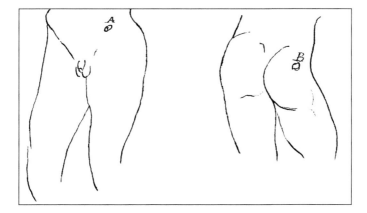

Regrettably, no detail of the severe damage done to this French prisoner's pelvis (bladder, bowel, blood vessels etc.) had been recorded. Likewise, there is no comment on his survival.

110. Blackburn

Jesuits

Musket ball entered right side at A & came out behind at B.

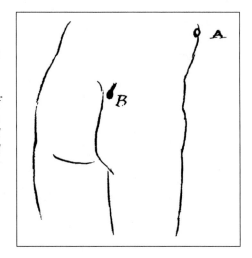

> *This is likely to refer to Thomas Blackburn of the Royal Horse Artillery, who had suffered a relatively superficial tracking wound around his right side and back. He was discharged from the army in 1816.*

111. Frenchman

Corderie
9 August

Musket ball passed from A to B.

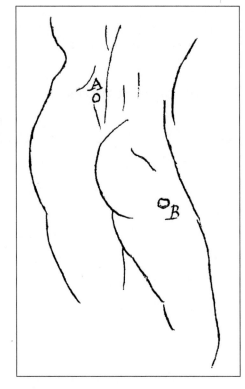

> *There is probably no deep penetration of this ball, which had tracked out to the right thigh.*

112. Richard Carpmeal – 1st Guards

Jesuits

Ball entered A & was cut out close to the anus at B on right side.

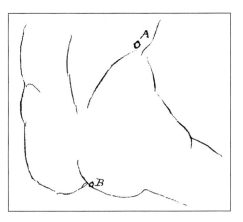

> *Actually, this drawing relates to Private Cartmeal of 2nd Battalion 1st Foot Guards. It is a similar case to the previous patient, but with clearly more risk of sepsis, from the proximity of the exit wound (with the surgical extraction) to the anus. He was discharged dead on 5 August 1815 (incorrectly shown as Cartmell in the Waterloo Medal Roll).*

113. Kenneth Macdonald – 79th Regiment

Jesuits

Musket ball entered at A and passed out at B.

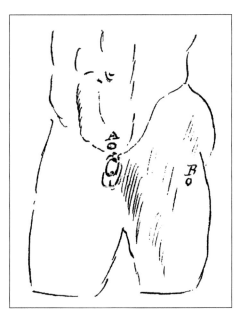

> *Private Kenneth Macdonald of Captain Peter Innes's No. 5 Company 79th Foot had been hit in the pelvic region. The ball has tracked in front near the root of the penis and exited in front of the major neurovascular structures deeper on the inner aspect of the thigh. There was extensive bruising as shown in the shading. The Waterloo Medal Roll states that MacDonald died on 6 March 1816. If this is the case, was it prolonged sepsis, or did the femoral artery get damaged and cause loss of the right leg (with or without amputation)? The Waterloo Prize Roll does not record his death and his Waterloo Prize Money was paid out in 1817, possibly to his family.*

114. John Haywood – 27th Regiment

Jesuits

This is Corporal John Haywood (spelt Heywood in the Waterloo Medal Roll). There is no comment about this patient whatsoever. This is a superficial wound damaging skin, fat and muscle. The shading suggests bruising over the left buttock, where blood, by gravity, had tracked down. When he retired on 16 September 1829 after nearly 25 years of service, he received a pension of 1 shilling 3½ d per day and resided at Uxbridge.

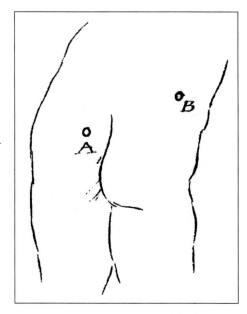

115. Hugh McLellan – 79th Regiment

Annonciate

Ball entered A & passed out at B, between the parietes[30]

Here we have Private Hugh McLennan of Captain James Campbell's No. 7 Company of the 79th Foot ('McLinnon' in the Waterloo Medal Roll). Hopefully, this was a superficial tracking wound. He certainly survived and received his Waterloo Prize Money in 1817.

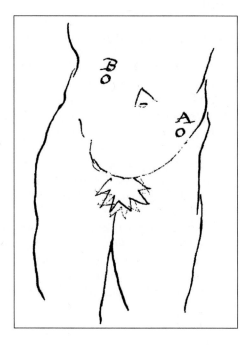

---

30 The constituents of the abdominal wall, i.e. the skin, fat, and three fine layers of muscle in the wall of the abdomen.

116. Pertrus Sprang

**Annonciate
9th August**

Ball passed from A to B. Doing well.

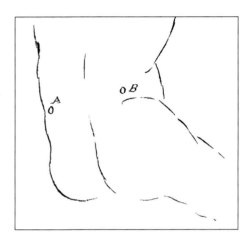

This was a superficial wound. It has proven impossible to discover anything regarding this person.

117. Peter Wardrop, 79th Regiment

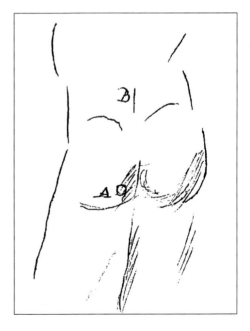

Musket ball entered at A & is lodged. Sharp pain is felt about B.

This is Private Peter Wardrop serving in Captain William Marshall's Light Company. The ball was retained and the pain felt at B as there had either been sacral nerve root irritation/damage or the ball had tracked up, after striking the ischial tuberosity (the pelvic bone we sit on). He survived and received his Waterloo Prize Money in 1817.

118. Captain Swinney – 1st Dragoon Guards

Was wounded by a Polish lancer on the right arm at A. The inside of the wrist was afterwards cut across by a sabre. The brachial artery was tied.

Severe pain in the arm which he inscribed to the lance wound attended with considerable swelling, constitutional symptoms severe.

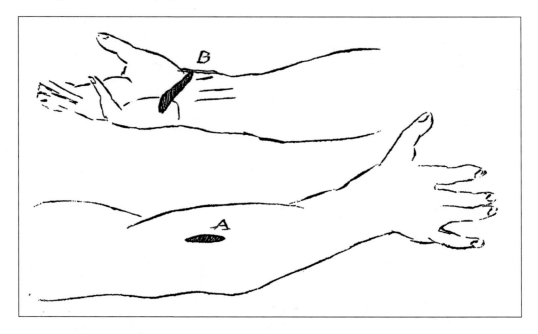

Actually this is Captain John Paget Sweeny of the 1st Dragoon Guards. He was probably injured in the left arm and wrist by either a lancer of the Imperial Guard or a cheveau–léger lancier *during the counter attack against the Union and Heavy Brigades. Body strikes with lances seemed to be less frequent than when inflicted on limbs, which probably reflects the wild manoeuvrings during the cavalry melées. From the above description, there may have been incipient sepsis in the lance wound. It is interesting that the brachial artery was ligated above the elbow, to control bleeding and to obviate any later secondary haemorrhage. There was a risk to this man's tendons, nerves, and arteries with the sabre strike. Sweeny survived and he became a major in August 1823, before he retired on half pay in 1825.*

119. Van de Boom

Annonciate
1 August

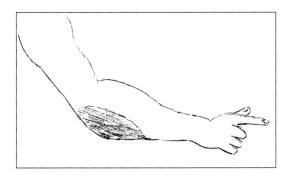

A piece of the muscles and integuments[31] cut off by a sabre, the forearm swelled to a prodigious size.

> *This probably refers to Private Herman Vanderbon of Captain George Hattorff's No. 1 Troop of the 1st KGL Light Dragoons. This was a painful and debilitating wound of the right arm and the back of the elbow. It was an open wound, so although there was much oedema (swelling), the sepsis was better controlled by allowing free drainage from it, into the dressings. His records show that he did not receive his Waterloo Prize Money and it is probable that he was discharged from the army.*

120. William Porteous – Scotch Greys

Elizabeth

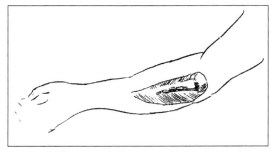

Was cut by a lance on the left arm, the head and a considerable proportion of the bone was laid bare by ulceration. He had also received seven pike [sic lance] wounds in different parts. The rotating motion of the bone was easily performed.

> *Sergeant William Porteous of Captain Barnard's No.1 or A Troop, 2nd Royal North British Dragoons suffered a painful wound, possibly in the counterstrike by the French cavalry after the famous charge of the Greys. This wound probably escaped sepsis and would have healed by second intention, leaving a deep scar. Many of the allied heavy cavalry casualties received multiple lance wounds from repeated stabbings, all of which is rather reminiscent of the aggressive behaviour of the Vistula Lancers at Albuera. The head and shaft of the radius are exposed and the head of the bone retained its rotational movements in its socket.*
>
> *Born in Stenten, Haddington, and a labourer by trade, Porteous had enlisted in 1794, when his height was recorded as 6ft 1in. He remained in Brussels until September 1815 and was discharged from the army in October 1816 because of the damage to his elbow. He appears to have received a pension of 1 shilling and 3d per day.*

31 Fat, tendon, and muscle.

121. James Bruce – 2nd Dragoons

Elizabeth
3 August

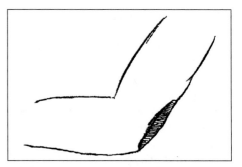

Had a slice cut off his left arm by a sabre. A musket ball passed through his right arm & he received 13 lance wounds. The left arm was swelled to a prodigious size.

Trooper James Bruce of Captain Poole's Troop of the Scots Greys suffered a slicing wound. Possibly this trooper had raised his left arm in defence and he might have been holding his sabre in his left hand, as his right had been disabled by the bullet wound. This large open would heal slowly with scarring. He was subject to repeated lance strikes, many of them received after wounding. Bruce was discharged on 2 November 1815 on a pension of 9d per day, although he did receive his Waterloo Prize Money in 1817. Bruce lived at Linlithgow in Stirlingshire and he was still living in 1865. James Bruce's Waterloo medal was reported as being sold from Colonel Gaskell's sale and resold at Christie's on 16 March 1965.

122. James Pierce – 32nd Regiment

Facon

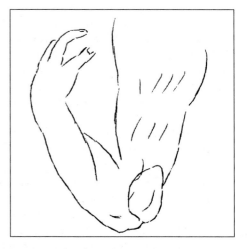

Sloughing sore from a g[un] shot wound in the left arm.

Private James Pearce of Captain John Crowe's no. 10 company 32nd Foot had been struck on the left arm. The ball has removed a chunk of skin, fat, and muscle just above Pearce's left elbow joint. The slough might have been trimmed away fairly painlessly by the surgeon and the wound dressed with damp lint and a roller bandage, using a sling to support the arm. Pearce survived and was awarded his Waterloo Prize Money in 1817. He had served 7½ years when he was wounded in the abdomen and bowels at Waterloo, the ball remaining, which bent him double. Surprisingly, this latter wounding had not been reported here. He was listed at his medical board to be an out-pensioner in August 1857 when he was 73 and living in Bath, also that he had served at Copenhagen, Corunna, Roliça, Vimeiro, the taking of Flushing, Salamanca, Pamplona, Pyrenees, Nive, Nivelle, and Orthez. He was on a pension of 6d per day. He claimed to have been a corporal, but is shown in the records as a private. He died on 9 May 1867.

123. Terance McCann – 32nd Regiment

Facon
3 August

Left arm wounded by a musket ball passing through at A. Sloughing sores on the parts separated by an isthmus almost entirely of integuments. Mr Blicke cut this band to make one ulcer.

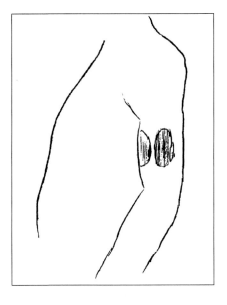

Private Terence McCann of Captain William Toole's no. 7 company of the 32nd Foot also suffered an arm wound. The ball has passed across and along the lateral (outside) of the biceps area and created a tunnel with a bridge of skin and fat and exposed or damaged some muscle. Staff Surgeon Blicke has cut away the bridge to expose the whole ulcerated surface, which would eventually have healed with dressings and patience. He was discharged from the army but did receive his Waterloo Prize Money in 1817.

124. Richard Amos – 32nd Regiment

Augustines

Two balls entered the same place of right arm. One went through. Pulsation of artery seen in the fluctuation of the surface of the pus at the wound at A.

Actually Private Richard Hamos of the 32nd Foot. Was this a fluke event with two separate missiles passing at exactly the same spot, or was this a double-shotted musket load? There is obviously a larger wound than would usually have occurred with a single missile, but we are not sure where the ball that 'went through' exited. Some muscle has been damaged. The brachial artery, which was observed pulsating at the base of the sloughy ulcer, had fortunately, thus far, escaped damage. He received his Waterloo Prize Money in 1817.

125. Maas – a German

Annonciate

A shell glanced over the right shoulder & occasioned extensive ulceration.

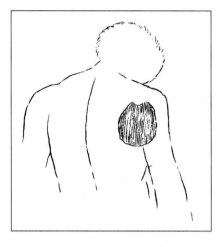

This is almost certainly Private Jacob Maas (incorrectly spelt Maafs in the Waterloo Medal Roll) of the Grenadier Company of the 5th KGL Line Battalion. Whether this was a glancing strike by a whole shell round or by a large fragment remains unclear. There had been a powerful shearing force, which had deprived the skin, some fat, and probably muscle of adequate blood supply. Those ischaemic (deprived of their blood supply) tissues have thus sloughed and probably remained smelling and adherent for a good while. However, the slough would have eventually separated or been cut away. Today the area would have received a skin graft to accelerate healing and improve cosmetic appearance. Jacob Maas appears to have been discharged and certainly did not receive his Waterloo Prize Money.

126. Colonel Bock

A cannon ball struck him on the posterior part of the left upper arm but [at the time of wounding] did not even discolour his skin or occasion any immediate apparent injury. A very extensive & troublesome ulceration with destruction of integuments on the posterior part of upper arm ensued & another is forming on the shoulder. Great debility and irritation.

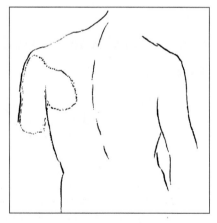

This is a truly fascinating case. I believe that this was a shearing and tangential strike, but what is strange is that there was originally no skin abrasion or subcutaneous bleeding and bruising. The damage has occurred to the skin fat and muscles on the back of his arm and shoulder, which would have been very painful. These tissues died and sloughed. The question of damage by the 'wind of the ball'; might creep into our thoughts, something that modern scientists declare is physically impossible. It just may be that the colonel's clothing had prevented worse shear but not the serious tangential force of the iron missile.

Surprisingly, given his rank, it has proven impossible to definitely identify him. It may refer to Lieutenant Colonel Hans von dem Bussche of the 1st KGL Light Battalion who is recorded as having been severely wounded and eventually had his arm amputated.

127. Joseph Badon – Royal Artillery

Elizabeth
2 August

Musket ball passed through the right shoulder. Joint rigid. Patient well.

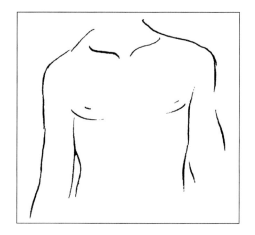

> *This was probably Private Joseph Barber of the Royal Artillery. The entry or exit wounds have been omitted from the sketch. Barber's shoulder would remain stiff for ever and he would have been lucky to escape sepsis. Barber did survive and received his Waterloo Prize Money.*

128. Thomas Draper – 1st Royal Dragoons

Elizabeth
3rd August

Musket ball entered at A & came out at B.

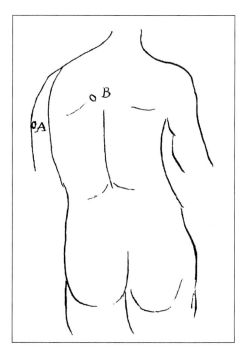

> *Private Thomas Draper of Captain Paul Phipp's No.5 or F Troop 1st Royal Dragoons escaped severe injury here, but the ball exited through the left arm, possibly injuring the triceps muscle, but the missile strike might have remained more superficial than this. He was discharged on 4 October 1816 with a pension of 1 shilling and 1d (penny) per day and he still received his Waterloo Prize Money in 1817. He died at Devizes on 14 June 1847 aged 77 years old.*

129. Robert Hyde – 1st Guards

Jesuits

Musket ball entered left shoulder at A & was cut out at B.

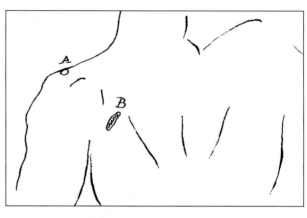

Private Robert Hyde of Captain Edward Staples No. 2 Company of 3rd Battalion 1st Foot Guards. There had been an incision over the area where the ball had been cut out. By and large, when compared with modern high energy transfer weaponry, musket ball exit wounds were not as large when compared with the entry wound. He was discharged from the army in 1816 but received his Waterloo Prize Money in 1817. Hyde was born in Ryall, Eden in Yorkshire enlisting at the age of 23. He served for just over 9 years with the 1st Foot Guards (including 2 years for Waterloo) before he was discharged because of a 'wound through the shoulder joint at Waterloo'. He had previously served 4 ½ years in the 6th Dragoon Guards. At his discharge on 22 May 1816, he was 30 years old, 5 feet 7¼ inches tall, light hair, grey hair and with a fresh complexion. His trade was previously a labourer and he was unable to write, marking his discharge papers with an X. He appears to have died at Halifax on 3 October 1850.

130. Quin – 27th Regiment

Elizabeth
2nd August

Musket ball entered the left shoulder at A & is lodged.

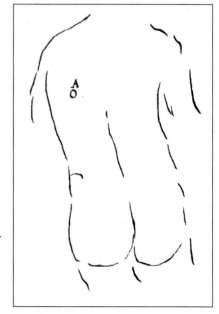

This was one of the two Privates named James Quinn of the 27th Foot. The wound was rather too deep to find easily, but the surgeon would have put his finger in to explore the accessibility of the buried missile. It might have been tricky to recover it from beneath the trapezius muscle (a large triangular muscle on the back). Quinn was pensioned as an out-patient on 11 June 1817 receiving a pension of 6d initially, slowly rising to 1 shilling per day. He died on 26 June 1849 aged 56.

131. Christian Schroder

Annonciate
1st August

A grape shot entered at A & passed out at B.

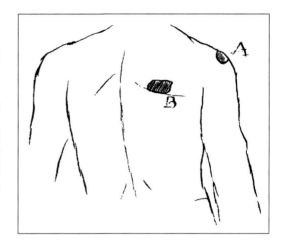

> *This is most likely Private Christian Schroder of 1st KGL Light Dragoons. There are seemingly larger than usual entrance and exit wounds, probably from resulting sepsis. He survived and received his Waterloo Prize Money in 1817.*

132. William Fish – 7th Light Dragoons

A canon ball carried away the integuments & muscles & shattered the head of the humerus, Mr Blicke cut out four inches of the bone disengaging the head from its socket having sawn the bone across. The head of the humerus had begun to exfoliate. The operation performed the 3rd Augt., the greater part of the processus acromion [the outer bone felt

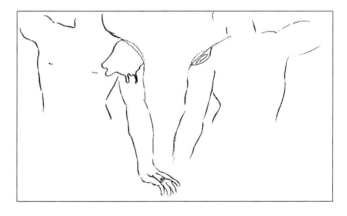

above the shoulder joint] carried away, Appearances favourable beyond what might have been expected. The incision from the sore part down to A [not marked in sketch] was healing.

This case afforded Mr Blicke an opportunity of shewing his dexterity in the application of sticking plasters[32] & bandages.

> *William Fish did not survive this fairly conservative operation of removal of the shattered head of Fish's humerus from the shoulder joint and was discharged dead.*

---

32   Adhesive plasters – strips of linen spread over with various sticky ingredients such as gum acacia.

133. John Young – 92nd Regiment

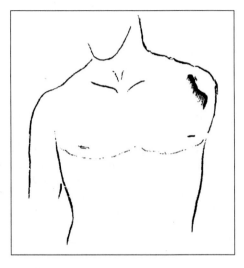

Left arm taken out at the socket by Staff Surgeon Hennen on the 18th day, after the arm was wounded. Healing rapidly 30th July.

Private John Young of Captain Donald McDonald's No.7 Company of the 92nd Foot was probably lodged at the Jesuits Hospital, since that is where John Hennen worked.[33] *The patient might have received a round shot injury to his left arm. The experienced surgeon John Hennen had removed his left arm at the shoulder joint – a disarticulation. The wound as shown is three weeks old and is a little wide. It was closed with tapes, with or without sutures. He recovered from his wound and received his Waterloo Medal and Waterloo Prize Money in 1817.*

134. An officer of artillery

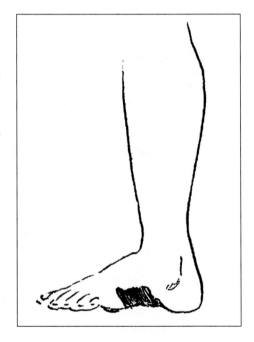

A nine–ounce iron grape shot was lodged in the side of the left foot twelve days. It was then extracted. The foot doing well.

This was a very painful and temporarily disabling injury, attended by the risk of tetanus from contamination by manured soil.

---

33   Dr John Hennen was a remarkably successful and well–known Irish surgeon, served initially with the 30th Regiment and was appointed as a staff surgeon in 1811. He served in the Peninsula, published widely, but tragically died of Yellow Fever in 1828.

135. John Gory – 52nd Regiment

Jesuits

Musket ball is lodged having entered at A.

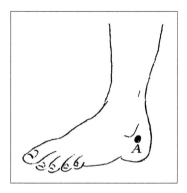

> *Private John Gorey of Captain Charles Diggle's No. 6 Company of the 1st Battalion 52nd Foot had an extremely painful wound and was also at risk from osteomyelitis of the calcaneum (heel bone) – and tetanus. He survived, receiving his Waterloo Medal and his Waterloo Prize Money in 1817.*

136. Lieutenant Colonel Beckwith

A musket ball lodged in the left leg. The tibia felt to be splintered, by the probe a fungus growth from the wound. Amputation performed on 31st July. The tibia was found [to be] splintered into many fragments, to a considerable extent.

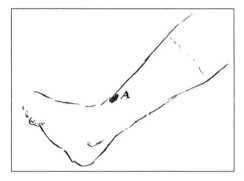

> *This was actually Major Charles Beckwith of the 95th Rifles who served at Waterloo as an Assistant Quartermaster General.*

Surgeon Hutchinson gives us more detail of this case.

> *My friend Lieutenant Colonel Beckwith, of the 95th, who underwent amputation of the left leg, both bones of which had been fractured close to the ankle joint, by a grape shot which lodged in the part. This gallant officer was totally unacquainted with his calamitous wound, till informed of it sometime after by a staff officer, who first called his attention to the circumstance, on perceiving a stream of blood flowing from the boot and stirrup iron to the ground; and after such a lapse of time, the loss of blood must have been considerable, which produced some degree of faintness.[34]*
>
> *Because of the comment about the 'fungus', we know that Beckwith has an unhealthy and infected wound. He is suffering from a chronic osteomyelitis. This would never have been cured except with the removal of all infected fragments of bone (sequestra). Without surgery this would prove to be a long and stormy progress, with risk to the colonel's life. A below knee amputation has been carried out – we can see a faint line drawn on the leg, which indicates the level of section of the leg. He died as a major general on 19 July 1862.*

---

34 A.C. Hutchinson, *Some Practical Observations in Surgery* (London: Underwood, 1816); he was Principal Surgeon at the Royal Navy Hospital in Deal.

137. General Adam

Musket ball entered at A right leg, passed between the bones & is lodged & two fragments of cloth pantaloon were extracted by a counter opening, in the calf of the leg.

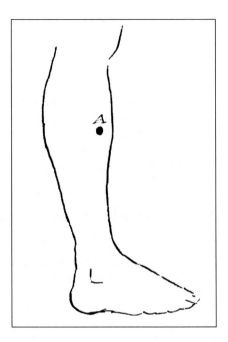

The patient was Major General Frederick Adam. It seems that the tibia and fibula (the two bones in the leg that the ball passed between) may have been intact – this was fortunate. Also it was commendable that the fragments of the pantaloons were successfully removed. These were a potent source of sepsis, although, admittedly, a senior officer's overalls (trousers) would likely be cleaner than a private soldier's! Counter incisions were made on the opposite side to the wound or original incision, often as an additional drainage procedure. This officer's brigade (3rd Brigade in Henry Clinton's 2nd Division) played a pivotal role in the final defeat of the Imperial French Guard. Adam retained his leg and survived until 17 August 1853.

138. Colonel Llewellyn

Musket ball entered front of right leg, shattered the tibia, many fragments of bone exfoliated and denuded bone still felt.

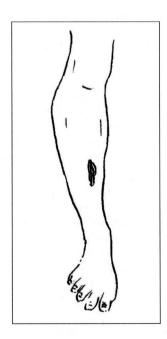

Actually the patient was Major Richard Llewellyn of the 28th Foot, he was made a brevet Lieutenant Colonel for Waterloo. This is a compound fracture with infection. The method of splinting has not been described. If his fibula was intact, the fracture would be in better alignment. This area is notable for its poor skin healing. He is believed to have retained his leg and later became a general, spelling his name Lluellyn. He died on 7 December 1867.

139. Lieutenant Douglas – 7th Hussars

Tibia right leg fractured, by a musket ball which went through.

Here we have Lieutenant Robert Douglas of the 7th Hussars. The same comments apply as in the last case. His leg was saved, but he quit the service in 1822.

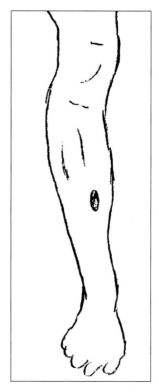

140. Pierre Louis

Elizabeth
2nd August

Musket ball fractured right tibia. Now doing well

There has been extensive skin loss here, possibly due to poor blood supply or infection.

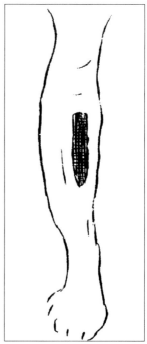

141. Thomas Fervel, 15th Light Dragoons

Elizabeth

Tibia & fibula fractured by grape shot. Doing well.

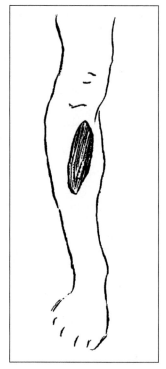

> *This probably refers to Private Thomas Fletcher of the 15th Hussars. We can see a large soft tissue loss here, since the missile strike wound has become infected. Thomas Fletcher survived and received his Waterloo Prize Money.*

142. John Dawson – Coldstream Guards

Facon
7 August

Sloughing ulcer on left leg.

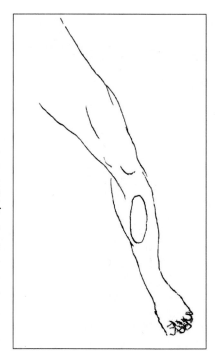

> *This patient was Private John Dawsel (Dawshell in the Waterloo Medal Roll – Dawshill in his pension papers) of Lieutenant Colonel the Honourable Hercules Pakenham's 6th Company of the 2nd Battalion Coldstream Guards. We have no idea of the cause of this man's injury, but it was probably secondary to a tangential small arms bullet strike that has become infected. There appears to be no bony injury. He survived and received his Waterloo Medal and his Waterloo Prize Money in 1817. He was at age 39, granted a pension of 9d per day in 1832 having served 18½ years as a private.*

143. John Robine – German Legion Light Battalion

Augustines

Wounded through left leg by a musket ball. Gangrenous sore with extensive sloughing on both sides, by which bones & blood vessels exposed to view. The surgeon could pass the forceps upwards from the cavity on the inside of the leg until they were entirely hid [sic] under the parts.

Possibly Private Jurgen Rohbern 2nd KGL Light Battalion. The soldier was fortunate if he kept his leg with this wound. There was extensive skin loss and muscle damage. The wounded part had much dead tissue on it and we do not perceive that there would have been débridement (cleaning the wound then removing all dead and dying tissues, the retention of which could lead to infection). The exposure of the blood vessels could mean secondary haemorrhage and a great threat to life. As skin cover would be difficult, the only two outcomes would be slow healing by second intention and scarring or above knee amputation. Rohbern survived and received his Waterloo Prize Money.

144. Mathew Kirkland – 3rd Guards

Minime[s]

Tibia laid bare by sloughing, hospital sore.

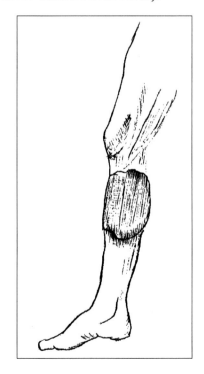

Private Mathew Kirkland of Lieutenant Colonel Charles Dashwood's No. 2 Company of the 2nd Battalion 3rd Foot Guards has received a wound resulting in extensive loss of skin, fat, and some muscle on his leg. Although there was a large sloughing area (i.e. covered in dead tissue and purulent material), this might eventually have healed with a scar covered with thin fragile skin. This area has a poor blood supply. He survived but was discharged from the army on 16 August 1816 living in Hinckley, he did receive his Waterloo Prize Money in 1817. He was still alive in 1864.

145. William Fitzpatrick – 92nd Regiment

Facon
6thAugust

Musket ball entered left leg at A and passed through, sloughing ulcers on both sides.

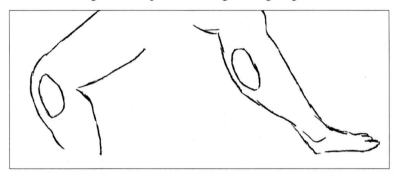

This case is that of Private William Fitzpatrick of Captain Angus Fraser's No. 6 Company 1st Battalion 92nd Foot. A is not marked, but it is likely that there would be a fracture of the upper tibia and fibula and/or the bones around the knee joint. An amputation was necessary. No note is made but he was not issued his Waterloo Prize Money. He was discharged from the service on 31 July 1816 and received a pension of 1 shilling and 3d per day and resided at Maryboro before moving to Liverpool. He was still living in 1864.

146. James Biggs – 4th Regiment

Facon
8 August

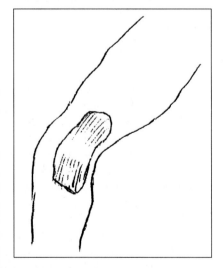

A musket ball slightly grazed the outside of the limb passing from A upwards without penetrating deep. A gangrenous ulcer now occupies the part.

This case relates to Private James Biggs of Captain Wood's Light Company 1st Battalion 4th Foot. Thankfully, the wound was superficial and an ulcer with dead (gangrenous) tissue had resulted. The slough would be treated with dilute mineral acids or lunar caustic (silver nitrate). With patience and dressing the wound would have healed. No note is made on his record, but he did not receive his Waterloo Prize Money. He retired on 15 May 1817 on a pension of 6d per day. He died at Windsor on 23 September 1849 aged 54.

147. Sergeant Alexander Sutherland – 2nd Battalion 3rd Guards

Facon
9 August

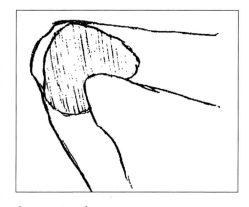

Was one of the many examples of bad ulcer where wounded men had been in private houses where they were indulged with the most unsuitable diet. He was brought from a private house to this hospital on the 6th July when the people who had acted from kindness found him getting rapidly worse.

Musket ball had passed through below the bone of the thigh upwards & out. The sore now clean & puts on a healthy appearance. Patient greatly emaciated.

Sergeant Alexander Sutherland of Lieutenant Colonel Charles West's No. 10 company was fortunate that the ball had passed below his femoral artery and missed the knee joint. The deep muscular wound had been treated and was 'now clean', but the sepsis and loss of protein had caused him great weight loss. It is an interesting case report as it castigates the kindness of the 'private house' dwellers for plying him with meat, wine etc., which in contemporary theory of early convalescence was not recommended and such relapses as did occur frequently, were often blamed on excess alcohol.

Sutherland is incorrectly ranked in the Medal Roll, as a private soldier. It is recorded that Sergeant Alexander Sutherland was discharged dead a few weeks later.

148. William Miller – 1st Battalion 79th Regiment

Facon
9 August

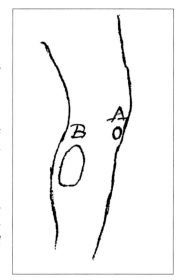

Musket ball had entered at A. The wound occasioned by it is now healed. A sloughing foul ulcer exists at B with constitutional symptoms. The sore is deep, wider in its circumference within than the aperture in the integuments show. The edges of the integuments hang loose & flabby over the hole which is precisely as if it had been what workmen call countersunk.

Private William Miller of Captain Thomas Mylne's No. 3 Company 79th Foot had been hit on his leg. We don't know if the tibia was fractured in this wound. Today the soft tissues would be thoroughly cored out and all dead and dying tissues excised. This is called débridement, which literally means 'unbridling' or releasing tension in the tissues, but in fact now means thoroughly cleaning out the wound cutting back to clean fresh tissues.

The infection must have got the better of Miller (Millar in the Prize Money Roll) as the medal roll lists him as dead on 28 December 1815. The Prize Money Roll records him discharged dead, but interestingly his Prize Money was still paid out, presumably to his family.

149. Thomas Bryan – 2nd Battalion 73rd Regiment

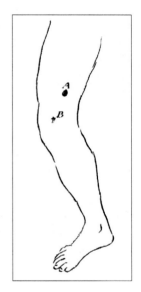

Ball lodged in the right thigh having entered at A. Complains of acute pain on the inner edge of the patella at B.

This is Private Thomas Bryant of Captain John Pike's no. 2 company 2nd Battalion 73rd Foot. The question must be, was the ball lodged near the patella (kneecap) or had it damaged the cutaneous nerves around that area, to give referred pain? He survived and received his Waterloo Prize Money in 1817. Bryant was born at Ware in Hertford. He enlisted at Hatfield on 21 April 1813 aged 17. He served 6 years (including 2 years for Waterloo). He was discharged on 4 June 1817 because of a wound to his right knee with a pension of 6d per day. On discharge, he was aged 21, he was 6 feet and ¼ of an inch tall, with brown hair, grey eyes and a fair complexion. His original trade was as a baker.

150. French Prisoner

Gens d'Armerie

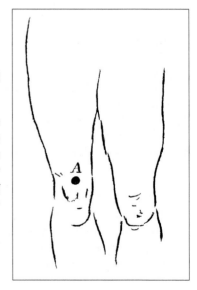

Musket ball entered at A and is lodged. Patient doing well.

The missile must have damaged the quadriceps tendon (the tendon which arises from all the large front thigh muscles, encloses the kneecap and inserts into the top of the tibial bone) and the suprapatellar bursa (a small lubricated sac which helps the gliding movements of the knee joint) and interfered considerably with flexion of the right knee joint.

151. John Milloato[?]

Jesuits

Musket ball entered at A and lodged.

We can add little here to the comments made for the last case.

152. Richard Macruerun– 27th Regiment

Facon
7 August

Musket ball entered [at A] & passed thro' B left knee. Copious Synovial discharge.

This must refer to Private Richard McCrakin. The knee joint has been damaged and the wound discharged synovial fluid, which is a clear viscous lubricating liquid that helps the joint move smoothly. This wound was painful and the soldier might well end up with sepsis, a stiff joint, or an above knee amputation. We are not told if there was any bone damage.

The Medal Roll shows him as 'discharged'. He was invalided out on a pension of 9d per day on 19 September 1816 (increased to a shilling per day in 1856). He died on 14 June 1860 aged 73.

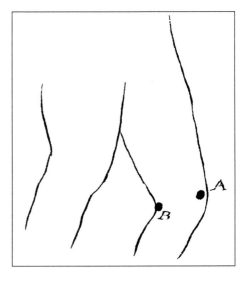

153. Anonymous

Corderie
9 August

Sabre cuts. Adhesion has taken place of the flap.

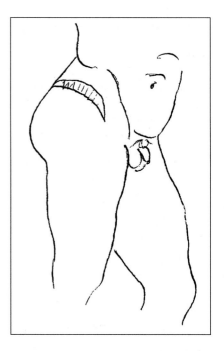

> *This wound had probably been caused by a downward stroke of a cavalry sabre and had cut through skin, fat, and some of the gluteal (buttock) musculature. The lower flap had retracted and has not been sewn or stuck together. This was a consequence of delay in presentation.*

154. John Adge – 42nd Regiment

Facon
9 August

Fascia sloughing on the upper wound at A.

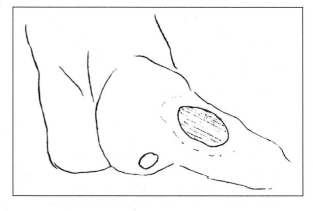

> *This is the case of Private John Adge of Captain Murdoch McLaine's No. 2 Company 42nd Foot. There may have been a gunshot wound or a sabre slash inflicted on the outer aspect of Adge's thigh. Alternatively, a ball had entered the buttock and exited from the thigh. The buttock ulcer could be a pressure sore with the man lying in bed for a long while. The fascia covering the large Vastus lateralis (the large muscle on the outside of the thigh) muscle is exposed and was sloughing through sepsis and a poor blood supply. The Medal Roll states that he was 'Discharged'. He was paid his Waterloo Prize Money in 1817.*

155. Victor – French Prisoner

Gens d'Armerie

Left Thigh wounded by a ball.

It looks as though the ball had scoured a relatively superficial groove in the outer aspect of this soldier's thigh and this had resulted in a long ulcer.

156. Kahle Trauberg a German

Annonciate

A cannon ball struck the left thigh on the outside slanting along it & deprived the muscles of their covering. The muscles protruded through the fascia to a great extent producing a most extraordinary appearance with as little promise of this sort of Hernia [of muscle tissue] being reduced as can be supposed. The judicial attentions of the Staff Surgeon Brownrigg were in the way of accomplishing a cure to which great progress had been made.

This is Private Charles Troberg of 1st Troop KGL Horse Artillery. This wound had resulted from a glancing blow by a round shot that sheared off the skin, fat and the fascia (the sheet of fibrous tissue covering the muscle). Deprived of its covering, the soft red muscle bulged as a large hernia through the skin. This would gradually become covered with granulation tissue and heal very slowly, leaving a large scar.

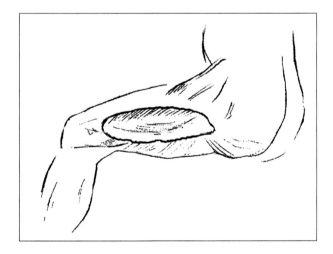

157. Lewis Blake – 32nd Regiment

Facon
8 August

Musket ball entered at A, passed through. He was well the wound however opened & became gangrenous & a second one took place at B.

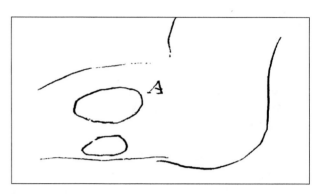

Private Lewis Blake of Captain John Crowe's No.10 Company 32nd Foot had a through and through thigh wound, with no obvious bony, arterial or nerve damage. Sepsis has set in and like most of the other similar wounds, the dead sloughy tissue had not been removed – further evidence that many of the wounds were not thoroughly cut back to viable and clean tissues (débridement). Larrey was supposed to have introduced this important procedure into the Service de Santé, but there is little evidence of it. Lewis Blake was discharged in 1816 but he did receive his Waterloo Prize Money in 1817. He was born at Great Torrington near Chiddlehampton in Devon. He served 13 years with the 32nd Foot (including 2 years for Waterloo) and having been discharged in 1817 as an out-pensioner for 18 months, he was allowed to join the 3rd Royal Veteran Battalion, in which he served from 12 November 1819 until 31 October 1820 when he was again discharged. In 1820 he was described as being 38 years old, 5 foot 8 inches tall, with brown hair, grey eyes and a brown complexion. His previous trade was recorded as a labourer.

158. Gilbert Ross – 92nd Regiment

Facon
8 August

Musket entered at the upper wound A [not marked] & passed out at B. Both are now sloughing sores.

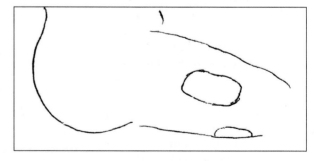

Here is Private Gilbert Ross of Captain Donald McDonald's No. 7 Company 92nd Foot. This is a soft tissue wound only – there is no comment on therapy. Ross was not paid his Waterloo Prize Money in 1817. He was invalided and granted a pension of 9d per day on 21 June 1816 and he resided at Inverness and then Thurso. He was still living in 1865.

159. Corporal Hall – 1st Royals

Facon
8 August

Musket ball passed through left thigh [marked 'outside of left Thigh' on line drawing] from A to B [not marked], sores are now gangrenous.

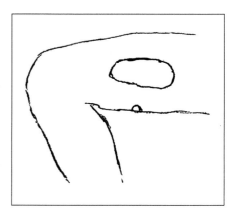

> *This is probably Corporal Michael Hart of Captain John McRa's company of the 1st Foot. This more superficial, rather than bone smashing small arms injury seems to be a fairly frequent type of wound. Whether there has been delay in transfer or any sort of neglect of treating the 'gangrenous' areas, we are not told.*

160. Anonymous

Corderie
9 August

One of the gangrenous sores of the greatest extent of surface occupying the right hip, upper part of the thigh up to [the] Ilium.[35]

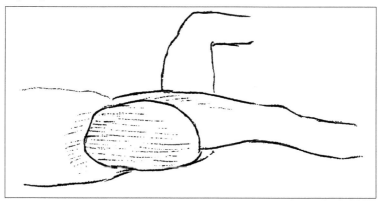

> *Just the same challenge as the preceding cases but with a greater risk from sepsis, particularly necrotising fasciitis. This is a rapidly spreading infected gangrene, which will overcome the patient with septicaemia (sometimes named 'hospital gangrene' or, by the French, 'Pourriture d'hôpital').*

35   The ridge of the bony pelvis, felt at the lower part of the flank

161. Philip Parker – 1st Guards

Jesuits

Musket ball entered left thigh above the knee at A & was cut out close to the Scrotum at B.

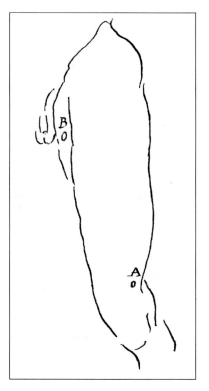

> *Private Philip Parkes of Lieutenant Colonel Sir Henry Harding's No. 2 Company 2nd Battalion 1st Foot Guards had an interesting wound. Since we can surmise that the missile strike was received whilst the soldier was kneeling. It had probably tracked fairly superficially, being a spent round, and ended up near the left side of the scrotum. This is not a particularly safe area for a wound as it is close to the moist perineum and anus, with inevitable septic risk from bowel bacteria. Philip Parkes was born at Unston in Derbyshire, and he enlisted at Sheffield on the 6 December 1813 at the age of 19 on unlimited service. He served just over five years (including 2 years for Waterloo). He was discharged on the 12 March 1817 because of a 'wound through the thigh received at Waterloo'. His conduct was noted as 'Very bad'. At his discharge he was 22 years old, 5 feet 8 inches in height, with light hair, hazel eyes, and a fair complexion. His previous trade was as a saw handle maker. He lived in Sheffield and he died on 10 January 1852.*

162. French Prisoner

Gens d'Armerie
31 July

Musket ball entered at A passed upwards & out at B. No bad symptom.

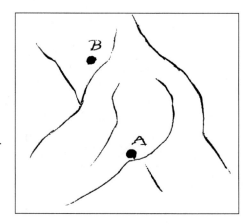

> *The ball, entering below the left buttock on its course, probably encountered the tough area of the left aspect of the greater trochanter (the bony protuberance at the upper end of the thigh bone) of the left femur, outside the hip joint. This was a deflecting factor driving the partially spent ball up onto the left flank.*

163. [A] German

Facon

Musket ball entered at A & passed out immediately above the hip joint. Many fragments of bone discharged at B.

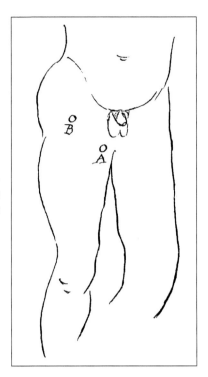

> *A serious case as, possibly, the upper end of the femur and/or the parts of the acetabulum (the concave 'receiving' surface for the head of the femur to rotate in, within the 'ball and socket' joint of the hip), may have been broken and fragments of infected bone were discharged. The surgeon could have helped here, by searching for and removing the dead bony fragments (this is called sequestrectomy).*

164. George Davis – 1st [sic] Battalion Royals

Facon
7 August

Musket ball entered at A and passed out at B.

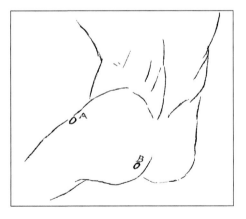

> *This is Private George Davis of Captain (brevet Major) George Dodd's No. 7 Company 3rd Battalion 1st Foot. Hopefully the missile avoided damaging the femur or hip joint, by passing outside these structures. Davis was invalided in 1816 but was paid his Waterloo Prize Money in 1817. He later served as an Assistant Warden at Aldershot.*

165. Smith – 33rd Regiment

Facon
9 August

Musket ball entered left groin at A & passed out through the left Hip at B.

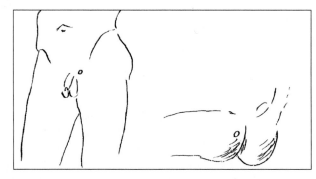

There were 10 'Smiths' in the 33rd Regiment. James, John x 2, Joseph x 2, Josiah, Samuel, William x 3 – (of these the two Johns, Josiah and one of the Williams were wounded). This must have shattered Smith's left hip joint, (though A & B are not marked) and caused a very significant and dangerous injury. Therefore, this most likely refers to the John Smith who did not survive and was discharged dead. His Waterloo Prize Money was paid out however, presumably to his family.

166. James Galloway

Annonciate

Musket ball entered at A fig 1 & was cut out from the left groin at B fig. 2 No alarming symptoms.

Here is the case of Private James Galloway of Captain Peter Innes's No. 5 Company 1st Battalion 79th Foot. If there were 'no alarming symptoms', then can we assume that the ball was spent and merely tracked around the front of the right groin across to the left groin? If the ball had smashed the right pelvic bones, crossed the abdominal pelvis, and exited through the left groin, the patient would have been pretty unwell! His wound, even if superficial, could still have been a risk to James. The long tracts made by the ball passing through soft tissues were a potential source of infection and small bits of clothing could be deposited along the way through. Galloway was discharged on 5 March 1816 receiving a pension of 6d per day (later increased to 9d. He lived in Glasgow and Belfast at times. He still received his Waterloo Prize Money in 1817. He died on 16 October 1862.

167. Captain Moray – 13th Light Dragoons

Musket ball entered at A anterior to the Joint & is lodged – The nerves were injured.

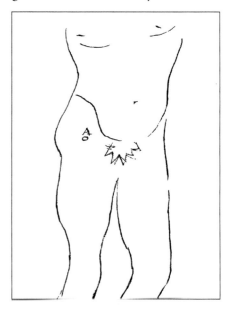

This is actually Captain William Moray 17th Light Dragoons, who was serving at Waterloo as aide de camp to Major General Sir Colquhoun Grant. The casual way in which the writer comments that, 'the nerves were injured' is remarkable. It is quite likely that it was the femoral nerve which was damaged – whether divided with permanent damage (neurotmesis) or merely bruised with neuropraxia (temporary paralysis and numbness only.) Neurotmesis would mean some numbness of the thigh, palsy of the quadriceps muscles, and possibly long-standing pain. If neuropraxia was the result of this injury, the sensation and motor functions would take between 6 and 12 weeks to recover. Moray was placed on half pay on 10 November 1821. He died on 9 February 1850.

168. Julius Floegem – Hanoverian

Jesuits

Musket ball entered right Thigh near the neck of the Trochanter and remained lodged. Patient doing well.

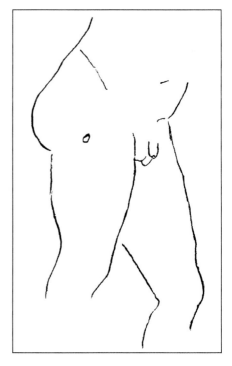

It would appear that the hip joint had been preserved with this injury.

169. James Quarry – Royals

Musket ball entered at A & is lodged in the Joint.
There is Synovial discharge which is diminishing.
Patient doing well.

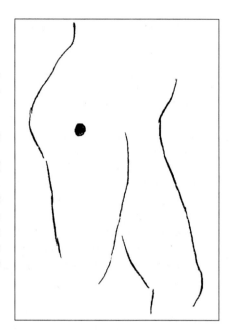

> *This is Private James Quarry of Captain James
> Cowell's no. 1 company 3rd Battalion 1st Foot.
> It would be interesting to learn if this wound
> healed with any preservation of joint function.
> Recurring bouts of sepsis in the future might
> have led to limb ablation. James Quarry was
> invalided out of the army on 20 March 1816 on
> a pension of 9d per day but did not receive his
> Waterloo Prize Money. He died on 17 January
> 1859 aged 66.*

170. The Hon[oura]ble. Capt. Brown

Had been wounded on [in] the Peninsula. A ball
fractured & splintered the left Femur at A. Profuse
discharge of bad matter. Constitutional symptoms
severe. Pulse quick. Loose fragments thought to be felt.
Extensive counter opening B [to] C made in the view
of attempting to remove loose pieces of bone & also of
giving issue to the matter which was sending upwards.
Great improvement in countenance and general symptoms on 12 August.

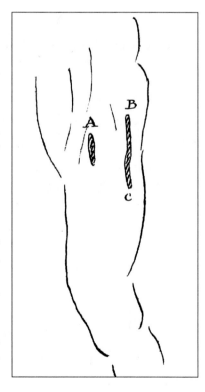

> *Lieutenant the Honourable Michael Browne of the
> 40th Foot was wounded in both the Peninsula and
> at Waterloo, but his was a serious head wound not
> a leg wound and therefore does not fit.*
> *Captain the Honourable William Frederick
> Browne commanded No. 3 or C Troop of the 6th
> (Inniskilling) Dragoons: he is a possibility but he
> did not serve in the Peninsula. This is a risky type
> of thigh wound, with the middle of the shaft of the*

*femur broken and involved in a compound fracture – the mortality rate here would
be around 60 percent. The use of counter incisions was essential to give an egress for
infected material. His recovery was clearly implicit on this measure.*

171. James Quin – 73rd Regiment

Facon
7 August

Right leg fractured by a grape shot & amputated. A musket ball entered at A [on the] left
thigh & is lodged.

*Private James Quinn of Captain
Duncan Dewer's No.9 Company, 2nd
Battalion 73rd Foot underwent a
below-knee amputation for his 'grape
shot' injury and hopefully the lodged
musket ball in his left hip region had
not damaged his joint. Unfortunately,
we do not know what percentage of
buried missiles were retrievable. If not
removed, a few could gradually shift
position around the body or suddenly
infection would manifest itself around
the ball or debris and later present with
an abscess, with discharge of the ball.
James Quinn did not survive, dying on
25 July 1815, and was discharged dead,
although his Waterloo Prize Money
was paid out, presumably to his family.
James Quinn was born at Adgerworth,
having formerly been a labourer. He
had enlisted on 5 August 1812, volun-
teering from the Westmeath Militia.
A Waterloo Medal was issued for him
but was returned to the Royal Mint on
5 May 1816.*

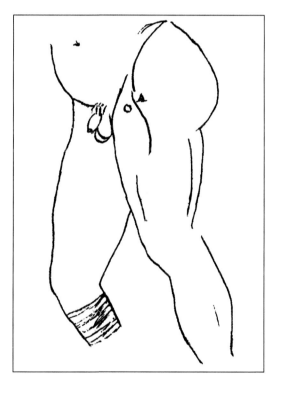

172. Christopher Matthews – 27th Regiment

Elizabeth
2 August

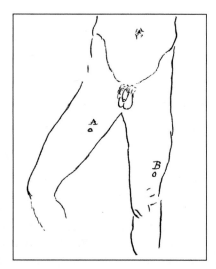

Musket ball entered right Thigh at A, passed upwards, wounded the urethra[36] below the Scrotum in [the] perineum. His left Thigh was also fractured by a musket ball at B.

> *Both of these injuries were potentially fatal. From the wound in the urethra, urine would have passed out of his perineum when Matthews voided. This would have ceased as the wound very slowly healed – such leakage was called a urinary fistula.*
> *Spreading sepsis was a real risk as the bruised tissues in the perineum were contaminated with blood and infected urine. As far as the second wound was concerned, he might have escaped amputation. By and large, the lower down the fracture in the femur (excepting involvement of the knee joint), the less is the surgical mortality rate. Matthews unfortunately did not survive and he was discharged dead. He was not issued a Waterloo Medal.*

173. Hamlin

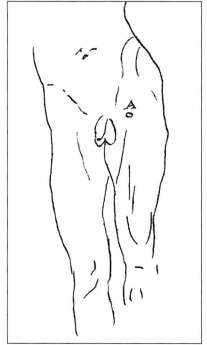

Musket ball entered at A passed through the thigh, & out of the sacrum.[37] Paralysis took place in the left thigh & leg.

> *It seems as though the ball missed the great femoral artery and vein, but injured the femoral nerve and possibly other nerves (e.g. the sciatic). The missile probably skirted the pelvic organs (rectum and bladder). The shot was fired quite close to the victim for it to take the tough course that it did.*

---

36   The tube that allows urine to flow from the bladder, out through the penis.
37   The tough tail bone forming the back of the bony pelvic girdle.

174. Neil Johnston – 27th Regiment

Facon

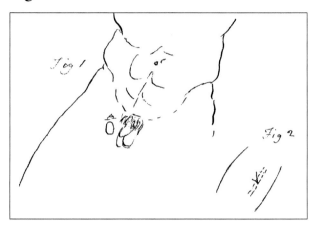

Was wounded at A on the right thigh & he was also wounded in several other parts by the splinters of a shell which exploded close to him. On examining the wound A the feather spring of a soldier's musket was found lying across the femoral artery & immediately pressing on upon it as in Fig 2.

Neil Johnston served in No. 2 company of the 1st Battalion 27th Foot. This is a good example – and one that has appeared in some contemporary texts – of a secondary missile injury. Coins, buttons, and body parts could frequently cause injury after the explosion of a common shell or a round shot strike. In this case, it was fortunate that the femoral artery was not injured. Presumably a large fragment of shell smashed his own or someone else's flintlock mechanism and the feather spring was driven into this man's groin. He was invalided in 1816 but he still received his Waterloo Medal and his Waterloo Prize Money in 1817.

175. Michael Ternanses – German

Annociate

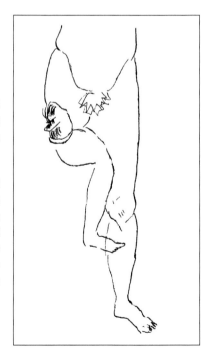

Very bad compound fracture [of the thigh – crossed out] from the wound of a ball. Threatening twitches of the face for many days. Protrusion of [part of] the femur. Patient sunk under it.

This soldier had a serious compound fracture at the upper end of his right femur, part of which protruded from the wound. He was suffering from a mild form of Tetanus (lockjaw), after the wound has been contaminated by horse manure and the organism Clostridium Tetani. *His leg was painfully distorted, with both hip and knee flexion from muscle spasms. He did not survive.*

176. François de Gay – French prisoner

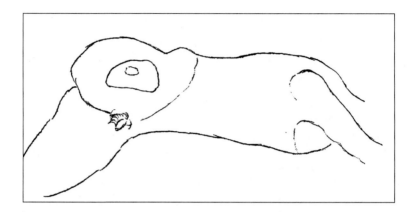

Right Thigh shattered by a cannon shot too high to admit of operation. He informed us that he lay where he was wounded four days & four nights on his back – his head was so placed that by turning it he could lap water from a pool. The limb was removed by Mr Guthrie at the hip Joint on the 7th July. Vast discharge of matter took place. The open surface is greatly diminished on 3rd August but the patient had lost strength. P[ulse] quick & rather feeble.

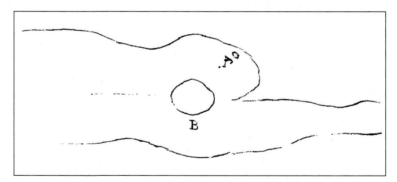

A back representation of the same patient. A was an opening of a sinus of some depth, but not communicating with the wound on the opposite side. B [is] an ulcerated surface from [sentence incomplete – should read, 'the patient lying for weeks on his back'].

Below is a detailed description of the most notorious surgical success story after Waterloo:

François de Gay, private in the 45e Regiment of French infantry, was wounded, at the Battle of Waterloo, by a musket ball, which entered behind, fractured the neck of the femur, and made its exit anteriorly, about four inches below the groin. He was admitted into the Elizabeth Hospital on the 5th of July, much exhausted, not having had until that period, any regular attendance. In addition to his wounds, which had put on a sloughing appearance, he suffered from an extensive sore on the sacrum, which was caused by lying on his back for five days. The wounds being cleansed, and the thigh placed in proper position, he remained until the 7th, when the operation of amputation at the hip joint was considered advisable. This operation was performed by Mr Guthrie at two o'clock of the 7th; nineteen days after the injury. His pulse was 120, and a considerable deviation was observed by Dr Hennen and Mr Collier, between the pulse at the wrist and at the groin, at the termination of the operation; his spirits good; he lost about twenty–four ounces of blood; was immediately put to bed and had an anodyne [pain killer] draught. In the evening his pulse was only 108; had lemonade for common drink. 8th Had milk for breakfast; beef tea for dinner. Evening, pulse 124. 9th Pulse 120 and soft; skin cool; countenance good; stump discharging good pulse, and in one part a quantity of sanies [thin, purulent material]. No particular appearance of inflammation or anything unfavourable. 10th Pulse 108, good; skin rather hot; countenance not so good as yesterday: the wound discharging healthy [thicker pus] in great quantity, especially from the centre; when there was considerable loss of substance: he was sponged all over frequently with vinegar and water; had some chicken broth and wine. 11th Pulse 112; skin and bowels open; slept four hours during the night. 12th Discharge lessened; skin rather hot; bowels open: pulse 110: the bedsore on the sacrum is sloughing, and obliges him to rest on one side; the stump is healing at the sides; the integuments of the fore part have contracted considerably towards the ilium; he is still supported with wine, chicken broth, tea &c. 13th Pulse 104, and good; discharge increasing; the external appearance of the stump healthy; he is rather irritable; bowels and skin open; the bed sore enlarging, had an anodyne at night, with sago and claret. 14th Slept well; skin hot and dry: he is a little purged; countenance not so good; discharge much less than yesterday: pulse 120, after dressing; bedsore still enlarging; dressed with spirit. The body frequently sponged with vinegar and water during the day. 15th Slept well; had a copious perspiration in the night; bowels perfectly open; discharge less, and of good quality; bedsore looks healthy, and is dressed with the spirit terebinthinae [turpentine] pulse this morning, after dressing, 108. 16th Countenance improving; no headache; bowels open; tongue clean: pulse 112 and good. The stump is looking well, and the discharge is not considerable; skin rather hot. 17th No change whatever; his body was sponged as before frequently in the day. 18th Discharge decreasing; general health improving; the bedsore is looking healthy but is very extensive. The dressing and nutriment continued. 19th Health improving; the hump and bedsore look healthy. Was visited by the Baron Larrey, who had been wounded and taken prisoner by the Prussians. 20th Slept well; granulations look healthy; the discharge more copious, but of good consistence; bowels and skin open; general appearance good and tranquil; pulse 104; dressings & continued. 26th No remarkable change since last report, either as to the discharge of the sores, or general health. 27th Passed a restless night; pulse feeble and 108; discharge considerably increased, but of good quality; granulations looking healthy; bedsore clean; countenance sallow, eyes suffused; bowels gently opened by castor oil, and had good broths, jellies, and wine, in the course of the day; dressing &c continued. 28th Slept a little during the night; pulse after dressing 130, small and feeble; countenance as yesterday; bowels and skin open, and head clear. In the course of an hour after dressing the pulse came down to 110, but still feeble; broths, jellies and wine continued. 30th No material change in the discharge; general health and pulse somewhat improved; same treatment continued. 31st Slept badly; pulse 120, and small; tongue somewhat furred; countenance sallow; eyes suffused; appetite bad; broths &c continued. August 1st. Pulse 120; countenance improved; had several stools during yesterday and last night, which were not very fetid; the discharge from the stump this morning is not so considerable; appetite somewhat improved; the bedsore still enlarging but looking healthy; it is dressed with diluted nitric acid; nourishing broths &c continued. 2nd Slept well. And feels himself much better; discharge less and good; skin and bowels open; pulse 110; usual diet &c continued. 4th to 20th No material change has taken place; his general health has been gradually improving; the sore and discharge lessening; during this period, he took the following mixture, from which he appeared to derive benefit. His appetite was, in every instance, studied and even solicited by cordial and nourishing diets. 20th Had a bad night; slept little; bowels constipated; sores looking well and healthy; had castor oil; diet &c continued. 21st Passed a good night; had several motions yesterday; discharge good; pulse 104; skin open; head clear; countenance considerably improved; appetite very good. 22nd No alteration as to general health; matters appear to be forming under the glutiae [buttock] muscles communicating with the original wound of the ball. 30th General health still continues good. Hitherto the matter from the abscess was discharged through the original wound, but, apprehensive of its extension, an opening was made through the glutiae muscles, and the abscess dressed from the bottom. September 1st General health still improving. The distance from the abscess healthy and diminished; feels heat about its edges; bedsore looking well, and its circumference diminished; the surface of the stump lessening; discharge healthy, the portion of the ligamentous edge of the acetabulum, which had not hitherto sloughed away, came away this morning: the ligatures would appear to have been thrown off with the discharge. 2nd A small abscess appears to be formed over the external iliac artery, communicating with the stump; the discharge from it is good; the granulations on the surface of the stump do not appear so florid as yesterday, nor is his countenance as good; pulse 108 and full; his skin is hot; tongue moist and white. Vespere [during an evening ward round]. Has had three motions since taking the medicine; thinks he is better and has had some sleep since its operation: his pulse is now 110; feels as if he would be again purged. A little jelly, tea, &c ordered for the night. 3rd Has had a good night; had one alvine [bowel] evacuations early this morning; pulse 110; measures taken by compress to obliterate the abscess over the iliac artery; his tongue is clean and moist; the granulations as yesterday; chicken broth &c to be given. 4th Has slept well: complains of tension of the abdomen, although his bowels are open; no alteration in the appearance of the stump or bedsore; the general health is somewhat better and his appetite is better. 6th Slept well and is equally tranquil; the abscess over the iliac artery is diminished in size, about two ounces of arterial blood was discharged from it today; the abscess, which was under the glutiae muscles, is nearly obliterated; the bedsore is stationary. Continue the pills. Pulse 109. 7th Was attacked during the night with diarrhoea, which is very troublesome; in other respects, the same as yesterday. Pulse 116. He is supported with cordials [usually wine and fruit juice], nourishing broths &c. 8th The purging continues, but not so harassing; granulations appear at the bottom of the acetabulum, which are florid; the remaining surface looks pale, and the discharge thin. Pulse 110. 9th Has had a very good night; feels himself very much and demands food; the surface of the stump looks better; the abscess much diminished, and

*no more arterial bleeding. Pulse 106. Three thin alvine evauations during the night.
11th Health mending gradually; wound closing in; the granulations in the acetabulum
luxuriant and florid; the abscess much less than yesterday; no alteration in the bedsore;
bowels regular. Nourishing diet, broths &c continued as before the attack. 15th Pulse
generally from 104 to 112: improving rapidly in every respect; the diet is well regulated
and continued as usual. 16th Did not sleep well, finds himself however strong and in
good spirits; had three evacuations since yesterday; the stump and abscess doing well.
Pulse remaining at 106; apprehensive of accumulation, the laxative bolus, was repeated.
18th The acetabulum [the socket part of the hip joint] is nearly three parts full of healthy
granulations; the stump and abscess closing, and the health good. 23rd He is gaining
strength; slept well; the bedsore looks more irritated in consequence of his constantly
remaining on his back; has been detained by force for four hours on his back; but more
was lost from the general irritation caused by this plan, than gained in the appearance
of the sore. 24th Still mending; had him placed at the window and supported by six men
for an hour and a half, which he bore very well and appeared to acquire additional
strength by it; bowels regular and appetite good. 25th Is perfectly tranquil; has slept
well, and talks with confidence of his recovery; his bowels are regular, skin moist and
soft; is free from all pain; stump &c are doing well; was supported at the window for the
same period as yesterday, he did not however bear it so well, some debility supervening;
in all other respects he continues to promise a favourable issue: had him changed to his
own room again in the evening. 27th Slept but little in consequence of an attack of diarrhoea, which is attributed to a salad he ate yesterday; his countenance is not so lively;
pulse 116, and irritable; he is careless as to food. 28th Had some sleep during the night
but feels himself not so well this morning; he is griped a little, and has no inclination to
eat; his pulse is 120, the wound does not look so healthy as yesterday. 29th Had a tolerably good night; bowels getting more regular; countenance better; the surface of the
wound is now only 2½ inches by 1½. October 1st Everything going on apparently well;
appetite good; sores healing. 5th Slept very well: there is an anasarcous [widespread
swelling of the body due to an accumulation of fluid in the tissues. This is a sign of
chronic malnutrition and illness] appearance of the scrotum this morning; his bowels
slightly affected during the night, otherwise doing very well. 8th Had four alvine evacuations last night; tongue clean; pulse 100; the pulse &c look well; there is a slight odema-
tous enlargement of the limb; it is carefully rolled up with a flannel bandage; the
acetabulum is now completely filled up, and on a level with the general surface of the
wound; the anasarcous swelling of the scrotum begins to disappear; his appetite
continues good. 9th The state of the bowels much better, the oedematous appearance of
the limb does not increase; the bandage continued, and frequent friction with flannel
and volatile liniment. 10th to 15th No alteration in the appearance of the extremity; his
bowels are regular, and his appetite good; tongue clean; pulse from 104 to 110 during
this period. This medicine agrees with him, and he is in good spirits. 17th to 22nd The
wound nearly closed, and the abscess is totally obliterated; pulse 110; bowels open; skin
cool, and head free; has a good appetite; is nourished with sago, wine, broths, tea &c;
complains of no pain; the swelling of the extremity is subsiding. 25th Had some sleep
during the night but complains of much pain in his knee; the limb is much diminished
this morning; has had two alvine evacuations during the night; has passed a*

considerable quantity of water during the last twenty–four hours; tongue clean; head clear; skin cool; pulse 120. Had a mutton chop for breakfast; is in good spirits. Chicken broth, beef tea &c; one bottle of porter, one pint of port wine; the limb to be frequently rubbed with flannel and volatile liniment. 27th Was removed to a more airy room: he had several alvine evacuations during yesterday and last night, which prevented his sleeping; no change in the appearance of the wound or bedsore; he is much more irritable; pulse 130 and feeble; skin hot and dry; the oedematous swelling of the limb remains much the same; the friction with volatile liniment to be repeated; the body to be sponged with vinegar and water; to have jelly and white wine, broths &c. Laxative bolus repeated. 28th Slept well and feels in every respect better; is anxious to eat. November 1st Feels himself quite well; his bowels are regular, and appetite good.

11th It would appear that matter is again forming under the glutiae muscles; in all respects doing well. 12th Complains of pain in the direction of the former abscess; is otherwise well. 13th The cicatrix of the glutaeal [sic] abscess opened spontaneously this morning; he is in other respects doing well. 14th The discharge from the abscess is very trifling; the bedsore looking healthy and healing. 19th During this period he has been sitting up before the fire two hours each day. There is no discharge from the abscess; his appetite continues good and is gaining strength; the unhealed part of the wound is not quite an inch in size. At this period he was brought to England by Mr Campbell[38] and sent to the York Hospital, where the remaining sore healed without inconvenience. His Royal Highness the Duke of York, on seeing the man, was pleased to interest himself in his favour with the French government, and on his return to France he was placed in the Hôtel des Invalides, where he now is. He is capable of walking as much as three miles at a time, the wooden leg which he has attached to his body being thrown forwards by an exertion of the muscles of the trunk. He is in very good health, not quite so fat as when in England, talks of getting married, and is not, as the French express it 'sage'.[39]

This must be the most notorious surgical case of such a large and ultimately successful operation on a private soldier. The case has been well recorded elsewhere. Surgeon George James Guthrie had travelled out late to Brussels to help with consultations and a few procedures. He was Britain's most experienced and skilful military surgeon. This patient had initially refused surgery which was not surprising as disarticulation at the hip joint was an almost certain death sentence. De Gay had a severe wound infection and also suffered a sloughing sacral pressure sore. He remains the only well-documented case of this operation in the history of the war. A similarly successful case had previously been carried out in the Peninsular War but the documentation is not there. The patient went back to France and communicated with Guthrie that he had married, which the French medical staff clearly had thought most unwise!

This dramatic and successful case, performed by Britain's most prestigious military surgeon of these times, brings to an end this collection of sketches relating a few of the casualties from the Waterloo campaign.

---

38   Possibly Staff Surgeon James Alexander Campbell, no. 1552 in Peterkin & Johnston *Medical Officers*.
39   Guthrie, *A treatise on gunshot wounds*, pp.332–341.

10

Some Specific Case Studies recorded by Dr Thomson

Case Reports

These case notes below are fairly detailed and emanate from the allied hospitals in Brussels and Antwerp. They would have formed part of a report on the medical services during and after the campaign. In general, they are representative of the various parts of the body wounded and are a mixture of patients reflecting successful and failed medical care. Amongst the 25 patients, 15 died (60 percent mortality), thus displaying a high proportion of more complex and challenging patients.

Some Casualties of Waterloo[1]

Case of Moses Wyse 33rd Regiment, Wound of the head[2]
Case of Charles Murray, 1st Foot Guards, Wound of the head
Case of William Rogers. 32nd Regiment, Wound of the head
Case of William Kitchen, 1st Foot (Royals) Wound of the head
Case of Dominique Maderie, Wound of the head
Case of James Beswick 4th Regiment, Wound of the pharynx
Case of Corporal Dunlavy 69th Regiment, Wound of the thorax[3]
Case of Thomas Stoppel French Prisoner – gunshot fracture of the thigh
Case of Adrian Mathian, French prisoner – gunshot fracture of thigh
Case of Corporal McDonald, 79th Regiment, Wound of the abdomen[4]
Case of John Dun, 79th Regiment, Wound of the abdomen
Case of William Godwin, 23rd Light Dragoons gunshot fracture of humerus
Case of William Fish, Fracture of head of humerus from cannon shot

---

1   Reference Thomson and Somerville (Ed University – Gen 595D).
2   This is the same Private Moses Wise, who appears as No. 2 in the line drawings.
3   This is actually Corporal Francis Donhavy, who appears as No.61 in the line drawings.
4   This is the same Corporal John McDonald, who appears as No.55 in the line drawings.

Case of Elien Patrel, 54e Regiment de Ligne, gunshot fracture of humerus
Case of Joseph Walters, 1st Guards, gunshot wound of the arm
Case of Benjamin Verinder, 32nd Regiment, gunshot wound of the elbow joint
Case of William Peachman, 1st Foot Guards, gunshot wound of the elbow joint
Case of Osten Cooper, 1st Guards, gunshot wound of the femoral artery
Case of John Bayen, Royal German Legion, gunshot wound of Iliac artery
Case of Angus Maclean, 79th Regiment gunshot fracture of thigh
Case of Mathias Joury, French prisoner, gunshot fracture of thigh
Case of Gillan Glander, 1st Chasseurs, gunshot fracture of thigh
Case of William Crosswell, 73rd Regiment, wound of the thigh
Case of Boiteux Langlet, leg carried off by cannon shot.
Case of Sergeant Sutherland, amputation at the hip joint[5]

Moses Wyse 1st [Battalion] 33rd Regiment

Was wounded on the 16th June about an inch and [a] half above the left superciliary ridge[6] or centre of the left protuberance by a musket ball which fractured the bone and depressed it into the cerebrum one inch & a half in diameter just as if a hammer had been struck against the part, & the cerebrum protruded through the fragments of bone; I saw him first early on the morning of the 17th, laying in the farmyard at Genappe, at which time he had rec'd no surgical aid, was perfectly senseless with grit on them[7], pupil dilated, bleeding gently at the nose and apparently had bled considerably from the wound – I removed all the little loose *spiculi*[8] of bone & took away 40 oz. of blood when he appeared triflingly relieved & having dressed the wound with lint and bandage left him to attend to others little expecting ever to see him alive again; and was much surprised to find him in my hospital. Here this day the 20th June; he is still uncollected, pupil contracted, does not see plain, cerebrum protrudes beyond the scalp, pulse hard & quick, respiration hurried and laborious, skin hot & dry, tongue parched, countenance flushed & cannot make out if he has had a stool. Some person has bled him since *V.S. ad drachm9 xxx [30]y Sumat Mag: Sulph. drachm ifs Statim* .

21st much relieved. Skin moist, breathing natural, perhaps rather quick, has had 4 loose stools with a large quantity of faeces in the first. Cerebrum more protruded [and] removed it with a knife when more bone was taken out, and one piece appeared as though there had been fissures in it & melted lead had been run into them so violent has been the force with which the ball came, in some parts of the bone it has penetrated more than ⅛ of an inch, ordered him the tartarised

5   This is the same Sergeant Alexander Sutherland, who appears as No.147 in the line drawings.
6   A bony ridge above the eyebrow.
7   Dirt in the wound.
8   Splinters or fragments.
9   An apothecary's measure, equivalent to 60 grains or one eighth of an ounce.

antimony[10] in small doses – 8 in the evening. The symptoms are returned bled him to *xx [20] oz. Cerebrum* is rising again but otherwise is tranquil & apparently doing well (the [infected and swollen part of the] cerebrum being removed by a knife every second day) till this evening, when he was attacked with epilepsy, ordered him to be bled immediately was relieved by taking away *xxx [30] oz.* of blood.

On the 1st July he was again attacked with epilepsy when v. once again had recourse to, to the extent of 16oz; & I examined the wound with my finger & found several more pieces of bone, which I carefully removed; from this period till the 8 he went on well, the cerebrum still being protruded and removed, afterwards to the present day September 2nd he had no recurrence of unpleasant symptoms or protrusion of cerebrum the wound has simply been dressed with dry lint, and occasionally small pieces of bone the size of pin's heads have been exfoliated. Osseous matter has been poured out,[11] but not in the centre, at least not sufficient to cover the cerebrum, for the pulsation[s] are still seen, the wound is now very small but deep and is evidently only prevented from healing by some remaining caries. It would be needless to add, the strongest antiphlogistic regimen[12] was enforced.

Comment

This case is that of Private Moses Wise who also appears as line drawing No. 2.

Wyse was struck at Quatre Bras on 16 June and received a penetrating brain injury through his frontal bone, above the left eye. A succinct contaminated circular wound was produced with fragments of skull driven into the frontal lobe of the brain, part of the cerebral substance protruded out. Seen, probably at Quatre Bras farm, by an unidentified surgeon the following morning and having received no treatment, he was noted to be unconscious and with one pupil dilated, indicating raised intracranial pressure. The surgeon, possibly the battalion medical officer, Robert Leaver, who had little hope of success in this case, cleaned up the wound, removed some bony splinters and bled Wise 40ozs blood (around 1.2 litres). He had improved from the intracerebral pressure rise but inevitably became febrile and was bled again and purged. As the brain had protruded more with the rise in intracranial pressure, it was pared with a knife on several occasions and the antiphlogistic (anti-inflammatory) regimen continued. Further surgical trimming and medication continued, interrupted by epilepsy. It seems the patient had survived and was alive almost three months later.

Charles Murray 1st Guards, (aet. 33)

Was wounded on the 18th June at the Battle of Waterloo, was admitted into the Minimes General Hospital on the 25th June. The skull was found to be extensively fractured and a considerable portion of the left Parietal Bone was depressed, the right arm only was paralysed.

---

10 Tartar emetic.
11 Some bony regeneration and healing at the edges of the wound had occurred.
12 Venesection, purgation, emesis and a low diet

On the 26th the external wound was dilated and the trephine applied the detached portion of bone removed, the depression raised. The paralysed arm immediately recovered its power and he brought it to his mouth before he left the operating room. All other symptoms of compression were removed, nothing untowards occurred to impede his perfect recovery. He embarked for England on the 28th of July.

J. Cole Surgeon to the Forces[13]

George Guthrie also commented on this man's case:

This is Private Charles Murray of Lieutenant Colonel Richard Cooke's company of 2nd Battalion 1st Foot Guards, aged thirty-three, was wounded on the 18th of June, at Waterloo, by a piece of shell that struck him on the superior part of the left parietal bone. He remained insensible about half an hour, and on recovering from that state, was affected with nausea and some bleeding from the left ear and found himself unable to move his right arm and right leg, which hung as if they were dead and had lost their feeling. Admitted into the Minimes General Hospital at Antwerp on the 29th; he suffered much from pain in the head, which was relieved by his being twice bled. The paralytic affection having remained without change from the moment he was wounded, a piece of the parietal bone, about three fourths of an inch long, and several smaller fragments were extracted four days after admission into the hospital, two perforations with the trephine having been necessary. Immediately after the removal of the bone he recovered the use of his right arm, and leg, so far as to be able to move them, and to be sensible of their being touched. He gradually recovered by the 14th of August, so as to be sent to the General Hospital at Yarmouth, never having a bad symptom, the only defect remaining on the right side being an ability to grasp anything in his hand with force. The pulsation of the brain was still visible at the bottom of the wound for about the space of half the circumference, of the crown of the trephine. September 16th 1815; the wound was filled up with healthy granulations and has nearly cicatrized. A small sinus remains at the superior part, through which the edge of the bone can be felt. His health has been invariably good, although he has suffered a good deal of pain twice previously to the coming away of little pieces of bone, and toward evening he has been generally subject to slight vertigo. Discharged cured.[14]

Comment

This man's head injury was typical of its kind, with depressed bone fragments sticking into the brain, and the patient's condition was instantly improved by elevating them with the improved access gained by trephination. The right arm was initially paralysed, as the spicule of bone pressed down on his motor cortex. As soon as the bone was lifted, the paralysis was

---

13   Staff Surgeon John Cole who was on half pay from 1812 (no. 1992 in Peterkin and Johnston, *Medical Officers*).

14   G.J. Guthrie, *Commentaries on the Surgery of the War, In Portugal, Spain, France and the Netherlands, from the Battle of Rolica to that of Waterloo in 1815; with additions relating to those in the Crimea in 1854-55.* (Philadelphia: Lippincott, 1862), p.309.

relieved. Murray would be at risk from epilepsy in later life, should his cerebral cortex have been significantly scarred. It is interesting to note that there was seemingly a dedicated operating room. Usually surgery was performed at a screened off area in the open ward. This latter was a practice encouraged by a later heroine of medical and nursing care 40 years later – Miss Florence Nightingale. Charles Murray survived and he received his Waterloo Prize Money in 1817.

William Rogers 32nd Regiment. Aged 19

Was wounded by a musket ball on the 16th June, which entered at the inferior angle of the left parietal bone He immediately fell and was senseless a few minutes, then perfectly recovered his recollection, but found himself incapable of speaking which (as he says himself) seem to arise not from the want of power to form words, but of giving them sound. His senses were perfect, as were his mental powers, he retired out of the reach of shot and lay down for the night. The following morning, finding the piquets retreating, he fell back himself to Bruxelles, where he was examined and superficially dressed. On the morning of the 18th [he] reached Antwerp on horseback, overwhelmed with fatigue & privation of food & rest. This was soon relieved after being put to bed in the *Minimes* Hospital where he fell fast asleep.

On the 19th June the ball was found to have passed obliquely upwards and backwards at least two inches & could be very distinctly felt with a probe. It gave me the idea of having raised the outer table instead of having depressed the inner [there are two thin layers of bone in the skull]. The power of speech was in some measure restored and this with giddiness was the only symptom of compression, a poultice was placed on the wound & a brisk purgative given.

20th the pain and giddiness having increased & being aggravated by light, twenty-six ounces of blood were taken from the arm. The following day the purgative was repeated & the patient very much relieved. A faltering in the speech continued for many days. The wound looked healthy & he was almost considered fit to be discharged, when on the 16th July, the wound began again to open. On the 18th it was dilated and a portion of cranium removed. 22nd Symptoms of *phrenitis*[15] appeared, twenty ounces of blood were taken from his arm, purgation and diaphoretics ordered and the strictest abstinence enforced.

23rd July. The bleeding was again repeated as well as the other means to reduce the inflammation.

24th Completely relieved. Saline mixture given and a little milk allowed.

26th another small piece of bone was removed. The dura mater[16] completely exposed, the patient in the best state.

---

15   Inflammation of the brain and its coverings, with the patient being delirious and disorientated.
16   The principal protective covering membrane of the cerebral cortex.

August 3rd. Up to this period was doing remarkably well the wound looks healthy, the pulsation of the brain still evident.[17] The power of speech perfectly restored, the ball is yet in, has gradually changed its seat as the patient imagines (who is a fine intelligent lad) has descended to the petrous portion of the temporal bone. Embarkation for England.

Presumably Staff Surgeon Cole was the author of the above report.

Comment

This patient showed a remarkable degree of fortitude and strength, reaching the Belgian capital and then after initial treatment, riding on horseback to Antwerp.

Rogers was wounded by a musket ball that hit the left side of his skull and most probably disrupted the linings of the brain, as there was soon some 'phrenitis' or meningism, i.e. there was probably some bleeding into the subarachnoid space (the space under the innermost delicate of three membranes covering the brain substance). This would produce neck stiffness, headache, and photophobia (aversion to light). This missile injury, whether completely penetrating or not, lay over the part of the brain controlling speech. This is now known as Broca's area. This region, located in the frontal part of the left hemisphere of the brain, was discovered in 1861 by French surgeon Paul Broca, who found that it served a vital role in the articulation of speech. There was either bruising or relatively minor damage of this part of the cerebral cortex, since recovery (despite the patient being purged, given diaphoretics and being bled around five pints of blood!). It is of note that, later, the patient may have been aware of slight downward movement of the ball.

Rogers was recorded as having been discharged from the army, but he did receive his Waterloo Prize Money. He was granted a pension of 1s/6d on 16 August 1816 and is recorded as having died on 5 September 1860 aged 63 at Bath.

William Kitchen 1st Regiment (or Royals) aged 40

Was wounded at the Battle of Waterloo on the 18th of June by a musket ball which fractured the cranium and depressed a considerable portion of the parietal bones, was admitted into the General Hospital of the Minimes on the 27th June, then labouring under symptoms of compression, the lower extremity completely paralyzed.

On the 28th the trephine was applied in two places and several large detached portions of cranium removed and the whole of the depressed [portion] raised. The symptoms were immediately alleviated, the paralyzed lower extremities gradually recovered their power and at the end of four weeks he embarked for England, nothing having occurred to retard his cure or to render at all doubtful his perfect recovery. In this case there was never any involuntary discharge of faeces or flow of urine, the three last cases produced ample matter for reflexion.

J. Cole Surgeon to the Forces

---

17   From the raised intracranial pressure.

Comment

The case of Private William Kitchen of Captain Robert Dudgeon's No. 8 Company 3rd Battalion 1st Foot, is another example of a compound skull fracture. This time, it would appear that the ball had somehow damaged both parts of the primary motor cortex, to produce complete paralysis of both lower limbs. This would be in the upper part of the motor area. Cole does refer to the 'Parietal Bones'. Thus, did the ball pass right across the upper brain through both sides of the skull? There was clearly a significant amount of bony damage. Like many brain injuries, once intracerebral pressure had been relieved, the motor function recovered. Kitchen was invalided out of the army but still received his Waterloo Prize Money in 1817.

Dominique Maderie aet. 27

Was wounded on the 18th June. He lay three days on the field of battle, without food, was taken to a village and from thence to one of the churches in Brussels. He was admitted into the Gens d'Armerie Hospital on the 30th June, he came under my care, on the 4th July. A musket ball had entered at the anterior part of the squamous suture of the right temporal bone, & passing outwards, & downwards, fractured the parietal bone & lodged in the brain. On the morning of the 5th the wound was laid open by Mr Charles Bell, three large pieces of bone were removed and the ball was found lodged in the posterior lobe of the right hemisphere of the brain immediately at the *tentorium cerebelli* superoexteriorly.[18] The ball when extracted was covered with the substance of the brain. Notwithstanding this extensive injuries of the brain, his condition could scarcely be said to be at all affected, his pulse before laying open the wound, was 72, & on the day after 80, he had no complaint, has a slight ache and deafness, slept well, appetite good, belly natural, tongue clean, skin cool.

The wound was carefully cleaned of blood & small portions of the substance of the brain.

The lips of the wound were then brought together, & retained by two stitches, and adhesive straps,[19] a uniform compress was applied over it to the whole head kept moist with cold water, the bowels were freely kept open, diaphoretic medicines [those substances that encourage sweating] administered, & he was put on the *lowest diet*.

Under this management (his bowels kept constantly loose) he continued free of all complaint, until the 16th when he complained of *lancelating* [sic] pains in the back part of the head, & increasing from the light of a candle & from noise, the wound looked extremely well, the lips nearly united, almost no discharge of matter but the pulsion [sic – pulsation] could be discerned at the different parts of the wound. A brisk cathartic entirely removed his complaints.

18   The tentorium cerebelli is a sheet of dura mater that supports the occipital lobes of the brain and lies above the organ of proprioception and balance – the cerebellum.

19   Strips of linen coated in adhesive gum-based paste.

From this time till the 24 hours continued free of all complaints, that day however, the expression of his eyes & the fullness of his countenance indicated to me new excitation in the system, the pulse for the first time was found as high as 96, and hard, the skin very hot with a disposition to sleep.

Upon making enquiry it was found that the officer under whose care he had been placed for the last four days, had omitted giving him his daily laxative, and had given him, wine, eggs and other extras.

These were immediately stopt [sic], & a brisk cathartic again administered, by which means he was, in the course of a few hours once more restored to his former state of convalescence. From this time, he has no complaint, except the slight deafness of the right ear and this he thinks is gradually diminishing. He says, that from his present sensations, that he could not know that he had been wounded. The wounds are closed, & to all appearances will be speedily cicatrised. He has all along been allowed to smoke tobacco, which he uses freely as a means of removing the sensation of hunger, but kept on a very spare diet, of the propriety of which, he himself is perfectly sensible.

Brussels, 30 July 1815

Henry Home Blackadder, Hospital Assistant to the Forces

Gens d'Armerie Hospital

Comment

Maderie was a relatively 'lucky' patient. He had survived a three-day sojourn uncared for on the field. Initially admitted to one of many churches in the city, he was later transferred to the Gens d'Armerie. The ball had hit him in a tangential fashion and had passed into the brain (probably not very deeply, since it was easily retrieved) eventually ending up in the rear part of the right hemisphere of the brain, in the right occipital lobe. The man was fortunate that the vital areas of the brain seem to have escaped injury. The missile had fractured areas of the parietal bone, likely giving enough access for civilian surgeon Charles Bell to remove them and the lead ball. His condition deteriorated roughly a month after admission, with irritation and probable infection of the brain and/or the membranes covering of his brain, the meninges. The deterioration was put down to failures of the attendant junior medical man to purge him and allow 'excitation' with items of rich diet. Maderie's scalp had eventually healed over the large defect in the skull.

James Beswick 4th Regiment [of] Foot aged 35

Was wounded on the 16th June by a musket ball at the Battle of Quatre Bras. It entered at the angle of the inferior maxilla[20] on the right side and passing across made it exit below the inferior angle of the same bone on the opposite side. In its course fracturing it as well as the *Os Hyoides*[21] and dividing the pharynx, trachea and some blood vessels as inferred by the escape of the food through the left wound,

---

20 The cheekbone.
21 The delicate hyoid bone at the top of the larynx – the voice box.

haemorrhage and loss of voice. He was admitted in this state into the Minimes General Hospital on the 27th June, eleven days after the wound was received.

The following morning (28th) the haemorrhage returned with such profusion by the amount as to fill vessel after vessel, and when I reached him the only remedy was clearly indicated, that of securing the carotid artery which was immediately done. The only difficulty arising from the pulsation of the vessel not being to be felt[22] so exhausted was the patient. A double ligature[23] was used, and a section [i.e. division] of the vessel, made nearly in a line with the cricoid cartilage.[24] The ends retracted immediately leaving an interval of more than half an inch between them. The sides of the wound were then brought together by adhesive straps. The haemorrhage was restrained and the patient tranquil.

June 29th Passed a comfortable night. Was supported by strong animal broths conveyed into the stomach by an elastic[25] tube and by nutritive clysters.[26] An opiate added to his evening mess.

30th Improved. Has lost no blood, chest a little oppressed dislikes the frequent questions put to him by Hospital Assistants. Strength seems to increase.

July 1st Progress to recovery uniformed and satisfactory – vespere[27] feels comfortable.

2nd Passed a good night received nutriment as before: pulse though small are [sic] good. Noon – to my great surprise and mortification, he was seized with stertorous breathing[28] and expired.

Dissection [post-mortem] showed us that the ball in its course had fractured the maxilla inferior & the *Os Hyoides*, had wounded in its passage the pharynx, trachea and some large branches of the carotid; the bronchiae[29] and air cells were found choaked [sic] with foetid pus, precisely of the same odour and appearance as that found in the wound, and which constantly trickling down the trachea, filled the lungs, producing death by suffocation. It [the pus?] entered, we remarked below the epiglottis and glided down without producing the smallest irritation. That extreme sensibility with which nature has endowed the immediate neighbourhood of the epiglottis above not being necessary is of course not found below. The right side of the heart was, as might be expected distended with black blood[30]. His great disinclination to try and speak, doubtfully arose from the increased sense of suffocation occasioned by the effort to inflate the lungs & which during the whole period was the only complaint made perhaps suffocation never so gradual before.

Here again as far as the necessity of the operation and its success can exist. The haemorrhage which it was the intention to restrain, was restrained & no other

22 As the patient's blood pressure was so low.
23 Of linen or silk.
24 The lowest of the three laryngeal bones of the larynx.
25 Gum-elastic.
26 Enemas, probably of broth.
27 Evening time.
28 Irregular and stuttering breathing.
29 Old term for Bronchi.
30 ie de-oxygenated venous blood.

mode could have been adopted to attain that end. Not a single bad symptom was produced by it. Not a drop of blood was lost after it. I could not have imagined that such a torrent of blood could have been so abruptly diverted from its natural course, with so little derangement of the system.

J. Cole, Surgeon to the Forces

Comment

It sounds as though the missile had passed through the upper neck, and fractured the delicate upper bone of the larynx: the hyoid bone. The pharynx was also breached. The shattered larynx and severe bruising negated speech and the pharyngeal wound allowed escape of swallowed material onto the exterior. The patient had had a long gum elastic catheter passed into his stomach to provide him with liquid nutrition, also administered by ineffectual 'nutrient' enemas. The sepsis and damage to blood vessels in the vicinity of the wound caused a secondary haemorrhage to occur on the 10th day after injury. Cole cut down on the carotid artery to control the bleeding. The operation was not made easier by the inability of the surgeon to feel the carotid pulsations, which would have directed him to the large blood vessel. Two ligatures were applied around the carotid artery a little further down the vessel. Despite the successful control of the bleeding, sadly the patient succumbed and the post mortem revealed wound infection and inhalational pneumonia. The patient clearly had made little effort to cough up the infected material.

Private James Beswick was not included in the Waterloo Medal Roll as he was discharged dead.

Corporal Dunlavey 1st [sic] Battalion 69th

Was wounded on the 16th by a musket ball which entered the thorax by fracturing the 7th rib near the sternum & lodged; lost a large quantity of blood in the field but had no medical or surgical aid till he was admitted, on the 19th into the Falcon. Had then a quick hard pulse, respiration difficult and anxious blood issuing from the wound on a full inspiration and had not any evacuation since the 16th. 44 ozs. of blood were immediately taken from him and a saline purge administered; from this period till the 29th of June (when he had a free suppuration) he lost at intervals 2 ozs. more blood and the saline purge with diaphoretics were constantly employed with of course a strict antiphlogistic regimen. The man was then put on a milk diet for 6 weeks and continued doing well the air circulated now and then and on which account he went back to England [on] August 31 when he was quite well with that exception and to use his own expression, had never been better in his life than he had been for the last month; no clue as to the direction of the ball could ever be ascertained.

W Blicke Surgeon to the Forces

Comment

This case report is that of Corporal Francis Donhavy (who appears as line drawing no. 61.). He had been struck in front, on the chest near the breastbone, by a ball which must have narrowly missed his heart. He had received no medical aid for three days and was seemingly taken to Antwerp. The ball had not exited. The patient, as was the way with chest injuries, was bled around 1300ccs of blood, then purged and put on a low diet. He was discharged home around two months after wounding. The corporal was a further example of survival after a non-exiting chest injury.

Thomas Stoppel, a French Prisoner

Received a gunshot wound in the back on the 18th June. The ball entered the thorax between the 8th and 9th ribs about the distance of two or three inches from the junction with the vertebrae. The patient was treated in the Gens d'Armerie Hospital till about the 10th October when he was transferred to the St Elisabeth. When in the Gens d'Armerie Hospital, the wound used to discharge about a pint of matter daily for a considerable time, but suddenly it ceased to flow by the external orifice excepting only a small quantity which oozed out upon coughing. It was conjectured that this matter must have taken another course and probably, passed off by the intestines a communication having betwixt[31] them and the lungs. On examining the stools which were now become more frequent a white fluid very much resembling pus floated on their surface.

10th October. Patient at present seems to suffer from the discharge, he is very much emaciated countenance pale and languid pulse small and intermitting, perspires frequently at night, has no appetite and complains constantly of pain in the upper part of the abdomen with want of sleep during the night. He was ordered, Decoct: Cinchona [Quinine] with a dose of Al. Ricini[32] occasionally and an opiate at bedtime, low diet, [then later] port wine, fowls and a few extras daily. His wound dressed with dry lint, compress and rollers.

By the 14th October the patient appeared to get weaker daily with no abatement of the symptoms, the discharge of matter by stool seemed to increase. Pain in the abdomen still remained. Pulse 50, at times imperceptible. The medicines were continued, his urine increased and a blister applied to the abdomen.

Till about the 28th there was little alteration excepting the pain in abdomen which abated but again returned. It felt hard and tense; was not was not increased by pressure.

On the 29th he complained of pain in the region of the pubis and inability to discharge his urine. These symptoms were relieved by warm cloths to the pubis. He likewise [was prescribed] two drachms [of] Tinct. Scillae[33] and one of Nitrous

---

31 An abscess must have formed in the chest and burst downwards in to the large bowel – the colon. This then would have constituted a fistula between bowel and abscess.

32 Ricinus Communis, Ricinoides or Pineus Purgans derived from an Indian tree that produced an oil – a purgative we know as castor oil.

33 A native coastal plant of Sicily, Syria and Spain, with properties of drying up the 'humours', also possessing emetic, purgative and diuretic properties.

Aether.[34] A severe cough without any expectoration now attacked him, with deficient respiration his stools became less frequent and contained none of the whitish matter. Pulse quick, small [volume] and intermittent.

Demulcent mixtures[35] with opium were used for the cough, the Pulv. Cinchona: was substituted in place of the decoction. He now was unable to eat, could only drink his wine. Aromatic confection was given as a cordial combined with Tict: Cinchona & Peppermint Water. He continued to sink every hour and by the first [of] November was almost insensible, his eyes shut, extremities cold, tongue dry and foul, his wound looked black and livid, of a putrid smell. He expired on 3rd November at 3 [in the] afternoon.

Dissection

On opening the thorax the general appearance of the lungs was healthy, the left lobe was found to adhere firmly to the Pleura Costalis,[36] the right lobe only slightly; the posterior part of the left lobe nigh the site of the wound was detached from the costa [ribs] for a considerable space of the wound forming a kind of sac where the matter had lodged, the surface of the lungs covering this space was ulcerated in several parts but did not seem to have been much injured by the ball. One part near the opening appeared to have been grazed by it. The sac contained very little matter. No communication could be traced between the lungs and intestines. A curious appearance presented itself at the diaphragm by a protrusion of a portion of the superior part of the stomach through an aperture situated at about the centre of the left side of the diaphragm; on the superior part of the space betwixt the spine and the false ribs of the left side. It protruded about three inches into the thorax carrying before it the peritoneum and the omentum, the latter only adhered to the lungs but no communication between the lung & stomach existed.[37] The ball was not to be found either in the chest or abdomen.

The heart appeared quite natural; the substance of the lungs when cut into contained a quantity of mucus mingled with pus and was very turgid with thick blood.

In the abdomen no morbid appearance could be observed except a slight degree of inflammation on parts of the small intestines. The internal surface of [the peritoneal cavity] was healthy only a small quantity [of pus or inflammatory change] was found on [the] colon about its termination in the rectum.

The urinary bladder was exceedingly small contracted and drawn up towards the Symphisis [sic] Pubis resembling very much in appearance an unimpregnated uterus.

---

34 Solution of spirit of ethyl nitrite, mixed with alcohol is a diuretic and diaphoretic.
35 Medications which are muco-protective. They coat an irritated, inflamed or painful mucosal surface to relieve symptoms.
36 The membrane forming the inner lining of the chest cavity.
37 Thus, interestingly, there was a smallish para-oesophageal hiatus hernia, but no sign of an internal fistula found between the chest abscess cavity and the large bowel, as strongly suggested in the clinical case report.

Andrew Gibson H[ospital] A[ssistant][38]
J. Boggie Staff Surgeon[39]
St Elisabeth, 20 November, Brussels

Comment

Clearly, for many weeks after the patient's non-exiting chest injury, the purulent material which had drained out from the entry wound in Stoppel's chest seemed to lessen and
only exude on raised intrathoracic pressure, i.e. coughing. It was surmised, since there was
some evidence of 'matter' being excreted with the patient's motions, that an intra thoracic
abscess had formed and discharged downwards into the patient's abdominal cavity, thence
outwards in the bowel motions. Curiously, there seemed no evidence at post mortem of any
fistula (or communication) between the lung pathology and the intra-abdominal gut. It is
feasible that this man actually had a bowel infection and died from this or pneumonia. The
only suggestion that there might have been a connection between the chest and bowel, was
that there was found a herniation (an upwards protrusion of the stomach into the chest) of
the stomach into the thorax, what we would term today as a para-oesophageal hiatal hernia.

Adrian Mathian French Prisoner

This man died on the 27th of October two days after he came under my care. I
found no case [notes] relating to him, he had been wounded on 18th June and had
a compound fracture of the superior part of the thigh, I found him exhausted by
excessive discharge from various sinuses running through the thigh.
    Dissection shewed nothing more than what usually appeared in such cases – a
partial union of the bone had taken place and abscesses and the remains of them in
many of the interstices of the muscles from the glutei to the knee joint.
    J Roche Staff Surgeon[40]
    19th November 1815

Comment

Mathian had a most dangerous and threatening wound. He had perished form acute and
chronic osteomyelitis. Situated in the upper part of the thigh, the mortality would be double
that of a similar wound lower down the femur. There seems to have been gross neglect in
the care of this man. The combination of continued and severe sepsis from the compound
thigh fracture had caused ultimate septicaemia and before that, four months of protein
loss and inanition, much reducing the patient's immunological response to infection. Dead
and infected portions of bone (sequestra), chronic abscesses in the large thigh muscles, and
poor attempts to heal and remodel the patient's shattered femur probably infer that, despite

---

38   Andrew Gibson had only become a Hospital Assistant on 3 June 1815 and was dismissed the service at Halifax Nova
     Scotia in 1821. He was readmitted to the service in 1825 and left the army around 1836. (Peterkin and Johnston No.
     3896 in *Medical Officers*)
39   Staff Surgeon John Boggie (no. 2064 in Peterkin and Johnston *Medical Officers*).
40   Staff Surgeon Jordan Roche (no. 1526 in Peterkin and Johnston *Medical Officers*).

its risks in cases of upper thigh injury, it might have made an attempt at high amputation worthwhile. Perhaps he had refused surgery.

Corporal McDonald of the 1st [Battalion] 79th Regiment

Was wounded on the 16th of June by a musket ball which entered the abdomen by splintering the 8th rib on the right side passed through the liver and supposed to be lodged in the left thorax, lost very little blood in the Field says he felt the ball strike his left side & cannot lay on it; was dressed superficially only till he was admitted into the Falcon on the 19th, when he was labouring under great Pyrexia.[41] Pulse quick and hard, skin hot, tongue dry, respiration short, labouring and extremely painful but had no evacuation since the 16th V.S. [?] ad oz. XXVI Sumal. Mag. Sulph.[42] Statim.[43] The V.S was continued for seven successive days from 12 to 6oz: when he had a large bilious suppuration colouring everything about him of a deep yellow and the inflammatory symptoms seemed to be entirely subsided till the 30th June when he had haemorrhage to the extent of 16 to 20 oz. in the night. He then continued going on well till, the 15th when the haemorrhage recurred and he had so much pyrexia that it was deemed necessary to take twenty ounces of blood. It was repeated the following day. From which period till September 2nd 1815 (when he was discharged) he continued improving with the exception of his requiring occasional purgative (of which class the saline was always used) and a little local irritation as the rib exfoliated. The bilious discharge ceased about 3 weeks previously & it should always be remarked that almost to the day of his discharge the respiration was affected by any great exertion.

W. Blicke, Surgeon to the Forces.[44]

Comment

Corporal McDonald appears as line drawing no. 55. He was wounded at Quatre Bras and was fortunate to survive. As the ball entered the upper abdomen, it fractured the 8th rib on the right side, passed through the right lobe of the liver and passed through to the left chest cavity, missing the heart. Admitted to the Facon Hospital in Antwerp, he was soon septic and was bled and purged for a week. As bile escaped into his abdominal cavity and through his wound site, some was re-absorbed and he became jaundiced. A fortnight after wounding, he had two secondary haemorrhages with the sepsis, from the wound, at a fortnight and a month after injury. The bile discharge from his wound ceased after about seven weeks.

41   Pyrexia – a fever.
42   Magnesium sulphate a drug to promote a liquid bowel action.
43   Immediately.
44   Staff Surgeon William Flamank Blicke (no.2488 in Peterkin and Johnston *Medical Officers*).

John Dunn 1st [Battalion] 79th

Was wounded on the 16th by a musket ball passing through the scrotum testicle & groin and out at the nates[45] was treated antiphlogistically with a cooling lotion firm and simple dressings afterwards & was discharged without any unpleasant symptom on July 31st.

    W Blicke

Comment

Private John Dunn of Captain William Marshall's light company of the 1st Battalion 79th Foot. He survived his wound and received his Waterloo Prize Money in 1817. Dunn was granted a pension on 27 June 1821 and was still living in Ayr and Paisley in 1854.

Often unconsidered, these types of painful and dangerous wounds were not that uncommon in warfare. Today they are likely to affect soldiers subjected to upward explosive episodes with anti-personnel mines or IEDs and appropriate body armour can now be provided. The

real risk later in the convalescent period, was the likely threat of infection by a concoction of mixed bacteria, extant in the groin, buttock, and perianal area. Provided one testis survived, the chances of procreation would not have been significantly affected. Such were the rigors of military life that, very occasionally, men would avulse (tear out) a testicle to obtain a discharge from the army!

William Go[o]dwin 23rd Light Dragoons, aged 21

Was wounded on the 18th June at the Battle of Waterloo & was admitted into the Minimes General Hospital on the 12th July. The ball had penetrated the inner side of the deltoid muscle, fractured the humerus & seemed to have penetrated the joint itself, the discharge was profuse and foetid, the patient already hectic and much debilitated, On the 15th July to ascertain the extent of the injury and thereby learn what further would be necessary, the wound was freely dilated upwards and downwards, the humerus was found shattered & diseased as far as the finger could reach in both directions. Sinuses extended themselves over the joint & under the pectoral muscle[s]. I was desirous of going on and removing the limb but the absolute refusal of the patient prevented me. The profuse discharge, constant pain & hectic fever was fast terminating his existence, when on the 26th of July he consented and indeed solicited the operation might be performed. It was therefore determined to remove the humerus and its articulation with the scapula. The situation of the wound left no alternative as to the mode, the deltoid flap [a flap created from the large muscle covering the shoulder joint] was the only one practicable & although very generally recommended is not the one in my opinion that merits a preference. On making the anterior [front] incision, a large quantity of foetid pus gushed out. The posterior

---

45 The buttocks.

incision being made & the deltoid raised, the capsular ligament divided, the head of the humerus was removed, or rather part of it, for it was so splintered that a portion remained adhering to the shattered glenoid cavity, indeed the frightful proof of the extent of the disease was appalling to the surgeon when coupled with the conviction of the hopelessness of the case. However, all the diseased detached portions of bone were removed, the blood vessels secured and the flap brought down which completely covered the surface. The patient was removed in a very exhausted state to his bed, which was placed in a separate room, in order that he might breathe his last, undisturbed. For never did a case occur that was less likely to repay the surgeon for his care and anxiety. In the evening he rallied exceedingly & walked unsupported to his former bed – to be in the neighbourhood of his companions (a feeling which prevailed in every case that was operated on). Has taken food & porter & is more cheerful than since his admission – nevertheless those favourable appearances, when reflected on the great injury the scapula had sustained, the numerous sinuses that had burrowed around the joint, & the shoulder emaciated state of the patient I could not indulge the faintest hope of ultimate recovery although from his quiet & tranquil condition & improved appetite a casual observer would v prognosticated a success – On the 4th August he expired – and the appearances on dissection confirmed all that remained undemonstrated of the case – the fracture of the Glenoid [the inner articulating surface of the shoulder joint] process extending down the body of the scapula.

Comment

Where this trooper had been cared for, for more than three weeks, is uncertain. Perhaps he had languished in a field hospital or a private house. His sepsis was far advanced and his operation was performed too late. Having explored the wound and correctly pronounced that removal of the upper limb with drainage of the sepsis was the only very slim chance that Goodwin had of survival, the surgeon (Blicke?), carried out the disarticulation through the shoulder joint a fortnight after the patient had been admitted to the Minimes Hospital. This further delay had been a consequence of the patient's initial refusal of amputation. After a temporary improvement, the patient wandered into the main ward from the room in which he had been isolated to talk to and have company with his fellow patients. Sadly, Goodwin died on the ninth day, worn out with infection and malnutrition. His scapula injury was worse than had been realised, extending into the blade of the bone. Much sepsis remained around the area.

Private William Goodwin was discharged dead, but his Waterloo Prize Money was still paid out in 1817, presumably to his family. He is not listed in the Waterloo Medal Roll but he certainly served there.

William Fish (aet 27)

Was admitted in to the Facon General Hospital – June 19th with the head of the humerus shattered by a cannon shot, the integuments over the pectoral [front of chest] muscle and deltoid with the muscle itself were torn away. The tumefaction, inflammations and febrile action very considerable was treated antphlogistically & poultices and fomiculations[46] applied to the part till the middle of July when he was supported by a generous diet and the wound dressed superficially.

August 4th The bone is much diseased, the arm elongated, two inches surface of the bone [exposed], glairy[47] profuse discharge tolerably good; the man much emaciated with hectic sweats and a large deep sloughing bedsore on the sacrum, the bone exposed, a healthy bed sore on the elbow. The head of the bone was now carefully dissected out and found black, soft, and spongy, a longitudinal incision was then made in the forepart of the arm down to the bone about half way to the elbow, & the muscles carefully dissected away from around till it was found healthy (which was about 4 inches from the head). Severed off, it was not found necessary to tie any artery, the bone was now brought so near to the glenoid cavity as to bag[48] the muscles a little; and the wound brought together as much as possible putting a piece of lint in the glenoid[49]cavity: the man's wine and porter were stopped for two days and gradually given him again. The bed sore on the sacrum was dressed every day and the arm every second day, shortening the arm as much as possible every day, till the second of August. The bed sore assumed a healthy appearance in the course of a few days and is gradually healing, but in spite of everything the arm could not be got into the glenoid cavity; for the copious [probably glairy infected joint fluid] matter was poured out so plentifully it bled every time after the 20th that I tried to raise it. It was therefore permitted to lay underneath on the ribs, from this period until the 16th Sept. it healed rapidly & he appeared to be doing remarkably well, the swelling in the hand and arm was considerably abated; on this day for the first time, I did not dress it and owing to the gentleman putting on the bandage too tight, haemorrhage took place in the night to a considerable extent; so much so, I was called up & on examining it the next morning, I found the sore itself looking as well as ever, but the granulations which had brought together at the top immediately under the acromion torn open by the haemorrhage, the integuments over the Latissimus Dorsi inflamed & swollen dressed it lightly and applied a cold solution to the part ordering him to take Mag. Sulphate[50] drachms Ip statim.[51]

September 20th. Had been going on well ever since except that I fear a small abscess will take place on the integuments but at present the repellent lotion is used the surface of the ulcer is now about ⅙ the original size the wound from the wound and ulcer up the arm being entirely healed.

---

46 Poultices.
47 A colourless discharge, which was synovial fluid from the joint.
48 Bunch up.
49 Shoulder joint.
50 Magnesium sulphate is a cathartic drug.
51 Immediately.

September 23rd. The bed sore and arm have assumed a phagedaemic[52] appearance and I think evidently from the confined room he has been necessarily put in on his removal to the 25th Regiment Hospital.[53]

24th was immediately removed and the ulcers have nearly recovered themselves this morning, but the tumour in the back is rather increased.

26th. The bed sore is not larger than a shilling: the ulcers have recovered their healthy appearance, the one on the elbow is prevented healing by its situation; the ulcer from the phagedaema and the tumour continued stationary but I think it will come forward & indeed now wishing it ordered a poultice to be applied.

29th. Perceiving a fluctuation opened it with a spear pointed lancet it discharged a thin foetid pus injected it with St Magarh [?] and applied a light bandage, since which upon the whole he has been [well], but such as his persuasiveness and obstinacy he tries & frequently succeeds in getting liquor & retards the cicatrisation, but I consider his recovery certain.

W Blicke Surgeon to the Forces

Comment

This refers to Private William Fish of the 7th Hussars who, despite the positive comments from his surgeon, unfortunately died and was discharged as dead. His Waterloo Prize Money was however issued and his Waterloo Medal issued, presumably to his family.

By the middle of July, a month or so after injury, the head of the arm bone (the humerus) was found to be shattered and infected. There was much bruising and destruction of the surrounding skin, fat and muscles of the shoulder region. By early August, the patient had developed a pressure sore over his sacrum, having lain with little mobilisation or movement in bed for around six weeks. This complication of immobility was common in such hospital patients and these ulcers soon became infected with a mixture of bowel organisms. Such ulcers could risk the patient's life. The diseased head of the bone was removed, leaving the limb in situ. The surgeon tried to shorten the arm length, to try and bring the remaining limb nearer to the shoulder joint. A dresser or orderly had bandaged the arm or shoulder wound too tightly and a secondary [venous] haemorrhage occurred. This was managed, but his various sores and the wound at the operation site appeared gangrenous around 3 months after admission. This was probably an indication of a new onslaught of sepsis and depressed immune response. Fish then developed a 'tumour'; in fact an abscess on his back, which was incised and some thin pus obtained. The patient had clearly ongoing infection, but was clearly, at this time, well enough to try and get 'liquor'. His fatal outcome was not recorded.

Elien Patrel 54e Regiment de Ligne

Was received by transfer from the 4th to the 2nd Division of the Gens d'Armerie Hospital on the 15th of August.

---

52   A spreading ulcer with dying – i.e. gangrenous tissue.
53   The 2/25th was part of the Antwerp garrison.

He had received a compound fracture of the humerus on the 18th June from a musket ball which entered about the middle and on the outer side of the arm & came out nearly opposite. No union had taken place and the constitution had begun to be severely affected. He complained also of pain in the same shoulder which had been injured in an encounter with the Russians about 18 months before. The head of the bone was found upon examination to the lower and to the inside of its natural situation. Some sloughing had taken place over the sacrum from the constant pressure. The arm was dressed in the usual way and supported with splints, spirituous fomentations were applied to the shoulder and warm dressings to the back, while opium, wine and generous diet were allowed.

On the 30th September he was transferred to the St Elisabeth and appeared to have suffered considerably from the motion. A large collection of matter soon formed around the shoulder joint and burst by two openings, one immediately above the clavicle [collar-bone] the other on the inner side of the arm a little below the axilla [armpit]. The quantity of matter discharged from there as well as the other openings of the arm was immense though as yet of good quality.[54] Sloughing shortly took place at the lower and inner part of the humerus, the sore on the back spread, the opening above the clavicle enlarged so as to expel nearly three inches of the bone covered only by a very thin layer of granulations and the matter discharged became vitiated in quality while it continued undiminished in quantity. His appetite now began to fail, his strength became very much reduced and sleep was only procured by large doses of opium. Nitric acid diluted in the proportion of drachm 1 to a quart of water was applied warm to the sloughing sores with the effect of arresting their progress and rendering them cleaner.

On the 20th of October a considerable quantity of blood was found on the sheets and bandages which being removed discovered a large coagulum [congealed matter] occupying the cavity above the clavicle. This was not removed for fear of renewing the haemorrhage but pieces of lint dipped in the cold nitric acid diluted as above, were laid over it. He continued to sink that day and next morning he died.

Dissection

On removing the coagulum of blood which had been formed on the day previous to death and laying open the parts the ulceration was found to have extended anteriorly to within an inch of the sternal extremity of the clavicle and downwards into [the] axilla communicating with a very extensive sinus which run between the scapula and the ribs and which contained purulent matter mixed with coagulated blood. None of these external sinuses though running close upon the pleura communicated with the cavity of the thorax, the only diseased appearance in which was strong adhesion on the side of the injury between the pleura costales & pulmonalis.[55]

---

54 Thick purulent matter.
55 i.e. the two layers of the pleura – the thin lining membrane covering the lung surface (pulmonalis) and the inside surface of the rib cage (costalis). These normally would glide over each other smoothly, so facilitating the smooth

A considerable number of loose pieces of bone were found in the situation of the fracture which was about the middle of the arm: no union had taken place. On examining the shoulder joint it was found that the head of the bone was situated on the lower & anterior margin of the glenoid cavity a proportion being formed on it corresponding to a depression on the head of the humerus. No other morbid appearances presented themselves.

Roderick Macleod Hospital Assistant[56]

J Boggie Staff Surgeon

Comment

We do not know when the patient, a soldier of d'Erlon's 1st Corps was admitted to the Gens d'Armerie. He had been moved from one 'division' of the hospital to another, possibly as he was deteriorating. A through-and-through lead musket ball had shattered his humerus around its middle part. The head of the arm bone was found to be dislocated. As in the last case, the patient had developed a sacral pressure sore. An unwelcome and probably unwise transfer to the St Elisabeth Hospital took place at the end of September. Patrel's wounds and pressure sore were clearly not improving and a portion of clavicle (collar bone) was expelled from the main wound. Sleep could only be procured with opiates and an attempt to remove slough etc. from the wound was made, using dilute nitric acid. A secondary haemorrhage occurred on the 20 October. The patient died the following day – four months after injury.

Joseph Walters, 3rd Battalion 1st Guards. Aet: 34.

Spare habit of body, sallow countenance, dark hair.

Received a gunshot wound on the 16th June, the ball entered the right forearm, passed through the elbow joint fracturing the olecranon – was admitted into the hospital on the 20th. The inflammation and swelling which were very great had extended to the shoulder, he was considerably debilitated from loss of blood, and had strong febrile symptoms pulse quick and small. A poultice from the hand to the shoulder was applied with antiphlogistic treatment.

In the evening of the 25th haemorrhage occurred, the inflammatory symptoms, not having sufficiently subsided, to admit of an operation being performed, the patient was removed, & cold applications, with a roller[57] from the shoulder down was applied, under this treatment, continued until the 4th July, the haemorrhage frequently occurring and the man's health perceptively declining, the operation was determined on. The upper part of the arm being now free from swelling & tensions; notwithstanding, the amputation was performed as high up as possible, the parts exhibited so much appearance of disease, as to exclude any expectation of the wound uniting by the first intention, upon removing the dressing on the 3rd day there was a considerable discharge and dark coloured sanguineous pus, but no

movement of the lungs on the inside of the chest wall.

56   Hospital Assistant Roderick Macleod (no. 3843 in Peterkin and Johnston *Medical Officers*).

57   A rolled linen bandage.

other unfavourable symptoms, he was ordered bark[58] & a more generous diet. The appearance of the stump daily improved, the pus discharged was well conditioned, the quantity not large, & the wound throwing out healthy granulations. His appetite was good, & his strength so much recovered, that he was able to sit up nearly the whole day, and walk about, he continued in a progressive state of amendment, until the 16th when he complained of shivering during the night pain in his head, thirst, his pulse was quick, skin hot b[reathing] regular. He took a saline purgative which was frequently rejected, & a diaphoretic mixture with Tart: Antim:[59] & was ordered a spare diet. No material change took place in the symptoms until the night of the 22nd, when he had another attack of shivering, which went through the usual stages of Int: fever[60], terminating in a profuse diaphoresis.

On visiting him in the morning of the 23rd his pulse was more regular & soft, skin moist. Tongue foul but moist. Belly[61] open. He was ordered a stimulating regimen, but no bark. In the evening, the febrile symptoms improving recurred, the former mode of treatment was again adopted. He now complained of pain in his left side, his skin and the Tunica Conjunctiva [the delicate lining of the eye] assumed a dark yellow appearance.[62] He was again freely purged the stools evidencing rather a super abundance of bile, but without any other peculiar appearance, the pain in his side continuing. a blister was applied but without any benefit. His bowels were kept open constantly & had pills with calomel[63] and antimony. He was removed to a different part of the hospital, to try the effects of change of ward but without any success, the symptoms still continued the same, no material remission being perceptible. On the 25th large quantities of mercury were rubbed into the body and an attempt made to induce salivation,[64] but the only effect produced was diarrhoea, his strength then declined, he had frequent occurrences of fever for two days previous to his death. He died on the 3rd July.[65] What is particularly remarkable in this case no material change took place in the stump during the whole progress of the disease, the fever indeed became rather worse.

The discharge became increasingly purulent & less in quantity but the wound evinced no disposition to slough nor [to show signs of] irritation. Appearance at dissection. The thorax contained a very large quantity of yellow viscid serum, but more particularly, on the left side, there was considerable inflammation & strong adhesions.[66] The spleen was rather larger than usual, but appeared healthy as did the liver, the coats[67] the descending branch of [the] colon were very much thickened.

58 Red or yellow Peruvian bark; cinchona containing quinine.
59 Anthony Tartrate – a diaphoretic, emetic and purgative.
60 Intermittent Fever.
61 Bowels.
62 ie the discolouration of the conjunctiva – with jaundice.
63 Mercurous chloride – a purgative.
64 A toxic side effect of mercury therapy!
65 This is an error – it should read 3rd August.
66 i.e. the two layers of pleura were fused together after inflammation and infection.
67 The peritoneal lining inside the abdomen.

Comment

Private Joseph Walters of Lieutenant Colonel Charles Thomas's company of the 3rd Battalion 1st Foot Guards died on the 3rd August 1815 and was recorded as having been discharged dead.

A lead musket ball had smashed his elbow and the bruising and inflammation had rapidly spread into the elbow joint. Joint wounds were always serious, painful and usually proved difficult to heal. Constitutional disturbance was common. The resultant scarring left a stiff or often an immovable joint. On the ninth day there was an almost inevitable secondary haemorrhage from a major arm vessel. On 25 June, since haemorrhage had recurred, a secondary amputation, high up on the arm was carried out. The infected stump left open, its healing gradually improved. On the 16 July, there were symptoms of septicaemia, with fever, sweating, rigors, headaches and unwellness. Various ineffectual drugs and remedies were applied. On the 23 July he complained of left sided abdominal pain (which was blistered) and he appeared jaundiced. In no way aiding his recovery, he was given, antimonials and mercury, both topically and systemically in the hope of curing the fever. Joseph died on the 3 August, leaving us slightly puzzled as to the final cause of his demise. At post mortem, the significance of the pleural effusion may have reflected left sided pneumonia. The pain in the side could have been due to inflammatory problems in the left colon (e.g. diverticulitis). An optional diagnosis, particularly terminally, might have been multi-organ failure, as a consequence of repeated sepsis.

Benjamin Verinder 32nd Regiment (aet 32)

> Was wounded on the 16th of June by a ball passing through the elbow joint and fracturing the olecranon[68] & humerus & when admitted into the Minimes General Hospital (21 June) the tension was considerable and extended high up the arm. Fomentations, poultices and a strict antiphlogistic regimen reduced the high action.
>
> July 9th Hectic fever impervened [sic] with rigors approaching in severity to that of the cold stage of an intermittent [fever]. General diet with bark and mineral acids were recommended however the patient was daily sinking.
>
> July 11th Excision at the shoulder joint was performed (for extensive sinuses and diseased integuments would have rendered any other operation nugatory [worthless]) vessels were secured without loss of blood the thumb perfectly commanding the event in the subclavian.[69] The flaps which nearly covered the surface were brought together by adhesive straps placed horizontally and a compress and bandage being applied, the patient was put to bed, feeling as released from a heavy burthen.
>
> 12th [July] Passed a more comfortable night than he has done since receiving the wound.
>
> 19th Health had improved since the operation and union is going on rapidly.

---

68   The tip of the elbow – the upper end of the ulna bone.

69   That is, the thumb pressed on the subclavian artery above the collar bone to temporarily shut off the blood supply to the arm.

27th Stump going well. Extensive & foul ulcer on the sacrum from constant pressure in so emaciated a subject.

July 31st Looks cleaner. He continued weak with night sweats.

August 1st Stump nearly well, debility very considerable.

6th [August] was transferred to the Falcon.

24th [August] Stump perfectly healed. Debility still considerable. The ulcer on the sacrum clean & healthy & of small size.

Comment

Private Benjamin Verinder of Captain Charles Wallett's company of 32nd Foot (incorrectly shown as Vumder in the Waterloo Medal Roll) was discharged from the army but still received his Waterloo Prize Money in 1817.

As in the last case, the elbow was shattered by the missile and after some anti-inflammatory measures had been prescribed, an amputation at the shoulder joint (i.e. a disarticulation) was carried out, since the fever and patient's debility were increasing. Interestingly, the haemostais was achieved easily by the assistant pressing down on the subclavian artery as it passed over the first rib. His stump healed well enough, but the patient gained a sacral pressure sore. His wounds became smaller and the stump healed. Profound weakness and weight loss would make convalescence prolonged, but, miraculously, Verinder lived.

William Peachman 2nd Battalion 1st Guards Aged 34

Was severely wounded by a musket ball in the battle of Quatre Bras, on the 16th June. The ball passed through the elbow joint, the fracture extending up the humerus. Tension and inflammation very considerable from the first moment there was no hope of saving the limb but from the high excitement and swelling although the most rigid antiphlogistic plan was persevered in [sic]. No good opportunity offered of removing it until the 5th of July and even then the extirpation of the humerus was the only practicable mode. This was therefore determined on. An assistant being placed behind the patient, in readiness, when necessary to compress the subclavian artery, with thumb above the clavicle diverging incisions with a scalpel were made from the point of the processus acromion[70] anteriorly and posteriorly, first through the skin and cellular membrane, and then (keeping the edge of the instrument close to the retracted edges of the Integuments) through the muscles down to the bone. The capsular ligament was next divided, the arm being withdrawn from the side, and the assistant then continued to compress with his thumb the large artery with one sweep of an amputating knife, the whole of the Soft parts were divided, & the limb disengaged – the compression of the subclavian was effectual. Only two ligatures were made on the blood vessels and those from their situation and equality in size, seem to have been axillary bifurcating so high up. The flaps were brought together by adhesive straps placed horizontally & were

---

70   A projection of bone of the shoulder blade, which abuts against the collar bone.

found neatly & completely to cover the surface. The patient was put to bed much tranquillised.

11th nothing untoward has occurred, adhesion rapid, pus healthy, strength recruited.

14th Union progressive, already the surface of wound reduced to a lump, a small abscess formed in the side which was punctured with a lancet. Ligatures not come away.

15th alarming haemorrhage during the night. He imagined it at first to be pus trickling down the side and did not call for assistance, until faint. The haemorrhage had ceased before the orderly medical officer reached him. But such extreme exhaustion was induced, that he died the following morning. It was found the artery had sloughed.

This was the only case of secondary active haemorrhage that occurred in my hospital, after an operation. In some subjects, attacked with intermittent fever, bleeding from the stump, during the hot stage, was not frequent. The mode adopted, I feel assured is preferable to that of preserving [i.e. using] the deltoid[71] flap. However, we must always be governed by the circumstances of the case. The compression with the thumb I think also preferable to that with a key or the handle of a tourniquet. In the one case, the assistant feels and is satisfied that he is on the vessel; in the other he is alarmed, presses with increased force and diminished advantage, for he has got on the side of it. The efficacy of the thumb was likewise exemplified in several cases of amputation of the arm so high up that no tourniquet could be employed but where the head of the bone did not require removal & which every surgeon must feel the necessity of avoiding, whenever it be practicable.

Comment

The description of another compound injury of an elbow joint perhaps points out that the surgeons were anxious to present these cases as being difficult to manage. The guardsman was hurt at Quatre Bras and the usual antiphlogistic remedies were applied. The patient clearly rallied just enough for amputation on the 5 July. Some details of the disarticulation are given with two flaps, fashioned with a scalpel, and a sweeping of a capital knife dividing the soft tissues under the armpit. An assistant steadied the patient, and, as in the last case, compressed the subclavian artery with his thumb. Despite securing the axillary artery, there was a fatal secondary haemorrhage. The surgeon comments that this was a unique complication in his current hospital experience. He also remarks that pressing on the subclavian artery with the thumb above the clavicle was superior to using a handle to do the same job, since the tip of the handle might slide off the vessel.

Private William Peachman of Lieutenant Colonel Richard Cooke's company of 2nd Battalion 1st Foot Guards was discharged dead and his Waterloo Prize Money was not paid out.

---

71   A large muscle running over the shoulder.

Osten Cooper of the 2nd Battalion 1st Regiment of Guards. Aged 30

Was wounded at the Battle of Waterloo on the 18th June by a musket ball which entered the left groin a little below Poupart's ligament,[72] passed through the thigh and was cut out the following day a little above the lesser trochanter.[73]

Nothing remarkable occurred until the 29 when the slough from the anterior wound came away and was followed by so frightful a haemorrhage as to leave no doubt as from whence it proceeded, nor (from the wound being so high up) any alternative as to the means to be adopted for stopping it. The external Iliac[74] was therefore immediately exposed secured by a double ligature and divided, the ends immediately retracted more than half an inch. The sides of the wounds being now brought together by adhesive straps, the operation was finished without loss of blood; increased arterial action was so high that twenty ounces of blood were taken from the arm and saline draughts recommended, the limb was rolled in flannel and warm Jars kept to the foot.[75]

June 30th Passed a good night; a tingling sensation in the limb amounting to pain in the heel. Has had free evacuation, no pain in the bowels or tension of the abdomen, Had, however, yesterday a severe rigor followed by heat and which was succeeded by profuse sweating which we call an ague fit; and of which there can be no doubt as he asserts having had a similar paroxysm every other day nearly at the same hour ever since he was wounded. A good deal of pus had collected in the gun shot[76] and some had insinuated itself into the incised [surgical] one, thereby in some measure loosening the straps and allowing the sides to open a little. In the evening excitement continued with thirst & nausea. The saline draughts in a state of effervescence, he remained on spoon diet with whey.

July 1st During the night the excitement was increased with oppressed respiration, 12 ounces of blood were taken from the arm, which gave relief. In the morning the pulse was rather feeble, the abdomen continued soft and free from pain. The bowels open, the pain of the chest was removed but the breathing was hurried. The discharge from the old wound sanious.[77]

Vespere – a peculiar pulse giving the idea of ebb and flow more than of the progression of a fluid – No rigors during the day, or tenderness of the Peritoneum.[78] The incised wound looking well but part of the sides kept from actual contact by the insinuation of pus from the old one.

2nd Pulse less tremulous. Low delirium occasionally but easily recalled to his recollection. Tongue moist. Had a copious evacuation after the laxative enema. The

---

72   The infolded termination of the external oblique muscular sheet of muscle at the groin.
73   A bony protrusion at the upper outer end of the femur.
74   Iliac artery – a major division of the aorta.
75   viz, 'hot water bottles' to promote the little blood flow, resulting from the tying off of the iliac artery.
76   Entry wound.
77   Purulent material tinged with blood.
78   Abdomen.

limb has acquired its natural temperature, and the abdomen continues free from pain or tension.

Vespere. The stroke of the pulse more distinct.

3rd. passed a tolerable night although the delirium is now constant. Belly free from pain soft and regular. The camphorated saline medicines were now succeeded by tonics and wine.

Noon countenance flushed, pulse very feeble.

Evening. Great exhaustion. Pulse scarcely to be counted. Tongue brown & parched. The temperature of the skin exceedingly high. Cold effusion. Increased quantity of Port wine & bottled Porter. Bark with mineral acids.

4th. The typhoid symptoms increased. Picking of the bed clothes. Subsultus Tendinum.[79] One involuntary stool. Tongue exceedingly parched. The temperature of the skin high. Cold sponging with vinegar. Stimulants and antiseptics.

Vespere, Stupor and increase of debility

5th. Insensibility and involuntary stools. Stertorous breathing. Cold extremities. Noon expired.

In this case the necessity of the operation is evident and as far as it went also its success. Not a drop of blood was lost after it. That the patient died from intermittent fever running into the continued form and that of the typhoid type (induced probably by the loss of blood) no one who has observed the endemic disease of this climate will be inclined to doubt.

J. Cole Surgeon to the Forces.

Surgeon George Guthrie commented on Cooper's case:

Private Austin Cooper of Lieutenant Colonel Henry Bradford's company of 2nd Battalion 1st Foot Guards, thirty years of age, was wounded at the Battle of Waterloo, on the 18th of June, by a musket ball, which entered the left groin a little below Poupart's ligament, passed through the thigh, and was cut out the following day a little above the smaller trochanter. Nothing remarkable until the 29th when the slough from the anterior wound came away and was followed by so frightful a haemorrhage as to leave no doubt from whence it proceeded, nor (from the wound being so high up) any alternative as to the means to be adopted for stopping it. The external iliac was therefore immediately exposed, secured by a double ligature, and divided; the ends of the artery immediately retracted more than half an inch. The sides of the wound being brought together by adhesive straps. Twenty ounces of blood were taken from the arm, the limb rolled in flannel, and warm jars kept to the foot. 30th June, a tingling sensation in the limb, amounting to pain in the heel. Has had free evacuations, no pain in the bowels, but suffered a severe sweating like a fit of ague, which reported having every other day since being wounded.[80]

---

79 Weak convulsive motions or twitching of muscles and tendons seen during severe febrile illnesses.

80 G.J. Guthrie, *On the Diseases and Injuries of Arteries with the operations required for their cure*, (London, Burgess & Hill, 1830), p.293.

Comment

This patient, whose identity is uncertain (see below), suffered a left groin injury at Waterloo. The ball had tracked through the groin and was cut out from the outer side of the upper thigh on the same side. The missile had partially damaged and weakened the arterial wall which, with added sepsis, had caused the femoral artery (the main artery supplying blood to the lower limb) to disrupt. The torrential haemorrhage necessitated the surgeon to cut down just above the groin and doubly ligate the external iliac artery, which, lower down, became the femoral vessel. The wound was closed with sticky tapes rather than stitches, and flannel bandages and warm water in porcelain jars were applied to the lower limb to promote blood flow as much as was possible. The only hope of limb survival after the principal blood supply had been cut off was that accessory blood vessels from above, around the hip joint and pelvic areas, could supply enough blood to keep the leg alive. Cooper developed an infection in the surgical and entry wounds. This was treated by venesection, catharsis and quinine. We are uncertain of the nature of the 'stimulants' or 'antiseptics' used. Staff Surgeon Cole was careful to point out that despite the success of the arterial ligation, the patient died from an irrelevant 'intermittent/continued' fever. It was far more likely that the sepsis from the wound and operated area and also the ischaemia (lack of blood supply and hence oxygen) evolving in the lower limb, ended the patient's life.

There is some doubt with the naming of this patient. There was only one Austin Cooper at Waterloo, but he was not Discharged Dead and was paid his Waterloo Prize Money in 1817. There was however a Private Edward Cooper whose entry in the Prize Roll remains blank, indicating he was missing, but has he been mixed up with Austin? Was it Austin or Edward who died?

John Bayen 1st Lt. Bn. K.G.Legion.

Received a grape shot in the groin which passed through the pelvis and out of the back was wounded on the 17th of June, on the 22nd I saw him, the foot, leg, and thigh were gangrenous & the man's countenance cadaverous, complains of nausea pulse small and weak & bowels costive; ordered him a glister[81] [sic] immediately with a generous diet, a cordial mixture with opium, & a Poultice to the part – 23rd & 24th continued the same.

25th. The man is sinking. Stomach rejects everything but brandy, & opium but a line of separation is commencing.

26th. Much the same, stomach rather better, took some Beef Tea.

27th. Sinking fast, 28th. Died last night.

<u>Appearance on Dissection</u>

The shot had divided the external iliac artery [and] about a pint of coagulated blood mixed with serum excessively foetid was found in the pelvis; both ends of the artery

---

81 Glyster – An enema.

had receded considerably and a coagulum [blood clot] formed in each; the upper mouth of the artery was slightly contracted but no adhesion, and the coagulum was easily pressed out of it, the ball had inclined upwards and shattering the superior spine of the Os Ilium[82] [and] passed out; there appeared to have been a little peritoneal & intestinal inflammation, but the intestines were not wounded.

W J Blicke, Surgeon to the Forces

Comment

This problem was a more severe injury than the last case. The canister round had gone right through the German's pelvis, shattering the wing of the pelvic bone and divided the main lower limb vessel higher up than the groin. There was no chance of new blood vessels opening up and the whole leg was gangrenous at five days post-injury. The divided artery was observed at post mortem. The cause of death was haemorrhage and infection in the depths of the wound cavity.

This must refer to Private Jacob Beyer of the 5th company 1st Light Battalion King's German Legion who was discharged dead, although issued a Waterloo Medal. His Waterloo Prize Money was also paid out in 1817, presumably to his family.

Angus MacLean 1st [Battalion], 79th Regt. Aet 28

Compound fracture of the right thigh. Received a musket ball on the 18th of June 1815 which, struck the right thigh about its middle in the direction of the Vastus Externus muscle[83] and made its exit exactly on the opposite side, a few lines above the situation of the femoral artery, fracturing the bone.

September 9th. He was transferred this morning from the 4th Division of the Elisabeth Hospital with between three or four inches shortening of the fractured limb, the lower end of the bone protruding out of the opening made by the exit of the ball, which is about an inch & a half in diameter and about two inches round this opening the integuments were highly inflamed, tumefied[84] and painful, the sore itself having a sloughing appearance, the discharge thin, mixed with a dark brown matter and very foetid; this protruded end of the bone seemed only one half of the main bone but is firmly attached, it was removed this morning with the common saw.

Extension and counter extension, is performed by applying Mr Guthrie's improved splints;[85] the wound is dressed with a solution of nitric acid to the bottom, over which is applied opiate ointment and Hay's wash[86] and the part well supported by a calico roller.

---

82 The main pelvic bone.
83 A large quadriceps muscle on the outside of the bulk of the thigh.
84 Swollen.
85 These splints were longer in length than usual.
86 We have been unable to trace the make-up of this solution

His general health has been very bad for some time, and about a fortnight before his admission into Ward 15, he was attacked with a vomiting & purging rejecting almost everything therapy was administered in the shape of nutriments or medicine except the tincture of opium and wine, these symptoms continued with increased violence and about ten days before his death there were extracted six very large portions of bone the least not weighing less than two drachms besides several of a smaller size and two days before his death the opposite side of the wound rose in blisters to the same extent and the toes became quite blue; he expired at 9 o'clock in the evening of the 2nd of November.

Dissection after Death

On making a longitudinal incision in the direction of the Rectus Femoris[87] down to the fractured bone, there appeared a large portion of bone of a square shape attached to the superior part of the fissure between the bones[88] this being removed the ends of the bones were exposed, of an irregular shape the superior end riding over the inferior one to the extent of about 3 inches, the lower end being the inferior half circle of the bone gradually terminating to a point; upon which the upper lay loose sharp and irregular[ly] pointed, the largest portion of which had been separated by splinters.

Ulcerative absorption of the bone had taken place to a considerable extent and necrosis of the bone at the extremity of the superior end there was found an irregular round piece which was nearly separated from the main bone by ulcerative absorption and was easily separated by the small forceps.

The disease of the soft parts extended from the knee up to the groin, the muscles had a dark lead colour the abscess was very large the face of which was like a condensed thick membrane covered with a dark viscid matter mixed with a black charred substance. On examining the stomach its coats were a little tumefied & hard near the pyloris [sic][89], and covered with a viscid brown secretion.

Charles Collier, Surgeon to the Forces[90]

Comment

Private Angus McClean of Captain Robert Mackay's company 79th Foot, was discharged dead. The Waterloo Medal Roll records that he died on 3 November 1815.

MacLean had suffered a compound thigh fracture from a musket ball. Fortunately, the missile had not injured the femoral artery, but the lower end of the broken femur was protruding through the exit wound. By 9 September, almost three months after injury, the patient for some reason (for a second opinion or further management?), had been transferred from the Elisabeth Hospital. Collier, an experienced man, cut away the protruding bone, which had started to heal, with subsequent leg shortening. The wound was infected and, since the two ends of the femur were then separated, George Guthrie's wooden long

---

87 The central of the quadriceps group of muscles.
88 Was this thin weak newly formed bone?
89 Sic – the pylorus is the narrow contractile exit to the body of the stomach.
90 Staff Surgeon Charles Collier (no. 2679 in Peterkin and Johnston *Medical Officers*).

leg splints (these had been introduced in the late stages of the Peninsular War and stretched from hip to ankle). This allowed a degree of stretching out of the limb, to hold it in a better position. Mineral acids were placed in the wound and interestingly, as sometimes was the case, topical opium ointment was spread over the wound, which was then dressed with a calico roller bandage. During his last few weeks, the wound discharged sequestra and one or more of the arteries in the leg had probably thrombosed (ie clotted), causing ischaemia of the toes. The patient succumbed in November. The post mortem revealed acute or chronic osteomyelitis, with bone re-absorbtion, sequestra, and deep sepsis involving muscle groups. The overlapping of the bone ends demonstrated the importance of strong traction that would be used in later conflicts, to keep the bone ends aligned. This hospital where Collier worked obviously had a large capacity, since the patient had been admitted to Ward 15.

Matthias Toury, French Prisoner

Came under my charge in the Gens d'Armerie Hospital Bruxelles about the 20th August 1815.

At this time he had a wound on the outside and upper part of the thigh from which there was an enormous discharge of matter daily: another wound with extensive excoriation[91] more posteriorly and the integuments[92] over the sacrum were in a sloughing state supposed to be from pressure. The thigh bone had originally been fractured by a musket ball which after having struck the bone had passed out not far from its entrance. By the probe you ascertained the presence of loose pieces of bone though not in great quantity. These were at various times extracted through the existing wounds, his health never admitting of incisions. During the treatment he at one period became so weak as to be considered by all dying. Gradually however & under the administration of stimulants his health improved [and] the discharge ceased & about the [date missing – probably in September] he could walk about. He was shown at this time as a case of recovery from fracture in the upper third of the thigh.

October 12th. During a week's leave of absence when Toury was consigned to another medical officer, he unfortunately became feverish, without any assignable cause, sunk rapidly & died on the 30th. His death having taken place unexpectedly his dissection was made.

Dissection

Nothing worthy of notice to be observed in any of the viscera, of the head, thorax or abdomen. A large callus or deposition of new bone had taken place all round the fractured part. There were still present some loose pieces of bone.

Robert Knox MD Hospital Assistant[93]

J Boggie Staff Surgeon

91   Ulceration and loss of tissue.
92   Skin, fascia, fat and muscle.
93   Hospital Assistant Robert Knox (no. 3911 in Peterkin and Johnston *Medical Officers*).

Comment

Toury had been cared for elsewhere in the city or in the countryside and had, as in the last case, sustained a compound fracture of the femur. This was a break in the upper part of the femur. He was admitted to the *Gens d'Armerie* Hospital around two months after wounding. There was sepsis and the presence of sequestra. The patient was never fit enough to undergo 'incisions', i.e. cutting open of the wounds to extract further pieces of dead infected bone. He also had an infected sacral pressure sore. By the middle of October he had rallied and was expected to recover. However, when the case was managed by other staff, the patient unexpectedly had a fever and died, probably from a flare up of sepsis from his deep-seated thigh infection. It is likely that the report was written by Knox and countersigned by Boggie. Knox was later to have a colourful and notorious career as a brilliant anatomist in Edinburgh, involved in the infamous 'Burke and Hare' murders.

Gillan Glande 1st [French] Chasseurs

Prisoner of War in the St Elisabeth General Hospital. Taken from the case Book of Hospital Assistant Robert Gillespie[94] under whose charge he was when he died. Had his thigh fractured nearly, in the middle on the 18th June 1815 by a musket shot which passed through it.

On the 22nd October he came under the care of Mr Gillespie. At that time the thigh through its whole extent was filled with abscesses which discharge matter of a most foetid nature. Had different sores on his thigh which were mostly in a gangrenous state. The bone was not at all united and the thigh extremely reduced. His strength had been sinking for some time previous and he has had a diarrhoea which could not be stopped. His stomach could bear nothing but a little port wine.

27th October. The patient is worse this morning. He had vomited in the night, three large common worms.[95].Some medicine was prescribed but immediately rejected. Pulse small and frequent, great emaciation of the whole body. Diarrhoea not so troublesome, no appetite whatever.

29th October The above symptoms continuing to increase – Died 7pm.

J Roche, Surgeon to the Forces

Comment

Glande was a French prisoner of war patient in the St Elisabeth Hospital and his presence emphasises the mix of patients in the city's hospitals. The case had been extracted from Hospital assistant Gillespie, who had been caring for the patient. The overwhelming septic episodes from the infected fracture site took four months to kill the patient. Patients with such severe infections in this series frequently suffered with intractable diarrhoea in their agonal moments. The infestation by parasitic roundworms was not that uncommon in European armies. This reflected poor meat supply and preparation.

---

94   Hospital Assistant Robert Scotland Gillespie (no. 3906 in Peterkin and Johnston *Medical Officers*).

95   These were round worms – ascaris lumbricoides. They are internal gut parasites with a complex life cycle. Infestation results from faecal contamination resulting from eating improperly cooked pork or other foodstuffs.

William Crosswell 2nd [Battalion] 73rd Regiment

Received by transfer from the 4th Division on the 1st November in the most debilitated state with abscesses formed the entire length of the thigh, lower extremities cold & gangrenous dropsical[96] and swelling of the cellular membrane of the entire body, pulse 120, tongue brown, regular exacerbations of hectic fever, discharge very extensive and foetid, tight bandaging was applied from the toes to the lower edge of the wound and from the groin to the upper, the wound was dressed with lint dipped in a solution of camphor and opium and compresses of linen kept constantly moist with vinegar and brandy, took boluses of camphor and opium and a bark mixture in the course of each day and dressed twice a day as above, Discharge more extensive and foetid day after day, constitution gradually sunk on the 14th.

Low muttering delirium, involuntary evacuations by stool – hiccup – died on 19th.

Appearance on Dissection

On opening the abdomen a quantity of green fluid escaped. Mysenteric [sic] glands much enlarged.[97] Membranous bands found round the intestines. On opening the capsular ligament of the knee joint a quantity of fluid escaped, crucial ligaments, semilunar cartilages and articulating surfaces perfect.

Charles Collier, Surgeon to the Forces

Comment

This refers to Private William Counsell of Captain Morgan Carroll's company of the 2nd Battalion 73rd Foot.

He had been injured over four months previously, presumably suffering from an infected compound thigh injury and was in nearly a terminal state. He was admitted from the '4th Division', which we do not know of, clearly another hospital, which may have been closing down. He was treated with tight bandaging (presumably to reduce the oedema or tissue swelling), various topical solutions, stimulants, opium and quinine. He was overcome by multi-organ failure, peripheral oedema and malnutrition, finally expiring five months after his injury. The post mortem revealed fluid escaping from various body areas, reflecting his body's 'waterlogged' state from organ failure and hypoproteinaemia.

Boiteux Langlet Aet 20

Was wounded on the 18th June and admitted into the Gens d'Armerie Hospital on the 30th.

A cannon ball carried away the left leg and the thigh was immediately amputated [i.e. the stump tidied up] on the field.

---

96   Gross swelling of the part, as witnessed in severe heart failure, otherwise called oedema.
97   The mesenteric lymph nodes of the intestine – part of the body's immune system.

He states that at the moment that the French were retreating, and, that, the surgeon not taking time to secure the arteries, merely applied a large quantity of Charpie,[98] and hastily bandaging it, left him to his fate.

For some days he had nothing almost either to eat, or to drink, and the stump, was not dressed till ten days after amputation. When admitted into hospital the granulations, had a healthy appearance but the bone protruded, and had become black[99] at its extremity, he complained of pain in the stump, while dressing it; his pulse quick, skin hot, appetite bad, belly rather costive, tongue white.

His bowels were freely opened, and Diaphoretic medicines administered, but the febrile conditions still continued and in the course of three days the granulations[100] became indolent and of a horny appearance. By the use of medicines, his skin became moist, & the pulse more soft; but general irritability with a disposition to spasmodic affections of muscles, particularly those of the face.

On the 22nd July he became restless & uneasy, & died on the 23rd

Upon examination after death, all the large veins of the stump were found to be inflamed, thickened, and uncommonly vascular with ulceration at the extremity of the femoral vein, unfortunately the state of the vena cava was not examined, but there cannot be a doubt that the inflammation extended to the heart.[101]

There was an abscess on the outer surface of the remaining portion of the femur, also one in the substance of the bone, near its cut extremity, around which was a considerable deposition of bony matter but no appearance of separation of sound from diseased parts.

Henry Home Blackadder &c. &c. &c.

Brussels, 30th July 1815

Comment

With this severe and life-threatening injury, the patient's surgery was interrupted by the precipitous French retreat. The surgeon, instead of securing the blood vessels with catch forceps or a tenaculum (a mounted fine sharp hook for teasing out blood vessels prior to ligation) and then ligatures, merely stuffed charpie (often used by the French medical staff) into the open wound and then bandaged it in. This was very risky to the patient, since torrential haemorrhage might soon have terminated Langlet's existence. The dilemma for the surgeon was to either finish the job properly or run from a likely death at the hands of ruthless pursuers! At any rate, 12 days later the patient was admitted to hospital, before which the dressings had been changed once. The wound had started to heal, but the protruding end of the cut femur had lost its blood supply. The patient was febrile and, as per usual, septic. He had diarrhoea, a problem often accompanying very sick patients. He then had spasmodic twitching of muscles, including his facial muscles. The sepsis had clearly travelled up the

98   Linen, as opposed to cotton waste.
99   Necrotic or gangrenous as it had lost its blood supply.
100 Exuberant and friable healing tissues forming around the stump.
101 Here there is clear clinical evidence of, firstly early or mild tetanic infection and also of septicaemia spreading along the venous channels. These observations on the spread of sepsis along veins had previously been observed by Surgeon George Guthrie.

veins from the abscesses described around the femoral stump. He died about a month after wounding.

Sergeant Sutherland (aet. 32) [2nd Battalion 3rd Foot Guards]

Has this day a large extensive sore on the leg and thigh with a sinus extending to the hip joint, discharging variably a thick or thin extremely foetid pus, highly irritable and painful leaving little or no doubt of a diseased head of femur independent of the general map of disease. Pulse 120 small and weak hardly perceptible at the wrist & impossible to count it. There, appetite good and no diarrhoea but has a little hectic exacerbation now and then with sweats. Has a large, deep ill conditioned bed sore on the sacrum & another on the left Trochanter but the latter is more healthy. ½ past two o'clock removed the limb from the socket at the hip with the loss of less than a pound of blood and in that is included what came from the limb. Was rather faint during the operation and took 4 ozs. of port wine; it was not found necessary to secure any of the circumflex, Ischiatic, or Obturator branches[102] but the branches from the Iliac [artery] were tied and Iliac which was bleeding profusely. Took Tinct. Opii. Gr. XI and was put to bed immediately. Countenance continued pale and sweat copiously for an hour and a half when the sweating began to decline, at half past six pulse fuller perceptible to be counted at the wrist 130 skin rather hot spirits good countenance restored & quite easy & tranquil. Stump had oozed considerably but appeared now to be checked.

August 23rd 8 o'clock passed an excellent night drank freely of lemonade, pulse gradually quickened to 126 by 4 o'clock. Commenced with the fever mixture at 4 o'clock and continued it during the day. Took some butter pudding, chicken broth and drank freely of apple water & lemonade. 7 o'clock has just had a rigor on inquiry found he would have the window open notwithstanding the repeated orders to the contrary and, I think from the slightness the rigor will prove of no great importance. Gave him Tinct. Opii Gns. XXX e [with] Ant. Tar[rate] of ½.

August 24th 8 o'clock. Continued rather warm all night drinking freely of gruel when he walked which was only 3 times for a few minutes, has had no stool since the operation, would have given him an enema but he had such an aversion to it thought it better to wait till the morning and while it was preparing had one with a few hard faeces. Ordered him Ol [oil]. Ricini [vide supra], drachm 1 statim, 7 o'clock in the evening was perspiring rather too much in the middle of the day when the vitriolic acid[103] was substituted in lieu of the Apple water & lemonade. Appetite had been very good & the sweating is now gone off except the back of the head and has had two good stools from the oil. P[ulse] 124 soft and regular throughout the day. Bed sores were much the same.

August 25th 8 o'clock. Had a severe and regular paroxysm of intermittent last night, shivering commencing 10 minutes before light, the sweating was profuse

102 The arterial branches.
103 Sulphuric acid.

has however slept well the whole night pulse 116 and is refreshed. Commenced at 5 o'clock this morning with Tinct. Cinchona drachm 11 e [with] Acid Sulph. Dilut. Grns XXX [30] and repeated at eight, eat [sic] his breakfast with avidity at 11 complained of nausea with a cold sweat on his face and soon vomited about a pint of greenish matter when it went off and he took his nourishment as usual and has taken a bottle of bottled porter in the day. The bed sores look rather better & on dressing the stump the integuments were found perfectly united at the lower part of the distance, in the centre they were about an inch open gradually closing again towards the upper part; about two or three drachms of fluid from I suppose the acetabulum[104] of a light beer colour was discharged, and although considering the situation he has been in it was astonishingly well; ordered him to take a dose of laudanum to prevent the paroxysm which had the desired effect.

August 26th Has slept soundly the whole night pulse 118 soft and regular. 8 in the Evening. Has been very well all day eat and drank heartily and been reading all day has had a stool ordered him to take Tinct. Opii grns. XX 6ta ggrorq. [?] Has not perspired anything like as much today as before.

Aug 27th Has passed an excellent night pulse 106 and eats really quite heartily, has no perspiration on his head this morning, at two o'clock he called for the urinal and on using it was in excessive agony so much so that his forehead and face were instantly covered with huge drops of sweat pulse 120 & intermitting ordered the bottled beer and wine to be stopped and milk substitutes, Habeat Pulv. grem drachm 11.

3, o'clock the perspiration has continued profuse ever since voids his urine mixed with blood, 5 o'clock the sweating continues, the strangury[105] appears to be getting better but still great. 9 o'clock the sweating is rather abated Ret. Tinct opii grns XX

August 28th Has been talking in his sleep this morning. Pulse sunk and has a cadaverous smell about him although bed linen &c are changed daily, took sago and milk this morning. Strangury still continues slightly. Pulse continued to intermit and is 126, the bed sores are worse but the stump looks well ordered him half a pint of wine with spices and raised up in bed so as to sit on the tuberosity of the ischium. ½ past 12 the sweating continues the wine has not altered his pulse, sumat. Camphorie gr. VIII, Ammon: carbon gr. III conf. aromal: statim Rept. Vini Rubri drachm V 6.h. [6 hourly]. 3 o'clock it is now necessary to rouse him a little to get a correct answer from him.

8 o'clock in the evening. Is somewhat rallied has had two stools & is more alert. Has taken his beef tea and pudding as usual but no meat Rep. Vin. Rubr 2dc gghom.

August 29th has passed a good night is quite collected and considerably rallied (pulse 120) but not so much as one could wish. Eat a couple of slices of cold roast Beef this morning with avidity and took his sago with wine in lieu of the milk. 11 o'clock has had another paroxysm of intermittent. Rept. Tin: opii e [with] aether: 5 o'clock. The sweating has been profuse.

104 The concave part of the ball and socket hip joint.
105 Painful urination with straining and painfully voiding small amounts of urine.

August 30th Is sinking fast ordered him brandy in lieu of the wine which raised him a little for an hour or two in the day but he sunk again in the evening and died at 10 o'clock at night

Dissection

The thoracic, and abdominal viscera were found healthy except the liver which was a little enlarged with the gall bladder distended and the right kidney which was very large, union by the first intention had taken place full[y]. One third the length of the stump [wound] at the lower part and was obliged to be cut, the remainder with some force was separated, & union was only partial, the muscles at one side of the Acetabulum and to all the edge had adhered the capsular ligament had been scarified it was of a pink colour and from that part where the gland[106] was removed there were decided granulations.

By accident afterwards in operating the large veins were found inflated so much so that in puncturing the subclavian vein the air rushed out with a hissing noise.[107]

W J Blicke, Surgeon to the Forces

Comment

This is only the second example of disarticulation at the hip joint in the records of this campaign.

There was only one Sergeant Sutherland who was discharged dead after Waterloo and thus this must be our man. The report refers to Sergeant Alexander Sutherland of Lieutenant Colonel Charles West's company of the 2nd Battalion 3rd Foot Guards. He is incorrectly shown as a private in the Waterloo Medal Roll. He was not issued his Waterloo Prize Money. He is recorded as No. 147 in the line drawings.

The exact track of the musket ball injury is a little unclear, but the ball may have entered the thigh and tracked upwards and outwards. It was fortunate that the ball had missed the femoral artery and the knee joint. There seems little doubt that the head of the femur in the hip joint was damaged. Thus, it would have been difficult to carry out any lesser procedure than a disarticulation of the whole lower limb, at the hip joint. The patient was admitted from a private dwelling into the Facon Hospital in Antwerp, on the 6 July. This was over two weeks since the injury. Well-meaning householders had plied him with rich foods, which were considered by Surgeon Blicke to be partly responsible for his feverish and poor state of health. In fact, inevitable and severe sepsis was the problem. In addition to the deep seated bony and muscular abscesses, the patient had two pressure sores, one in the sacral area and the other on the upper outer thigh lateral to the hip joint, on the side opposite the injured thigh. The deep muscular wound had been treated and was 'now clean', but the sepsis and loss of protein had caused him great weight loss. It is an interesting case report as it castigates the kindness of the 'private house' dwellers for plying him with meat, wine etc., which

---

106 The head of the femur.
107 This is certain evidence of anaerobic wound in infection, with gas-forming organisms.

in contemporary theory of convalescence was not recommended and such relapses as did occur frequently, were often blamed on such indulgences.

It is unclear as to when this large operation was carried out but there may well have been a delay of over six weeks. This may have been to settle the patient and wait for the hectic fevers to abate. This was a delayed operation with all its attendant risks and it was performed on the 22 August. We get some idea of the surgery from Blicke's description. How long the operation took, we do not know, but probably about half an hour. His assistants were given the tasks of pressing on the minor blood vessels with their fingers, whilst the main arteries were tied off. The patient was faint afterwards, but given cordials and opium. He had lost another pint of blood during the operation. His pulse came down a little and became stronger and Sutherland was able to take various refreshments. His wound appeared to be partly healing.

On day five, post operatively, he had painful urination and passed blood. He may have had some bladder stones or gained a bladder infection. His bedsores had not improved, so the sepsis from the wound site, bedsores, and possibly the cystitis terminated his life on the eighth post-operative day. At post mortem, the only fact of interest, apart from the sepsis in the wound and removed limb, was air escaping from the subclavian vein in the thorax – clear evidence of infection with anaerobic gas-forming bacteria.

11

Other Named Cases from Waterloo

After the wars had ended, many surgeons wrote up their experiences or produced articles and textbooks, passing on what had been learnt regarding how best to proceed with certain battlefield wounds, in the light of their experiences in the hospitals of Spain and Belgium. A number of named and selected cases of casualties from the Waterloo campaign were treated in Brussels, Antwerp, and later there were some reports from British hospitals, such as Colchester and the York Hospital in Chelsea. These cases were recorded in the texts written by two eminent military surgeons George James Guthrie and John Hennen These have been collected into this book, without much detailed medical commentary, to further illustrate the later experiences of others who were wounded in the campaign of 1815.

Second Lieutenant John Prendergast Walsh, 2nd Battalion 95th Foot[1]

> After the Battle of Waterloo my opinion was requested on the case of a very young officer of the rifle corps, who has since entered the church, who was struck, as was supposed, by a canister shot on the knee, which had lodged in the head of the tibia, although it could not be felt. I examined the joint, found a large external opening with the bone broken within, as if a ball had entered deep into its substance; the whole joint was in a state of suppuration, the pulse 130 and he was much emaciated. Amputation was performed with great dexterity and despatch by Staff Surgeon Lindsey[2] and the patient's life was only saved by this gentleman's unwearied diligence. I examined the joint, after the operation, but no ball could be found; it had never lodged.[3]
>
> Walsh remained in the army until 1833, when he was a lieutenant (half pay) in the 6th Foot. He took Holy Orders afterwards.

1 Guthrie, *A treatise on gunshot wounds*, p.20.
2 Staff Surgeon Owen Lindsey, a late arrival after Waterloo.
3 The ball had conceivably been ejected on joint movement – amputation was mandated here.

Captain Henry Dumaresq, 9th Foot, aide de camp to Major General Sir John Byng[4]

Lieutenant Colonel Dumaresq,[5] aide de camp to Sir John Byng, was wounded at the Battle of Waterloo by a musket ball, whilst in the act of turning round, after having made a successful charge with some advanced light infantry at the farm of Hougoumont; the ball passed in through the scapula, penetrated and was lost in the chest. The symptoms of thoracic inflammation were almost irrestrainable [i.e. untreatable], and he barely escaped with life. A swelling was then discovered in the axilla, and it is now fully ascertained to be the ball, which lodged in the rib, I should suppose without destroying the periosteum [the nutrient membrane tightly enclosing evert bone], and which has formed a quantity of bony matter around it. At one time an operation for its removal was talked of, but he always dissented from such a proceeding, and he now enjoys good health, although occasionally subject to spasms in the chest.

Dumaresq described his own wounding on 2 July 1815[6]

While turning round, after a successful charge of infantry, at Hougoumont on the 18th of June 1815, I was wounded by a musket ball, which passed through the right scapula, penetrated the chest, and lodged in the middle of the rib in the axilla, which was supposed to be broken. When desired to cough by the medical officer who first saw me, almost immediately after receiving [me], some blood was inter-mixed with the saliva. I became extremely faint and remained so about an hour and a half, after which I rode four or five miles to the village of Waterloo, where I was bled, which relieved me from the great difficulty; this difficulty was accompanied by a severe pain down my neck, chest and right side. I was much easier until the evening of the 19th; but in the course of the night, the difficulty of breathing becoming much greater, and the spasmodic affection having very much increased, I was bled seven times, until the middle of the next day. 20th I continued better but was then seized with the most violent spasms imaginable in my neck, chest and stomach. I could scarcely breathe at all and was in the greatest possible pain; I was again bled twice very largely, and my stomach and chest fomented for a length of time with warm water and flannels. I passed a very tolerable night and continued very well until two o'clock the following day, when I was again very largely bled, by which I was very much relieved [this demonstrates the placebo effect of a treatment which was of little value]. I continued pretty well, and free from much pain; but my pulse having very much increased, and having a good deal of fever, on the 23rd I was bled again; after this I continued from much pain or difficulty of respiration, and on the 26th was removed into Bruxelles, when I came under your care. I forgot to mention that when I was so violently attacked I had two lavements [sic] most vigorously applied; salts etc proving of no avail, took digitalis [as a stimulant],

4   Guthrie, *A treatise on gunshot wounds*, p.93.
5   Dumaresq became a lieutenant colonel in June 1817.
6   Guthrie, *Commentaries on the Surgery of the War, In Portugal, Spain, France and the Netherlands*, p.440.

commencing with ten drops every four hours, increasing to fifteen from the second day. NB Up to this period, the 2nd of July, the devil a bit have I eaten [i.e. he was on a low diet].

Dumaresq married Elizabeth Danvers in 1828 and died in New South Wales on 5 March 1838, aged 46, when a manager of an Australian Agricultural company.

Lieutenant Colonel John Ross, 3rd Battalion 95th Foot[7]

Colonel Ross of the Rifle Brigade was wounded at the Battle of Waterloo by a musket ball which entered at the upper part of the arm and injured the bone. More than one surgeon had pointed out the way by which it had passed under the scapula and lodged itself in some of the muscles of the back. About a year afterwards, I extracted it close to the elbow, the ball lying at the bottom of an abscess, which was only brought near the surface by the use of flannel [poultices], and by desisting from all emollient applications.

Ross died on 21 April 1835.

Private John Hodges, 2nd Battalion 3rd Foot Guards[8]

John Hodges, 3rd Foot Guards [of Lieutenant Colonel Master's company], aged 21, was wounded on the 18th June by a musket ball, which entered a little below the anterior part of the right shoulder, passing out behind; it went on favourably until 15th July, both wounds having a healthy appearance, and discharging good pus, when the arm became tumid and painful; he had rigors and other symptoms denoting the formation of matter, but it did not reach the surface till the 21st, when it was opened, and a very large quantity of offensive pus was evacuated. During the period specified, he constantly laboured under more or less fever, with slight cough and expectoration, for which he took saline purgatives and febrifuge medicines [medications or substances to reduce fever eg cooling drinks, cinchona (bark) and angostura]. At the time of opening the abscess, the fever was much abated, and what little he had was of a low type. 24th Passed a very restless night, and for a few hours was delirious; complains of pain in the chest and expectorates a considerable quantity of purulent sanguineous matter; pulse quick; but notwithstanding he was very low, six or eight ounces of blood were drawn from the arm. 25th He passed another restless night, but his pains and fever were much abated; blood drawn yesterday did not exhibit the inflammatory appearance; expectorates [coughs and spits] freely; the discharge from the abscess continues very offensive, and the original wounds have assumed an unhealthy appearance. A pectoral mixture was

---

7   Guthrie, *A treatise on gunshot wounds*, p.97.
8   Guthrie, *A treatise on gunshot wounds*, p.256.

ordered, and acidulated barley water prescribed him for common drink. 26th He had little or no fever; expectoration diminished, and no pain whatever in the chest; he was extremely low. Wine and sago and a pint of milk were ordered him. About 11 pm there was a discharge of blood from the abscess to the quantity of about half a pint, from the effect of which he never rallied. He died at three o'clock on the morning of the 27th.

Private John Lomax, 2nd Battalion Coldstream Guards

It appears he was wounded at the Battle of Waterloo, and in consequence suffered amputation of the right arm on the 23rd of August, the operation was performed midway between the shoulder and elbow joints, was admitted into the general hospital at Colchester [this garrison hospital received many Waterloo cases], on the 27th of August. On his admission he was in a state of high fever of the typhoid type and was unable to give any very distinct account of himself; he stated, that in hospital at Antwerp he had the ague for many days, which left him for a short time; but returned again on his passage on board ship to this country, that on the 25th he was attacked with pain in the side, which was very severe on the 26th, on which day a blister [a form of counter irritation using, for example, dried up and powdered very irritating cantharides insects] was applied to the affected part, which greatly relieved him. The stump had an unhealthy appearance and evinced a disposition to separate. On the 28th he was free from pain; but his febrile symptoms were not abated, and there was a tendency to delirium. He continued with little alteration on the 29th, but sunk rapidly on the 30th, notwithstanding the use of the most powerful stimuli, and died on the evening of the 31st.

The Waterloo Prize Roll confirms that he was Discharged Dead, but his prize money was paid to his wife, Jane Lomax.

Private George Burnett, 1st Battalion 92nd Foot[9]

George Burnet, of the 92nd Regiment [Captain S. Maxwell's company], was wounded at the Battle of Waterloo by a musket ball, which entered near the anterior edge of the deltoid muscle [the large muscle running over the shoulder], passed through the head of the humerus, and came out near the posterior edge of the same muscle. He was treated successively in the general hospitals at Antwerp, Yarmouth, Colchester and Chatham, and was admitted into the York Hospital of the 13th November 1816. A great many pieces of bone had been extracted at different times previously to this date, and they were evidently portions of the head of the humerus. The motion of the shoulder joint was lost, but the pronation and

---

9   Guthrie, *A treatise on gunshot wounds*, p.478.

supination [rotational movements of the arm] of the hand could be readily effected, as well as the movements of the fingers, and nearly of the elbow joint. The opening of the entrance of the ball, and one that was made towards the back part, in August 1815, by incision, were discharging freely. The place where the ball had passed out was marked by a circatrix [scar]. In December the shoulder became inflamed, and incision was made into it and a piece of bone extracted, from which he obtained considerable relief. In January 1817, the probe could still be passed, but no pieces of bone could be felt, the discharge diminished, and he suffered little or no inconvenience from it. In May the probe could not be passed, the discharge was very trifling, and the openings were closing. In July 1817, two years after the receipt of the injury, he was discharged, with a pension of 9d per day, free from inconvenience, save that which arose from the loss of motion in the joint, but which he did not mind, as he had use of the forearm, and a certain movement of the shoulder, depending on the greater power he had acquired of moving the scapula.

He lived in Inverness and Aberdeen for many years and he was still living in 1865.

Private Anthony Chitty, 1st Battalion 95th Foot[10]

Anthony Chitty, of the 95th Regiment [of Captain E. Chawner's company], when he presented himself at the York Hospital in 1817, was perfectly cured. The wound had been at the upper part of the right arm and implicating the head of the humerus; the deficiency of which could be distinguished through the cicatrix. This man had been principally under the care of Staff Surgeons Blicke and Swallow[11], who had removed the portions of the bone, and to whose ability he was indebted for his recovery. He retained a considerable degree of motion in the shoulder joint [i.e. although the patient had eventually suffered a false shoulder joint, most of which had been destroyed by his injury, he had retained some useful movement].

He received his Waterloo Prize Money, but is recorded as Invalided out of the army in the Waterloo Medal Roll. He was granted a pension of 6d per day on 6 March 1816 and was living in South London. He died on 6 July 1854 at Deptford, aged 67.

Private Thomas Ellard, 18th Hussars[12]

Thomas Ellard, a private in the 18th Hussars [of Captain J. Lloyd's troop], aged 32, muscular and apparently free from any kind of disease, was admitted a patient of York Hospital, September 18th, 1815, for a gunshot wound of the left shoulder,

---

10 Guthrie, *A treatise on gunshot wounds*, p.478.
11 Staff Surgeon Robert Swallow, who retired on Christmas Day 1815 and died in December 1836 (No. 2068 in Peterkin & Johnston *Medical Officers*).
12 Guthrie, *A treatise on gunshot wounds*, p.479.

received at the Battle of Waterloo. The ball had passed through the head of the os humeri, about an inch and a half below the scapular extremity of the clavicle [collar bone], as may be seen by a reference to the annexed plate.

In addition to the two wounds made by the entrance and exit of the ball, there was a third occasioned by an abscess which had formed, and which had been opened, and from which some small fragments of bone had been extracted. The situation of this latter opening was a little below the insertion of the pectoralis major, and upon examination with the probe was found to communicate with two former ones. In whatever direction the instrument passed, shattered pieces of bone could be felt. From the long and constant irritation kept up by the fractured portions of the head of the bone, and the profuse discharge of offensive matter which they occasioned, the health of the patient was evidently on the decline, and as it clearly appeared that nature of herself was unable to remove the offending cause, there remained the alternative of either removing the member at its articulation with the scapula, or of attempting to preserve it by cutting out the shattered portions of the bone. On the 22nd November, in the presence of most of the medical officers of the York Hospital, and other gentlemen, an assistant having made pressure with a boot hook wrapt [sic] up in a piece of lint, upon the subclavian artery, as it passes over the first rib, I made an incision through the integuments and deltoid muscle; commencing at the upper orifice, and continuing it in a semilunar direction to the opposite side, with the intention of forming a flap, similar to that which is made when the arm is to be removed at the articulation. This operation took up nearly three quarters of an hour. Two arteries only required the ligature. On sawing through the posterior portion of the bone, an artery sprang from the interior substance of it; but the haemorrhage was immediately suppressed by a dossil of lint dipt in spirits of turpentine. I should suppose that the man might lose during the operation about two pounds of blood, an occurrence to be considered rather as favourable than otherwise [ie this was the equivalent to a vigorous therapeutic venesection!]. He bore the operation with great firmness; was carried to his bed; the shoulder and arm ordered to be kept constantly wet with cloths dipt into cold water, and in the evening an opiate was administered. 23rd I visited him about ten o'clock this morning; found him in good spirits; slept but little during the night and complained only of soreness; skin moist; tongue clean; countenance cheerful; pulse about 120. He was put upon spoon [ie a sloppy] diet, and the opiate ordered to be repeated. 24th Slept very well, and said he was not in any one respect than he was before the operation. This morning I removed the dressings, which from their stiffness had occasioned some uneasiness, and found all quiet; perfectly free from pain, inflammation, or tension; edges of the wound in contact; skin temperate; pulse 102; tongue clean; slept a little at intervals; rather languid. Not having had an evacuation since the operation, I gave him half an ounce of sulphate of magnesia in a little peppermint water and repeated the opiate in the evening; a small quantity of broth was allowed.

There followed some further minor details of Ellard's recovery, dealing with diet, bowel function and wound care. He was discharged from hospital in early January 1816. Thomas was invalided from the army, but still received his Waterloo Prize Money in 1817.

Trooper Ellard by Charles Bell. (Courtesy of the Museum of Military Medicine)

Private Owen Sweeney 2nd Battalion 95th Foot[13]

Owen Sweeney, 2nd Battalion, 90th [sic – 95th] Regiment[14] [of Captain F. Le Blanc's company], aged 19, was wounded by a musket ball, on the 18th of June, which carried off a great portion of the little finger of the left hand and wounded the ring finger; the former was amputated at its metacarpal articulation, on the following day. Between the period of his quitting Brussels, July 5th, and his arrival at Colchester, on the 14th, a collection of matter had formed above the annular ligament of the carpus, which broke spontaneously and discharged freely; he had at this time a most unhealthy aspect; but his appetite was good and he did not complain. Bark was prescribed for him, and a pint of porter allowed daily. On the 24th, a second collection of matter pointed about the middle of the back of the forearm, which was evacuated; and on the 26th, a third, about an inch higher up, which was treated in like manner. The whole discharged good healthy pus, and his health rather improved. As he was not confined to bed, but walked a good

13   Guthrie, *A treatise on gunshot wounds*, p.531.
14   Guthrie constantly states that he was in the 90th Regiment, although that regiment was not at Waterloo; he was actually in the 95th.

deal about, there being many more severe cases, I only occasionally saw him. On the 29th, I was informed that in the preceding night there had been a haemorrhage from the several abscesses, which however, was soon supressed; I found him looking extremely ill; the discharge very fetid and mixed with blood. The limb was enveloped in cold compresses, and a tourniquet applied loosely by way of security. Haemorrhage recurring in the night, the arm was removed on the 30th. On dissection the whole of the muscles were found in a state of disease, the flexor ones particularly were entirely separated from their attachment to the bones; the integuments (with the exception of the parts where the abscesses had pointed) were perfectly sound. He continued extremely well after the operation till the afternoon of the following day (31st), when he was seized with rigors, which continued for about fifteen minutes, and were succeeded by febrile symptoms and a tendency to vomit. Effervescing draughts were prescribed. On the following morning he was considerably better, and continued going on perfectly well till the 6th of August, when he was again attacked with symptoms of fever. Small doses of the sulphate of magnesia were ordered him. Early in the morning of the 7th he was attacked with griping of the bowels, followed by purging and vomiting; it was many hours before the latter could be overcome, and he was very much reduced by it. On the 9th he was very low and complained of pain and tenderness on pressure of the abdomen, which was in some degree relieved by fomentations and an enema; his stump continued to look extremely well, and discharged healthy [i.e. thick pus, laden with white blood cells] pus, in small quantity; the ligature on the brachial artery, which had been cut short, came away this day. On the 10th, the fullness and tension of the abdomen had returned, and not having had an evacuation since the preceding day, the enema was directed to be repeated. His tongue and teeth were covered with a dark sordes [ulcers]; chicken broth and wine were ordered to be frequently given him, in small quantities. During the night of the 10th he was very restless, and he had low delirium; and on visiting him, on the morning of the 11th, I found him collected, but very low, and with the complete facies hippocratica [the so called 'Hippocratic Facies was that of a person near to death, with sunken, sallow and pallid features]; two injections had failed to procure a motion, and he was ordered a pill of hyd submur [probably sublimated dilute hydrochloric acid] which he swallowed with some difficulty; he continued to take small quantities of wine till one o'clock when he died.

This case highlights the risks incurred even with the smallest wounds.

Trooper Thomas Haynes, 23rd Light Dragoons[15]

Thomas Haynes, 23rd Light Dragoons [of Captain McNeill's No. 3 troop], aged 19, was wounded on the 18th of June, by a spear [lance] on the back of the left forearm, about an hand's width above the wrist; it did well until the period of his departure from Brussels; on his march from that place to Ostend it assumed an unfavourable appearance, and on his arrival at Colchester, on the 14th of July, it was completely in a sloughing state. I first saw him on the 16th; the sore was then circular, and about three inches in diameter; the integuments were entirely destroyed, and the whole of the extensor muscles were deeply involved in the disease; he had considerable fever, accompanied with a strong hard pulse. Attention to the state of the bowels had been the only constitutional treatment employed; the local applications consisted of emollient poultices only. The pain was excessive, and the tenderness around the whole circumference of the sore was so great, that he could not suffer the smallest pressure with the finger. I directed him to be largely bled, and instead of the poultices, a solution of the sulphuric acid, to be applied twice a day to the whole surface; to allay the burning heat that constantly prevailed in the surrounding parts, he was directed to keep them continually wet with cold water; that treatment was pursued to the 21st, during which period he was bled five times, and the quantity of blood drawn each time amounted to be about twenty ounces; his bowels were kept open by saline purgatives, and he drank plentifully of acid drinks. The sore had not increased in size; several portions of sloughs had been detached, leaving healthy granulations; there was still however, much to be thrown off; the strength of the solution was directed to be increased; care was taken in the application, that the sloughing portions only were touched with it; his health was considerably amended, and on the whole a favourable result was expected. About two o'clock on the morning of the 22nd, a sudden and unexpected haemorrhage took place; it was most profuse, amounting I should consider, at least to three pints. I found him at my hour of visit with his countenance extremely pallid, and pulse very frequent and weak; sore continuing to improve; it was difficult to pronounce with certainty from whence the bleeding came; the extent of disease rendering it possible that it might be from any of the great vessels of the forearm. The same treatment was directed to be pursued, and a loose tourniquet was applied on the limb, by way of security. A second haemorrhage ensued on the morning of the 23rd, which was immediately supressed. Notwithstanding the patient was very low, I amputated the arm; scarce a drop of blood was lost during the operation. The pulse continued quick, in other respects he was perfectly well until the 25th, when he had some accession of fever, for which a saline purgative was prescribed; on visiting him on the evening of the same day, I found that the cathartic had operated briskly; notwithstanding, his fever had increased and his pulse was become fuller and harder; in consequence of which he was bled to the amount of ten ounces. On the following day he had somewhat less fever, but his pulse remained very frequent. The outer dressings and a portion of the straps were removed; adhesion by the first intention appeared to have taken

15 Guthrie, *A treatise on gunshot wounds*, p.534.

place nearly throughout the whole extent of the stump. On the 27th he remained much the same, and had no unpleasant symptom, with the exception of the frequent pulse, which now beat 140 strokes in the minute; he was free from pain of every kind. On removing the centre strap which had been suffered to remain yesterday, a large collection of matter (of good quality) issued. On the 28th the frequency of the pulse was not diminished, but it was less full than the preceding day; no other untoward symptom as yet manifested itself; from the centre of the stump (the only part where adhesions had not taken place) a similar quantity of healthy pus was again discharged. In the evening he remained much the same; but having had no motion for twenty-four hours, a common purgative injection was prescribed. On visiting him on the morning of the 29th, I was instantly struck with the alteration in his countenance, which had assumed a deathlike paleness; his pulse was less frequent (120), but intermitted about every fifth pulsation; his breathing very short and laborious, with some pain in the chest, and every symptom of effusion having taken place; stump continued to discharge good matter, but much less in quantity. He got rapidly worse and died at two o'clock pm six days after the amputation.

Thomas was Discharged Dead and his Waterloo Prize Money was not paid out.

Private Alexander Clark, 1st Battalion 79th Foot[16]

Private A Clarke, 79th Regiment, had his thigh broken by a musket ball a little above the knee joint, at Waterloo, and was admitted into the clinical ward of the York Hospital in London in November 1816. The bone being in a state of necrosis, Mr Guthrie amputated the thigh high up, on the 20th January 1817. Pulse before and after the operation 104. On the 25th pulse 120; skin cool, tongue moist, appeared weak and irritable. During the 26th and 27th symptoms of low fever came on. 28th, suffered severely from vomiting, general fever, greater prostration of strength; stump had not united, but discharged good [ie thick] pus. 30th skin assumed a yellow tinge. On the 1st of February had a rigor resembling a fit of ague, and Mr Guthrie declared his suspicion of the formation of matter, probably in the liver, and of inflammation of the veins of the stump. The symptoms gradually assumed the character of typhus gravior [ie symptoms resembling a serious case of Typhus fever], and on the 8th he died. On dissection the liver was found enlarged and weighing six pounds, the other viscera were sound. On examining the stump an abscess containing four ounces of good pus was found in the under part, near the bone. The femoral vein and those going to that part of the stump were inflamed, and contained coagulated blood, lymph, and purulent matter, the disease extending from the femoral to the vena cava.

Septicaemia and multi-organ failure had claimed another victim.

16   Guthrie, *Commentaries on the Surgery of the War, In Portugal, Spain, France and the Netherlands*, p.64.

Private Charles Brown, 1st Battalion 92nd Foot[17]

Charles Brown 92nd Regiment, forty years of age, at that time a healthy man, was wounded on the 18th June by two musket balls in the right hand and wrist; he was admitted into the hospital at Antwerp on 25th June. On the 5th July, the arm was swollen above the elbow; discharge profuse and fetid; countenance sallow and dejected; fever. 8th arm amputated above the elbow. 9th, 10th, 11th, A little increase of fever. 12th A paroxysm of intermittent, to which he had been subject occasionally since he had been at Walcheren. On removing the dressing, the edges of the stump were retorted [shortened and conical like a retort]; discharge copious and fetid; respiration hurried; thirst; skin hot and yellowish; pulse 90. 14th Intermittent returned; head [ache] affected in consequence of long continuance in the hot bath. 15th complains today of fullness and pain in the left side; pulse 100; skin of a deeper tinge of yellow; a sense of suffocation when in the horizontal position. A blister was applied to the whole side of the chest. 16th; Was delirious during the night; vomited frequently; became insensible at the hour when the paroxysm of intermittent fever was expected to return; and died in the evening.

It is difficult to ascertain whether the patient had a flare up and recurrence of malaria that he had contracted in the Walcheren campaign, or was just severely septic, with all the sequelae. Charles Brown was Discharged Dead but his Waterloo Prize Money was paid out.

Private William Mitchell, 1st Foot[18]

William Mitchel, of the Royals, aged forty, was wounded by a musket ball on the 18th of June at Waterloo; it struck the side of the head near the vertex, and passing across through the sagittal suture, fractured and depressed both parietal bones. When he had recovered his senses, he suffered great pain in the part and found that he had lost the use of both his legs and was benumbed even from the loins and the lower part of the chest; he was often sick and felt low and ill. He was brought to the Minime Hospital at Antwerp on the 27th August. On the 28th, ten days after the battle, the trephine was applied in two places, and the whole of the detached and depressed portions of bone were removed. The sickness, lowness of spirits, and general illness immediately subsided, and the loss of power in the lower extremities gradually began to diminish, but he was not able to walk without assistance until the first week in August. On the 10th he arrived at Yarmouth, not having had a bad symptom after the depressed bone had been removed; and by the end of September he was discharged, able to walk well with the assistance of a stick.

17   Guthrie, *Commentaries on the Surgery of the War, In Portugal, Spain, France and the Netherlands*, p.67.
18   Guthrie, *Commentaries on the Surgery of the War, In Portugal, Spain, France and the Netherlands*, p.310. There was no one of this name in the 1st (Royals) Foot, but there were four men of this name at Waterloo. Only one of these four was discharged after the battle, a private William Mitchell in Captain James Stirling's Company of the 42nd. Therefore, it is most likely to be this man – was the regiment wrongly named in the case note?

This was indeed an impressive result of the trephining. Mitchell was given a pension of 1 shilling per day from 27 June 1821 when he resided at Dundee and died on 6 March 1858.

Private Thomas O'Brien, 1st Battalion 28th Foot[19]

Thomas O'Brien, 28th Regiment [of brevet Lieutenant Colonel Sir Frederick Steven's company], aged twenty-three, was wounded by a musket ball on the 16th of June at Quatre Bras; the bullet entered the occipital bone below and to the right of the junction of the lambdoidal and sagittal sutures [two of the skull fissures at the back of the cranium]. On his arrival at Colchester, the wound was healthy in appearance and healing rapidly. It appeared from his own account that for some hours after the injury he was totally deprived of sight; since that time he has been constantly more or less affected with headaches, for which he has been prescribed occasional cathartics and low diet. He has also been affected with pain and weakness in both eyes, but more particularly in the right. While at Brussels, and during his progress to Ostend, he lived very irregularly and was frequently intoxicated. The external wound was entirely healed on the 20th of July and no suspicion existed that the ball was lodged in the brain. On the 25th matter was perceived under the scalp and was evacuated yesterday. Today the 27th, he complains of increase of headache, pulse small and quick. 28th in the course of this day his symptoms have become very urgent; he is restless with a very quick pulse; an extensive crucial incision was made in the site of the original wound, and now for the first time it was discovered that the ball had penetrated the brain; several loose pieces of bone were extracted; a considerable quantity of arterial blood was suffered to flow from the small vessel divided in the incision. His bowels had been well opened by the cathartic. The most vigorous treatment was continued, but the symptoms notwithstanding increased and he died on the morning of the 29th of July. The ball was found lodged nearly two inches deep in the substance of the right posterior lobe of the brain [the visual cortex is situated at the posterior end of the cerebrum].

O'Brien was Discharged Dead but his Waterloo Prize Money was paid out.

Private William Birkett, 1st Life Guards[20]

William Birkett of the Life Guards, a middle aged, muscular man, of full habit, was wounded by a musket ball at the Battle of Waterloo; it fractured the third and fourth ribs behind on the left side and broke the left arm. He was brought to Brussels, where the inflammatory symptoms were subdued by repeated general and local bleedings, and the other ordinary but strictly antiphlogistic means, during the first six weeks, by which time the external wound had nearly closed, and no trace of the ball could

---

19   Guthrie, *Commentaries on the Surgery of the War, In Portugal, Spain, France and the Netherlands*, p.333.
20   Guthrie, *Commentaries on the Surgery of the War, In Portugal, Spain, France and the Netherlands*, p.450.

be perceived. At the end of this time, Staff Surgeon Collier, now Inspector General of Hospitals, under whose care he was, finding that his symptoms became worse, that he had rigors and evening exacerbations, and that the difficulty of breathing had increased almost to suffocation, decided on opening into the cavity of the chest and following the course of the ball. This he did by a deep incision, which enabled him to remove some pieces of the ribs, which were denuded but not detached. A bag like protrusion was then felt between the ribs, near their angles, which was opened, and nearly two pints of thick, fetid pus escaped, the relief which followed being as complete as sudden. The wound sealed and a second evacuation was needed. He gradually recovered, and was sent to England, cured, in November.

It was not that frequent that this chest drainage procedure was carried out. In this case it proved highly successful. William was born at Netherslade in Westmorland and enlisted at Kendal on 5 December 1807. He was discharged on 18 May 1818 for serious pulmonary complaints.

Private James Wilkie, 12th Light Dragoons[21]

James Wilkie, 12th Light Dragoons, aged thirty-four, received a puncture wound from a sword on 18th of June at Waterloo. The sword entered about an inch below the inferior angle of the scapula on the left side, penetrated the thorax, appeared to have passed through the diaphragm, the point of the weapon coming out on the opposite side of the chest, between the first and second false ribs. The wounds were quite healed and he apparently enjoyed good health, when he arrived from Brussels in August. He was suddenly attacked at four pm of the 6th September 1815, with violent pain in the umbilical and epigastric regions, accompanied with nausea and great irritability of stomach; pulse small, rapid and regular. Assistant Surgeon Egan[22] visited him half an hour after the attack, bled him freely and caused the abdomen to be fomented with hot water; a large blister was applied to the seat of pain, an ounce of castor oil was given, and emollient and laxative clysters were occasionally administered. At night the symptoms abated, and he slept about three hours. The next morning his countenance exhibited that appearance of haggardness and anxiety which have always been alarming indications, pulse feeble and rapid; the pain severe; at noon he vomited from two to three ounces of black, fetid blood in a fluid state; the pulse became very feeble. At four pm the pain increased, he ejected from his stomach from four to six ounces of dark, fluid blood that had less fetor; and at six the same evening he expired in pain. On dissection the entire intestines were inflamed, and the stomach found full of black fetid blood.

21 Guthrie, *Commentaries on the Surgery of the War, In Portugal, Spain, France and the Netherlands*, p.461.
22 Patrick Egan was the assistant surgeon to the 12th Light Dragoons. We are not certain of his presence at Waterloo. At some stage he had been in a duel with a superior officer and had had to change regiments no. 2941 in Peterkin and Johnston, *Medical Officers*).

The sword had initially not wounded any vital organ. It may have partially injured the stomach wall, which after many weeks had given way, leading to secondary bleeding and possibly a degree of perforation, accounting for the inflamed intestines. James Wilkie was Discharged Dead, but his Waterloo Prize Money was still paid out in 1817.

Trooper Henry Dierking, 3rd Hussars KGL[23]

J [H] Dierking, a stout muscular man, of the 3rd Regiment of German Hussars [of Captain Goeben's troop], was wounded at the Battle of Waterloo, by a lance, which penetrated the chest between the fifth and sixth ribs and was then withdrawn. He fell from his horse, lost a good deal of blood by the mouth and some by the wound and was carried to Brussels without any particular attention being drawn to the injury. His strength not being restored, while he suffered from palpitations of the heart and other uneasy sensations in the chest, he was sent to England to be invalided; and in November 1815 was admitted into the York Hospital Chelsea, in consequence of an attack of pneumonia of which he died in two days. On examining the body, it was discovered that the lance had passed through the inferior lobe of the left lung, and also penetrated the pericardium [the sac containing the heart] under the heart, and sliced a piece of the outer edge of the right ventricle. It also penetrated the central tendon of the diaphragm and then entered the liver.

This was about as near to a fatal heart wound that one could sustain! Henry Dierking's record is blank, not recording an outcome, but confirming that he was not issued his Waterloo Prize Money.

Major General Sir Colin Halkett[24]

General Sir Colin Halkett KCB, was wounded on the 18th of June at Waterloo; when in front of his brigade, which was formed in squares for the reception of the French cavalry, by a pistol ball, fired by the officer commanding them, which struck him in the neck, and gave him great pain, but without doing much mischief. A second shot shortly afterwards wounded him in the thigh, and he was obliged to leave the field towards the close of the day, by a third musket ball, which struck him on the face when standing sideways to the enemy. It entered a little below the outer part of the cheek bone on the left side and taking an oblique direction downward and forward, shattered and destroyed in its course several of the double teeth [that is the premolars and molars] of the opposite side in the upper jaw, fracturing the palate from its posterior part forward to the front teeth. The ball then took a direction obliquely upward, destroying the teeth on the opposite side of the upper jaw, which bone it also broke, and lodged under the fleshy part of the cheek of the

---

23   Guthrie, *Commentaries on the Surgery of the War, In Portugal, Spain, France and the Netherlands,* p.470.
24   Guthrie, *Commentaries on the Surgery of the War, In Portugal, Spain, France and the Netherlands,* p.479.

opposite side. These wounds gave great pain, and until the ball was removed, the left ear was totally insensible to sound and all external impressions, although the general suffered much from distressing noises in his ear [tinnitus]. These subsided on removal of the ball some days afterwards. JP Tupper MD,[25] Antwerp July 1815. The general had to undergo a number of subsequent operations to remove pieces of bone and he suffered from regular horrendous headaches.

Halkett actually had four horses shot under him at Waterloo. He died on 24 September 1856 when he was Governor of Chelsea Hospital.

Colonel Sir John Elley, Royal Horse Guards, Deputy Adjutant General[26]

General Sir John Elley was wounded in the last charge of heavy cavalry at Waterloo, by the point of a sabre, which entered nearer the extremity of the ensiform [xiphoid] cartilage than the umbilicus, causing a wound about two inches in length, penetrating the stomach. From this he recovered in due time without any severe symptoms bit with a small hernia of that organ, which remained until his death, giving rise occasionally to some gastric inconvenience when he did not keep a gentle pressure on it by a retaining bandage.

Sir John Elley lived until 23 January 1839 still unmarried.

Private John Richardson, 1st (Royal) Dragoons[27]

John Richardson, of the 1st Dragoons [of Captain A. Clark's No.8 or G troop], was wounded at the Battle of Waterloo by a musket ball, which entered two and a half inches above the umbilicus and passed out on the left side, close to the lumbar vertebrae. He threw up a considerable quantity of blood, and the stomach was so irritable that nothing would remain on it. He complained of pain, which cut him right across, as he termed it; his eyes were suffused and face flushed; had headache; pulse 130. Thirty ounces of blood were taken from the arm, emollient injections [enemas] thrown up the rectum, and poultices applied to the wounds. June 20th. Some blood came away with the injections during the night; great pain in the right side and shoulder; saline draughts are returned tinged with bile and blood; pulse 130. Bled to sixteen ounces; injections and poultices continued. 21st. A draught was ejected mixed with blood, and a quantity of bilious blood; diarrhoea during the night; the faeces were mixed with blood; pulse 120; skin hot. Bleeding to twelve

25 James P. Tupper joined Guy's Hospital in 1794-5 as a Dresser under Mr Cline. He did not join the Army medical corps and therefore must have attended the hospitals in Belgium as a volunteer.

26 Guthrie, *Commentaries on the Surgery of the War, In Portugal, Spain, France and the Netherlands*, p.490.

27 Guthrie, *Commentaries on the Surgery of the War, In Portugal, Spain, France and the Netherlands*, p.517.

ounces; blood sizey [thick, viscous]. 22nd. Slept a little during the night; had several alvine [bowel] evacuations of a bilious fluid mixed with blood. The tension of the belly is not so great. He still complains of pain. Tea remains on his stomach. Bleeding to twelve ounces; fomentations and poultices to the belly; chicken and beef broths; injections frequently. 24th. Feels considerable relief from the tension of the abdomen having subsided; threw up his tea and a quantity of clotted blood this morning. 26th. Had a bad night; pulse 125 and full. Complains of great pain in the hepatic region, and backward toward the spine. Bleeding to sixteen ounces. 30th. Vomiting in the night, mixed with blood; tea &c remain on the stomach this morning; pulse 108. 5th July. The adnatae [sic] have a yellow tinge; in other respects, he is doing well. 20th. The wound perfectly healed; is cleaning his accoutrements, boots etc.

Richardson had a wound of his gut, which must have leaked into his belly, since he had a fever, distended abdomen and shoulder pain, suggesting diaphragmatic irritation from leaking blood and bowel contents. He was discharged on the 28th of July 1815, perfectly recovered. John Richardson received his Waterloo Prize Money in 1817.

Private Owen Connelly, 1st Battalion 95th Foot[28]

Owen McCaffrey aged thirty-three, first battalion 95th Regiment, was wounded on the 18th of June at the Battle of Waterloo, by a musket ball, which penetrated the cavity of the abdomen on the right side about midway between the superior anterior spinous process of the ilium [i.e. near the prominent pelvic bone below the waist], and the linea alba [i.e. the mid line of the abdomen]. When admitted into the Minimes General Hospital, three days after, he was in the most deplorable state; the whole abdomen was tense and exquisitely tender [he had peritonitis] the pulse small and wiry; vomiting incessant, with hiccough and ghastly visage. From this period to the 24th, he was thrice largely blooded, and the strictest antiphlogistic plan was laid down and rigidly adhered to. Laxative injections were administered, the whole of the abdomen was frequently fomented and opiates were administered to allay the irritability of the stomach, and to procure ease and rest. On the 25th the wounded intestine sloughed, and the faeces escaped by the external orifice, *the adherence of the two surfaces of the peritoneum,* preventing any, even the smallest portion, getting into the cavity of the abdomen. 26th. The high inflammatory action having been reduced, milk, rice, and sugar, and the farinaceous part of the potato were allowed. 1st July. No very alarming symptom remains. Half a fowl ordered for his dinner, and the greatest attention to personal cleanliness directed to be paid. 7th. Strength slowly but gradually returning. The action of the large intestines is daily kept up by stimulating injections. 14th. Progress to recovery satisfactory. The

28   Guthrie, *Commentaries on the Surgery of the War, In Portugal, Spain, France and the Netherlands,* p.518. Notwithstanding that Guthrie calls him McCaffrey, Private Connelly the only Owen in the 1st Battalion and there is no McCaffrey or similar name in any of the three battalions of the 95th at Waterloo.

injections are daily repeated, and the discharge by the natural passage increases. The wound contracts and looks healthy. Is enabled to sit up and has recovered his cheerfulness. 28th. Still improving; ultimately recovered.

NB This patient who was transferred from Antwerp to the naval hospital at Yarmouth he was admitted on the 10 August (to Yarmouth) from Antwerp; health a little impaired; countenance pallid; tongue white; without thirst; appetite good; wound looking healthy. Until the 1st September, faeculent [matter] was discharged from the wound, which was dressed with a simple compress; it then ceased. He takes a mild aperient every other day and is now nearly well. Robert Muir, Hospital Assistant to the Forces,[29] September 16, 1815.

The ball had perforated the gut, whose wounded edges had become adherent to the abdominal wall, preventing worsening peritonitis. The faeces could then 'safely' escape onto the abdominal surface. The situation of the ball was never ascertained. Owen received a pension of 9d per day from 15 April 1819, increased to 1 shilling per day in 1853. He lived in Monaghan, Ireland, and died there on 26 August 1856.

Private Jonathan Brown, 2nd Battalion 1st Foot Guards[30]

John [Jonathan] Brown, private 2nd Battalion, 1st Foot Guards, was wounded at Waterloo, on the 18th of June 1815, by a fragment of a shell, which produced a considerable degree of laceration of the glutaei [sic – buttock] muscles of the right side, passed over the spine or semi-circular edge of the ilium [the largest curved pelvic bone], and lodged itself between the internal oblique and transverse muscles of the abdomen [two of the thin sheets of muscle making up the abdominal wall]. The orifice of the wound, which was dressed with dry lint, soon assumed a healthy appearance, and showed a disposition to cicatrize [narrow down and form a scar]; but as the patient's health gradually declined, and as he frequently complained of obtuse pain in his abdomen, accompanied by a sense of weight and pressure, there was reason to suspect that these complaints originated in some cause which had hitherto escaped detection. This idea was rendered more probable by the immense purulent discharge which issued from the wound, when the patient was turned on his right side; the integuments however of the abdomen still preserved their natural colour, and no hardness, swelling, or extraneous [foreign] body was perceptible to the touch. Three weeks after the injury had been received, the patient informed me, when dressing his wound, that he felt a hard substance in his abdomen, which changed its place to a certain degree according to the position in which he placed himself. He was now visited by Dr Thomson of Edinburgh, and by Mr Brownrigg, Surgeon to the Forces, who agreed in opinion, that an incision should be made directly over the hard body alluded to, which was now distinctly perceptible to the

29   Hospital Assistant Robert Muir, (or Moir) no. 3914 in Peterkin & Johnston *Medical Officers.*
30   Hennen, *Principles of Military Surgery*, p.82

touch, in the centre of the right lumbar region. An incision, four inches in length, and about half an inch in depth was accordingly made, which enabled the operator, Mr Brownrigg, to discover and extract a piece of shell, of an irregularly quadrangular form, weighing nine ounces and a half avoirdupois, together with several pieces of bone, which had been detached from the ilium. The wound was kept open by the insertion of dry lint, in order to promote the discharge from the cavity which had been formed by the piece of shell, and to excite the process of granulation in the contiguous surfaces. The discharge, which was purulent and healthy, from this time gradually diminished; and the patient's health and strength improved rapidly. On the 20th of August, the original wound on the ilium was completely cicatrized, and the purulent discharge from the incision was almost imperceptible. The patient's health was now quite good; and from the favourable manner in which the cure proceeded, I have no doubt, but it was soon after completed.

Unknown Hanoverian soldier[31]

A Hanoverian soldier received a severe wound from a grape shot on the 18th of June 1815, at Waterloo, which struck him on the external part of the thigh, producing very extensive laceration. On the second day he was brought into the hospital, and the usual dressings were applied. On the fifth day a long narrow passage was discovered by the probe, seeming to run nearly the whole length of the vastus externus muscle [the large muscle on the outside of the thigh]. On cutting into this, three pieces of coin (which, from the very curious mode in which they were compacted together, I thought worthy of presenting to the Director General of Hospitals) were extracted from the parts. This poor fellow, a raw recruit, had no money whatever about him, nor even a pocket to contain it, and fervently protested against his right to this forced loan. He accounted for it by supposing that the money was carried from the pocket of his comrade, who stood before him in the ranks, and who was killed by the same shot which wounded him.

This is a good example of a wound caused by a secondary missile.

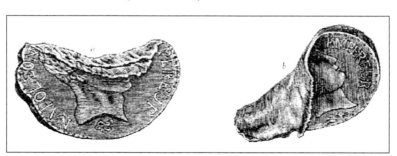

French silver coins which acted as secondary missiles. (Courtesy of the Royal College of Surgeons of England)

---

31   Hennen, *Principles of Military Surgery*, p.86.

Major Charles Edward Radclyffe 1st (Royal) Dragoons[32]

Lieutenant Colonel Radclyffe Dragoons recorded his own injury and treatment on 26th July 1816.

Owing to circumstances of the service on the 16th of June, 1815, I had a common tea breakfast, and at night, after a fifty-mile march, a piece of bread, with a little spirits and beer. On the 17th I had a meat breakfast, and, throughout the day, was employed in a very severe skirmish in heavy rain. At night I took a small piece of bread, and a little spirits. On the 18th, I took for breakfast, at seven o'clock in the morning, a very small quantity of meat, and one glass of wine.

Sunday 18th June, Waterloo. About two o'clock I received a musket shot in the outside part of the right knee joint; a surgeon who saw it almost immediately, was prevented cutting out what was then thought to be the ball, protruding on the opposite side of the knee pan [joint], by the heavy fire of the enemy. I moved back towards the village of Waterloo, and on the road met with another surgeon, who looked at my wound and it was decided that amputation above the joint was the only means of saving my life. The instruments were brought for the purpose, when a reiterated attack from the enemy's cuirassiers caused orders to be issued for our immediate removal. I moved on to Brussels, where I arrived at half past eight pm. I had my limb washed, was stripped, and put to bed. No dressing or application whatever was used, but I received a caution from a medical gentleman, who accidentally saw me, to take only lemonade; my diet, therefore, this day, was water and lemonade.

Monday 19th. I was recommended to send for Mr Hennen, the principal medical officer of the Jesuit's Hospital, who was entrusted with the general charge of the wounded officers and staff. I was taught to place the most perfect confidence in him, and I accordingly wrote to him. My diet this day was entirely confined to lemonade.

Tuesday 20th. Mr Hennen did not come till towards evening, and then placed me on his own private list of patients. Before his arrival the assistant surgeon of my own corps brought a staff surgeon to remove the limb; but the latter gentleman, after carefully examining it, said he did not feel justified in amputating it without a consultation. Mr H[ennen] ordered me immediately to lose sixteen ounces of blood, from the arm, to apply twenty-four leeches to the knee, and to purge copiously with Epsom salts, keeping the part covered with cloths dipped in cold water, and preventing inflammation by all possible means. His directions were complied with, and I felt relieved, but much debilitated; diet, water and lemonade.

Wednesday 21st. The assistant surgeon called in the morning and applied fifteen leeches; Mr Hennen called in the evening and ordered thirty to be applied instantly by a native surgeon [a Dutch-Belgian practitioner], which was done effectually and reiterated his direction to live low and keep down inflammation by all possible

---

32   Hennen, *Principles of Military Surgery*, p.149.

means. I now felt very languid and in addition to my water and lemonade, took one basin of gruel and one small roll (weight two ounces) of very fine white flour.

Thursday 22nd June. Bled again with thirty leeches in the morning, and thirty in the evening; some of the orifices continuing to discharge from one bleeding, to the other; diet as yesterday, with tea to my roll.

Friday 23rd. Sixty leeches applied this day, and the cold application continued as usual night and day. Breakfast, tea and half a roll; dinner, a very little vegetable, and half a roll; supper gruel and a roll. Mr Hennen made a very cautious opening on the spot where I fancied the ball was; he found a large portion of bone but did not extract it. This whole day I had much pain and some fever.

Saturday 24th. The same treatment continued, but I had only thirteen leeches; in the morning fever less; pulse very low, hard and wiry, diet as yesterday. During the whole morning I felt very cold, and changed my bed linen, as everything was wet about me. In the evening Mr H[ennen] came. The cold I had complained of had become excessive; I was much shook by it and felt wretchedly. He ordered an immediate change of application to hot fomentation continued for two hours at a time; and after that a large warm poultice to the knee. The hot fomentation increased my pulse so much, that after midnight it was more than 100 per minute. I perspired however, and my breathing was free; and though the pulsation in my head was violent, I had no pain or other symptom of fever. The pain in the knee was much lessened, and from that period gradually diminished.

Sunday 25th. Mr H[ennen] and the assistant[33] saw me in the morning; all going on well, and all alarm removed. Ordered to strengthen my diet, breakfast, gruel and one roll; dinner, vegetable soup (no meat) one roll, coffee; supper, gruel and one roll.

Wednesday 28th. The two last nights have had slight night sweats; again ordered to strengthen my diet. A healthy discharge now came from the wound; some small pieces of bone had been removed; eleven leeches were applied on Monday evening; diet – breakfast, gruel, one roll; basin of veal soup and one roll at eleven o'clock; dinner, peas soup and one roll; evening, basin of veal soup and one roll; supper, gruel and one roll.

Thursday 29th June. There had been a swelling and pain on the inside of the knee, and above the joint where I fancied the ball had lodged. This morning on removing the poultice, a considerable aqueous and bloody discharge was found on it. The swelling was reduced, and the pain diminished. The veal soup, added to my vegetable diet, had the desired effect, and I had no more night sweats.

Friday 30th. Discharge less, and of better quality; ordered to take a little meat and a glass of wine. Diet as on the 28th, with the addition of one ounce of solid meat, and one ounce of claret.

Saturday 1st July. A healthy discharge and doing well; about the 5th or 6th of July, cold goulard [a solution of lead acetate and lead oxide, to act as an astringent] was applied to the part, which removed a heat of the skin caused by the poultices and

33   Either a hospital assistant at that hospital or, possibly, Assistant Surgeon Thomas Prosser 1st (Royal) Dragoons.

fomentation. Diet was now gradually increased to about three ounces of meat, and two ounces of claret. I have gradually and rapidly improved in bodily strength, and the knee goes on as well as possible. The wound is closed up and seems quite sound.

Private Michael Mackinley, 2nd Battalion 3rd Foot Guards[34]

Michael M, 3rd Regiment of Guards, had the right lower extremity amputated below the knee, on the 11th of July 1815, in the Jesuit's Hospital, at Brussels. On the 18th the stump became very painful, and his bowels were costive. On the 27th, inflammatory fever set in, which resumed a remittent form, but by the 29th became continued and much aggravated in violence. Bark, which had previously been employed, was now left off, and the heat of skin being great, he was sponged with vinegar and cold water, which soon lowered its temperature. During these appearances of general disease, the stump assumed an unhealthy appearance; and on one day slight haemorrhage took place; a bed sore also formed on his back. By the 1st of August, the febrile symptoms became very severe. Delirium took place, attended with great prostration of strength and he died on the 3rd. His body was inspected by Hospital Assistant Nichol, the left lung showed signs of disease and a large amount of material collected around the right hip joint, but no clear disease around the stump.

Corporal James Cocking, 33rd Foot[35]

Corporal J Cockeyne [sic], 33rd Regiment, received a wound from a musket ball at Waterloo, which struck the right parietal bone at its junction with the occipital, close upon the union of the lambdoidal and sagittal sutures, and fractured the bone to an extent exactly corresponding with its own size. The ball was split into two portions, forming nearly right angles. It was easily removed, but from the narrowness of the passage, and from the depth to which the fractured portion of bone had been driven into the brain, (being exactly an inch and one-fourth from the surface of the scalp) no operation was performed on the field; and, as no one bad symptom occurred in the hospital, I did not allow the wound to be meddled with there, although much and frequently solicited by some of my medical friends. I trusted to venesection, a most rigid abstinence, open bowels, and mild easy dressings. On the 14th July, or 26th day, the wound was nearly closed, without any one untoward symptom, and the functions were in every respect natural. In a few weeks after, the man was discharged cured.

---

34 Hennen, *Principles of Military Surgery*, p.277. This is the only man in the battalion with these initials who was Discharged Dead after the battle.
35 Hennen, *Principles of Military Surgery*, p.290.

It is rather surprising that this patient did not suffer more with the small disc of bone fragment. He was lucky and may have suffered later with post-traumatic epilepsy. Cocking was born in St Mary's, Nottingham, and he enlisted at Dublin on 1 April 1813 for seven years' service, having previously been a framework knitter. He is recorded as having been severely wounded at Waterloo and did receive his Waterloo Prize Money. He retired on 10 April 1820 with a Good conduct, when he was 26 years old. He is described as having been five feet eight inches tall, with brown hair, hazel eyes and fair complexion and living at Nottingham.

Favre, a Chasseur of the Guard[36]

Favre, a Chasseur of the Imperial Guard of Napoleon, who had fought at Borodino, distinguished himself most gallantly on the field of Waterloo. No mounted British soldier was enabled to unhorse him that day; but he at length fell, and a shower of musket balls, one of which penetrated his left temple, at the junction of the three sutures. Staff Surgeon Laisne and my friend Dr Knox, who favoured me with the heads [important details] of the case, it was obvious that he had lain insensible for three days and nights, and that violent inflammation had taken place before he was brought into the British hospital [the Gens d'Armerie]. The entrance of the ball, and its course within the brain, were very evident to the eye and probe. In October, four months after the battle, this man was alive and without any constitutional injury, or disturbance of any one function, was performing the part of an assistant and orderly to his less fortunate colleagues. He returned to France with his recovered comrades shortly afterwards.

Private Francis Wade [sic], 1st Battalion 95th Foot[37]

Actually Francis Wilde, 1st Battalion 95th Regiment, aged 28, was wounded by a musket ball, in the action of the 16th June 1815, at Quatre Bras. The ball struck the frontal bone, about an inch above the right eyebrow, and passed in a direction towards the squamous suture of the temporal bone [a large skull bone at each side of the cranium]. He walked from the field of battle to Brussels by the help of two of his comrades. He was first seen by a native surgeon, who cleaned and dilated the wound, and then sent him to the *Jesuits* Hospital, where a longitudinal fracture was discovered, of an inch and a half long, and one broad, but no depression. The fractured bone was divided into four small pieces which were easily picked away, leaving the surface of the dura mater uncovered. In dressing him on the third day, fully a dessert spoonful of the brain, and some loose splinters, were discharged, but he did not appear to suffer the slightest inconvenience. On the 10th day, I found Wilde in his general health and appearance the same as before. No particular change occurred until the 38th day, when a greyish coloured spongy fungus [dead

36   Hennen, *Principles of Military Surgery*, p.296.
37   Hennen, *Principles of Military Surgery*, p.316.

spongy infected cerebral matter], containing much coagulated blood, was observed to protrude from the wound, strangulated [i.e. squeezed the brain protrusion so tightly that its blood supply had been cut off], as I may say, by the edges of the fracture, which had fairly formed a groove in it. He now complained of severe pains darting from ear to ear; bot the pupils were dilated with a slight degree strabismus in each eye; skin natural; tongue whitish; thirst urgent; appetite impaired; and occasional nausea. The fungus was still protruding on the 40th day to the size of an egg and it was determined to remove it with a scalpel, on inspection it was found to be brain matter. It was later found necessary to tie his hands to prevent him tearing his dressings off, but the wound continued to ooze matter and blood at each change of his dressings. On the 45th day at 4 pm he expired in the greatest agony. Professor Thomson and Dr Sommerville assisted at the autopsy. The right hemisphere of the brain mass merely a bloody pulp.

Wade was Discharged Dead from the army and his Waterloo Prize Money was not issued.

Private Amos Bower, 33rd Foot[38]

AB of the 33rd Regiment received a wound from a musket ball, which brushed along the root of the nose, and onwards towards the right eye brow, but without producing any injury to the bone, and so little general derangement, that the wound healed in a very few days. Immediately on being struck by the ball, double vision took place. I did not see him until the wound was nearly healed. He then saw the double objects at the same moment, and both with equal distinctness. In about two months the disease was removed, but on running into some excess in drinking, it returned again, and the wound burst out afresh; a recurrence to a more rigid regimen perfected the cure in a fortnight, and he was discharged entirely from hospital.

Amos received a pension of 9d per day and is recorded as having died on 16 April 1873 at Halifax.

Captain George Henry de [or von] Hattorf, 1st Dragoons King's German Legion[39]

A most remarkable instance of a sabre wound to the face occurred to Captain De H at the Battle of Waterloo. My friend Staff Surgeon Dease[40] dressed him on the field

---

38 Hennen, *Principles of Military Surgery*, p.349. Two individuals had these initials in the 33rd. Amos is the most likely, as the other, Adam Bamford, did not receive his Waterloo Prize Money and probably did not survive.

39 Hennen, *Principles of Military Surgery*, p.354. Hatorff is No. 93 in Ludlow Beamish, *History of the King's German Legion* (London: Boone, 1837), Vol.2, p.540.

40 Staff surgeon James Dease, no. 3487 in Peterkin & Johnston *Medical Officers*.

and sent him into Brussels to my care. The wound was from a sabre, which struck him nearly across the eyes, one of which it destroyed, and cut obliquely inwards and outwards, so as to admit of a view of the pharynx. In the multiplicity of engagements, I did not see him for several days, and not before a Belgian barber [possibly a civilian surgeon] had cut out the ligatures and removed the straps by which the lower portion of his face was kept in position and had stuffed the parts with charpie [linen waste]. The parts were brought back into apposition by [adhesive] straps and bandages, but with great pain to the patient, and consequent delirium. The cicatrix now forms one right line from ear to ear, the soft parts united, but the bones not.

Lieutenant Colonel Arthur Clifton, 1st (Royal) Dragoons[41]

My friend, Lieutenant Colonel A.C. received a wound from a musket ball on the evening of the 18th June, at Waterloo. The man who fired at him was so close, that he could perfectly well see him, the distance probably about 70 yards. On receiving the shot he instantly dropped, not, however, perfectly senseless, but very much stunned. He felt as if he had received *three* distinct wounds, the most severe of which he referred to the arm of the wounded side, the two others, of nearly similar severity, to his throat and stomach [abdomen]. There were probably just the two balls which hit the patient [possibly the musket was double-shotted]. He was carried to the rear, where a light dressing was applied by an hospital assistant, and a very copious bleeding employed. He was then sent into the city of Brussels, where he arrived at two in the morning. On his arrival I was called to see him expire; and truly, I did not suppose he could possibly survive till daylight. The ball had entered the sternal portion of the sterno-cleido-mastoideus [the prominent muscle lying diagonally on each side of the front of the neck] of the left side and had passed inwards towards the thorax; but no trace of its route could be discovered. The wound had obviously discharged an enormous quantity of blood, which also gushed copiously from it at every effort to cough or vomit. His left arm hung nearly lifeless, with a pulse scarcely perceptible. [One ball had tracked down into the neck and damaged his brachial nerve plexus – so causing a paralysis of his left arm. Also the ball may have damaged the subclavian or axillary artery] On the second day, when the bustle, consequent on the arrival of the wounded, had subsided, I called upon him and much to my surprise, found him comparatively calm, sensible and free from any pain in the wound; but with such an oppression all along the course of the diaphragm, that he urged me to cut for the ball, as he was certain it was the source of the pain. Third day. The symptoms as before, but towards the evening the pain became torturing, but was relieved by copious bleeding. On the fourth day, he lost his voice, and the following day the cough and spitting of blood eased and the bowels were free. On the sixth evening, his sufferings were dreadful, his face was almost purple. Thirty ounces of blood were taken, and the symptoms eased, but

41   Hennen, *Principles of Military Surgery*, p.362.

returned again two days later, but after another bleeding he improved greatly over many days. On the thirtieth day he was seized by violent vomiting and convulsive jerks, by which large quantities of bilious matter were thrown up [he may have had some trauma to his liver as one of the missiles had passed through the upper abdomen]. On the thirty first day the arm became less painful, within a few days he was visiting his brother officers and at the end of July he received leave of absence to proceed to England.

Lieutenant Colonel John Humphrey Hill 23rd Foot[42]

Lieutenant Colonel H received a grape shot of eight ounces weight on the day of Waterloo, just as the action was decided. The ball entered precisely under the centre of the clavicle, of the left side; raised the periosteum and passed through the spine of the scapula close to its neck, lodging between the skin and his flannel waist-coat. His haemorrhage was described by his servant and nearby soldiers as 'enormous beyond example' and he lay as if dead for some time. On recovery, he found himself in the hands of a foreign surgeon [a civilian or military Dutch /Belgian doctor] in a village adjacent to the field, his arm numb but very sore to the touch. Placed under my superintendence on the ninth day, I removed the dressings, keen to view the state of the artery, which was laid bare for some two inches, all pressure on the 'dead' arm being accompanied with extreme torture. A triangular piece of the scapula lay in the posterior wound and was easily removed with the fingers. Nothing interrupted the cure until the 14th day, when there was acute pain in the vicinity of the kidneys, but warm fomentations and drinks eased this and the cure continued. A few days later, the arm was released from its support and immediately there was great pain and a great discharge, but returning the arm to its original position and strapping the wound it again settled. His general health was restored and he returned to England three months after the wound.

Hill recorded in his Statement of Service:

A splinter of bone from some other body driven in the orbit of the right eye, two splinters of stone in my cheeks, a graze of a bullet on the left lower jaw, and an half pound iron grape shot entered my left breast and materially injured the shoulder joint and passed out through the centre of the shoulder blade and lodged in my cloathes[sic].

This refers to earlier wounds suffered on Peninsular service by Hill. He added further details of the Waterloo injury in a letter to his brother-in-law:

---

42   Hennen, *Principles of Military Surgery*, p.394.

The four and three-quarter [ozs.] ball (iron ball) entered under the collar bone and came out through the blade bone behind. The wound is beginning to heal and the discharge is trifling. The front wound still continues to discharge very much, he [sic – it] is a most confounded ugly fellow, with a nasty red and blazoned face as big as a tea cup.[43]

Augustus Labiche 7e Dragons[44]

Augustus Labiche, 7th French Dragoons, was wounded 18th of June 1815, by a musket ball, which entered directly under the left rib, and came out to the left of the 2nd vertebra of the loins. Some blood flowed through the urinary tract the first few days after the wound. Up to the 13th of July, the discharge through the wound in the back was copious, and mixed with thin faeces, and the seeds of fruit he had swallowed. On the 14th of July, for the first time, had the sensation of air passing through the urethra, with a gurgling sound after discharging urine. On the 16th, the wound on the back was healing and faeces ceased discharging. On the 20th, the bed clothes and bandages revealed a ruinous smell and it was observed leaking from the rear wound, but the noises heard previously had largely stopped. On the 8th of August or 51st day, the wounds were much diminished, but a few days after, he complained he wanted to pass winds and he felt an acute pain in the wound. The pain continued to increase and the wound assumed a fistulous disposition, till on the 57th day, the air began to pass from the urethra and wound, [this was air from the bowel passing into the thin tube leading from the man's kidney into his bladder. The ball had damaged both bowel and urinary tract. If the patient survived the first effects of the injury, these fistulae between the bowel, ureter and skin should have healed], he then began to recover fast. Dr Gordon believes that the man recovered.

Lieutenant Colonel James Hay, 16th Light Dragoons[45]

June 18th 1815 Lieutenant Colonel H received a musket shot, which, entering between, and partially fracturing the 8th and 9th ribs, posteriorly [and exiting at] at about two and a half inches from the sternum. The haemorrhage which continued for three days, from both wounds, was so excessive that he could not be moved from the neighbourhood of the field of battle. The 11th day he was brought into Brussels, when I saw him, with Deputy Inspector Gunning, Surgeon in Chief and Mr Robinson,[46] Surgeon of the 16th Dragoons. His pulse was then about 90, and hard; his countenance pale and sunk; his eyes glazed, and with difficulty kept open; his skin of a dusky yellow [he was jaundiced] and bedewed with a clammy

---

43   J. Currie, *Letters to a Vicarage 1796-1815 the Letters of Lt Col JHE Hill* (Exeter: Oriel, 1988), p 37.

44   Hennen, *Principles of Military Surgery*, p.431.

45   Hennen, *Principles of Military Surgery*, p.435

46   Surgeon Isaac Robinson 16th Light Dragoons, no. 1444 in Peterkin & Johnston *Medical Officers.* .

sweat; the respiration difficult and interrupted by frequent singultus [hiccoughs]. This might indicate damage to the diaphragm or surface of the liver – if the wound was on the right side]. Mr Robinson had bled the patient five times and had kept his bowels regular with a solution of neutral [mineral] salts. 12th day, extremely low and weak, barely able to reply, pulse 80, tosses incessantly, discharge, thick copious and a deep bilious tinge and coughing up a yellow bitter tasting mucous. 13th day, the symptoms became aggravated, Assistant Surgeon Mr Bingham,[47] bled him for 12 ounces of blood. Up to the 24th day of July, or 37th after wounding, very little hopes of his recovery were entertained and he had griping in his bowels. 40th day, seized with a severe itching [the patient was jaundiced, which can cause itching] all over his body. On the 41st day the discharge became much less. On the 1st of September he had recovered almost perfect health.

Private James Murphy, 1st Battalion 28th Foot[48]

James Murphy of the 28th Regiment [of Brevet Major Richard Llewellyn's company], 22 years of age, was wounded at the Battle of Waterloo by a musket ball, which passed through the thigh below its middle and in the course of the femoral artery, which was not wounded at the time [i.e. not completely divided]; but as the wound began to heal, it gave rise to an aneurismal swelling in the part, for which the usual operation for aneurism above the seat of disease was performed by Staff Surgeon Cole, on the 22nd of July 1815, two ligatures being placed below the artery, which was divided between them. The pulsation in the swelling immediately ceased. 23rd the discharge from the wound noticeably increased but everything else seemed improved. 25th the gun-shot wound discharged good matter. Temperature of limb normal, no pulsation in the swelling. 1st August. The dressings much soiled by discharge, and when removed the wound discharged about 2 ounces of matter discoloured with blood. 6th Has suffered pain in the wound for the last two days, the discharge is considerable, but the wound looks healthy. 8th the discharge from the aneurismal wound is thin and watery, mixed with what appeared to be coffee grounds. No pain in the wound. 11th Matter collecting in the thigh. 13th A counter opening made in the thigh, in the line of the aneurismal tumour, and over the exit wound of the ball. Two ounces of purulent bloody fluid were extracted, four ounces of blood were extracted in the evening. 25th Has been doing well since the 13th, until this morning, when on rising to get out of bed, an arterial haemorrhage took place from the counter opening, pressure by tourniquet could not stop it, but it was arrested by compress and bandage. The thigh in the evening appeared swollen. 26th the bleeding recurred this morning, but again arrested by pressure, but the

---

47   Second Assistant Surgeon John Bingham of the Ordnance Medical Department, no. 3819 in Peterkin & Johnston *Medical Officers*.

48   G.J. Guthrie, *On the Diseases and Injuries of Arteries with the operations required for their cure* (London: Burgess & Hill, 1830), p.284.

thigh is enlarged and seems injected with blood. Amputation was determined upon and performed. The man sunk and died two and a half hours afterwards.

James Murphy died from haemorrhage and ischaemia of his leg after its blood supply was cut off with the ligation of his aneurysm. He was discharged dead, but his Waterloo Prize Money was paid out.

Jean Debret[49]

Jean Debret, a French prisoner of war, came under the care of Staff Surgeon Collier, in the beginning of September, having been wounded at the Battle of Waterloo by a musket ball, which broke both bones of the left leg, and requiring several incisions to be made into the soft parts, which were greatly implicated by disease. Towards the end of the month, the wound assumed the character of the hospital sore or gangrene, which spread rapidly over all parts down to the tibia. On 4th of October, haemorrhage took place about two inches and a half above the ankle joint, which was arrested by pressure. On removing this and some coagula which covered the artery, it bled furiously; a little dissection laid the artery bare and inch and a half above this spot, when a ligature was passed around it, and the bleeding never returned; the ligature came away on the sixth day. The man recovered and was sent to France, with a serviceable leg, although lame.

Private John Henry Vogeler, 4th Line Battalion KGL[50]

Henry Vigarelie, a private in the German Legion, was wounded on the 18th of June, at the Battle of Waterloo, by a musket ball, which entered the right leg immediately behind and below the inner head of the tibia, inclining downwards, and under or before a part of the soleus and gastrocnemius muscles [the two large calf muscles, making up the bulk of the calf], and coming out through them, four inches and three quarters below the head of the fibula, nearly in the middle, but towards the side of the calf of the leg. In this course, it is evident that the ball must have passed close to the posterior tibial and peroneal arteries [two of the three principal arteries of the leg]; but as little inflammation followed, and no immediate haemorrhage, he was considered to be one of the slighter cases. On the latter days of June, he occasionally lost a little blood from the wound and on the 1st of July a considerable haemorrhage took place, which was suppressed by the tourniquet. It bled however at intervals during the night; and on the 2nd it became necessary to re-apply the tourniquet, and to adopt some means for his permanent relief. Having gone to Brussels after the Battle of Waterloo, this man was shown to me by my

---

49   Guthrie, *On the Diseases and Injuries of Arteries*, p.292.
50   Guthrie, *On the Diseases and Injuries of Arteries*, p.296.

friends Messrs Campbell[51] and Hill,[52] [both late arrivals in Brussels] surgeons to the forces, under whose care he was, and who were desirous of avoiding an amputation, if possible, although the site of the wound, and the uncertainty of the vessel wounded, as it bled from both openings, rendered it doubtful. The man had lost a large quantity of blood, pulse 110, skin hot, tongue furred, the limb was swelled. On passing the finger into the outer opening, and pressing it against the fibula, a sort of aneurismal tumour [i.e. the artery was damaged and was bleeding into a small cavity – it needed tying off, but access was difficult] could be felt under it and the haemorrhage ceased, indicating that the peroneal artery [the deepest of the three leg arteries] was in all probability the only vessel wounded. The man being laid on his face, with the calf of the leg uppermost, I made an incision near seven inches in length in the axis of the limb, taking the shot hole as a central point, and carried by successive strokes, towards the peroneal artery. The artery was tied in a healthy portion, the cavity washed out and the wound drawn together by two or three adhesive straps. The limb was wrapped in cloths and constantly wetted with cold water. The patient was placed on a milk diet. On the 4th, two days after the operation, the wound looked well; the weather being very hot, two straps of plaster used to close the wound [the straps had been replaced]. On the 5th a poultice was laid over and on the 6th the plasters were removed and poultices only continued. On the 10th or eight days after the operation, the ligature came away. From this period the cure continued without accident. The wound was entirely healed within three months. The wounded limb ended up two inches shorter than the other. The man is now at York Hospital, Chelsea and can walk short distances only, without appearing lame.

This was one of two operations carried out by Surgeon George Guthrie on his somewhat reluctant visit out to Waterloo. He acted largely in a consultative role. This technically challenging operation, which avoided an amputation, acquired a nickname, 'Guthrie's bloody operation!' Henry Vogeler is the most likely candidate in the KGL records to match the name given. He received his Waterloo Prize Money.

Private Richard Morrisey, 2nd Battalion 30th Foot[53]

John Morrisy, of the second battalion of the thirtieth regiment, aged 24, of a full and masculine habit, was admitted into St Elisabeth's Hospital, under my care, Thursday August 24th, for aneurism [ballooning out of a part-damaged artery] of the femoral artery of the right side; the tumour was about three inches in length, and two in breadth, and extended to within an inch of Poupart's [inguinal – at the fold of the groin] ligament. There was a cicatrix where a ball had entered on the top, about two and a half or three inches from Poupart's ligament. I learned that the

---

51   Staff Surgeon James Alexander Campbell, no. 1552 in Peterkin & Johnston *Medical Officers.*
52   Staff Surgeon William Hill (Peterkin & Johnston *Medical Officers* no. 1684), died London 23 March 1833.
53   Guthrie, *On the Diseases and Injuries of Arteries,* p.310.

patient had been wounded by a musket ball on the 18th of June, and the ball had remained in the limb, but he had healed well and was discharged from the hospital, apparently cured, on the 12th of July. On the 17th of July he was placed as [an] orderly in the Notre Dame Hospital, where he continued, being at times very dissipated [drunk], until the 18th of August, when unable to continue his work, showed his tumour to the medical officer in charge. This hospital being broken up, was the cause of him coming under my charge on the day stated. The aneurism I considered to have been formed by the injury done to the vessel, in the passage of the ball, it was decided not to delay securing the external iliac artery, which I judged to be requisite in order to save life. He was confined to bed, kept on a spare diet, and the bowels evacuated preparatory the operation, which I performed on Monday 28th August, in presence of Mr Gunning, Surgeon in Chief, Mr Niel, Deputy Inspector, Dr Wray, Physician to the Forces, and most of the medical officers at Brussels. After the operation the foot was numb and cold, followed by severe pain and want of power in the limb. Through the day of the 29th and the 30th the same issues continued, on the 31st the wound was highly inflamed and pain in the abdomen, 12 ounces of blood was taken. The limb had a cadaverous odour. The following day he took a little wine, but his constitutional powers gradually sunk, and he died at four o'clock in the afternoon, of the 1st of September. On dissection the whole limb was in a state of gangrene [the tying off of the large artery at the groin, deprived the leg of its blood supply and, in this case, the leg died for lack of oxygen and nutrients].

The only Morrisey in the 30th Foot at Waterloo was named Richard and he was discharged dead in the Waterloo Prize Money Roll, this is most likely our man.

Drummer William Ball, 2nd Battalion 44th Foot[54]

William Ball, drummer, belonging to the 44th Regiment, aged between nineteen and twenty, of a spare habit, was wounded by a spear or sword, on the 17th of June, which passed in at the angle of the left jaw, and penetrated the mouth, lacerating the tongue severely in three or four places. He was brought into St Elisabeth's Hospital on the 19th and had by his account lost a considerable quantity of blood on the way. On the evening of the 22nd I was sent for to see him and found arterial blood jetting up with considerable force from the bottom of a narrow deep wound. As all efforts to trace the sources of bleeding were fruitless, as compresses simply diverted the flow of blood through the mouth and the coagula had to be removed to prevent suffocation. My opinion was that the patient's safety depended on securing the common carotid artery [i.e. ligating the main artery to the head, neck and brain on the affected side, performed by cutting into the neck – see image below]. I performed the operation at eight o'clock that evening; the haemorrhage ceased the instant the ligature was applied. On the 23rd I found him perfectly sensible

54   Guthrie, *On the Diseases and Injuries of Arteries*, p.323.

and easy. On the 26th he complained of a ringing noise in his left ear [known as tinnitus], and numbness on the left side of the face. On the 5th of July the ligature came away from the artery and the cure continued. The man was discharged cured the 12th of August.

William Ball received his Waterloo Prize Money in 1817.

Private John Butler, 1st Battalion 71st Foot[55]

John Butler, 71st Regiment, was wounded on the 18th of June, at Waterloo, by a musket ball, which fractured the underpart of the right clavicle, a little to the outside, injured the brachial plexus of nerves, without affecting the vessels, passed obliquely downwards, backwards and inwards through the chest, injuring the superior part of the lung, and came out about an inch and a half from the base of the scapula, opposite the spine. He spat blood in moderate quantity, breathed with some difficulty, suffered from pain in the part, and from total loss of the use of the right arm. He was bled largely several times during the first fortnight; during which period some little blood and matter were discharged from both wounds. They gradually, however, closed, and on the 20th of August 1815, he was sent to England, cured, with the exception of some slight difficulty of breathing on exertion, or walking quickly, and with paralysis of the right arm.

John Butler received his Waterloo Prize Money in 1817 and is not recorded as having been discharged from the army. In the Waterloo Medal Roll he is recorded as having been invalided from the army.

Private Thomas Stilfox, 1st Life Guards[56]

Antwerp, July 28th, 1815. Thomas Stilfox, of the 1st Life Guards, aged 40, received a puncture wound of the thorax on the 18th of June at Waterloo. The wound was inflicted by a lance, which penetrated the cavity of the thorax, between the second and third ribs, about four inches from the sternum, and wounded the right lung. He remained on the field of battle four days without assistance [an incredibly long time to suffer without help!], during which period he had frequent attacks of haemorrhage. On his admission, considerable haemorrhage recurred. There was emphysema [this is where air from the punctured lung escapes from the lung and goes into the chest and is forced out into the tissues puffing up the patient's skin and chest wall tissues] of the chest, difficulty of breathing of which the air rushed forcibly from the lung. He had also received a sabre wound which extended from the temporal end of the zygomatic [cheekbone] process, to below the left ala [side] of the nose.

55   G.J. Guthrie, *On Wounds and Injuries of the Chest* (London: Renshaw, 1848), p. 9.
56   Guthrie, *On Wounds and Injuries of the Chest*, p.84.

He had several slighter wounds in different parts of the body, and a considerable one of the thigh; bowels constipated, not having had an evacuation for some days. 29th June, a roller [linen bandage] applied round the chest; the wound covered with simple dressings; those of the thigh and face brought together with adhesive straps. 30th June, the discharge from the thorax resembles blood mixed with water. July 1st, passed a restless night, severe cough and pain in chest, twelve ounces of blood taken from arm. July 2nd, Cough and respiration relieved, July 3rd, Delirious through the night, no sleep and incoherent. 4th a considerable sinus [blind-ending tract] formed in the thigh; 6th attacked with severe cough and vomiting, Bark and demulcent mixture continued. 7th coughing and pain abated, but he appears to be gradually sinking. 10th, Obtuse pain in the side, difficulty of breathing and bowels confined. A blister was applied at the seat of the pain, a mixture of squills [Drimia maritima, a historically important medicinal plant, native to the Mediterranean region] and camphorated tincture of opium and had a purging enema. 11th pain relieved, air passing through the wound causing a peculiar sound. 12th Immense discharge of pus from the chest, intolerably offensive and acrid. The infusion of bark was continued. 14th Died at seven o'clock in the morning.

Thomas Stilfox was Discharged Dead, but his Waterloo Prize Money was still paid out in 1817.

Thomas Dobson, 2nd Battalion, Coldstream Guards[57]

Thomas Dobson, of the 2nd Battalion, 2nd Foot Guards, received a gun-shot wound, on the 18th June, at the battle of Waterloo, which entered about three inches above the umbilicus, in the right side, wounding the liver, as was evident from the discharge of a fluid of a green colour [i.e. bile], and in the consistence resembling bile, and for which he has been bled. But little else had been done, until he came to Antwerp, on the 29th June. He then complained of pain in the region of the liver, extending to the shoulder [i.e. the bile in his belly was irritating his diaphragm, which has the same nerve supply of the skin of the shoulder]; countenance anxious; tongue white; eyes yellow [ie he was jaundiced]; pulse quick and hard; belly tumid and constipated. Twenty-four ounces of blood were drawn from the arm, and a cathartic mixture of infus. [infusion] of sennæ and sulphate of magnesia, was desired to be taken, until some effect was produced. The abdomen was fomented. And simple dressings were applied to the wound.

Over the next month, Dobson clearly improved and his wound healed. On August 2 he was sent back to Brussels as the hospital at Antwerp was being 'broken up'; that is to say, closed.

---

57   G.J. Guthrie, *On Wounds and Injuries of the Abdomen and the Pelvis* (London: Churchill, 1847), p.52.

Jean Sordis A French prisoner of war[58]

Was wounded, at battle of Waterloo, by a ball which entered about an inch and a half from the root of the penis, and immediately above Poupart's ligament [a crease formed by a muscular infolding in the groin] on the right side, passed through the bladder, and made its exit near the tuberosity of the ischium [the hard bony lump felt in the buttock, which one sits upon – part of the bony pelvic girdle] of the left side. He was sent to Antwerp and was placed under the care of the civil surgeons, who were in charge of the French hospital at the Corderie, until the 14th of August, when the wounded were given over to the British. Very little had been done for him surgically, and when he came under my care, the original wound was still open, as well as a fistulous, which had formed and gave exit to the urine in [through] the left groin; his health had suffered considerably. An elastic gum catheter was introduced into the bladder the following day, and retained, being removed occasionally; the neighbouring parts, scrotum &c. were defended from the acrimony of the urine, which had previously caused considerable excoriation (erosion and superficial ulceration of the skin and consequent soreness), and a light diet was ordered him.

August 28. – [two weeks on] At present the fistulous opening [between the bladder and the groin skin] is healed, the original wound is doing well, and the quantity of urine that escapes through it is inconsiderable; his health has much improved, and I am of [the] opinion, if no unforeseen accident occurs, this man will do well. Samuel B. Bruce Surgeon to the Forces[59]

Charles Murray, 2nd Battalion 1st Foot Guards[60]

Charles Murray, a private in the 2nd battalion of the 1st Foot Guards, aged thirty-three, was wounded on the 18th June at Waterloo by a piece of shell which struck him of the superior part of the *left* parietal bone. He remained insensible about half an hour, and on recovering from that state was affected with nausea and some bleeding from the left ear and found himself unable to move his *right* arm and *right* leg, which hung dead and had lost their feeling. Admitted Minime[s] General Hospital at Antwerp on the 20th; he suffered much pain in his head, which was relieved by being twice bled. The paralytic affection having remained without change from the moment he was wounded, a piece of the parietal bone about three-fourths of an inch long, and several smaller fragments, were extracted four days after admission into the hospital, two perforations of the trephine having been necessary. Immediately after the removal of the bone he recovered the use of his right arm and leg, so far as to be able to move them and to be sensible of their being touched. He gradually recovered by the 14th of August, so as to be sent to the

---

58   Guthrie, *On Wounds and Injuries of the Abdomen and the Pelvis*, p.66.
59   Samuel Barwick Bruce – initially trained as an hospital mate, then as an apothecary, he became a staff surgeon on 25 May 1815.
60   G.J. Guthrie, *Injuries of the Head affecting the Brain* (London: Churchill, 1842), p.50.

General Hospital at Yarmouth, never having had a bad symptom; the only defect remaining on the right side being an inability to grasp anything in his hand with force. The pulsation of the brain was still visible at the bottom of the wound for about the space of half the circumference of the head of a trephine. September 16, 1815. The wound has filled up with healthy granulations and has nearly cicatrized. A small sinus remains at the superior part, through which the edge of the bone is felt. His health has been invariably good, although he has suffered a good deal of pain twice previously to the coming away of little pieces of bone, but towards evening he has been generally subject to slight vertigo; this however is not so much the case as it has been and appears to be almost daily decreasing. Discharged cured.

12

Repatriation of the Wounded and Beyond

Mention has been made regarding the initial moves by the Allied medical staff towards repatriation of British and Dutch/Belgian, German and French casualties, which of necessity, had started early for those fit enough to travel.

The British were evacuated in the main via Antwerp and to the 5,000 wounded who remained in Brussels by 30 June, we have to also add 3,346 patients who were sick with fevers. By April 1816, 6,851 British patients had been repatriated, the remaining 2,000 wounded survivors going home during the remainder of 1816.

French casualties, mainly concentrated in Brussels, Antwerp and Louvain, were either sent as prisoners (particularly officers) to Britain or home via Dunkirk. Whilst some were repatriated to France during the autumn of 1815, most were taken, as prisoners, to Dartmoor Prison, whilst a number of others were held at Liège and Maastricht. The last French patients left the convent of St Agatha in Liège on 17 November 1815 to return to their homeland. However, some French patients preferred to stay on in Belgium, rather than returning to a royalist France. Larrey relates that on his visit to Belgium in October 1831, at the request of King Leopold I, he was asked to inspect the Belgian military hospitals. He found at Louvain a small group of French soldiers who had been wounded at Waterloo! These men recognised Larrey who had carried out surgery on a few of them.

Prussian casualties had principally been accommodated in Louvain, but some had also been scattered in Brussels and Antwerp, Namur, Tirlemont, St Tron, Lier, Ghent and even as far as the Hague, Leyden and Amsterdam. The military hospital of St Laurent at Liège served as an important base for repatriation of Prussian patients. From June 1815, this place acted as a sorting house for the wounded. The Prussian casualties continued to be cared for by a mixed team of Prussian and Dutch military doctors, supported by local civilian medical staff. Some convoys of Prussian wounded were diverted to Maastricht and from here they went on to military hospitals in Germany. The last Prussian patients were evacuated from Belgium in March 1816.[1]

The British and Prussian armies had occupied Paris on 7 July 1815. A British military hospital was opened at St Denis, and later during the years of occupation at Cambrai and

---

1   M-C de Graaf, 'Metamorphose de Saint-Laurent de Liège sous Guillaume 1er, Roi des Pays-Bas (1815-1830)', in *Saint-Laurent, église, abbaye et hôpital militaire. Mille ans d'histoire* (Liège: Soledi, 1968), pp.391-392.

Valenciennes. Unfortunately, the British army, including its medical department soon underwent a major reduction with the 'peace dividend'.

Provided only with a small pension, barely adequate to live on, most of the badly wounded were pensioned off as unfit to continue to serve in the forces, average pensions were between 6 pence and 1 shilling per day, at a time when an average farm labourer earned nearer 2 shillings per day[2]. There was no welfare system for these old soldiers, apart from the few, lucky enough to be admitted to the Military Hospitals of Chelsea or Kilmainham in Dublin as in-pensioners. The majority of the remainder lived out their lives in abject penury, often being too badly injured to work to supplement their meagre pensions.

A group of men, mostly merchants, bankers and brokers, gathered at the City of London Tavern on 28th June 1815 to discuss a public subscription for the widows, orphans and wounded after the Battle of Waterloo. A committee was immediately formed, including such men as John Julius Angerstein, Chairman of the Society of Lloyd's; William Mellish MP Governor of the Bank of England, Alexander Baring the banker, John Parr Welsford, Robert Shedden, Joseph Marryat and banker William Henry Hoare amongst them. Five thousand pounds was pledged that afternoon and, confident of success, the newly-appointed committee ordered that accounts be opened at all the major city banks, without delay.

Within a week of its establishment, the City of London subscription had raised £62,640 10s 10d. A month later the total exceeded £107,000. In 2017, this sum was equivalent to around £9 million. While this included several large donations, not least £10,000 in 3% consols from the Society of Lloyd's and £5,000 from the Bank of England, the vast majority of donations consisted of just a few pounds or even shillings each from the general public. An official thanksgiving prayer, read out from the pulpit of every church, regardless of denomination, resulted in a flood of locally organised collections. Among the many paid in via Hoare's Bank were offerings from Porlock in Somerset (£2); Spalding in Bedfordshire (£11 15s 6d); Hawarden in Flintshire (£49 12s 6d); Steeple cum Tyne (£27 13s 0d) and the Wesleyan Chapels of London's East and West Circuits (£116 5s 6d).

At a packed public meeting in Edinburgh, Sir Walter Scott proclaimed his faith in the inhabitants of that city. Edinburgh raised £18,000 in a matter of weeks. Not that the subscription's contributions were confined to Britain alone. Thousands of pounds poured in from the farthest reaches of the Empire and beyond from Dublin, Calcutta, Bengal, Ceylon, Canada, St Petersburg, Java and Montserrat.

By December 1815, the City of London Committee had started dispensing cash sums to cases of particular distress. Its members were anxious to ensure that the Fund would benefit those who needed it most and to that end, they drew up forms aimed at discovering as much as possible about those who had been killed or wounded, asking for their name, age, rank, place of birth, address and details of any dependent relatives. Copies of these forms were then forwarded both to the commanding officer of each regiment that had served at Waterloo and to the minister of every parish in the country.

Given this painstaking diligence, progress was inevitably slow and a year after the battle there was still no definite scheme in place; by this time the fund had topped £290,000

---

2   Gregory Clark, *Farm Wages and Living Standards in the Industrial Revolution, England 1650-1850* (Thesis, University of California, 2001).

(almost £27 million in 2017) and there were voices of complaint. The Committee therefore seized the opportunity presented by the anniversary to publicly declare their plans. After much deliberation, they announced that it had been decided to issue annuities, which would not only make the best use of the money raised, but protect widows from fraud, children from neglect and the spendthrifts from their own improvidence. The first annuities were issued during the autumn of 1816. The widows of privates received life annuities of £10 for as long as they remained unmarried, as well as £4 p.a. for each child under seven. Children aged between seven and fourteen were entitled to fixed term annuities, payable to nominated trustees, usually a local clergyman or magistrate. At fourteen, these annuities would cease, but each child would then be presented with £10 and the promise of an additional £50 at the age of twenty-one (or earlier if a girl married). Larger sums were allocated to widows and children of officers or non-commissioned officers, according to rank. Additional life annuities were awarded to disabled privates and non-commissioned officers, most of whom had been blinded or lost limbs, and lump sums to those who were discharged on account of their wounds. Nor were the families of Britain's allies forgotten; £62,000 being remitted to Berlin, Hanover, Amsterdam and Brunswick for the relief of the families of the dead and the wounded.

By the summer of 1817, a total of £168,051 9s 11d had been paid out, but recipients were warned that any attempt to sell, mortgage or pawn the annuities would result in instant forfeiture.

Nearly £500,000 had been subscribed by 1817, of which £338,000 was invested in government securities. Not only did this money require active management, but the Committee's decision to issue life annuities had created an onerous and decades long commitment. Nearly twenty years later, the Committee's remaining members lobbied the government for permission to formally end their connection with the fund, which by then stood at nearly £1 million. In their petition they pointed out that they had administered over 1,000 life annuities and nearly as many fixed term annuities, besides dispensing 6,000 lump sums. Much to their relief, the government agreed and management of the remaining 700 surviving annuities passed to the National Debt Office in 1838.

Another fund started with a conversation at an Edinburgh coffee house in 1812 and collected moneys throughout Scotland for the families in need, who had lost their husbands and fathers in the Great War (as the Victorians called the wars of 1793-1815). Eventually in 1815 it became the *Scottish Widows Fund and Life Assurance Society*, the *Scottish Widows* we know today.

In Britain, many medical officers went onto half pay and started seeking out gainful civilian practice. This was often hampered by a need to catch up with the current ways of civilian medicine and obtain more qualifications. The number of soldiers and medical staff were cut down in a massive effort to reduce expense and work off the enormous National Debt (£744.9million by the end of 1815) that the nation had incurred. In a similar manner, the medical services of the Low Countries witnessed a period of parsimony and reorganisation soon after Waterloo. Junior surgeons in the Kingdom of the Netherlands were ordered to be examined for promotion and were required to write a doctorial these. Unfortunately, all three of the university medical schools re-established in August 1815 were situated in the northern portion of the Netherlands, at Groningen, Utrecht and Leyden. The latter, having also the school of military medicine and was the preferred university for the Belgian military students. Three further faculties of medicine in Belgium, at Louvain, Ghent and Liège did eventually open in October 1817. The Belgian *Service de Santé* then underwent a further major reorganisation that year, Brugmans and his staff, who were responsible for medical care, were subjected to the unwelcome control of an *Intendant Général de l'Administration de la Guerre* and two assistant inspectors were appointed to help the Director General, one posted at Leyden and the other at Louvain.

In Brussels, the Jesuit's, which had housed so many casualties after the Waterloo campaign, was closed down in 1816 as it was simply too large for the military garrison and the buildings were taken over by the Ministry of Justice. Politically, the decision was made to make the Royal Hospital at Louvain the principle military hospital for the southern provinces of the Netherlands Kingdom. This left only a small military hospital in Brussels, at the Annonciate barracks.

During the year of the Waterloo campaign, by an unfortunate twist of fate, the Low Countries were afflicted with a severe outbreak of opthalmia (trachoma). The original eye infection had arisen in the Egyptian campaigns of 1798-1801, which had affected thousands of men serving in the French and British armies. This highly contagious disease had crossed to Europe with them and it had then passed on to the Austrian, Prussian and Russian troops who imported it into Belgium in 1813/14.

Unlike Britain, the forward thinking post-war Belgian administration soon created a cadre of permanently appointed military nurses and a system of instruction for army medical students. Twenty garrison hospitals were permanently established in the Netherlands and a reserve force of civilian doctors was inaugurated. Regimental medical staff could provide help in military and civil hospitals (wherever military casualties or sick were admitted) or when emergency care was needed in times of crises.

These medical provisions remained in place until 1830, when the Belgians revolted against what they saw as the Dutch supremacy. On 21 July 1831 Leopold of Saxe-Coburg was appointed King Leopold I of Belgium and Belgium followed its own path.

Appendix

List of Pensions for Awarded to Officers for Wounds Received at the Battles of Quatre Bras and Waterloo

Pensions were awarded for damaged men and officers. The officer patients were examined at the Royal College of Surgeons of London by military and medical doctors. The majority of the pensions were not awarded as a permanent legacy, but were temporary and thus would need to be reviewed at the Royal College at appropriate intervals. If the wounds had healed and there was little if any residual disability, the pension might then be rescinded. The men who had the most severe wounds, with continuing disability, particularly those with limb loss or blindness in one or both eyes, would retain their pensions for life. Temporary pensions, which would have come under review by an appropriate medical board, are marked in the list below with an asterisk.

Royal Horse Guards	Lt Col Sir Robert Hill	For a wound	Waterloo	*£300
Royal Horse Guards	Lt Col Sir John Elley	For wounds	Waterloo	*£300
Royal Horse Guards	Quarter Master Thomas Varley	For a wound	Waterloo	*£50
1st Dragoon Guards	Major Michael Turner	For a wound	Waterloo	*£200
1st Dragoon Guards	Captain Thomas Noel Harris	Loss of an arm	Waterloo	£200
1st Dragoon Guards	Captain John Paget Sweny	For wounds	Waterloo	*£100
1st Dragoons	Captain Charles Edward Radclyffe	For a wound	Waterloo	*£100
1st Dragoons	Lieutenant George Gunning	For a wound	Waterloo	*£70
2nd Dragoons	Major Robert Verner	For wounds	Waterloo	*£200
6th Dragoons	Major (commanding) Fiennes S Miller	For a wound	Waterloo	*£300
6th Dragoons	Captain William Frederick Browne	For wounds	Waterloo	*£100
7th Light Dragoons	Captain Peter Augustus Heyliger	For a wound	Waterloo	*£100
7th Light Dragoons	Lieutenant Frederick Beatty	For a wound	Waterloo	*£70
12th Light Dragoons	Colonel Frederick C, the Hon. Ponsonby	For wounds	Waterloo	*£300
13th Light Dragoons	Lieutenant Charles Robert Bowers	For a wound	Waterloo	*£70

15th Light Dragoons	Lt. Colonel Leighton C Dalrymple	Loss of a leg	Waterloo	£300
15th Light Dragoons	Major Joseph Thackwell	Loss of an arm	Waterloo	£300
16th Light Dragoons	Lt Colonel James Hay	For a wound	Waterloo	*£300
18th Light Dragoons	Lieutenant Charles Hesse	For a wound	Waterloo	*£70
23rd Light Dragoons	Lieutenant Thomas Barker Wall	Loss of a leg	Waterloo	£70
1st Foot Guards	Captain & Lt Colonel Richard Harvey Cooke	For a wound	Waterloo	*£300
1st Foot Guards	Captain & Lt Colonel William Gordon Cameron	Loss of an arm	Waterloo	£100
1st Foot Guards	Captain & Lt Colonel Somerville W Burges	Loss of a leg	Waterloo	£100
1st Foot Guards	Colonel Lord Fitzroy Somerset	Loss of an arm	Waterloo	£300
1st Foot Guards	Colonel the Hon. William Stuart	Loss of an arm	Quatre Bras	£300
2nd Foot Guards	Lt Colonel Henry Wyndham	For a wound	Waterloo	*£300
3rd Foot Guards	Lieut. & Captain George Evelyn	For a wound	Waterloo	*£100
1st Foot	Captain Robert Macdonald	For a wound	Waterloo	£250
1st Foot	Ensign Leonard Morse Cooper	For wounds	Quatre Bras	*£50
1st Foot	Lieutenant William Clarke	For a wound	Quatre Bras	*£70
1st Foot	Lieutenant George Lane	Loss of an arm	Waterloo	£70
1st Foot	Lieutenant Charles Mudie	Ruptured	Waterloo	£50
4th Foot	Lieutenant George Richardson	For a wound	Waterloo	£70
4th Foot	Lieutenant John Browne	For a wound	Waterloo	£100 2nd pension
9th Foot	Captain Henry Dumaresq	For wounds	Waterloo	*£100
23rd Foot	Major JHE Hill	For a wound	Waterloo	*£200
27th Foot	Lieutenant William Henderson	For a wound	Waterloo	*£100
27th Foot	Lieutenant George Macdonald	For wounds	Waterloo	*£70
27th Foot	Lieutenant John Millar	Loss of an eye	Waterloo	£70
27th Foot	Lieutenant William Faithful Fortescue	For a wound	Waterloo	£70
28th Foot	Captain William Irving	For a wound	Quatre Bras	*£300
28th Foot	Captain Richard Llewellyn	For wounds	Waterloo	*£300
28th Foot	Captain John Bowles	For a wound	Waterloo	£100
32nd Foot	Lieutenant Henry Quill	For a wound	Quatre Bras	*£70
32nd Foot	Captain George Barr	For wounds	Waterloo	*£100
32nd Foot	Lieutenant Jonathan Jagoe	For a wound	Waterloo	*£70
33rd Foot	Lieutenant John Alderson	Loss of an arm	Quatre Bras	£70
33rd Foot	Lieutenant William Bain	For a wound	Waterloo	*£70
33rd Foot	Lieutenant James Forlong	For a wound	Quatre Bras	*£70
33rd Foot	Lieutenant Richard Westmore	For a wound	Waterloo	*£70
33rd Foot	Lieutenant Samuel Alexander Pagan	For a wound	Waterloo	£70
40th Foot	Lieutenant James Anthony	For wounds	Badajoz Toulouse Waterloo	£70

40th Foot	Lieutenant the Hon. Michael Brown	For a wound	Waterloo	£70
40th Foot	Ensign William Aldworth Clarke	Loss of an arm	Waterloo	£50
40th Foot	Ensign Richard Thornhill	For a wound	Waterloo	*£50
42nd Foot	Major Archibald Menzies	For wounds	Quatre Bras	*£200
52nd Foot	Brevet Major Charles Diggle	For a wound	Waterloo	*£200
52nd Foot	Lieutenant Matthew Anderson	Loss of a leg	Waterloo	£70
61st Foot	Brevet Major Algernon Langton	For a wound	Quatre Bras	*£200
69th Foot	Volunteer Charles Christopher Clarke	For wounds	Quatre Bras	*£50
69th Foot	Lieutenant Henry Anderson	For a wound	Waterloo	*£70
69th Foot	Captain Henry Lindsay	For wounds	Quatre Bras	*£100
69th Foot	Lieutenant Edward Hodder	For a wound	Waterloo	*£70
71st Foot	Lieutenant Robert Lind	For a wound	Waterloo	*£70
73rd Foot	Captain John Garland	For a wound	Waterloo	£100
79th Foot	Captain William Marshall	Loss of an arm	Quatre Bras	£100
79th Foot	Lieutenant William Maddock	For a wound	Quatre bras	*£70
79th Foot	Captain Thomas Brown	For a wound	Quatre Bras	*£100
79th Foot	Major Andrew Brown	For a wound	Quatre Bras	*£200
92nd Foot	Lieutenant George Mackie	For wounds	Quatre Bras	*£70
92nd Foot	Ensign Robert Hewitt	Loss of a leg	Quatre Bras	£50
92nd Foot	Lieutenant John McKinley	For a wound	Quatre Bras	*£70
92nd Foot	Lieutenant Ewan Ross	For a wound	Quatre Bras	*£70
92nd Foot	Ensign John Bramwell	For a wound	Quatre Bras	*£70
92nd Foot	Lieutenant Ronald Macdonald	For a wound	Quatre Bras	*£70
92nd Foot	Lieutenant Donald Macdonald	For a wound	Waterloo	*£70
Rifle Brigade 95th Foot	Lt Colonel Alexander Cameron	For wounds	Waterloo	£300
Rifle Brigade 95th Foot	Lt Colonel Alexander Cameron [further award]	For wounds	Waterloo	£200
Rifle Brigade 95th Foot	Lieutenant William Humbley	For a wound	Waterloo	*£70
Rifle Brigade 95th Foot	Major John Garlies McCullock	Loss of left arm	Waterloo	£200
Rifle Brigade 95th Foot	2nd Lieutenant John Prendergast Walsh	Loss of a leg	Waterloo	£50
Rifle Brigade 95th Foot	Lieutenant Colonel George Wilkins	For a wound	Waterloo	*£300
Rifle Brigade 95th Foot	Brevet Lieutenant Colonel Charles Beckwith	Loss of a leg	Waterloo	£300
Rifle Brigade 95th Foot	Major Amos Godsil Robert Norcott	For wounds	Tarbes and Waterloo	*£250
Rifle Brigade 95th Foot	Lieutenant George Simmons	For wounds	Waterloo	*£70
Rifle Brigade 95th Foot	Lieutenant Joseph Lynam	For a wound	Waterloo	*£70
Staff	Major General Sir Thomas Bradford	Loss of an arm	Waterloo	£350
Staff	Major General Sir George Cooke	For a wound	Waterloo	£350

Clearly, the amount of pension was related to seniority. Thus, for a general or field officer the range of award would be several hundreds of pounds, whilst junior officers, usually up to £100. However, the severity of the wound would be taken into account. By correction for inflation over the years, £100 awarded in 1815 would, in 2017, be worth £8,400

To re-gain employment in the post-war austerity and the increasing mechanisation of industry was hard. For some, an injury would be a source of pride and a badge of honour, for others it represented continued ill-health. For the military medical profession, particularly the surgical fraternity, long service at war would bring, in some cases, exhaustion and disease and for others wealth, as their profound experience gave them the confidence and ability to rise to dizzy heights in their profession.

However, too many heroes of the campaign fell on hard times and continued a very meagre living, until they succumbed to an early death. Britain had yet to learn to care for its old soldiers properly, perhaps it is still learning.

Bibliography

Archival Papers

Gen 594 Coll -535 *Line drawings and reports from Brussels by John Thomson MD 1815* University of Edinburgh Archives

Printed Sources

Anon. [probably J. McGrigor], *Instructions for the regulation of Military Hospitals and the Sick with Divisions* (Lisbon: A.R. Galhardo printers, 1813).

Beamish, L.N., *History of the King's German Legion* (London: Boone, 1837).

Brice, Docteur, and Bottet, Capitaine, *Le Corps de Santé Militaire en France, 1708-1782* (Paris: Berger-Levrault, 1907).

Callataÿ, P. de, 'Napoleon et Medicine, Evolution du Service de Santé Militaire 1815-1997', *Medic,* 1997, pp.37-8.

Cantlie, N., *A History of the Army Medical Department,* (London: Churchill Livingstone, 1974).

Chaboulon, F. de, *Les Cent-Jours. Mémoires pour servir à l'histoire de la vie privée, du retour, et du règne de Napoléon en 1815* (London: Roworth, 1820).

Clark, G., *Farm Wages and Living Standards in the Industrial Revolution, England 1650-1850* (Thesis, University of California, 2001)

Crumplin, M. & Starling, P., *A Surgical Artist at War, The Paintings and Sketches of Sir Charles Bell, 1809-1815* (Edinburgh: Royal College of Surgeons, 2005).

Crumplin, M., *Men of Steel, Surgery in the Napoleonic Wars* (Shrewsbury: Quiller, 2007).

Currie, J., *Letters to a Vicarage 1796-1815 the Letters of Lt Col JHE Hill* (Exeter: Oriel, 1988).

Dible, J.H., *Napoleon's Surgeon* (London: William Heinemann Medical Books Ltd, 1970).

Eaton, Charlotte *A Near Observer of the Battle of Waterloo* (London: Murray, 1816)

Evrard, E., *Esculape aux Armées – 500 Ans de Médecine Militaire en Belgique* (Brussels: Société scientific du Service Médical Militaire 1997).

Evrard, E, 'Breve Histoire de l'organisation des soins dispenses aux blesses militaires dans les hôpital belges,apres la derniere campaign napoleonienne (juin 1815)' *Histoire des Sciences Medicales*, Tome XXVII, No. 1, 1993.

Field, A., *Waterloo Rout & Retreat, The French Perspective* (Barnsley: Pen & Sword, 2017).

Graaf, M.C. de, 'Metamorphose de Saint-Laurent de Liège sous Guillaume 1er, Roi des Pays-Bas (1815-1830)', in *Saint-Laurent, église, abbaye et hôpital militaire. Mille ans d'histoire*. (Liège: Soledi, 1968).

Gurwood, Lt. Col. (ed.), *The Dispatches of Field Marshal the Duke of Wellington* (London: John Murray, 1852),

Guthrie, G.J., *A treatise on gunshot wounds, on injuries of nerves, and of wounds of the extremities requiring the different operations of amputation* (London: Burgess & Hill, 1820).

Guthrie, G.J., *On the Diseases and Injuries of Arteries with the operations required for their cure* (London: Burgess & Hill, 1830).

Guthrie, G.J., *Injuries of the Head affecting the Brain* (London: Churchill, 1842).

Guthrie, G.J., *On Wounds and Injuries of the Abdomen and the Pelvis* (London: Churchill, 1847).

Guthrie, G.J., *On Wounds and Injuries of the Chest* (London: Renshaw, 1848).

Guthrie, G.J., *Commentaries on the Surgery of the War, In Portugal, Spain, France and the Netherlands, from the Battle of Rolica to that of Waterloo in 1815; with additions relating to those in the Crimea in 1854-55* (Philadelphia: Lippincott, 1862).

Hassenforder, J., 'Le Service de Santé Militaire pendant la Révolution et l'Empire', in J-L des Cilleuls, J. Pesme, J. Hassenforder et G. Hugonot, *Le Service de Santé Militaire de ses Origines à nous jours* (Paris: SPEI, 1961).

Hathaway, E., *Costello, The True Story of a Peninsular War Rifleman* (Swanage: Shinglepicker, 1997).

Hay, W. (ed. Mrs S.C.I. Wood), *Reminiscences under Wellington, 1808-15* (London: Simpkin, 1901).

Haythornthwaite, P.J., *Waterloo Men – the Experience of Battle 16-18 June 1815*, (Marlborough: Crowood Press, 1999).

Hennen, J., *Principles of Military Surgery comprising Observations on the arrangement, police, and practise of hospitals* (London: Wilson, 1829).

Hodge, W.B., 'On the Mortality arising from Military Operations', *Journal of the Institute of Actuaries*, Volume 7, Issue 2, 1857, pp.80-90.

Howard, M., *Napoleon's Doctors: The Medical Services of the Grande Armée* (Stroud: Spellmount, 2006).

Howard, M., *Walcheren 1809, the scandalous destruction of a British Army* (Barnsley: Pen & Sword, 2012).

Howard, M., *Wellington's Doctors* (Stroud: Spellmount, 2008).

Hutchinson, C., *Some Practical Observations in Surgery* (London: Underwood, 1816).

Larrey, J.D. (Translated from the French by R.W. Hall), *Memoirs of Military Surgery and Campaigns of the French Army* (Baltimore: J. Cushino, 1814).

Mercer, C., *Journal of the Waterloo Campaign kept throughout the Campaign of 1815 by the Late General Cavalié Mercer, commanding the 9th Brigade Royal Artillery* (London: Blackwood, 1870).

Peterkin, A., Johnston. W., *Commissioned Officers in the Medical Services of the British Army, 1660-1960* (London: Wellcome Historical Medical Library, 1968).

Rothenberg. G.E., *The Art of Warfare in the Age of Napoleon*, (Bloomington: Indiana University Press, 1980).

Thomson, J., *Report of Observations made in the British Military Hospitals in Belgium, with some remarks upon Amputation* (Edinburgh: Blackwood, 1816).

Vansittart, J., *Surgeon James's Journal 1815* (London: Cassell, 1964).

Wellington, 2nd Duke of (ed.), *Supplementary Despatches, Correspondence and Memoranda of Field Marshal Arthur Duke of Wellington KG* (London: Murray, 1863).

From Reason to Revolution – Warfare 1721-1815

http://www.helion.co.uk/series/from-reason-to-revolution-1721-1815.php

The 'From Reason to Revolution' series covers the period of military history 1721–1815, an era in which fortress-based strategy and linear battles gave way to the nation-in-arms and the beginnings of total war.

This era saw the evolution and growth of light troops of all arms, and of increasingly flexible command systems to cope with the growing armies fielded by nations able to mobilise far greater proportions of their manpower than ever before. Many of these developments were fired by the great political upheavals of the era, with revolutions in America and France bringing about social change which in turn fed back into the military sphere as whole nations readied themselves for war. Only in the closing years of the period, as the reactionary powers began to regain the upper hand, did a military synthesis of the best of the old and the new become possible.

The series will examine the military and naval history of the period in a greater degree of detail than has hitherto been attempted, and has a very wide brief, with the intention of covering all aspects from the battles, campaigns, logistics, and tactics, to the personalities, armies, uniforms, and equipment.

Submissions

The publishers would be pleased to receive submissions for this series. Please contact series editor Andrew Bamford via email (andrewbamford@helion.co.uk), or in writing to Helion & Company Limited, Unit 8 Amherst Business Centre, Budbrooke Road, Warwick, CV34 5WE

Titles

No 1 *Lobositz to Leuthen: Horace St Paul and the Campaigns of the Austrian Army in the Seven Years War 1756-57* (Neil Cogswell)

No 2 *Glories to Useless Heroism: The Seven Years War in North America from the French journals of Comte Maurés de Malartic, 1755-1760* (William Raffle (ed.))

No 3 *Reminiscences 1808-1815 Under Wellington: The Peninsular and Waterloo Memoirs of William Hay* (Andrew Bamford (ed.))

No 4 *Far Distant Ships: The Royal Navy and the Blockade of Brest 1793-1815* (Quintin Barry)

No 5 *Godoy's Army: Spanish Regiments and Uniforms from the Estado Militar of 1800* (Charles Esdaile and Alan Perry)

No 6 *On Gladsmuir Shall the Battle Be! The Battle of Prestonpans 1745* (Arran Johnston)

No 7 *The French Army of the Orient 1798-1801: Napoleon's Beloved 'Egyptians'* (Yves Martin)

No 8 *The Autobiography, or Narrative of a Soldier: The Peninsular War Memoirs of William Brown of the 45th Foot* (Steve Brown (ed.))

No 9 *Recollections from the Ranks: Three Russian Soldiers' Autobiographies from the Napoleonic Wars* (Darrin Boland)

No 10 *By Fire and Bayonet: Grey's West Indies Campaign of 1794* (Steve Brown)

No 11 *Olmütz to Torgau: Horace St Paul and the Campaigns of the Austrian Army in the Seven Years War 1758-60* (Neil Cogswell)

No 12 *Murat's Army: The Army of the Kingdom of Naples 1806-1815* (Digby Smith)

No 13 *The Veteran or 40 Years' Service in the British Army: The Scurrilous Recollections of Paymaster John Harley 47th Foot – 1798-1838* (Gareth Glover (ed.))

No 14 *Narrative of the Eventful Life of Thomas Jackson: Militiaman and Coldstream Sergeant, 1803-15* (Eamonn O'Keeffe (ed.))

No.15 *For Orange and the States: The Army of the Dutch Republic 1713-1772 Part I: Infantry* (Marc Geerdinck-Schaftenaar)

No 16 *Men Who Are Determined to be Free: The American Assault on Stony Point, 15 July 1779* (David C. Bonk)